KT-232-293

CAMBRIDGE STUDIES IN LINGUISTICS

Georgian syntax

A study in relational grammar

In this series

1 DAVID CRYSTAL: *Prosodic systems and intonation in English**
2 PIETER A.M.SEUREN: *Operators and nucleus*
3 RODNEY D.HUDDLESTON: *The sentence in written English*
4 JOHN M.ANDERSON: *The grammar of case**
5 M.L.SAMUELS: *Linguistic evolution**
6 P.H.MATTHEWS: *Inflectional morphology**
7 GILLIAN BROWN: *Phonological rules and dialect variation**
8 BRIAN NEWTON: *The generative interpretation of dialect**
9 R.M.W.DIXON: *The Dyirbal language of North Queensland**
10 BRUCE L.DERWING: *Transformational grammar as a theory of language acquisition**
11 MELISSA BOWERMAN: *Early syntactic development**
12 W. SIDNEY ALLEN: *Accent and rhythm*
13 PETER TRUDGILL: *The social differentiation of English in Norwich**
14 ROGER LASS and JOHN M.ANDERSON: *Old English phonology*
15 RUTH M.KEMPSON: *Presupposition and the delimitation of semantics**
16 JAMES R.HURFORD: *The linguistic theory of numerals*
17 ROGER LASS: *English phonology and phonological theory*
18 G.M.AWBERY: *The syntax of Welsh*
19 R.M.W.DIXON: *A grammar of Yidiɲ*
20 JAMES FOLEY: *Foundations of theoretical phonology*
21 A.RADFORD: *Italian syntax: transformational and relational grammar*
22 DIETER WUNDERLICH: *Foundations of linguistics**
23 DAVID W.LIGHTFOOT: *Principles of diachronic syntax**
24 ANNETTE KARMILOFF-SMITH: *A functional approach to child language**
25 PER LINELL: *Psychological reality in phonology*
26 CHRISTINE TANZ: *Studies in the acquisition of deictic terms*
27 ROGER LASS: *On explaining language change*
28 TORBEN THRANE: *Referential–semantic analysis*
29 TAMSIN DONALDSON: *Ngiyambaa*
30 KRISTJÁN ÁRNASON: *Quantity in historical phonology*
31 JOHN LAVER: *The phonetic description of voice quality*
32 PETER AUSTIN: *A grammar of Diyari, South Australia*
33 ALICE C.HARRIS: *Georgian syntax*

**Issued in hard covers and as a paper-back*

GEORGIAN SYNTAX

A study in relational grammar

ALICE C. HARRIS

Research Assistant Professor of Linguistics, Vanderbilt University

CAMBRIDGE UNIVERSITY PRESS

CAMBRIDGE

LONDON NEW YORK NEW ROCHELLE

MELBOURNE SYDNEY

Published by the Press Syndicate of the University of Cambridge
The Pitt Building, Trumpington Street, Cambridge CB2 1RP
32 East 57th Street, New York, NY10022, USA
296 Beaconsfield Parade, Middle Park, Melbourne 3206, Australia

First published 1981

Printed in Great Britain by Western Printing Services Ltd, Bristol

British Library Cataloguing in Publication Data

Harris, Alice C.
Georgian syntax. – (Cambridge studies in
linguistics; 33 ISSN 0068-676x)
1. Georgian language
I. Title II. Series
499.996 PK9105 80-41497

ISBN 0 521 23584 7

FOR JIM

Foreword

This book addresses a number of central issues in linguistic theory.

The first and most fundamental issue is that of the relevance of the notions 'subject', 'direct object', and 'indirect object' to syntactic description. Georgian has been claimed to be a language to which these notions are not relevant. It therefore provides a particularly good test of the basic claims of relational grammar. The issue of the relevance of grammatical relations to Georgian syntax also affects other issues. These include: (i) the viability of linguistic universals stated in terms of grammatical relations, and (ii) the extent to which Georgian is different from other languages.

In this book, Dr Harris brings out generalizations in Georgian grammar that can be captured in terms of grammatical relations, but not in terms of case or word order. She penetrates the complexities of Georgian morphology to reveal the underlying syntactic generalizations. The result is a striking confirmation of the relevance of grammatical relations to grammatical description. At the same time, Dr Harris shows that Georgian has constructions such as Passive, Object Raising, Causative Clause Union, and others found in better-known languages. Thus, Georgian is not as different from other languages as has been claimed in earlier work on Georgian. Indeed, Georgian is shown to have exactly the constructions and kinds of phenomena that have been claimed in relational grammar to characterize natural languages and to require description in terms of grammatical relations.

The analysis of Georgian presented in this book also bears on what promises to be another central issue in syntactic theory in the 1980s: the question of whether or not it is necessary to posit more than one syntactic level. Working in a derivational framework, Dr Harris shows that there are rules and generalizations in Georgian that refer to distinct syntactic levels. Most striking here are the rules that refer to the initial level, those that refer to the final level, and those responsible for the marking of 'retired terms' – nominals that bear a term relation at one level and a non-term relation (chomeur or emeritus) at a subsequent level. These results constitute a significant challenge to theories that claim that a single level is sufficient for syntactic description.

This book illustrates the kinds of contributions that theory can make to the understanding of individual languages, and the study of individual languages to the development of linguistic theory. One of the principal problems this book addresses is that of the Georgian case system. Traditional descriptions state that transitive clauses in Georgian occur in three distinct case patterns. Dr Harris argues convincingly that Georgian has the Inversion construction, in which the subject is demoted to indirect object and the direct object promoted to subject. Once Inversion is recognized in Georgian grammar, the three case patterns are reduced to two. Another traditional problem in the Georgian case system concerns intransitive clauses. Intransitive verbs are divided into two classes, each of which is associated with a different case pattern. This raises two questions: (i) What determines the class assignment of intransitive verbs? (ii) Are there generalizations uniting the case patterns in intransitive clauses with those in transitive clauses? Dr Harris analyzes the case patterns of intransitive clauses in terms of the Unaccusative Hypothesis, under which there are two fundamentally different types of initially intransitive clauses: one with an initial subject and the other with an initial direct object. She shows that under this analysis, the assignment of intransitive verbs to the two classes is not arbitrary, and that there are indeed generalizations uniting the case patterns in transitive and intransitive clauses. This book thus shows how theoretical constructs can illuminate language-particular phenomena such as the Georgian case system. At the same time, the Georgian data provides evidence for these theoretical constructs.

In addition to its contributions to linguistic theory and its exemplification of relational grammar, this book also gives a good picture of what a portion of the grammar of a morphologically complex language looks like. It provides clear, refutable analyses of syntactic phenomena in what initially appears to be an unusually complex language. These analyses are in a form that facilitates comparison with other languages and the study of linguistic universals. Indeed, this work provides one of the best and most thorough studies yet available in English of the syntax of a non-Indo-European language. The interplay of theory and description that has produced this extensive documentation of Georgian syntax is a model of syntactic investigation itself.

DAVID M. PERLMUTTER

San Diego, California
12 *June*, 1980

Contents

Preface

This investigation of Georgian syntax originated as my 1976 dissertation at Harvard University; additional chapters were written in the fall of 1977. The work is based on interviews with native speakers of Georgian. The interviews were conducted during a twelve-month stay in Tbilisi in 1974–5 and a short research visit in 1977 and were supplemented by work with Georgians in the United States from 1973 to 1978. The research was supported in part by the International Research and Exchanges Board, by a Sinclair Kennedy Fellowship from Harvard University, and by the National Science Foundation.

Although I have had occasion in this monograph to question many assumptions and claims made by traditional Kartvelologists, I view my work as a continuation, not a contradiction, of theirs. Without the foundation laid by Chikobava, Shanidze, Topuria, Tschenkéli, Vogt, and many other specialists, this work would have been impossible.

I am deeply indebted to David Perlmutter for ideas about language universals that helped inspire the research reported here; his insights and criticism have improved this work in many ways. I am grateful to Dee Ann Holisky for her willingness to debate with me any aspect of the structure of Georgian and for her fine eye for the detail of language. I wish also to extend a special thanks to my Georgian teacher for her long-suffering tolerance of my ideas about the structure of her language.

I am grateful to Bernard Comrie for criticism that was extremely valuable in revising this work. I wish to thank Stephen Anderson for introducing me to the problems of ergativity, which led to my working on Georgian. In addition, Judith Aissen, Winfried Boeder, Jorge Hankamer, George Hewitt, Susumu Kuno, Paul Postal, Hans Vogt, the students in my class on Georgian syntax and other members of the Department of Linguistics at Harvard University have read parts of the analysis presented here and have given valuable comments. They do not necessarily agree with the views presented.

A great many Georgians, in the United States and in Georgia, have helped me – as informants, as teachers, as colleagues, and as friends. I am grateful, too, to the libraries of the Georgian Academy of Sciences, of Tbilisi State University, and of the Linguistics Institute of the Georgian Academy of Sciences for helping me to acquire research materials.

Earlier or different versions of three chapters of the present work have been separately published; these are:

Chapter 8, as 'Inversion as a Rule of Universal Grammar: Georgian Evidence,' *Studies in Relational Grammar*, ed. David M. Perlmutter (to appear).

Chapter 11, as 'Marking Former Terms: Georgian Evidence,' *Proceedings of the Seventh Annual Meeting of the North Eastern Linguistic Society*, 81–98 (1977).

Chapter 15, as 'Number Agreement in Modern Georgian,' *The Classification of Grammatical Categories* (*International Review of Slavic Linguistics* 3. 1–2), ed. Bernard Comrie, 75–98 (1978).

Notes on presentation

1 *Transliteration.* The following system is used:

Georgian letter	*Phonetic equivalent*	*Transliteration*
ა	a	a
ბ	b	b
გ	g	g
დ	d	d
ე	e, ε	e
ვ	v, w, f	v
ზ	z	z
თ	t‘	t
ი	i, ɪ	i
კ	ḳ	ḳ
ლ	l	l
მ	m	m
ნ	n	n
ო	o	o
პ	p̣	p̣
ჟ	ž	ž
რ	r	r
ს	s	s
ტ	ṭ	ṭ
უ	u	u
ფ	p‘	p
ქ	k‘	k
ღ	γ	γ
ყ	q̣	q̣
შ	š	š
ჩ	č	č
ც	c (ts)	c
ძ	dz	ʒ

Georgian letter	*Phonetic equivalent*	*Transliteration*
წ	c̣ (ṭs)	c̣
ჭ	č̣	č̣
ხ	x	x
ჯ	ǰ	j
ჰ	h	h

2 *A note on glosses*

The morphology of the Georgian verb is very complex, and there is no way to escape the use of examples with complicated verb forms. In addition to the lexical meaning of the root, a single verb form may code the following information:

person of subject
person of direct object
person of indirect object
number of subject
number of direct object
number of indirect object
tense
aspect (complete/incomplete, habitual/non-habitual)
voice
mood
direction and orientation
causative/non-causative (cf. ch. 5)
version (cf. ch. 6)
etc.

In this work, the gloss of a verb will not include all this information for two reasons: (i) A great deal of it is irrelevant to the topic of this monograph and would simply overwhelm the reader with a mass of material not necessary for interpreting particular examples. (ii) Although Georgian is generally agglutinative, the information necessary to interpret particular examples cannot always be attributed to any particular morpheme. Therefore, the principle behind my glosses is that they should give only that information which will enable the reader to understand the example in the context of the point under discussion. Since one of the main concerns of this monograph is the correspondence between case and grammatical relation, case is always clearly marked. Since case varies with Series and Class of the governing verb, those are always marked in the verb gloss. The grammatical relation is not marked in the gloss, but it is discussed at length in the text. Particulars are given below.

2.1 *Analytic gloss*. In the analytic gloss, which is directly below the Georgian example, the information carried by one word is hyphenated together in English; e.g. *daçera* 'he-wrote-it'. Analytic glosses are not generally given for examples quoted in the text itself.

2.1.1 Nouns. Plurality is indicated by plurality in the English word, not by a 'PL'; e.g. *ʒaɣlebi* 'dogs', not 'dog-PL'.

Case is noted separately in capitals; genitives are indicated separately, not by an English genitive; e.g. *ʒaɣlis* 'dog-GEN', not 'dog's'. An exception to this is the possessive reflexive, *tavis-*, which is genitive with secondary case marking; it is glossed 'self's'.

While nouns and most pronouns have a complete declension in Georgian, first and second person personal pronouns and a few others do not. These personal pronouns use a single form for the cases of greatest concern to us, the ergative, nominative, and dative. For example, *me* represents the ergative, nominative, and dative of 'I, me'. In the examples, a case is always specified for these pronouns, on the basis of the case used in the comparable sentence for a noun or third person pronoun.

Positionals (adpositions) in Georgian are all postpositions. Some are written together with the noun in Georgian and are hyphenated to the noun in the English gloss; e.g. *saxlši* 'house-in' from *saxl-* 'house'. A few postpositions are not written with the noun in Georgian; I have followed the Georgian spelling conventions, both in the Georgian example and in the English gloss; e.g. *ʒaɣlis mier* 'dog by'. Postpositions govern particular cases, but these play no part in the discussion, and so are generally not included in the glosses.

The Georgian alphabet has no capitals, so proper names are not capitalized in Georgian. I have followed this spelling convention in the examples transliterated here, but have capitalized the English gloss so that the reader can identify those words as proper names; e.g. *goča* 'Gocha-NOM.'

2.1.2 Verbs. Because case patterns vary with Series and Class of the verb, and because these characteristics would not otherwise be apparent to the reader, they have been included in the gloss of every verb. They are always the last two elements in the analytic gloss. Series is always indicated with a Roman numeral, in text and gloss alike; Class is always indicated with an Arabic numeral. For example, *dac̣era* 'he-wrote-it-II-1; *rčeba* 'he-stays-I-2'. (These elements are not relevant to the rules discussed in §4 of the Introduction, and therefore are not included until ch. 1.)

Person Agreement is indicated by the appropriate pronouns in the following order: subject, verb root, indirect object, direct object; e.g. *gcem* 'I-give-you-it-I-1'. All terms are indicated in the gloss, though they may be disguised in Georgian by zero markers or morphophonemic rules (cf. ch. 1, § 3).

Gender is included to aid the reader, although it is not indicated in Georgian. Third person singular subjects are glossed 'he' except when a female name is used, or when the subject must be inanimate. Objects are glossed 'it' except when animacy is indicated by a noun in the clause, or when an animate would be more natural.

Number Agreement is indicated in the gloss only when it is clearly marked in the Georgian.

maʒlevs	*sačukrebs.*
he-gives-me-it-I-1	gifts-DAT

'He gives gifts to me'.

Although 'gifts' is plural, it does not trigger Number Agreement; this fact is reflected in the 'it' of the analytic gloss of the verb. In the following example, number of the indirect object is indicated morphologically and is glossed:

gvaʒlevs	*sačukrebs.*
he-gives-us-it-I-1	gifts-DAT

'He gives gifts to us.'

Tense is indicated in analytic glosses only by the present, past, and future forms of the English verb; e.g. *dac̣ers* 'he-will-write-it'. The simple (habitual) present in English is used in analytic glosses for the present; this is used for brevity only and implies no claim as to the nature of this tense in Georgian.

When it is important that some morpheme be identified in the verb form, as in the discussions of agreement, the important morphemes will be isolated by hyphenating or using heavy type. In some instances the corresponding element in the gloss is in heavy type also; e.g. *mo***m***c̣era* 'he-wrote-**me**-it-II-1'. Otherwise, parts of the verb will not be separated by hyphens.

2.1.3 Adjectives. In Georgian, attributive adjectives do agree with the nouns they modify, but the case is not fully apparent. For this reason and because it is not important to the discussion, no case is indicated for adjectives that precede their head nouns.

2.2 *Final gloss.* The final gloss gives the sentence which corresponds most closely in English, including the tense, which is the appropriate one in English. In some instances, English has no corresponding syntactic rule, and the sentences in which the rule has applied and those in which it has not have the same gloss.

Final glosses are sometimes omitted from ungrammatical sentences, since those sentences do not always have a meaning. But if it would not be clear what the ungrammatical sentences show, a final gloss is given in parentheses, that corresponds to the intended meaning of the sentence.

2.3 *Quotational form.* When a noun is referred to in the text, it is usually quoted in its nominative case form or in its stem form (without case marking). A verb will be quoted in its masdar (nominalized) form, unless that is inappropriate, in which case it will be given in a finite form; this will be made apparent by the gloss.

3 *Diagrams*

This work uses the conventions of the 'network' diagramming developed for relational grammar (Perlmutter & Postal 1977). A clause and the elements which constitute it are represented as nodes. Arrows connecting the clause node with other nodes indicate that the latter are dependents of the clause. Labels on the arrows indicate the grammatical relations which various elements bear to the clause; only the central grammatical relations (cf. p.5 below) are indicated in network diagrams. The predicate relation is labeled 'P'. The subject relation is marked '1', the direct object relation '2', and the indirect object relation '3'. Benefactives are marked as 'B'. For example, network (1)

(1)

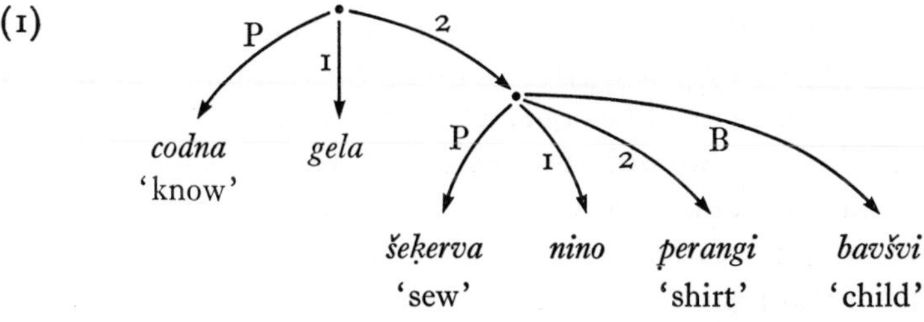

should be read as '*gela* is the subject of the matrix clause (or of the verb, *codna* "know"); and its direct object is the clause consisting of the predicate *šeḳerva* "sew", the subject *nino*, the direct object *perangi* "shirt", and the benefactive *bavšvi* "child".' This corresponds to the sentence (2).

(2) *gelam icis, rom nino ḳeravs perangs bavšvistvis.*
Gela he-knows that Nino she-sews shirt child-for
'Gela knows that Nino is sewing a shirt for the child.'

Levels are indicated as in (3), where Benefactive Version has applied to make the benefactive an indirect object.

(3)

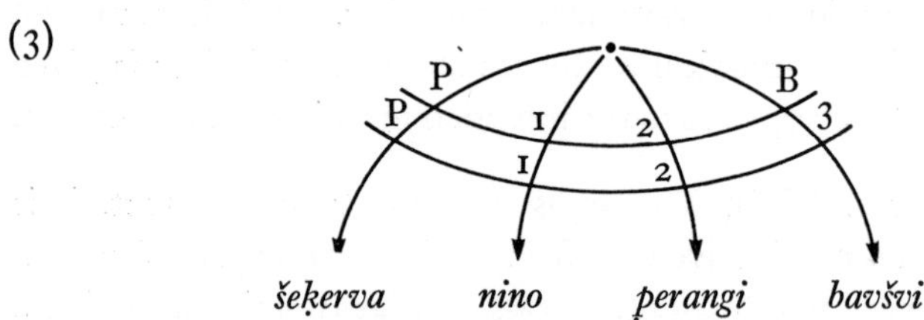

This network indicates, among other things, '*bavšvi* is an initial benefactive and a final indirect object'.

Retired subjects, direct objects, and indirect objects are marked 'R-1', 'R-2', and 'R-3', respectively. Other symbols used are introduced where appropriate.

4 *The reader*

The monograph is written primarily for syntacticians who know little or nothing of Georgian. For this reason, material that will be of interest only to the Georgian specialist is put, as often as possible, into notes or appendices. The complexities of case marking and verb agreement are introduced gradually.

5 *The dialect described*

This monograph is based on work with informants in Georgia and the United States from 1973 to 1978. The dialect described here is that spoken in the capital city of Georgia, Tbilisi (Tiflis). In those instances where I have isolated two dialects among my informants, I have made reference to this fact in the text or in a footnote. No attempt is made to account for divergences found in dialects outside Tbilisi or in earlier periods, or for phenomena restricted to written Georgian.

Introduction

1 Posing the problems

To many general linguists, Georgian has long seemed an inscrutable language. The main difficulty has been that the apparent subject of a given clause is not always in the same case, as it is in most languages. The sentences in (1) illustrate the problem of the case differential.

(1) (a) *glexi* *tesavs* *siminds.*
peasant-NOM he-sows-it-I-1 corn-DAT
'The peasant is sowing corn.'

(b) *glexma* *datesa* *simindi.*
peasant-ERG he-sowed-it-II-1 corn-NOM
'The peasant sowed corn.'

(c) *glexs* *dautesavs* *simindi.*
peasant-DAT he-sowed-it-III-1 corn-NOM
'The peasant has sown corn.'

The traditional names are used for cases; the names themselves are not intended as a claim about the real structure of the language. The nominative case is marked by *-i* (ø after a vowel), the ergative by *-ma* (*-m* after a vowel), and the dative by *-s*. The three case marking Patterns possible for a given clause are stated in (2).

(2)

	Subject	*Direct Object*	*Indirect Object*
Pattern A	ERGATIVE	NOMINATIVE	DATIVE
B	NOMINATIVE	DATIVE	DATIVE
C	DATIVE	NOMINATIVE	*tvis*-nominal

A second obvious problem in case marking is that the case marking Pattern does not vary for all verbs in the same way. The distribution of Patterns A, B, and C is stated in (3).

(3)

		Series I	II	III
Class	1	B	A	C
	2	B	B	B
	3	B	A	C
	4	C	C	C

Moreover, in Georgian Pattern A, with ergative subjects, is by no means limited to transitive verbs. In order to predict the case of a subject in Georgian, one must know the Series and Class of the governing verb form. The three Series are groups of tense-aspect-mood categories; these are listed in the appendix to ch. 2. In this work, the Class of the verb is defined morphologically; the precise criteria used are given in ch. 16, Appendix A. It is shown below that the Classes correlate with specific syntactic and semantic properties.

Looking at (1) again in light of (2–3), and knowing that the governing verb is a Class 1 verb, we can see that in (1a), which is in a Series I tense, the subject must be in the nominative and the object in the dative. In (1b), which is in a Series II tense, the subject is in the ergative, the object in the nominative. And in (1c), we see the Series III variant: subject in the dative and object in the nominative.

I have been using the labels 'subject' and 'direct object' in the way they are usually used in the description of more familiar languages. In fact, it is not at all obvious that these notions are even appropriate ones for Georgian. This is the primary problem that this monograph addresses: Are the notions 'subject', 'direct object', and 'indirect object' relevant to Georgian?

The difficulty in approaching the notion 'subject' in Georgian is that there is no agreement among the three most obvious criteria for defining this concept – case, verb agreement, and some intuitive idea of subject. In general, in order to make a claim about which nominals are subjects, linguists have had to choose between these criteria on an arbitrary basis. Shanidze (1973: 195–7) and Tschenkéli (1958: 497) select the intuitive idea, and would call *glexi* 'peasant' the subject in all of the sentences in (1). Vogt (1971: 81) chooses instead Person Agreement; this means that *glexi* is subject in (1a–b), and *simindi* 'corn' in (1c). Chikobava (1968) and Aronson (1970) define the subject as that nominal which always triggers Number Agreement in the verb.[1] Marr and Brière (1931: 244), writing mainly of Old Georgian, say that the 'nominative indicates the grammatical object – in fact the real subject' in (1b–c). Pätsch (1952/53) considers 'subject' an Indo-European notion and therefore confusing in Georgian. Sommerfelt (1937) suggests that 'subject' is an inappropriate notion for a language like Georgian.

Each of the above-mentioned analyses of 'subject' in Georgian is unsatisfactory because the choice of the criterion used is not clearly motivated. It is not clear, for example, why Chikobava considers Number Agreement to be the most important criterion, while Vogt considers Person Agreement to be.[2]

No analysis of the notion 'subject' in Georgian can be adequate if it is based upon a single criterion. Recent work on language universals has shown that the following syntactic characteristics are typical of subjects: they trigger reflexivization, they trigger coreferential deletion, they trigger verb agreement, they undergo Unemphatic Pronoun Drop, etc. (cf. Anderson 1976; Keenan 1974, 1976; Postal & Perlmutter 1974). But no one of these criteria is sufficient to establish the notion 'subject' for any language. In this monograph, I use, among others, the following syntactic rules to argue for the notion 'subject':

(a) *Tav*-Reflexivization (full-pronoun reflexivization)
(b) *Tavis*-Reflexivization (possessive reflexivization)
(c) Person Agreement
(d) Number Agreement
(e) Unemphatic Pronoun Drop
(f) Coreferential Version Object Deletion.

Additional phenomena will also be used to argue for the existence of a subject in Georgian, as well as for a direct object and indirect object.

Nor could an analysis of the notion 'subject' in Georgian be adequate if it failed to recognize distinct levels of derivation. A large portion of this work is devoted to an analysis of the major rules that change grammatical relations in Georgian. Because Georgian has rules like Passivization, Object Raising, Causative Clause Union, and Inversion, the notion 'subject' cannot be adequately characterized by reference to a single level of derivation.[3]

This leads us to the second major problem addressed by the present work: What is the nature of the rules that change grammatical relations in Georgian? This question is addressed from several points of view. From the language-internal viewpoint, individual rules provide additional criteria for identifying the grammatical relations 'subject', 'direct object', and 'indirect object'. Further, analyses of these rules lead to a consideration of rule interaction in Georgian. From the point of view of language universals, it is hoped that a detailed study of individual rules in Georgian will contribute to a better understanding of the ways in which particular rules vary and ways in which they are the same, across language.

The third major problem considered here is how to account for case marking, given the complexities represented in (2–3). Even after the subject, direct object, and indirect object are identified on various derivational levels, it is not obvious how nominals get marked with particular cases.

Finally, the discussion of these questions raises another problem: What is the nature of the verb Classes, which play an important role in determining case marking? In this work, the membership of the verb Classes is determined on the basis of morphological criteria (see ch. 16, Appendix A).[4] The syntactic and semantic nature of the Classes is investigated in the final chapter.

2 The approach taken: theoretical framework

This study is an exploration of the adequacy of relational grammar for describing the syntax of a language. The version of relational grammar used here has been modified to make the work more accessible to those interested primarily in Georgian. Only those parts of relational grammar are discussed here that are most important to this research on Georgian; other concepts are introduced in the text as they become relevant. The theory of relational grammar is discussed in detail in Johnson (1974, 1977, to appear), Perlmutter (1978, 1979, to appear a, b, c, d), Perlmutter & Postal (1974, 1977, to appear a, b, c), Postal (1977), and other works cited below.

2.1 *Some principles of relational grammar*

The central claim of relational grammar is that the processes of human languages are best described by rules operating, not on strings of ordered elements, on cases, or on constituent structure trees, but on grammatical relations. It is held that grammatical relations are the most appropriate basis for stating generalizations, both for universal rule-types and principles, and for language-particular data. For example, the rule of Passivization is best described universally as a rule that promotes direct objects to subjecthood, not as a rule that moves the second NP from the left all the way to the left, etc. (cf. Perlmutter & Postal 1977).

A fundamental principle of this theory is that the structure of a clause is the set of *grammatical relations* obtaining between the elements of a clause. The predicate bears the *predicate relation* to its clause. Three types of nominal-clause relations will figure in this work. (i) *Terms* or *term nominals* bear a *subject relation*, a *direct object relation*, or an *indirect object relation*. Subjects and direct objects together constitute the *nuclear terms*. (ii) The second type of nominal-clause relations are *oblique relations*; among these, only the *benefactive relation*, *instrumental relation*, *superessive relation*, *locative relation*, and *comitative relation* will be referred to here. (iii) The third type is *retirement relations* – *chomeurs* and *emeritus terms*. Nominals bearing one of these relations are terms that become *non-terms* through the application of some syntactic rule, as specified by the Chomeur Law (below) or some other condition (cf. ch. 7, §3 and ch. 11, §1). The notion 'non-term' includes nominals bearing oblique relations and those bearing retirement relations. Predicates and nominals are said here to be *dependents of the clauses* to which they bear grammatical relations. The nominals bearing grammatical relations to a clause are said here to be *governed by the verb* of that clause. The predicate relation, term relations, and oblique relations are undefined primitives of the theory; chomeur relations and emeritus relations are defined by the theory.

Only the central nominal-clause relations are investigated in this work. The *overlay relations*, such as *question* and *topic*, are not treated here. The internal structure of nominals must also be ignored here; only the relations of whole nominals to their clauses are investigated. A number of other elements, such as adverbs, are completely ignored in order to study in depth the relations named above.

The following hierarchy among nominal-clause grammatical relations is posited:

(4) subject
    direct object
    indirect object
    non-terms

This hierarchy plays a role in a variety of processes of natural language (cf. Keenan & Comrie 1977 and other recent works).

Rules that change grammatical relations are of three types: (i) *Revaluations* include *advancements* and *demotions*. An advancement is the promotion of a nominal dependent of a clause up the hierarchy (4). A familiar example of this is Passivization, the advancement of a direct object to subjecthood (Perlmutter & Postal 1974, 1977, and ch. 7). A demotion lowers a nominal dependent of a clause on the hierarchy (4). One demotion is discussed here; Inversion is the rule that demotes subjects to indirect-objecthood (cf. Harris (to appear a), Perlmutter (to appear b), and ch. 8). (ii) *Ascensions* raise a nominal out of an embedded clause, making that nominal a dependent of the higher clause. A familiar example of this is Non-Subject Raising (*Tough*-Movement), the ascension of an object from a sentential subject to subjecthood of the higher clause (cf. ch. 4). (iii) *Clause Union* makes all dependents of an embedded clause dependents of the matrix clause. Clause Union is discussed here in relation to organic causatives (ch. 5) and inceptives (ch. 16, §2.2.3 and n. 14).

Since the structure of a clause is the set of grammatical relations holding between the elements of a clause, and since syntactic rules may act on nominals to change grammatical relations, the theory recognizes distinctions in derivational *levels*, or *strata*. It is found in this work that, for Georgian, reference to *initial* and *final* levels is adequate for the formulation of most rules. Intermediate levels, however, are also recognized. (The schematic representation of levels of derivation is discussed in the introductory Note on Presentation.) An important principle of relational grammar is that a particular grammatical relation is not simply a bundle of properties; rather, the syntactic rules of a particular language predict precisely which properties are associated with initial and which with final termhood (cf. Johnson 1977). For example, we will find that in Georgian the derived subject of a passive can trigger Subject Person Agreement, a property of final subjects, and cannot trigger *Tav*-Reflexivization, a property restricted to initial subjects.

The theory of relational grammar defined in the works cited above puts a number of constraints on each of the types of rules that exist and thus the types of human language that can exist. Three of these are central and are stated informally here. Others are introduced in relation to a specific rule as they become relevant. Some are not relevant to this work and are not discussed here (cf. works cited above, especially Perlmutter and Postal (to appear c), for a more detailed discussion of constraints).

The Oblique Law requires that if a nominal bears an oblique relation$_i$ at any level, it bears that relation$_i$ initially. This rules out the possibility of any term or non-term nominal changing to an oblique relation, while permitting the possibility of an oblique being promoted to a term relation.

The Stratal Uniqueness Law, informally stated, requires that at each stage of derivation no more than one nominal bear a given term relation in a clause. That is, at any stage of derivation, a clause may have no more than one subject, one direct object, and one indirect object (cf. ch. 5, §4.2 and ch. 6, §6 for additional discussion).

The Chomeur Law, or Chomeur Condition, informally stated requires that if a nominal$_i$ assumes the term relation borne by nominal$_j$, nominal$_j$ becomes a chomeur. For example, in English the advancement of the direct object under Passivization puts the initial subject *en chomage.* Here the subject chomeur, unlike a subject in English, cannot trigger Reflexivization, cannot trigger Verb Agreement, cannot trigger Equi, cannot undergo Subject-to-Subject Raising, etc.

2.2 *Why relational grammar?*

Georgian is a language with 'free' word order; that is, the order of words in a sentence does not directly indicate grammatical relations. For this reason, formulating the rules of Georgian syntax on the basis of word order would not be as straightforward as for a language like English. The simplest way to do so would be to formulate rules on the basis of the most unmarked order, then have 'scrambling' rules apply in recognition of the artificiality of that order. Similarly, it would be possible to formulate rules on the basis of cases. But each rule of syntax would essentially have to incorporate the case marking differential represented in (2–3). Grammatical relations, on the other hand, provide the basis for a simple formulation of the rules of Georgian syntax and for the capturing of linguistically significant generalizations about the syntax and semantics of the language.

A second reason for working within the theory of relational grammar is that a major concern of this work is universal grammar, in the sense that it is an investigation of the appropriateness of certain proposed universals in a language with a typologically unusual structure. A number of universals have been proposed concerning rules like Passivization (cf. Keenan 1975, Perlmutter and Postal 1977, etc.) and causative formation (cf. Aissen 1974a, b; Comrie 1975; Perlmutter & Postal 1974;

and Shibatani 1976). Testing these proposals on Georgian data is one purpose of this work. Since various languages have various word orders, universals of rules of this type are most simply stated on the basis of grammatical relations, not on the basis of movement of constituents. Relational grammar thus provides the best framework for a comparative investigation of this sort.

Finally, it is well known in linguistics that a theory of language may highlight certain problems, and that a theory itself may point to solutions. In this instance, relational grammar provides the keys to the central problem of Georgian linguistics – the case differential sketched above. In particular, the two rules of Inversion and Unaccusative, defined within this theory, lead to the realization that case marking in Georgian is not as complex as it appears to be (cf. §3.3 below and chs.8, 9, 16). Relational grammar also highlights problems in Georgian that had not previously been addressed. For example, because relational grammar identifies a class of retired terms, we can confront the problem of how this class behaves and how it is marked (cf. §3.2.2 below and ch. 11). Thus, the theoretical framework in part shapes the investigation.

3 Results of the investigation

3.1 *The notions 'subject', 'direct object', and 'indirect object'*

It is established in chs. 1 and 2 that, although the dependents of a clause may be marked with different cases when the governing verb is in Series I and II (as illustrated in (1a–b)), one nominal has in both Series a particular set of syntactic characteristics, which are associated with 'subject'. Another nominal has in both Series a set of characteristics which can be associated with 'direct object', and a third has ones associated with 'indirect object'. In ch. 1, various syntactic phenomena are introduced and associated with particular grammatical relations in Series I. In ch. 2, it is shown that the *same* nominal is involved in the same phenomena in Series II, even though its case marking is not the same as in Series I.

Chapters 2–8 and 10 establish the simplicity of a grammar in which syntactic rules refer to grammatical relations. Each of the chapters 4–8 and 10 introduces one or more rules that change grammatical relations. In each instance it is shown that a nominal that bears a particular grammatical relation undergoes the rule, regardless of its other syntactic or morphological characteristics. Thus, while these rules may be simply stated on the basis of grammatical relations, in Georgian it would be impossible to capture the linguistically relevant generalizations on the basis of case.

3.2 *The nature of the rules that change grammatical relations*

3.2.1 *Inversion.* In ch. 8 it is shown that Georgian has a rule of Inversion, which demotes the subject to indirect-objecthood. Phenomena of this type have been discussed under the names 'Flip', 'Psych Shift', or 'Subject–Object Inversion' for other languages; but the evidence supporting a syntactic rule of this type has generally been sparse (cf. Davison 1969; Harris 1973; G. Lakoff 1970; R. Lakoff 1968; N. McCawley 1976; Postal 1970, 1971; Rosenbaum 1967; Sridhar 1976a, b; and Ziv 1976). In Georgian, on the other hand, the evidence is very strong. In Georgian the rule is not restricted, as in many languages, to a class of so-called 'affective' verbs. It applies also if triggered by a particular mood (the evidential) of the governing verb. The construction in this environment provides a kind of evidence rather different from that found in other languages.

3.2.2 *Retired Term Marking.* At least six different rules in Georgian – Object Raising, Causative Clause Union, Passivization, Inversion, Masdar Formation, and Infinitive Formation – create retired terms (cf. above §2.1). In ch. 11 it is shown that the rules that mark retired terms can be stated in a completely general way on the basis of grammatical relations, without reference to the rule that creates the particular retired term.

3.2.3 *Rules that refer to both initial and final termhood.* Chapters 14–16 establish that the rules of *Tav*-Reflexivization, Number Agreement, and two of the rules that assign cases are stated on initial and final termhood; that is, they are so-called 'global rules'. (*Tav*-Reflexivization is stated more simply in ch. 1 and refined in ch. 14 on the basis of facts considered in intervening chapters.)

3.2.4 *Rule interaction.* It is found to be unnecessary to impose conventional extrinsic ordering on syntactic rules. In general, rule interaction can be handled simply by stating rules on initial termhood, on final termhood, with reference to termhood at more than one level (cf. §3.2.3), or without restriction (cf. Epilogue, §4).

3.3 *Accounting for the case marking differential*

In ch. 8 it is shown that a syntactic rule, Inversion, applies just where Pattern C is found in (3). Thus, Pattern C is shown to be derived from Pattern B by a regular synchronic rule. In ch. 9 it is established that no such rule relates Pattern A to Pattern B, and that these two case Patterns must be assigned by different sets of rules. Finally, ch. 16 shows that the rules of case marking for Series II can be most simply stated if they take into account both the initial and final grammatical relations established in this work.

3.4 *The nature of the Georgian verb classes*

In early chapters verb Classes are treated as arbitrary groupings of verbs, morphologically defined. It is established that verbs of Classes 1 and 3 have two important syntactic characteristics:

(a) They govern Pattern A in Series II.
(b) They govern Inversion in Series III.

In ch. 16 it is shown that these two characteristics are related to a single semantic–syntactic trait that distinguishes these verbs from those of Classes 2 and 4. The fact that the semantic–syntactic nature of each verb can be predicted on the basis of universals means that Class membership is not arbitrary, as has been thought; it is therefore not necessary to have a lexical listing of Class membership.

3.5 *Georgian data from the point of view of universals*

Because of its structure, Georgian provides evidence that differs in an interesting way from that given by other languages. For example, it has been claimed that Causative Clause Union creates simplex clauses (Aissen 1974a, b; Comrie 1975, 1976e; Postal & Perlmutter 1974; etc.). In Georgian the evidence for this is particularly strong. First, each term, not just the subject, triggers Person Agreement. Second, the nominals in the causative are assigned cases according to (2–3) above. This is evidence that the rule that forms causatives is not a rule that assigns particular cases to the initial terms of the embedded clause, but that it actually makes them dependents of the matrix clause (cf. ch. 5).

Discussion of the nature of nominalizations has generally been based on selection restrictions, productivity, and nominal-like structure (cf. Chomsky 1970; Comrie 1976d; G. Lakoff 1970; Lees 1963; and McCawley 1970). Georgian provides a different kind of evidence that certain nominalizations are derived from clauses. In Georgian, retired terms are marked regularly (cf. §3.2.2). The fact that this marking is also used in nominalizations enables us to identify the grammatical relations involved. An analysis that did not derive these nominalizations from full clauses would be claiming that the generality of this marking was an accident (cf. chs. 10 and 11).

3.6 *Relational grammar*

This work constitutes a powerful argument for relational grammar. Georgian presents a complex problem in terms of case marking. I have shown here that the facts of case marking in simple sentences and in the major complex constructions of the language can be stated in a simple and elegant fashion on the basis of grammatical relations. A straightforward statement of the case marking facts cannot be made on the basis of linear order and dominance relations.

Second, it is shown throughout that Georgian, a non-Indo-European language whose syntax is not well known outside Georgia, behaves as predicted by relational grammar. There are some points on which the wrong prediction or no prediction at all is made by the theory; these are pointed out in the text. But the fact that the majority of the data are correctly predicted is a very strong argument for some form of this theory. Clause Union and Inversion provide particularly good examples of the fact that the universal core of a rule can be simply stated on the basis of grammatical relations, but not on the basis of linear order or case. Case marking rules are particularly good examples of the fact that language-particular rules may be stated most simply on the basis of grammatical relations.

Third, among current theories, only relational grammar defines a class of retired terms. As pointed out above and as shown in detail in ch. 11, any analysis of Georgian that fails to recognize this class of nominals will miss a set of significant generalizations about the language. Thus, any analysis written in terms of a theory that does not define such a class of nominals will be giving an inadequate account of Georgian.

3.7 *The systematicity of Georgian*

Georgian has been characterized by some general linguists as a language in which every verb is an exception, as a language that is 'totally irregular'. I believe that this monograph, because it shows the consistency in a large number of syntactic–semantic phenomena, establishes that

Georgian is systematic. Like any other language, it has irregularities; but these should not be permitted to obscure the general, regular patterns of the language.

4. Some necessary preliminaries

In this section several rules and phenomena are introduced. The first has no theoretical importance to this work, but it is necessary to the understanding of some of the data presented below. The second is Question-Word Question Formation; its importance derives from the fact that it is used as a test of constituency. Suppletion is introduced in §4.3; it will be the basis for arguments concerning termhood in later chapters. Finally, a statement is made concerning word order in Georgian.

4.1 Aris-*Cliticization*

In Georgian, there are pairs of sentences like (5–8), where *aris* 'he/she/it is' alternates with its clitic form, *-a*.

(5) (a) *es aris čemi çigni.*
this is my book
'This is my book.'
(b) *es čemi çignia.*
book-is
'This is my book.'

(6) (a) *sad aris čemi çigni?*
where is my book
'Where is my book?'
(b) *sadaa čemi çigni?*
where-is
'Where is my book?'

(7) (a) *es çigni čemi aris. / es çigni aris čemi.*
'This book is mine.'
(b) *es çigni čemia.*
'This book is mine.'

(8) (a) *gela aris ekimi.*
Gela is doctor
'Gela is a doctor.'

(b) *gela ekimia.*
doctor-is
'Gela is a doctor.'

As we can see by comparing (6) with (5) and (7–8), *-a* occurs after vowels, *-aa* after consonants.

It is most natural for the cliticization rule to apply wherever its input conditions are met, except when the word *aris* is emphasized. Because *-a* is more natural than *aris*, most of the examples given in this work use *-a*; it will be glossed as in the (b) examples above.

I have called *-a* a clitic because it can never bear stress; nor can there be a pause between the enclitic and the word to which it attaches.

This rule applies to reduce only the third person singular form only in the present tense; there are no clitic (i.e. unstressable) forms of the other persons and numbers in the present or of any person in other tenses.[5]

That this rule is clause-bounded is shown in (9). In (a) the *-a* has attached to a constituent of its own clause, *ekimi* 'doctor'. In (*b) and (*c) it has cliticized to constituents of the higher clause.

(9) (a) *gelam icis, rom anzori ekimia.*
Gela knows that Anzor doctor-is
'Gela knows that Anzor is a doctor.'
(b) **gelam icisaa, rom anzori ekimi.*
Gela knows-is that Anzor doctor
('Gela knows that Anzor is a doctor.')
(c) **gelama icis, rom anzori ekimi.*
Gela-is knows that Anzor doctor
('Gela knows that Anzor is a doctor.')

The *-a* most often cliticizes to a predicate nominal or predicate adjective, but it may attach to other constituents as well. In (a) of (10) it is on a participle, in (b) on the subject.

(10) (a) *es noxi gaçmendilia.*
this rug cleaned-is
'This rug has been cleaned.'
(b) *es noxia gaçmendili.*
rug-is cleaned
'This rug has been cleaned.'

4.2 *Question-word Question Formation*

In this section I describe the formation of Q-word questions in Georgian. Because of constraints described in §4.2.3 and 4.2.4, this rule serves as a test of clause constituency (cf. §4.2.6).

For forming content questions, Georgian uses question pronouns, an adjective *romeli* 'which', and a variety of adverbs.

4.2.1 *The position of the Q-word in a simple sentence.* In general, the Q-word in a simple sentence in Georgian occurs in the position immediately preceding the finite verb. Since the position of the verb relative to other constituents is fairly free, the Q-word may be sentence-initial or sentence-internal. The sentences of (11) differ only in the relative order of their constituents.

(11) (a) *sad çavida nino?*
where she-went Nino
'Where did Nino go?'
(b) *nino sad çavida?*
'Where did Nino go?'
(c) **sad nino çavida?*
(d) **çavida nino sad?*

Those sentences are ungrammatical (*11c, d), in which the Q-word does not immediately precede the verb.

There is one constituent which, if present, must intervene between the Q-word and the finite verb that governs it; this is the negative particle: *ar* 'not', *aɣar* 'no more', *nu* – negative imperative, *rodi* – emphatic negative, or *ver* 'cannot'.[6] (12) gives variant word orders; only (12a) is grammatical, with the order Q-word NEG VERB. Any other order is ungrammatical.

(12) (a) *sad ar ginda çasvla?*
where not you-want going
'Where do you not want to go?'
(b) **ar sad ginda çasvla?*
(c) **ar ginda sad çasvla?*

I will refer to the proper position of the Q-word as 'immediately preceding the finite verb', in spite of the intercession of these particles.

4.2.2 *Multiple Q-words.* Multiple Q-words, when they occur in a single clause, are all attracted to the verb as described above. They occur in preverbal position in the same order that the full nominals for which they substitute occur most naturally in clauses, that is, SUBJECT OBJECT. (13a) gives a declarative sentence; (13b) is its grammatical counterpart with Q-words as both subject and direct object. (*13c–e) give variant word orders.

(13) (a) *nino p̣urs qidulobs.*
Nino bread buys
'Nino is buying bread.'
(b) *vin ras qidulobs?*
who what buys
'Who is buying what?' cf. *Who what buys?
(c) **ras qidulobs vin?*
(d) **vin qidulobs ras?*
cf. Who buys what?
(e) **ras vin qidulobs?*

(13b) differs from the ungrammatical examples in that its subject and object Q-words both precede the verb and occur in the order SUBJECT OBJECT.

4.2.3 *What constituents may be questioned?* In Georgian any constituent may be questioned in a simple sentence. In (14a) the subject is questioned, in (14b) the direct object, in (14c) the indirect object, in (14d) the object of a postposition, and in (14e) a non-term in the instrumental case.

(14) (a) *xval vin midis kalakši?*
tomorrow who he-goes city-in
'Who is going into the city tomorrow?'
(b) *bebia ras ačukebs švilišvils?*
grandmother what she-gives-him-it grandchild
'What will grandmother give (her) grandchild?'
(c) *vis elaparaḳeba vano?*
who he-talks-to-him Vano
'Who is Vano talking to?'
(d) *vistan midixar?*
who-at you-go
'To whose house are you going?'

(e) *rit aris is saxli ašenebuli?*
what-INST it-is that house built
'What is that house built out of?'

In unmarked order in non-interrogative sentences, all attributives precede the head of the nominal, except the relative clause, which follows. When a constituent of a nominal is questioned, the whole nominal precedes the verb. In (15a) the possessive precedes its head, the whole nominal immediately preceding the verb. In (*15b) the nominal-internal order is reversed so that the possessive (the Q-word) immediately precedes the verb; in (*15c) the head follows the verb.

(15) (a) *visi švili xar šena?*[7]
whose child you-are you
'Whose child are you?'
(b) **švili visi xar šena?*
(c) **visi xar šen švili?*

(16) illustrates similar facts, this time with *romeli* 'which'. Again, (16a) differs from (*16b) and (*16c) only in word order.

(16) (a) *romeli çigni ginda?*
which book you-want
'Which book do you want?'
(b) **çigni romeli ginda?*
(c) **romeli ginda çigni?*[8]

Thus, for nominals of all kinds, the whole nominal must immediately precede the verb, the questioned constituent preceding its head noun.[9]

4.2.4 *A constraint on Question Formation.* As in English and other languages, the question-word remains in its own clause in indirect questions. (17b) illustrates an indirect question with a (direct) question in the matrix clause also; (17a) illustrates the same embedded clause without the matrix question.

(17) (a) *marinam icis, ķreba sad ikneba.*
Marina she-knows meeting where it-will-be
'Marina knows where the meeting will be.'
(b) *icit, sad ikneba ķreba?*
you-know where will-be meeting
'Do you know where the meeting will be?'

In Georgian, Q-words in direct questions cannot move out of embedded clauses (cf. §4.2.5 for the exception to this generalization). In (18) and (19), the (*b) sentences are ungrammatical attempts to move the questioned constituent into the matrix clause. The (*c) sentences show that it is also ungrammatical to leave the Q-word in the embedded clause.

(18) (a) *(ase) vpikrob, rom nino moigebs.*
thus I-think that Nino will-win
'I think that Nino will win.'
(b) **vin pikrob(,) (rom) moigebs?*
who you-think
('Who do you think will win?')
(c) **pikrob, (rom) vin moigebs?*
('Who do you think will win?')

(19) (a) *gelam tkva, rom mama ċavida kalakši.*
Gela said that father went city-in
'Gela said that Father went into the city.'
(b) **sad tkva gelam, (rom) mama ċavida?*
where
('Where did Gela say that Father went?')
(c) **gelam tkva, (rom) mama sad ċavida.*
('Where did Gela say that Father went?')

(*19b) is ungrammatical in the intended meaning, but has a grammatical reading, on which the Q-word originated in the higher clause. The grammatical meaning, then, is 'Where was Gela when he said that Father left?' (18–19) show that in Georgian it is impossible to question a constituent of an embedded clause with a direct question.

The meaning intended for (*18b) may be expressed by (20a) or (20b).

(20) (a) *ras pikrob? vin moigebs?*
what you-think who will-win
'Who do you think will win? / What do you think? Who will win?'
(b) *rogor pikrob? vin moigebs?*
how
'Who do you think will win?'

I know of no arguments to suggest that (20a) is a single sentence, or that (20b) is. Each has two intonation peaks, one on each Q-word: *ras, vin, rogor, vin.*

4.2.5 *An exception to the clause-boundedness of Question Formation.* When a clause is embedded in a matrix clause containing an independent modal verb, a constituent of the embedded clause may be moved out, contrary to the generalization stated in §4.2.4. There are three such independent, finite modals in Georgian: *unda* 'he wants it', *šeuʒlia* 'he can, he is able', and *sč̣irdeba* 'he needs it'. (21) illustrates the questioning of a constituent of an embedded clause and the movement of the questioned constituent to the matrix verb. (21a) is a declarative sentence, (21b) a properly formed question, and (*21c) a question with an improperly positioned Q-word.

(21) (a) *es minda, rom ninom moigos.*
this I-want that Nino will-win
'I want Nino to win.'
(b) *vin ginda, rom moigos?*
who you-want
'Who do you want to win?'
(c) *(*es*) *ginda, rom vin moigos?*

(21) differs from (18) only in the governing verb. (The different form of the verb of the dependent clause and concomitant change of case is governed by the matrix modal verb. This should not concern the reader now; it is the topic of the main part of this monograph.)

4.2.6 *Question Formation as a test of constituency.* Keeping in mind the single exception noted in §4.2.5, we can use Question Formation as a test of constituency in a clause, since it generally applies only within a clause, as shown in §4.2.4. This test will be used, for example, in ch. 5, to show that the derived structure of an organic causative is a simple sentence.

The fact that nominals are treated as inseparable wholes, as shown in §4.2.3, provides us with a test for the constituency of a nominal. This will be used, for example, to show in ch. 4 that the *tvis*-nominal ('for'-nominal) is not a constituent of the chomeur of the sentential subject in object-raised sentences.

4.3 *Suppletion*

In Georgian there are certain verbs that are suppletive for animacy of the direct object, number of the direct object, or number of the subject.[10] Three of these are described below, since they will form the basis for arguments about grammatical relations in subsequent chapters. In addition, there are verbs that are suppletive for tense; one of these is described in §4.3.4, as it will be the basis of an argument in ch. 8.

4.3.1 *Animacy of direct object.* The verb *miṭana/ç̣aqvana* 'take' is suppletive for the animacy of its direct object, such that the former occurs only with inanimates and the latter only with animates, as shown in (22) and (23). In the (a) sentences, the direct object is animate, in the (b) sentences, inanimate. (22) contains the form *miiṭana*, and is grammatical only with an inanimate direct object; (23) contains *ç̣aiqvana*, and is grammatical with an animate.

(22) (a) **anzorma gela miiṭana sṭudkalakši.*
Anzor Gela took student-compound-in
('Anzor took Gela into the student compound.')
(b) *anzorma ḳoḳa miiṭana sṭudkalakši.*
jug
'Anzor took the jug into the student compound.'

(23) (a) *anzorma gela ç̣aiqvana sṭudkalakši.*
took
'Anzor took Gela into the student compound.'
(b) **anzorma ḳoḳa ç̣aiqvana sṭudkalakši.*
('Anzor took the jug into the student compound.')

(*22a) is grammatical if Gela is a corpse. In spite of this, these two forms do *not* have the meanings of 'carry' and 'lead', respectively, in English. This difference shows up in (24), where the notion 'lead' would be inappropriate, but where *ç̣aqvana* is grammatical, not *miṭana*.

(24) (a) **gela miviṭane mcxetaši mankanit/ uremit.*
Gela I-took Mtsxeta-in car-with/ ox-cart-with
('I took Gela to Mtsxeta by car/by ox cart.')
(b) *gela ç̣aviqvane mcxetaši mankanit/uremit.*
I-took
'I took Gela to Mtsxeta by car/by ox cart.'

Moreover, *ç̣aqvana*, not *miṭana*, is used with the direct object *bavšvi* 'child', whether the child is led or carried:

(25) **bavšvi mivitane.*
child I-took
('I took the child.')

(26) *bavšvi çaviqvane.*
I-took
'I took the child.'

The noun *mankana* 'car' is a systematic exception – a grammatical animate – with all verbs that are suppletive for the animacy of their direct objects.

(27) (a) **mankana mivitane mcxetaši.*
car I-took Mtsxeta-in.')
(b) *mankana çaviqvane mcxetaši.*
I-took
'I took the car to Mtsxeta.'

The same suppletion occurs for this verb root with other preverbs, verbal prefixes which indicate, among other things, differences of direction; for example, *šetana/šeqvana* 'take in', *motana/moqvana* 'bring'. Most of the examples will use the preverbs used in the example sentences above.

4.3.2 *Number of direct object.* The verb *gadagdeba/gadaqra* 'throw' is suppletive for the number of its direct object, such that the former form occurs with singular direct objects, and the latter only with plurals. These facts are established by (28) and (29), which contain *gadagdeba* and *gadaqra*, respectively. The (a) sentences have singular direct objects, the (b) sentences plurals.

(28) (a) *bavšvma gadaagdo kva.*
child he-threw stone
'The child threw the stone.'
(b) **bavšvma gadaagdo kvebi.*
stones
('The child threw the stones.')

(29) (a) **bavšvma gadaqara kva.*
he-threw
('The child threw the stone.')
(b) *bavšvma gadaqara kvebi.*
'The child threw the stones.'

4.3.3 *Number of subject.* The verb *jdoma/sxdoma* 'sit' is suppletive for the number of its subject, such that the former occurs with singular subjects and the latter only with plurals.[11] (30) shows that this is so: (*30a) has a singular subject, (30b) a plural.

(30) (a) **bavšvi dasxda.*
child he-sat-down
('The child sat down.')
(b) *bavšvebi dasxdnen.*
children they-sat-down
'The children sat down.'

4.3.4 *Tense/Class.* The verb 'take' discussed in §4.3.2 is actually multiply suppletive – for animacy of its direct object and for tense. In some tenses the verb is a Class 1 verb, in some Class 4. The distribution of these characteristics and of the roots is summarized in the chart below. Finite verb forms are given so that the different roots will show up; the roots are in heavy type. All forms express 'I take it/him' in the various tenses.

(31)

	Inanimate Object		Animate Object	
Present	*mima***kvs**	Class 4	*mim***qavs**	Class 4
Aorist	*mivi***ṭane**	Class 1	*ç̣avi***qvane**	Class 1

The fact that the final grammatical relations in the Class 4 verb forms differ from those in the Class 1 forms will be used as one argument to motivate the rule of Inversion in ch. 8.

4.4 *Number Agreement*

For many speakers, only animate nominals trigger Number Agreement, even if the nominal otherwise meets the conditions to be a Number Agreement trigger (ch. 15). This can be seen in (32), where the animate subject in (a) triggers Number Agreement, but the inanimate subject in (b) fails to do so.

(32) (a) *ḳnuṭebi goraven.*
kittens they-roll
'The kittens are rolling.'
(b) *burtebi goravs.*
balls it-rolls
'The balls are rolling.'

Although this dichotomy is required by prescriptive norms, the rule is not always followed by speakers. Most of the examples given here do follow the rule, and the verb is glossed in the *singular* when a plural fails to trigger Number Agreement, as in (32b). Nominals that occur with a quantifier are in the singular in Georgian and also fail to trigger Number Agreement, as shown in (33).

(33) (a) *sami ḳnuṭi goravs.*
three kitten it-rolls
'Three kittens are rolling.'
(b) *ramdeni ḳnuṭi goravs.*
how-many
'How many kittens are rolling?'

4.5 *Word order*

There is considerable freedom of word order in Georgian. The following orders are very frequent and natural: S V DO IO, S DO V IO, and S IO DO V. It is clear that the subject usually precedes other major constituents, but it is not clear that Georgian is more 'basically' either OV or VO. A detailed discussion of word order can be found in Vogt (1974) and in works cited there.

I *Syntactic tests for termhood*

In this chapter I will introduce several tests for termhood (subjecthood, direct-objecthood, indirect-objecthood).

In Georgian the problem of isolating the notion 'subject' is particularly complex. As discussed in the Introduction, §1, an adequate analysis cannot be based on a single criterion. In this chapter, preliminary tests for subject are introduced; additional tests for subjects are defined in later chapters. An adequate analysis of the notion 'subject' must also take into consideration all Classes of verbs and all Series (cf. Introduction, §1). In this chapter, I deal with Classes 1–3 in Series I. In ch. 2, Series II will be introduced. Treatment of Series III and Class 4 verbs, both of which govern Case Pattern C, is deferred until ch. 8.

1 Tav-**Reflexivization**

In this section I will examine the rule that governs the occurrence of the reflexive pronoun *tav*-. It will be shown that this pronoun may be coreferent only to the subject of its clause and that it therefore serves as a test of subjecthood.[1]

1.1 *Morphology*

Reflexivization is expressed in Georgian with the pronominal element *tav*-. This root also functions as an independent noun meaning 'head' or 'source'; it will be glossed here as 'self' when it functions as a reflexive. The forms *tavis*- (singular) and *taviant*- (plural) serve as possessive reflexives. The first person singular reflexive is *čemi tavi* 'my self', the second *šeni tavi* 'your self', and the third person reflexive is *tavisi tavi* 'self's self', that is, 'himself, herself, itself', without distinction of gender.[2] The possessive element, *tavisi*, is deleted from the third person reflexive under certain circumstances (cf. ch. 6). The reflexive phrase is grammatically third person and triggers third person agreement. The conditions on the independent occurrence of *tavis-*/*taviant-* are different from those on *tav-*, and they are described in §2 below.

1.2 *Subjecthood of the trigger*

The reflexive pronoun *tav-* is always coreferent with the subject of its clause. That the subject may be coreferent with *tav-* can be seen in

(1) (a) *vano* *irçmunebs* *tavis* *tavs.*[3]
Vano-NOM he-convinces-him-I-1 self's self-DAT
'Vano is convincing himself.'

(b) *vano* *elaparaḳeba* *tavis* *tavs.*
Vano-NOM he-talks-him-I-2 self's self-DAT
'Vano is talking to himself.'

(c) *vano* *pikrobs* *tavis* *tavze.*
Vano-NOM he-thinks-I-3 self's self-on
'Vano is thinking about himself.'

(2), (3), and (4) show that the reflexive pronoun is not coreferent with the direct object, the indirect object or the object of a postposition.

(2) *mxaṭvari* *daxaṭavs* *vanos* *tavistvis.*
painter-NOM he-paints-him-I-1 Vano-DAT self-for
'The painter$_i$ will paint Vano$_j$ for himself$_i$.'

(3) (a) *nino* *ačvenebs* *ṗaṭara* *givis* *tavis*
Nino-NOM she-shows-him-him-I-1 little Givi-DAT self's
tavs *sarḳeši.*
self-DAT mirror-in
'Nino$_i$ is showing little Givi$_j$ herself$_i$ in the mirror.'

(4) *vano* *givize* *elaparaḳeba* *tavis* *tavs.*
Vano-NOM Givi-on he-talks-him-I-3 self's self-DAT
'Vano$_i$ is talking to himself$_i$ about Givi$_j$.'

In (2) *tav-* can refer only to *mxaṭvari*, not to *vanos*; the direct object, *vano*, cannot trigger *tav-*. Similarly in (3a), *tav-* refers only to *nino*, the subject, never to *givis*, the indirect object. The coreference that obtains between the subject and *tav-* is independent of the relative positions of the pronoun and antecedent, as can be seen in (3b) and (3c), which differ from (3a) only in word order.

(3) (b) *nino paṭara givis tavis tavs ačvenebs sarḳeši.*
(c) *sarḳeši paṭara givis tavis tavs ačvenebs nino.*
'Nino$_i$ shows little Givi$_j$ herself$_i$ in the mirror.'

In (4) the reflexive pronoun can refer only to the subject, *vano*, never to *givi*, an oblique nominal.

Since the coreference of *tav-* with the subject has been illustrated for a Class 1 verb in (1a), a Class 2 verb in (1b), and a Class 3 verb in (1c), we can conclude that in general *tav-* is triggered by the subject-nominal.[4]

1.3 *Clausemate constraint*

The rule of *Tav*-Reflexivization is governed by a clausemate constraint, which requires that the pronoun and its antecedent be dependents of the same clause. Thus in (5a) there is no ambiguity as to the meaning-reference of *tav-*; it can refer only to *nino*, the subject of its own clause.

(5) (a) *vano pikrobs, rom nino saçmels*
Vano-NOM he-thinks-I-3 that Nino-NOM food-DAT
amzadebs tavistvis.
she-prepares-it-I-1 self-for
'Vano$_i$ thinks that Nino$_j$ is preparing food for herself$_j$.'

In spite of the fact that *vano* is also a subject, it cannot be the antecedent of *tav-*, since these two nominals are not dependents of the same clause. We can see from (5b) that this is independent of relative word order, since here *tav-* precedes *nino*, yet nevertheless is unambiguously coreferent to it.

(5) (b) *vano pikrobs, rom tavistvis nino saçmels amzadebs.*
'Vano$_i$ thinks that Nino$_j$ is preparing food for herself$_j$.'

The lack of ambiguity in (5) shows that *tav-* in a postpositional phrase cannot be triggered by the subject of a higher clause; the ungrammaticality of (*6) shows that this is not possible, even where identifying the reflexive pronoun with the embedded subject would produce nonsense.

(6) **vano icvams axal ḳosṭiums, romelic*
Vano-NOM he-puts-on-it-I-1 new suit-DAT which-NOM
tavistvisaa šeḳerili.
self-for-it-is-I-2 sewn
('Vano is putting on the new suit, which was made for him.')

There is no sensible grammatical reading for (*6).

The ungrammaticality of (*7) shows that it is equally impossible for the reflexive pronoun to be the subject of the lower clause, triggered by the subject of the higher clause.

(7) (a) **vano* *pikrobs,* *rom tavisi tavi* *tamada*
Vano-NOM he-thinks-I-3 that self's self-NOM toastmaster-NOM
ikneba.
he-will-be-I-2
('Vano thinks that he will be toastmaster.')
(b) **rom tavisi tavi tamada ikneba, ase pikrobs vano.*
thus
('Vano thinks that he will be toastmaster.')

(*7b) differs from (*7a) only in that in the latter the lower clause is first, the pronoun thus preceding its antecedent.

Similarly, *tav-* in the higher clause cannot be coreferential to the subject of the lower clause:

(8) (a) **tavisi tavi* *pikrobs,* *rom vano*
self's self-NOM he-thinks-I-3 that Vano-NOM
tamada *ikneba.*
toastmaster-NOM he-will-be-I-2
(*'Himself thinks that Vano will be toastmaster.')
(b) **rom vano tamada ikneba, ase pikrobs tavisi tavi.*
thus

(*8b) differs from (*8a) only in that in the former the embedded clause is first, and the trigger thus precedes the target of reflexivization. In (*8) *tav-* in the matrix clause is triggered by *vano*, the subject of the embedded clause.

1.4 *Coreference with dropped pronouns*

The nominal with which the *tav-* is coreferent may be omitted in the final structure of the sentence, if its referent has been established in the discourse. This is accounted for by the rule of Unemphatic Pronoun Drop, which is described in §4 below. It is nevertheless clear that *tav-* is coreferent to the subject, for the person and number of the pronoun correspond to those of the subject marked in the verb form (cf. §3 on marking subjects in the verb). This can be seen in the glosses of (9), which represent the only possible interpretation of these sentences.

(9) (a) *čems tavs vakeb.*
my self-DAT I-praise-him-I-1
'I praise myself.'
(b) *šens tavs akeb.*
your-SG self-DAT you-praise-him-I-1
'You (sg) praise yourself.'
(c) *tavis tavs akebs.*
self's self-DAT he-praises-him-I-1
'He praises himself.'

1.5 *Summary*

Since the full pronoun *tav-* may have as its antecedent only the subject of its own clause, it provides us with a test for subjecthood within a single clause.

2 Tavis-**Reflexivization**[5]

In this section, the rule that governs the occurrence of the possessive reflexive pronoun will be described. The distribution of *tavis-/taviant-* is different from that of the full pronoun *tav-*; we must therefore account for these phenomena in terms of two distinct rules. It will be shown that *tavis-/taviant-* may be coreferent only with terms; it therefore serves as a test for termhood.

Any third person term can trigger *tavis-/taviant-*. The subject is the trigger in (10), the direct object in (11), and the indirect object in (12).

(10) *deda bans tavis švils.*
mother-NOM she-bathes-him-I-1 self's child-DAT
'The mother$_i$ is bathing her$_i$ child.'

(11) *nino azlevs bavšvs tavis dedas.*
Nino-NOM she-gives-her-him-I-1 child-DAT self's mother-DAT
'Nino$_i$ is giving the child$_j$ to its$_j$ mother.'
'Nino$_i$ is giving the child$_j$ to her$_i$ mother.'

(12) *ras ačukebs gela ias tavis*
what-DAT he-gives-her-it-I-1 Gela-NOM Ia-DAT self's
dabadebisdγeze?
birthday-on
'What does Gela$_i$ give Ia$_j$ on her$_j$ birthday?'
'What does Gela$_i$ give Ia$_j$ on his$_i$ birthday?'

In (11) and (12) either term may be the antecedent. Thus, any term may be coreferential with *tavis-*.[6]

A non-term cannot trigger *Tavis*-Reflexivization, as established by

(13) *gela* *saubrobs* *giastan tavis çignze.*
Gela-NOM he-chats-I-3 Gia-at self's book-on
'Gela$_i$ is chatting with Gia$_j$ about his$_i$ book.'

(14) *babua* *ķmaqopilia* (*misi*) *švilišvilit*
grandfather-NOM pleased-he-is-I-2 his grandchild-INST
tavis korçilši.
self's wedding-in.
'The grandfather$_i$ is pleased with his$_i$ grandson$_j$ at his$_i$ wedding.'

In (13) *tavis-* cannot refer to *gia*, which is the object of a postposition and not a term. Nor can the non-term instrumental-NP, *švilišvilit*, trigger the possessive reflexive in (14), even though it is semantically more natural that way than with the grammatical reading. Thus, we see that all and only terms can serve as antecedents of *tavis-*.

3 Person Agreement

In Georgian any one of the terms governed by a verb may trigger Person Agreement; subjects trigger Subject Person Agreement, direct objects trigger Direct Object Person Agreement, and indirect objects trigger Indirect Object Person Agreement. The term 'Person Agreement' will be used to refer to these three rules together, since they apply under similar circumstances. Each rule serves as a test for specific termhood.

3.1 *Description of the basic morphology of Person Agreement*

Paradigms (15), (16), and (17) represent the intersection of the categories of person and number. But these two agreement categories must be described by distinct rules in Georgian, since the conditions under which a given nominal triggers Number Agreement are different from the conditions under which it triggers Person Agreement. The rules of Person Agreement are simple and can be described now, but the rule of Number Agreement must take into account various other factors and will not be described until ch. 15.[7]

(15) *Subject markers*

	singular	plural
1. person	*v*—	*v*—*t*
2. person	ø	—*t*
3. person	—*s*/*a*/*o*	—*en*/*es*/*nen*, *etc.*

(16) *Direct object markers*

1. person	*m*—	*gv*—
2. person	*g*—	*g*—*t*
3. person	ø	ø

(17) *Indirect object markers*

1. person	*m*—	*gv*—
2. person	*g*—	*g*—*t*
3. person	*s*/*h*/ø—	*s*/*h*/ø—*t*[8]

The dash represents the position of the verb stem, which includes the root and various formants. The alternation between third person subject markers is governed by the tense-aspect and Class of the verb form. The alternation in third person indirect object markers is phonologically determined. The latter alternation, first clarified in Shanidze (1920), is also described in Tschenkéli (1958: vol. 1, 370–2), Vogt (1971: 83), and Shanidze (1973: 184–5). For some speakers the third person indirect object marker is always zero, or has become part of the verb root, thus making (16) and (17) nearly identical. Because the use of the third person indirect object markers is not consistent, I will not use the difference between them to argue that a given nominal is a direct object as opposed to an indirect object, or vice versa. But the markers in (16) and (17) will be used to argue that a given nominal is an object, without distinguishing on the basis of marking alone between direct and indirect. Because of the similarity between (16) and (17) and the confusion between them, they will often be referred to jointly as 'object markers'. Since I had informants who adhered strictly to the rules distinguishing (16) and (17), and others who did not distinguish them, my examples will not necessarily be consistent; but these facts will never be crucial to any argument.

Below, (18) illustrates the use of subject markers, (19) the use of direct object markers, and (20) the use of indirect object markers; each occurs with verbs of Class 1, 2, and 3.

(18) (a) *namcxvars* **v**-*acxob.*
pastry-DAT **I**-bake-it-I-1
'I am baking pastry.'
(b) *namcxvari cxveb*-**a**
pastry-NOM **it**-bakes-I-2
'The pastry is baking.'
(c) *sṭven?*
you-whistle-I-3 (zero marker)
'Are you whistling?'

(19) (a) *gela* **g**-*içvevs* *supraze.*
Gela-NOM he-invites-**you**-I-1 table-on
'Gela is inviting you to the banquet.'
(b) *mama motxrobas uqveba ninos.*
father-NOM story-DAT he-tells-her-**it**-I-2 Nino-DAT (zero)
'Father tells Nino a story.'
(c) *ia ipovis satvales.*
Ia-NOM she-will-find-**it**-I-3 glasses-DAT (zero marker)
'Ia will find (her) glasses.'

(20) (a) *mi*-**s**-*cems* *sasmels sṭumars.*
he-gives-**him**-it-I-1 drink-DAT guest-DAT
'He is giving drink to the guest.'
(b) *mama motxrobas* **g**-*iqveba.*
father-NOM story-DAT he-tells-**you**-it-I-2
'Father is telling you a story.'
(c) *gela* **m**-*pasuxobs.*
Gela-NOM he-answers-**me**-I-3
'Gela is answering me.'

The paradigms (15–17) represent an abstraction of the categories of person and number from all verb forms. Derived indirect objects show some superficial variations from (17); these are described with their morphology in chs. 6 and 8.

3.2 *Conditions on the occurrence of subject and object markers*

In Georgian, Person Agreement may be triggered by any term of the verb. Yet the reader will not always see the morpheme that marks agreement with a particular term. This may be due to any one of several factors. First, the zero markers in (15–17) may disguise agreement.

Second, there are morphophonemic rules that govern the co-occurrence of particular affixes:

(21) +v+ → ø/—— +g+
The morpheme **v** deletes before the morpheme **g**.
+s+ → ø/+v+ ——
The morpheme **s** or its variant **h** deletes following the morpheme **v**.

(22) +s+ → ø/ —— +t+
The morpheme **s** deletes before the morpheme *t*.

(21) describes the co-occurrence of personal prefixes; *v* is the first person subject marker, *g* the second person object marker, and *s* or *h* the third person indirect object marker. (22) describes the co-occurrence of the suffixes *s*, third person subject, and *t*, a marker of plurality.[9]

Third, there are syntactic rules which affect the occurrence of person markers on final forms of the verb. The first such rule is *Tav*-Reflexivization, which is described above in §1. The reflexive pronoun is itself third person, though it may be coreferential to a first or second person. Being third person, it triggers a zero marker in most instances (cf. paradigms 16–17). This rule thus insures that we never get sequences like **v–m*—, where *v* is a first person subject marker, and *m* is a first person object marker. The second syntactic rule that affects the occurrence of person markers will not be discussed in detail until ch. 3, but it is stated here for the reader's convenience.

(23) *Object Camouflage*
If a clause contains an indirect object, a first or second person direct object is realized as a possessive pronoun + *tavi*, where the possessive reflects the person and number of the input form.

Here, too, the possessive + *tavi* phrase is third person and triggers third person agreement. Thus, this syntactic rule insures that we never get sequences like **g-m*—, where *g* and *m* are second and first person object markers, respectively.

Because of the conditions described above, there is not always a one-to-one correspondence between terms and their markers in the verb form. But every final term triggers Person Agreement, the realization of which is specified by (15–17), (21–23), *Tav*-Reflexivization, and the low level rules required to select the forms of third person subject markers, depending on plurality, tense-aspect, Class, and morphological sub-group of the verb form.

3.3 *Implications of Person Agreement*

Keeping in mind the conditions (21–23) and *Tav*-Reflexivization, we can determine which nominal in a clause triggers Subject Person Agreement, and which ones trigger Object Person Agreement. Subject Person Agreement then serves as a test for subjecthood: only subjects trigger the markers in (15). Object Person Agreement will not be used as a test for specific termhood, since the conditions on it vary with the speaker, but it does provide a test for general objecthood.

4 Unemphatic Pronoun Drop

Compare the sets of sentences (24) and (25). The examples show that *miçera/moçera* 'write' takes an indirect object, and is always interpreted as having an indirect object even when there is none on the surface. *Daçera* 'write', on the other hand, does not take an (initial) indirect object, and is interpreted as having a direct object, but not an indirect.[10]

(24) (a) *çerils mivçer ʒmas.*
letter-DAT I-will-write-him-it-I-1 brother-DAT
'I will write a letter to my brother.'

(b) *çerils mivçer.*
'I will write a letter to him.'

(c) *mivçer.*
'I will write it to him.'

(25) (a) **çerils davçer ʒmas.*
I-will-write-it-I-1
('I will write a letter to my brother.')

(b) *çerils davçer.*
'I will write a letter.'

(c) *davçer.*
'I will write it.'

The root of both verbs is *çer*; *da-*, *mi-*, and *mo-* are preverbs, the presence of which indicates completed aspect. The difference between *mi-* and *mo-* is determined by the grammatical person of the indirect object (cf. ch. 6, example (19)); first and second person require *mo-*, third *mi-*. In addition, the difference between *da-* on the one hand, and *mi-* and *mo-* on the other, corresponds to the glossed difference between (24) and (25).

To account for the interpretation of the non-overt terms in (24–25),

I propose (i) the lexical specification that *miçera/moçera* takes an obligatory initial indirect object, while *daçera* does not take an initial indirect object, and (ii) a rule of Unemphatic Pronoun Drop, which applies only to terms.[11] The rule drops first, second, and third person independent personal pronouns unless they are either emphatic, or else non-terms. In the following sections I will demonstrate that such a rule affects only terms. Additional evidence to support a rule of Unemphatic Pronoun Drop is given in ch. 3, n. 3.

4.1 *Motivating Unemphatic Pronoun Drop and the proposed inventories of initial terms*

4.1.1 *Person Agreement.* The rule of Unemphatic Pronoun Drop is needed to account for the fact that verbs are marked to agree with a particular person, even when the corresponding nominal is absent from the surface structure. The verb form *vçer* 'I write', for example, will always be associated semantically with a first person subject, not a second or third. Similarly, when the subject pronoun is stressed, we necessarily get *me vçer* 'I write', not **šen vçer* 'you I-write', or **is vçer* 'he I-write'.

The inventories of initial terms proposed above are necessary to explain the fact that *miçera/moçera* requires Indirect Object Person Agreement, while *daçera* does not. This fact is established in (26–29). (26), in which *miçera/moçera* occurs with indirect object markers, is grammatical.

(26) (a) *vanom* *mo***m***çera* *çerili.*
Vano-ERG he-wrote-**me**-it-II-1 letter-NOM
'Vano wrote me a letter.'
(b) *vanom mo***g***çera* *çerili.*
he-wrote-**you**-it-II-1
'Vano wrote you a letter.'
(c) *vanom mi***s***çera* *çerili.*
he-wrote-**him**-it-II-1
'Vano wrote him a letter.'

(*27), where there are no markers of indirect object agreement, is ungrammatical.

(27) (a) **vanom moçera çerili.*
('Vano wrote me/you a letter.')
(b) **vanom miçera çerili.*[12]
('Vano wrote him a letter.')

With the verb *daçera*, on the other hand, the indirect object agreement marker must *not* occur. This is shown by the ungrammaticality of the examples in (*28), which are parallel to (26), and the grammaticality of the example in (29), which is parallel to (*27).

(28) (a) **vanom da*m*çera çerili.*
('Vano wrote me a letter.')
(b) **vanom da*g*çera çerili.*
('Vano wrote you a letter.')
(c) **vanom da*s*çera çerili.*
('Vano wrote him a letter.')

(29) *vanom daçera çerili.*
'Vano wrote a letter.'

These four sets of sentences show that *miçera/moçera* must take an indirect object marker and that *daçera* must not. This can be accounted for in a straightforward manner if (i) these verbs are assigned the initial terms claimed for them above, and (ii) Unemphatic Pronoun Drop drops the pronominal indirect objects in (26) after they have triggered Indirect Object Person Agreement. Since *daçera* will not have an initial indirect object, nothing will trigger the rule, and the sentences of (*28) will not be produced.

4.1.2 *Number Agreement.* Although the rule of Number Agreement has not yet been introduced, we may observe here that first person terms always trigger the rule (cf. ch. 15). Unemphatic Pronoun Drop is needed to account for the fact that the meaning of the form *vçert* is always 'we write', not 'I write'. Similarly, this rule explains the fact that when the subject is emphatic, it is always the pronoun *čven* 'we' that occurs with this verb form, not *me* 'I'.

4.1.3 Tav-*Reflexivization.* The rule of Unemphatic Pronoun Drop is needed to explain why we get (30a), but not (*30b, c). In the first, the verb agrees with a first person subject and has a first person reflexive. The two ungrammatical examples also have first person Subject Person Agreement, but have second and third person reflexives, respectively.

(30) (a) *čems tavs vakeb.*
my self-DAT I-praise-him-I-1
'I praise myself.'

(b) **šens tavs vakeb.*
your self-DAT
(*'I praise your self.')

(c) **tavis tavs vakeb.*
self's self-DAT
(*'I praise himself.')

In order to account for the ungrammaticality of (*30b) and (*30c), we must have initial structures with personal pronouns, a rule of *Tav*-Reflexivization, and a rule of Unemphatic Pronoun Drop.

4.1.4 Tavis-*Reflexivization.* In (31a) below, the possessive reflexive *tavis-* is triggered by *vano*; but in (31b), where the reference of *tavis-* is the same, the antecedent is not present.

(31) (a) *vanos vugzavni tavis çigns.*
Vano-DAT I-send-him-it-I-I self's book-DAT
'I am sending $Vano_i$ his_i book.'

(b) *vugzavni tavis çigns.*
'I am sending him_i his_i book.'

Since *tavis-* is triggered by a coreferential nominal, a pronoun *mas* 'him-DAT' must be posited for initial structure, with a rule of Unemphatic Pronoun Drop to account for the absence of the pronoun in (31b)

4.2.1 *Terms.* (30) illustrates the dropping of the subject pronoun, (31) the dropping of the indirect object. (32) shows that the direct object pronoun is also dropped.

(32) *čems megobars, gelas, icnob? ḳi, vicnob.*
yes I-know-him-I-I
'Do you know my friend, Gela? Yes, I know him.'

The inclusion of the pronoun *mas* 'him' would imply a contrast, for example: *ḳi, mas vicnob, mis das ḳi ara.* 'Yes, I know him, but not his sister.'

4.2.2 *Instrumentals.* Instrumentals can never be dropped. (33) is a statement with a nominal in the instrumental case.

(33) *xmas čavçer magniṭaponit.*
voice-DAT I-will-write-it-I-I tape-recorder-INST
'I will record (my) voice.' Lit: 'I will write my voice with a tape recorder.'

In reply to the question, *es magniṭaponia?* 'Is this a tape recorder?', (34a) is a possible response; (34b), while grammatical, is unnatural because it makes no reference to the tape recorder, as indicated in the translation.

(34) (a) *ḳi, xmas čavçer amit.*
yes it-INST
'Yes, I will write my voice with it.' i.e. 'I will record my voice with it.'

(b) *ḳi, xmas čavçer.*
'Yes, I will write down my voice.'

This shows that instrumentals cannot be dropped, even when they are unemphatic pronouns.

4.2.3 *Nominals marked with a postposition.* (35) illustrates the use of the complex postposition *-tan ertad* 'with, together with'.

(35) *mcxetaši çavedi gelastan ertad.*
Mtsxeta-in I-went-II-2 Gela-with
'I with to Mtsxeta with Gela.'

In answer to the question, *gelas icnob?* 'Do you know Gela?', (36a) would be a natural response; but (36b), while grammatical, would be highly unnatural as a response.

(36) (a) *diax, çavedi mcxetaši mastan ertad.*
yes him-with
'Yes, I went to Mtsxeta with him.'

(b) *diax, çavedi mcxetaši.*
'Yes, I went to Mtsxeta.'

(36b) shows that the postpositional phrase containing *mas* cannot be dropped; (*36c) shows that it is also impossible to drop the unemphatic pronoun out of a postpositional phrase, leaving the postposition.

(36) (c) **çavedi mcxetaši tan ertad.*
(*'I went to Mtsxeta with.')

4.2.4 *Conjoining.* In (37), the subject is *ia da gela* 'Ia and Gela', not *ia*, and not *gela*.

(37) *ia da gela çavidnen mcxetaši.*
Ia-NOM and Gela-NOM they-went-II-2 Mtsxeta-in
'Gela and Ia went to Mtsxeta.'

Even when the referent is established in discourse, as in answer to a question, one of these conjoined nouns cannot be dropped. For example, in answer to the question *ia sad aris?* 'Where is Ia?', a possible answer would be (38a); but (*38b) with one conjoined nominal omitted is totally ungrammatical.

(38) (a) *igi* *da gela ç̣avidnen mcxetaši.*
she-NOM
'She and Gela went to Mtsxeta.'
(b) **da gela ç̣avidnen mcxetaši.*
('She and Gela went to Mtsxeta.')[13]

Changing the order of elements will not save (*38b), as (*38c) shows.

(38) (c) **gela da ç̣avidnen mcxetaši.*
('Gela and she went to Mtsxeta.')

The subject of (37), if its referent has been established in discourse, and if it is unemphatic, can be dropped, as in (39).

(39) *ç̣avidnen mcxetaši.*
'They went to Mtsxeta.'

The sentences above show that while terms may be dropped, a member of a conjoined set that constitutes a term may not be dropped.

4.2.5 *Possessives.* The subject of (40) is *givis ʒma* 'Givi's brother'.

(40) *givis* *ʒma* *čemi megobaria.*
Givi-GEN brother-NOM my friend-NOM-he-is-I-2
'Givi's brother is my friend.'

If the referent of *givi* has been established in discourse, it may be pronominalized, but not dropped, as shown in (41). In this case, because of the necessity of interpreting the relation 'brother' as belonging to someone, the meaning of the sentence is entirely different if the possessive pronoun is dropped; but (41b), lacking the possessive, is not natural.

(41) (a) *misi ʒma čemi megobaria.*
his
'His brother is my friend.'
(b) *?ʒma čemi megobaria.*
'My brother is my friend.'

I conclude that although subjects may be dropped, a possessive that is a constituent of a subject may not be dropped.

4.3 *Conclusion*

We have seen that the rule of Unemphatic Pronoun Drop applies to terms generally and not to a variety of nominals that are not terms; I conclude, therefore, Unemphatic Pronoun Drop can be used as a test for termhood, since it applies only to terms.[14]

5 Summary

In this chapter I have introduced four processes that provide us with several tests for termhood. While none of these traits is universally characteristic of terms, all of them are typical of terms (cf. Anderson 1976; Keenan 1974, 1976; and Postal & Perlmutter 1974). The level at which the nominals identified by these tests are terms has not yet been specified. This will be considered in later chapters, as we consider the interaction of these rules with other rules of the grammar.

Chapter 2 will be concerned mainly with a different problem, but a test for termhood will be a by-product of that analysis also. Chapters 3 and 4 will describe two rules, each of which is a further test for direct-objecthood. In later chapters, the tests discussed here will provide evidence as to the termhood of particular nominals in more complex constructions.

2 *Case marking in Series I and II*

All of the examples in ch. 1 were in tenses which belong to Series I (cf. Appendix, 'Constituent screeves of Georgian Series'). Sentences with verbs in tenses of Series II exhibit different patterns of case marking. In ch. 1 I established that the nominative-nominals of clauses containing verbs of Classes 1–3 in Series I share a set of syntactic properties, which are associated with the notion 'subject'. In Series II we might expect to find (i) that the nominative-nominal has those properties, (ii) that the nominal which corresponds to the intuitive notion 'subject' has the subject properties, regardless of its case, or (iii) that the subject properties are divided between those two nominals. A variety of different approaches have been taken with regard to this problem (cf. Introduction, §1). In this chapter I will present syntactic evidence to support (ii); that is, I will show that in Series II the nominal which corresponds to the intuitive notion 'subject' has all of the syntactic subject properties established in ch. 1.

1 The case marking differential

The sentences in (1) contain intransitive verbs in Series I; those in (2) contain transitive verbs in Series I. The (a) sentences contain Class 1 verbs, the (b) sentences Class 2 verbs, and the (c) sentences Class 3 verbs. In each, the subject is in the nominative, the direct and indirect objects are in the dative.

(1) (a) *nino* *amtknarebs.*
Nino-NOM she-yawns-I-1
'Nino yawns.'

(b) *vaxṭangi* *ekimia.*
Vaxtang-NOM doctor-NOM-he-is-I-2
'Vaxtang is a doctor.'

(c) *vano pikrobs mariḳaze.*
Vano-NOM he-thinks-I-3 Marika-on
'Vano is thinking about Marika.'

(2) (a) *nino ačvenebs suratebs gias.*
Nino-NOM she-shows-him-it-I-1 pictures-DAT Gia-DAT
'Nino is showing pictures to Gia.'

(b) *mama uqveba motxrobas ninos*
father-NOM he-tells-her-it-I-2 story-DAT Nino-DAT
'Father is telling Nino a story.'

(c) *kartuli ena sesxulobs siṭqvebs*
Georgian language-NOM it-borrows-it-I-3 words-DAT
rusulidan.
Russian-from
'The Georgian language borrows words from Russian.'

(3) and (4) give the same sentences in the aorist, which belongs to Series II. Notice the different cases used here.

(3) (a) *ninom daamtknara.*
Nino-ERG she-yawned-II-1
'Nino yawned.'

(b) *vaxṭangi ekimi iqo.*
Vaxtang-NOM doctor-NOM he-was-II-2
'Vaxtang was a doctor.'

(c) *vanom ipikra mariḳaze.*
Vano-ERG he-thought-II-3 Marika-on
'Vano thought about Marika.'

(4) (a) *ninom ăcvena suratebi gias.*
Nino-ERG she-showed-him-it-II-1 pictures-NOM Gia-DAT
'Nino showed the pictures to Gia.'

(b) *mama mouqva motxrobas ninos*
father-NOM he-told-her-it-II-2 story-DAT Nino-DAT
'Father told a story to Nino.'

(c) *kartulma enam isesxa siṭqvebi*
Georgian language-ERG it-borrowed-it-II-3 words-NOM
rusulidan.
Russian-from
'The Georgian language has borrowed words from Russian.'

In the sentences which contain Class 2 verbs, the case pattern is the same in Series II as in Series I, as can be seen by comparing (3–4b) with (1–2b). (3a, c) and (4a, c) show that in sentences that contain verbs of Class 1 or 3, on the other hand, the case pattern is different in Series II from that used in Series I, regardless of the transitivity of the verb. (The question of whether the transitivity of the verb is relevant to case marking in Georgian is addressed in chs. 12 and 16.) In §2 below, I will present syntactic arguments to show that in clauses containing Class 1 or 3 verbs in Series II, the ergative-nominal is subject. The exact correspondences I am arguing for are summarized in (5).

(5) *Georgian Series II*

	Subject	Direct Object	Indirect Object
Class 1	ERGATIVE	NOMINATIVE	DATIVE
2	NOMINATIVE	DATIVE	DATIVE
3	ERGATIVE	NOMINATIVE	DATIVE

2 Evidence for the analysis of case in Series II

In this section I will show that, in spite of the case marking differential, the subjects of sentences containing Series II verbs correspond to the intuitive notion of subject and to the subjects of Series I. These arguments are based on the tests for termhood established in ch. 1. In each instance I will demonstrate that for each verb Class, the ergative-nominal, the nominative-nominal, and the dative-nominal have all the properties of the grammatical relation indicated for them in (5).

2.1 Tav-*Reflexivization*

It was established in ch. 1 that *tav-* can be coreferential only to the subject of its clause. In (6) we see that *tav-* is coreferential to the nominal bearing the case appropriate to the subject as stated in (5). That is, *tav-* is coreferential to the same nominal as in Series I, though its case is different in Series II. (6) is parallel to (1) of ch. 1; only changes in the tense and concomitant changes in case marking have been made.

(6) (a) *vanom* *dairçmuna* *tavisi tavi.*
Vano-ERG he-convinced-him-II-1 self's self-NOM
'Vano convinced himself.'

(b) *vano* *elaparaḳa* *tavis tavs.*
Vano-NOM he-talked-him-II-2 self's self-DAT
'Vano talked to himself.'

(c) *vanom ipikra tavis tavze.*
Vano-ERG he-thought-II-3 self's self-on
'Vano thought about himself.'

Thus, *tav-* is coreferent to the ergative-nominal in (6a, c) and the nominative-nominal in (6b). In each instance, the antecedent is the nominal claimed in (5) to be subject.

The sentences in (7) show that *tav-* cannot be coreferential to nominals other than the subject. The sentences are parallel to (2), (3a), and (4), respectively, of ch. 1.

(7) (a) *mxaṭvarma daxaṭa vano tavistvis.*
painter-ERG he-painted-him-II-1 Vano-NOM self-for
'The painter$_i$ painted Vano$_j$ for himself$_i$.'

(b) *ninom ačvena paṭara givis tavisi tavi sarḳeši.*
Nino-ERG she-showed-him-him-II-1 little Givi-DAT self's self-NOM mirror-in
'Nino$_i$ showed little Givi$_j$ herself$_i$ in the mirror.'

(c) *vano givize elaparaḳa tavis tavs.*
Vano-NOM Givi-on he-talked-him-II-2 self's self-DAT
'Vano$_i$ talked to himself$_i$ about Givi$_j$.'

(7a) is particularly important, since it shows that the nominative-nominal, *vano*, does not trigger *Tav*-Reflexivization, rather the ergative-nominal does.

The fact that it is the ergative-nominal of Class 1 and 3 verbs and the nominative-nominal of Class 2 verbs that trigger *Tav*-Reflexivization confirms the analysis of subjects made in (5). The fact that other nominals do not trigger the rule, as shown in (7), is weaker confirmation of the analysis of objects in (5).

2.2 Tavis-*Reflexivization*

In ch. 1, §2, it was established that *tavis-* can be triggered by any term. (8) shows that *tavis-* can be coreferential in Series II with those nominals identified as terms in (5) above. In (8a) a subject triggers *tavis-*, in (8b) a direct object, and in (8c) an indirect object. (8) is parallel to (10–12) in ch. 1, only the tense and cases being different.

(8) (a) *dedam dabana tavisi švili.*
mother-ERG she-bathed-him-II-1 self's child-NOM
'The mother$_i$ bathed her$_i$ child.'

(b) *ninom misca bavšvi tavis dedas.*
Nino-ERG she-gave-her-it-II-1 child-NOM self's mother-DAT
'Nino$_i$ gave the child$_j$ to its$_j$ mother.'
'Nino$_i$ gave the child$_j$ to her$_i$ mother.'

(c) *ra ačuka gelam ias tavis*
what-NOM he-gave-her-it-II-1 Gela-ERG Ia-DAT self's
dabadebisdγeze?
birthday-on
'What did Gela$_i$ give Ia$_j$ on his$_i$/her$_j$ birthday?'

Though the examples given here illustrate only Class 1 verbs, they show that the nominals identified as terms in (5) can trigger *Tavis*-Reflexivization. This is consistent with the fact that all and only terms can trigger this rule.

2.3 *Subject Person Agreement*

In ch. 1 I established the following paradigm of person and number markers for subjects of verbs in Series I:

Subject markers

	singular	plural
1. person	*v—*	*v—t*
2. person	ø	*—t*
3. person	*—s/a/o*	*—en/es/nen, etc.*

The same markers indicate the person of the subject in Series II. The examples in (9) are parallel to those in (18) of ch. 1; only the tense and cases have been changed.

(9) (a) *namcxvari gamo-***v***-asxve.*
pastry-NOM **I**-baked-it-II-1
'I baked pastry.'

(b) *namcxvari gamocxv-***a***.*
pastry-NOM **it**-baked-II-2
'The pastry baked.'

(c) *istvine?*
you-whistled-II-3 (zero marker)
'Did you whistle?'

In (9a) the first person subject triggers *v-*; and in (b) the third person subject triggers *-a*. The second person subject in (c) triggers the zero marker. This agreement pattern is constant in Series II, irrespective of the case of the subject. This confirms the analysis of subject in (5).

2.4 *Object Person Agreement*

The markers of Object Person Agreement are repeated below:

Direct object markers

	singular	plural
1. person	*m—*	*gv—*
2. person	*g—*	*g—t*
3. person	ø	ø

Indirect object markers

1. person	*m—*	*gv—*
2. person	*g—*	*g—t*
3. person	*s/h/ø—*	*s/h/ø—t*

(10) and (11), which repeat (19) and (20) of ch. 1 in tenses of Series II, show that the nominals analyzed as objects in (5) are indeed those that trigger Object Person Agreement.

(10) (a) *gelam* *mo-***g***-içvia* *supraze.*
Gela-ERG he-invited-**you**-II-1 table-on
'Gela invited you to the banquet.'

(b) *mama* *motxrobas* *mouqva* *ninos.*
father-NOM story-DAT he-told-her-**it**-II-2 Nino-DAT
(zero marker)
'Father told Nino a story.'

(c) *iam* *ipova* *satvale.*
Ia-ERG she-found-**it**-II-3 glasses-NOM (zero marker)
'Ia found her glasses.'

(11) (a) *mi-***s***-ca* *sasmeli* *stumars.*
he-gave-**him**-it-II-1 drink-NOM guest-DAT
'He gave drink to the guest.'

(b) *mama* *motxrobas* *mo-***g***-iqva.*
father-NOM story-DAT he-told-**you**-it-II-2
'Father told you a story.'

(c) *gelam* **m***-ipasuxa.*
Gela-ERG he-answered-**me**-II-3
'Gela answered me.'

The fact that the same nominals trigger Object Person Agreement in (10) and (11) as in their Series I counterparts, regardless of the case marking they bear, shows that these nominals are indeed objects, as stated in (5).

2.5 *Unemphatic Pronoun Drop*

It was established in ch. 1, §4.2, that only terms can undergo the rule of Unemphatic Pronoun Drop. The analysis summarized in (5) predicts that the nominals listed there can all undergo this rule. (12) illustrates the dropping of a variety of nominals; in each instance the gloss indicates that something has been dropped, not merely omitted.

(12) (a) *mivc̣ere* *c̣erili.*
I-wrote-him-it-II-1 letter-NOM
'I wrote him a letter.'
(b) *dac̣era.*
he-wrote-it-II-1
'He wrote it.'
(c) *darča.*
he-stayed-II-2
'He stayed.'
(d) *gelam* *gip̣asuxa.*
Gela-ERG he-answered-you-II-3
'Gela answered you.'

In (12a) the ergative-nominal and dative-nominal have been dropped from the surface, in (12b) the ergative-nominal and nominative-nominal (cf. ch. 1, §4), in (12c) the nominative-nominal, and in (12d) the dative-nominal. In each instance the person-reference is recoverable. Since all and only the nominals analyzed as terms in (5) can be dropped by this rule, the proposed analysis is again confirmed.

3 Case as a test for termhood

The subject properties established in ch. 1 are borne by the same nominal in Series I and II, but the case marking is different in these two Series. The case pattern used in Series II, moreover, is governed by the Class of the verb form. In (13) and (14) I combine the facts summarized in (5) above with those established for Series I in ch. 1.

(13)

	Subject	*Direct object*	*Indirect object*
Pattern A	ERGATIVE	NOMINATIVE	DATIVE
B	NOMINATIVE	DATIVE	DATIVE

(14)

	Series I	II
Class 1, 3	B	A
2	B	B

I have shown that an analysis that made use of case *a priori* to establish grammatical relations would be inadequate. That is, subject properties in Georgian are not always related to one particular case; nor are direct object properties. An analysis of Georgian based on the assumption that the nominative-nominal (or the ergative-nominal) was always subject would be inadequate.

However, now that the case–grammatical relation correspondences have been established through syntactic tests, case can be used as an argument for grammatical relations. For example, it can be stated that the nominative-nominal associated with a Class 1 verb in Series II must be its direct object. Thus Case Marking provides a further set of tests for termhood. It will be used as evidence for final subjecthood, direct-objecthood, and indirect-objecthood in all of the syntactic constructions considered in this work.

Appendix: Constituent screeves of Georgian Series

I use the word 'tense' or 'tense-aspect' throughout this work to refer to a conjugational unit, traditionally called a *mc̣ḳrivi*. There are ten or eleven *mc̣ḳrivi* in Georgian, divided among the three Series. Each is a unique collocation of tense, aspect, and mood. For example, the present 'tense' is in Series I and represents present time, incomplete aspect, either continuous or non-continuous aspect, and indicative mood. The aorist, on the other hand, is in Series II, and represents past time, complete aspect, and indicative mood. I refer to the *mc̣ḳrivi* as 'screeves' or 'tenses', since this word has no satisfactory translation in English.

The reader may be curious about the tenses which constitute the different Series. Therefore, although these will not be essential to the discussion, I list them here. Series III is introduced in ch. 8.

Constituent tenses of Series I

present
future

imperfect
conditional
present subjunctive
future subjunctive

Constituent tenses of Series II

aorist
optative (second subjunctive)

Constituent tenses of Series III

perfect (first evidential)
pluperfect (second evidential)
third subjunctive (third evidential)

The use of these tenses is described in Shanidze (1973: 215–23), Tschenkéli (1958: chs. 8, 10, 12–13, 18–19, 39–40), and in other handbooks.

3 *Object Camouflage*

This chapter describes a rule that determines the surface form of first and second person direct objects in clauses that also contain indirect objects. This phenomenon will provide a further test for direct-objecthood and for the presence of an indirect object.

1 The facts to be considered

(1) illustrates a simple sentence with third person subject, direct object, and indirect object; (a) is in a Series I tense, (b) in a Series II tense.

(1) (a) *vano anzors adarebs givis.*
Vano-NOM Anzor-DAT he-compares-him-him-I-1 Givi-DAT
'Vano is comparing Anzor to Givi.'[1]
(b) *vanom anzori šeadara givis.*
Vano-ERG Anzor-NOM he-compared-him-him-II-1 Givi-DAT
'Vano compared Anzor to Givi.'

(*2) is exactly parallel to (1), but the second person singular personal pronoun has been substituted for the third person direct object, and the corresponding marker of Direct Object Person Agreement has been added to the verb form.

(2) (a) **vano (šen) gadarebs* givis.[2]
Vano-NOM you-DAT he-compares-him-you-I-1 Givi-DAT
('Vano is comparing you to Givi.')
(b) **vanom (šen) šegadara givis.*
Vano-ERG you-NOM he-compared-him-you-II-1 Givi-DAT
('Vano compared you to Givi.')

(*2) is ungrammatical whether or not the pronoun *šen* 'you-SG' is dropped by Unemphatic Pronoun Drop.

The sentences of (3) are like (*2) except that the expression *šeni tavi* 'your-SG self' has been substituted for *šen* 'you-SG'.

(3) (a) *vano šens tavs adarebs givis.*
your self-DAT he-compares-him-him-I-1
'Vano is comparing you to Givi.'
(b) *vanom šeni tavi šeadara givis.*
your self-NOM he-compared-him-him-II-1
'Vano compared you to Givi.'

Notice that the meaning of these grammatical sentences is what (*2) was meant to express. The verb in (3) agrees with *šeni tavi* as a third person direct object; that is, it has a zero marker (cf. paradigm (16) in ch. 1). (*4) shows that the verb cannot agree with *šeni tavi* as a second person direct object, which would require the marker *g*.

(4) (a) **vano šens tavs* **g***adarebs givis.*
he-compares-him-you-I-1
('Vano is comparing you to Givi.')
(b) **vanom šeni tavi še***g***adara givis.*
he-compared-him-you-II-1
('Vano compared you to Givi.')

In (*5) and (6) we see that the same constraint that governs the occurrence of the second person also governs the first person; (*5) and (6) differ from (*2) and (3), respectively, only in that the former have first person direct objects instead of second person.

(5) (a) **vano (me) madarebs givis.*[2]
me-DAT he-compares-me-him-I-1
('Vano is comparing me to Givi.')
(b) **vanom (me) šemadara givis.*
me-NOM he-compared-me-him-II-1
('Vano compared me to Givi.')

(6) (a) *vano čems tavs adarebs givis.*
my self-DAT he-compares-him-him-II-1
'Vano is comparing me to Givi.'
(b) *vanom čemi tavi šeadara givis.*
my self-NOM he-compared-him-him-II-1
'Vano compared me to Givi.'

The plurals of the first and second persons are also governed by this constraint, but the relevant examples need not be given here.

It remains to be shown that this rule applies to direct objects only when there is an indirect object in the clause. (7) and (8) give paradigms that change for the person of the direct object in Series I and II, respectively.[3] It is clear from these that the simple pronoun forms of the first and second persons as well as those of the third person occur as direct objects, as long as there is no indirect object.

(7) (a) (*me*) **m***arçmunebs.*
me-DAT he-convinces-**me**-I-1
'He is convincing me.'
(b) (*šen*) **g***arçmunebs.*
you-DAT he-convinces-**you**-I-1
'He is convincing you.'
(c) *vanos* *arçmunebs.*
Vano-DAT he-convinces-**him**-I-1
'He is convincing Vano.'

(8) (a) (*me*) *da***m***arçmuna.*
me-NOM he-convinced-**me**-II-1
'He convinced me.'
(b) (*šen*) *da***g***arçmuna.*
you-NOM he-convinced-**you**-II-1
'He convinced you.'
(c) *vano* *daarçmuna.*
Vano-NOM he-convinced-**him**-II-1
'He convinced Vano.'

(5–6) and (2–3) show that Object Camouflage must apply to first and second persons, respectively; (1) shows that it does not apply to third persons. (7–8) show that it operates only if an indirect object is present in the clause.[4]

2 An analysis

I propose to account for the facts discussed above by permitting the rules that generate initial structures to specify first and second person direct objects, as for any other grammatical relation, and by including in the grammar the rule of Object Camouflage.

(9) *Object Camouflage*
If a clause contains an indirect object, a first or second person direct object in that clause is realized as a possessive pronoun + *tavi*, where the possessive reflects the person and number of the input form.

Such an analysis is needed to account for the fact that first and second person pronouns, which occur freely as subjects and indirect objects, and which occur as direct objects when there is no indirect object, do not occur only when there is an indirect object. Further, this rule is needed to account for the fact that *misi tavi* 'his self' is not found in this situation.[5]

3 Interaction with some rules previously considered

3.1 *Person Agreement*

It was observed above that the verb agrees with the phrases *čemi tavi* and *šeni tavi* as third person nominals, not as first and second persons. This can be accounted for by insuring that Person Agreement apply to the output of Object Camouflage. In chs. 4–8 I will establish that Object Camouflage applies generally to the output of rules that change grammatical relations.

3.2 *Unemphatic Pronoun Drop*

In the chapters that follow, we will see evidence that Unemphatic Pronoun Drop, too, is stated on final terms. We can account for the fact that camouflaged objects are never dropped by insuring that Unemphatic Pronoun Drop always applies to the output of Object Camouflage. However, the same fact might be handled equally simply by limiting Unemphatic Pronoun Drop to personal pronouns;[6] this would also correctly prevent this rule from applying to reflexive *tav*-, question-words, relative pronouns, indefinite pronouns, negative pronouns, etc.

3.3 *Case Marking*

The camouflaged object has the same case marking as any direct object would have, as determined by Series and Class of the governing verb.

4 An alternative analysis

The expressions *čemi tavi* and *šeni tavi* are used both as camouflaged objects and as reflexive pronouns (cf. ch. 1, §1.1). Because of this, it might be proposed that Object Camouflage and *Tav*-Reflexivization are a unified phenomenon. However, these phenomena cannot be accounted for with a single syntactic rule, since the rules apply under different conditions, including the following:

(i) *Tav*-Reflexivization requires coreference between the trigger and the target; Object Camouflage has nothing to do with coreference.
(ii) *Tav*-Reflexivization applies to any nominal dependent of the clause which contains its antecedent; Object Camouflage applies only to direct objects.
(iii) Object Camouflage applies only to first and second persons; *Tav*-Reflexivization has no such constraint.
(iv) Object Camouflage applies only in the presence of an indirect object in the same clause; *Tav*-Reflexivization has no such constraint.

I conclude that there is no way to unify the rules of *Tav*-Reflexivization and Object Camouflage.

5 Object Camouflage as a test for termhood

Because Object Camouflage applies to direct objects in the presence of indirect objects, it constitutes a test for direct-objecthood and for indirect-objecthood. In the chapters that follow, Object Camouflage will be the basis of arguments that the initial direct objects of passive and inversion constructions are not final direct objects. It will also be the basis of an argument that indirect objects created by Causative Clause Union and by the so-called 'Version' rules do indeed bear this particular final grammatical relation. Object Camouflage also provides evidence with respect to final direct and indirect objects in other syntactic constructions.

4 *Object Raising*

In this chapter I will argue for a rule, Object Raising.[1] Analyses of similar rules in other languages have shown that a variety of restrictions may be put on this type of rule. In English, for example, any non-subject may be raised to subject (Postal 1971). Chung (1976b) shows that in Indonesian only initial direct objects that are derived subjects may undergo this rule. In Portuguese, an initial direct object may undergo the rule, whether or not it has undergone Passivization (Perlmutter, ms.). In Georgian only initial direct objects that have not changed their grammatical relation can undergo this rule. For this reason, Object Raising provides us with a test for the direct object in Georgian.

Berman (1974) presents evidence that the *for*-nominal in

(1) Tadpoles are easy *for children* to raise.

originates, not as the subject of the embedded clause, but as a dependent of the matrix clause. She argues that this *for*-nominal is coreferential with the embedded subject, which gets deleted by Equi. In §5 below, and in ch. 11, I give two arguments to support a similar analysis for Georgian. The Georgian arguments are of a type very different from the ones which Berman presents for English. Chung (1976b) argues for an analogous structure in Bahasa Indonesia. The fact that languages as different as English, Georgian, and Bahasa Indonesia offer evidence for this analysis suggests that it is universal, regardless of superficial constraints of the kind mentioned above.

1 A description of the data in Georgian

Certain adjectives, such as *advili* 'easy', *ʒneli* 'hard, difficult', and *sasiamovno* 'nice, pleasant', occur with *qopna* 'be' in sentence pairs like those in (2–4). In the (a) examples, the subject is a masdar, or deverbal noun, together with the nominals it governs.[2] The (b) examples contain infinitives. Both masdars and infinitives are treated more completely in ch. 10.

(2) (a) *am gvelis moḳvla ʒnelia.*
this snake-GEN killing-NOM hard-it-is-I-2
'Killing this snake is difficult.'
(b) *es gveli ʒnelia mosaḳlavad.*
this snake-NOM to kill
'This snake is hard to kill.'

(3) (a) *amanatebis miɣeba saxlidan sasiamovnoa.*
parcels-GEN receiving-NOM home-from pleasant-it-is-I-2
'It is pleasant to receive parcels from home.'
(b) *amanatebi sasiamovnoa saxlidan misaɣebad.*
parcels-NOM to-receive
'Parcels are nice to receive from home.'

(4) (a) *čemtvis ʒnelia, ḳargi magalitebis moʒebna.*
me-for hard-it-is-I-2 good examples-GEN finding-NOM
'It is hard for me to find good examples.'
(b) *ḳargi magalitebi ʒnelia mosaʒebnad čemtvis.*
examples-NOM to-find
'Good examples are hard for me to find.'

The **a** which cliticizes to the adjectives in (2–4) is the enclitic form of the third person singular present tense *aris* 'is'; cf. Introduction, §4.1. For the failure of inanimate subjects to trigger Number Agreement, see Introduction, §4.4. The (b) sentences are analyzed in the next section.

2 An analysis

Below I will argue that the grammatical relations in object-raised sentences are partially represented by (5) and (6)[3] and that the rule of Object Raising can be informally described as (7).

(5)

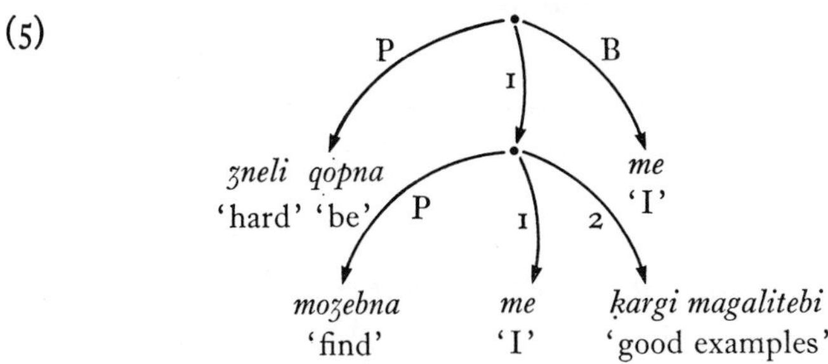

(6)

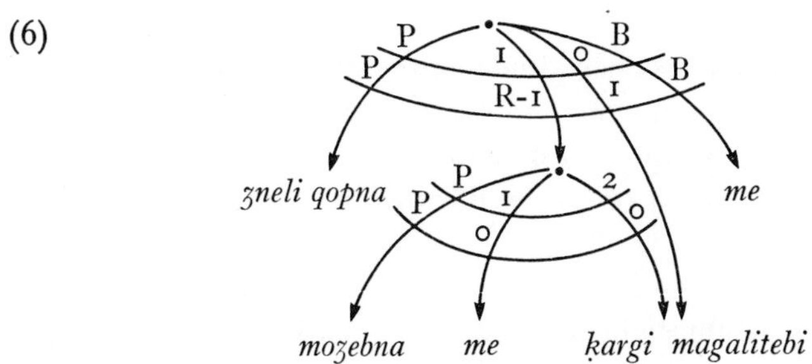

(See Notes on Presentation on the principles of diagramming used here.)

(7) With matrix verbs of the type, *advili aris* 'is easy', the direct object in a sentential subject may ascend.

This analysis is based on Postal & Perlmutter's proposal for a class of rules called 'ascensions', defined in the Introduction, §2.1 (cf. Perlmutter & Postal 1974 and Perlmutter (to appear c)). The Relational Succession Law, not yet stated in this monograph, requires that the ascending nominal (here *ḳargi magalitebi*) assume the grammatical relation borne by its host (here **me ḳargi magalitebi moʒebna*), in this instance becoming subject (cf. Perlmutter & Postal (to appear b)). The Chomeur Law (cf. Introduction, §2.1) predicts that the displaced subject, the embedded clause, will become a chomeur. Since it is suggested that these processes are universal, it is not necessary to state them in a grammar of Georgian. In the grammar, we need only observe that Georgian has this particular rule, and state the language-particular fact that only direct objects may undergo it (cf. §6).

3 Facts concerning the nominative-nominal

In this section it is argued that the nominative-nominal must be the initial direct object of the embedded clause and a final dependent of the matrix clause, rather than the initial subject.

3.1 *Suppletion*

The first step is to argue that *ḳargi magalitebi* 'good examples' of (4b) is initially the direct object of the embedded clause, as in (5). The arguments will be based on suppletion of the verb root for number or animacy of the direct object. The arguments will be of the following form:

(i) In simple clauses that have undergone no change of grammatical relations, there is suppletion of verb roots such that one root is used if the direct object meets a certain criterion (on animacy or plurality), and a different root is used if the direct object fails to meet this criterion.
(ii) In object-raised sentences, the same suppletion is observed with respect to the animacy or plurality of the nominative-nominal.
(iii) If the nominative-nominal is, at some stage of derivation, the direct object of the suppletive verb, the simple sentences and the object-raised sentences can be accounted for by a single rule. If, on the other hand, the nominal in question is not the direct object of the suppletive verb, the grammar must contain two rules to account for these facts.
(iv) The nominative-nominal must therefore be a sometime direct object of the suppletive verb.
(v) Since it is shown below that the nominative-nominal is final subject of *aris* 'be', and since it could not simultaneously bear a grammatical relation to two verbs, it must be at the initial level of derivation that it is direct object of the suppletive verb.

This analysis requires that the rules of suppletion be stated on initial terms; this is confirmed by additional data in later chapters.

3.1.1 *Suppletion for number of direct object.* In Georgian there are several verbs that are suppletive for the number of the direct object; that is, one verb root is used with singular direct objects, and another with plural direct objects. One such pair is *gadagdeba*/*gadaqra* 'throw';

gadagdeba (root *gd*) is used with singulars, while *gadaqra* (root *qr*) occurs only with plurals. Evidence to support this and a complete discussion is given in the Introduction, §4.3.2.

The root alternation in this verb is also governed by the plurality of the nominative-nominal in object-raised sentences, as shown in (8). In (*8a) the final subject of *ʒnelia* 'it is hard' is singular. (8b) differs from (*8a) only in that the final subject of the former is plural, and the sentence is grammatical.

(8) (a) **es didi kva ʒnelia gadasaqrelad.*
this big stone-NOM hard-it-is-I-2 to-throw
('This big stone is hard to throw.')
(b) *es didi kvebi ʒnelia gadasaqrelad.*
stones-NOM
'These big stones are hard to throw.'

(8) may be compared with (29) of the Introduction. (*8a) is ungrammatical because it violates the suppletion condition on the number of *didi kva/kvebi.*

If (8) has an initial structure in which *kva/kvebi* 'stone/stones' is the direct object of the verb 'throw', as proposed in §2, then we can predict the ungrammaticality of (*8a) with the same rule that predicts the ungrammaticality of (*29a) in the Introduction; otherwise the rule must be complicated.

3.1.2 *Suppletion for animacy of direct object.* In Georgian some verbs are suppletive for animacy of the direct object. One such verb is *miṭana/çaqvana* 'take'; *miṭana* (root *ṭan*) is used only with inanimate direct objects, while *çaqvana* (root *qvan*) occurs only with animate direct objects. This suppletion is established in the Introduction, §4.3.1, where this verb is discussed at length.

The root alternation in this verb is also governed by the animacy of the nominative-nominal in object-raised sentences, as shown in (9). Where an animate nominative-nominal is matched with *çaqvana*, as in (9b), the sentence is grammatical; but where it is paired with *miṭana*, as in (*9a), the sentence is ungrammatical. Similarly, where an inanimate nominative-nominal occurs with *çaqvana*, as in (*9d), the sentence is ungrammatical; but where it occurs with *miṭana*, as in (9c), the result is grammatical.

(9) (a) **gela advili ikneba sṭudkalakši misaṭanad.*
Gela-NOM easy it-will-be-I-2 student-compound-in to-take
('Gela will be easy to take into the student compound.')
(b) *gela advili ikneba sṭudkalakši çasaqvanad.*
to-take
'Gela will be easy to take into the student compound.'
(c) *es ḳoḳa advili ikneba sṭudkalakši misaṭanad.*
this jug-NOM
'This jug will be easy to take into the student compound.'
(d) **es ḳoḳa advili ikneba sṭudkalakši çasaqvanad.*
('This jug will be easy to take into the student compound.')

(9) may be compared with (22–23) of the Introduction. The comparison shows that the suppletion that occurs in verbs in simple sentences with respect to animacy of their direct objects also occurs in infinitives of object-raised sentences with respect to the animacy of the nominative-nominal.

According to the proposed analysis, where *gela* and *es ḳoḳa* 'this jug' are initial direct objects of the verb 'take', the sentences of (9) are accounted for by the same principle needed to account for suppletion in simple sentences, such as (22–25) in the Introduction. An analysis in which *gela* and *es ḳoḳa* were not direct objects of 'take' would have to complicate the suppletion rule unnecessarily.

3.2 *Selection restrictions on the matrix subject*

In Georgian, concrete nouns cannot normally occur as the subjects of 'be' plus a predicate adjective such as *advili*, etc.; this is shown in (10).

(10) (a) **anzori advilia.*
Anzor-NOM easy-it-is-I-2
('Anzor is easy.')
(b) **es sḳami advilia.*
this chair-NOM
('This chair is easy.')
(c) *es mušaoba advilia.*
work-NOM
'This work is easy.'

In (*10a) and (*10b) the subject of 'be'+*advili* is concrete; in (10c) it is abstract.

But the subject in object-raised sentences may be concrete; indeed, it is concrete in all the examples of object-raised sentences given above.

These facts are handled in a natural way under the proposed analysis. The constraint is stated on initial structures. The derived subjects of 'be'+predicate adjective originate in initial structures as the direct object of another verb, and hence do not violate the constraint. But a grammar that did not derive object-raised sentences by a rule that changed grammatical relations would have to state that predicate adjectives+'be' do not allow concrete subjects unless accompanied by certain kinds of complements. Thus, I conclude that the final subjects in object-raised sentences are not subjects in initial structures.

3.3 *Question Formation*

Question Formation insures that the questioned constituent immediately precede the verb that governs it. The rule cannot, however, move constituents out of a clause; cf. Introduction, §4.2.4. For this reason, it provides a test for constituency.

The sentences in (11) show that the nominative-nominal, if questioned, must immediately precede *aris* 'is'. In (*11b, c) the questioned nominative-nominal does not immediately precede *aris*.

(11) (a) *ra* *aris* *ʒneli mosaʒebnad?*
what-NOM it-is-I-2 hard to-find
'What is hard to find?'
(b) **ra ʒnelia mosaʒebnad?*[4]
(c) **ra mosaʒebnad aris ʒneli?*[5]

Because a questioned constituent cannot move out of its clause, *ra* 'what-NOM' must be a dependent of the clause containing *aris* 'is'. This is consistent with our analysis, (6), as long as Question Formation applies to the output of Object Raising. In later chapters, we will see additional evidence that Question Formation must apply to the output of relation-changing rules.

3.4 *Case Assignment*

The verb *qopna* 'be', like all Class 2 verbs, governs the nominative case for its subject in all Series. In the sentences of (2–4b), *es gveli* 'this snake', *amanatebi* 'parcels', and *ḳargi magalitebi* 'good examples' are in the nominative case. This supports the analysis above, where these nominals are derived subjects of the verb 'be'.

3.5 *Subject Person Agreement*

The nominative-nominal triggers Subject Person Agreement (cf. paradigm (15), ch. 1). (12) gives a paradigm of an object-raised sentence changing for the person of the nominative-nominal.

(12) (a) *ʒneli var dasarçmuneblad.*
hard I-am-I-2 to-convince
'I am hard to convince.'

(b) *ʒneli xar dasarçmuneblad.*
you(SG)-are-I-2
'You(SG) are hard to convince.'

(c) *gela aris ʒneli dasarçmuneblad.*
Gela-NOM he-is-I-2
'Gela is hard to convince.'

The verb *qopna* 'be' is irregular, and the subject agreement markers listed in paradigm (15) of ch. 1 are not realized in exactly the same form in this verb. But the *v-* of the first person is obvious in the *var* 'I am' of (12a). The *-s* of the third person shows up in the full form *aris* 'is'.

It was observed in ch. 3 that Person Agreement applies generally to the output of rules that change grammatical relations. The proposed analysis predicts therefore that Subject Person Agreement will apply to the output of Object Raising, treating the raised nominal as subject. Thus, (12) confirms the proposed analysis, in particular the final subjecthood of the nominative-nominal.

3.6 *Summary*

It has been shown that the nominative-nominal in the (b) sentences of (2–4) has the properties of the initial direct object of the verb which is realized as an infinitive, and the properties of a non-initial (§3.2) subject of *aris* 'is'. The obvious way to account for these facts is with a rule that makes the initial direct object of the embedded clause the subject of the matrix clause.

4 Facts concerning the infinitive

In §4.1 it is argued that the infinitive, together with the nominals it governs, constitutes a subject chomeur. In §4.2 it is shown that the infinitive and the nominals it governs are a constituent and that these nominals do not become dependents of the matrix clause.

4.1 *Case Assignment*
In ch. 2 I showed that in Series I and II in Georgian, all terms are marked with one of the following cases: nominative, dative, or ergative. The infinitive bears none of these cases. This supports the proposed analysis, according to which the infinitive is a chomeur, not a term of the matrix clause. Nor could the infinitive be a predicate nominal, since predicate nominals are marked with the nominative case in all Series.[6]

4.2 *Question Formation*
In Question Formation, the Q-word immediately precedes the verb of the questioned clause, unless the Q-word is part of a larger nominal, in which case that entire nominal must immediately precede the verb of the questioned clause (cf. (15–16) in Introduction). In (13a) the Q-word *vis* (in *visgan*) does not immediately precede the matrix verb *aris* 'is'. Instead, the whole nominal containing *vis*, namely *visgan misaɣebad* 'from whom to receive', precedes *aris*. This shows that *visgan misaɣebad* is a nominal constituent of the matrix clause. In (*13b, c) *visgan* itself immediately precedes the matrix verb; the fact that these orders are ungrammatical shows that *visgan* is not governed by *aris*. In (*13d) *visgan* precedes *misaɣebad* as in (13a), but the whole fails to precede *aris*. The fact that this order is ungrammatical rules out the possibility that *visgan misaɣebad* is an indirect question, comparable to (17a) in the Introduction.

(13) (a) *amanatebi visgan misaɣebad aris sasiamovno?*
parcels-NOM who-from to-receive it-is-I-2 pleasant
'From whom are parcels nice to receive?'
(b) **amanatebi visgan aris sasiamovno misaɣebad?*
(c) **visgan aris sasiamovno amanatebi misaɣebad?*
(d) **amanatebi sasiamovnoa visgan misaɣebad?*

Thus, (13) shows that *visgan* must be governed by *misaɣebad* and that *visgan misaɣebad* is a nominal governed by *aris*, as proposed in §2.

(14) gives an example of a similar kind, which shows that the *tvis*-nominal is governed by *misacemad* 'to give'.

(14) *sačukrebi vistvis misacemad aris ʒneli?*
gifts-NOM who-for to-give it-is-I-2 hard
'To whom is it hard to give gifts?'

Notice that the interpretation of the *tvis*-nominal in (14) is very different from that of the *tvis*-nominal in (4b). I assume that the former is the initial indirect object of *micema* 'give'. The *tvis*-nominal of (4b) is discussed below in §5.

4.3 *Summary*

In this section I have shown that the infinitive behaves as predicted by the analysis proposed in §2: it is a non-term (§4.1) nominal governed by *aris* (§4.2); the nominals it governs initially are not finally governed by *aris* (§4.2).

5 Facts concerning the tvis-nominal

In this section I will discuss the *tvis*-nominal which occurs in (4b). I will argue against the analysis usually given for Object Raising in most languages, with respect to the *tvis*-nominal ('for'-nominal). The usual analysis makes this nominal the initial subject of the clausal subject. Berman (1974) proposed for English that the *for*-nominal originate in the matrix clause, be coreferent to the subject of the embedded clause, and trigger the deletion of the latter by Equi. It is this analysis I wish to propose for Georgian.

If the *tvis*-nominal originated as the subject of the embedded verb, it would nevertheless not have the properties of a superficial subject. In ch. 10 it is shown that the initial subjects of non-finite verb forms do not have superficial subject properties. Therefore, I will not bother to show here that this nominal fails to trigger Subject Person Agreement, fails to undergo Unemphatic Pronoun Drop, and is not assigned a subject case.

I will, however, show that the *tvis*-nominal is not governed by the infinitive. If the *tvis*-nominal had originated as the subject of the embedded verb, we would expect it to remain a non-term dependent of that clause. In chs. 10 and 11 it is shown that the initial dependents of non-finite clauses continue to be dependents of those clauses, even though they cannot have the properties of superficial terms. Thus, a demonstration that the *tvis*-nominal is the dependent of a different clause will show that it cannot have been the initial subject of the embedded clause.

In §4.2.4 of the Introduction it was shown that only the questioned dependents of a questioned clause occur immediately before the verb of that clause. The fact that *vistvis* 'for whom' immediately precedes the verb in

(15) *sačukrebi vistvis aris ʒneli misacemad?*
gifts-NOM who-for it-is-I-2 hard to-give
'For whom is it hard to give gifts?'

shows that it is governed by the verb, *aris* 'is'. The English translations capture the difference in the meanings in Georgian; (14) asks *toward* whom gift-giving is difficult, (15) asks who *finds* gift-giving difficult. English uses *to* in the former function, and *for* or *to* in the second. In Georgian *tvis* is used for both purposes. Both (14) and (15) are unambiguous in Georgian, because of the constituent structure; but (16) is ambiguous.

(16) *sačukrebi ʒnelia anzoristvis misacemad.*
gifts-NOM hard-it-is-I-2 Anzor-for to-give
'Gifts are hard to give to Anzor.'
'Gifts are hard for Anzor to give.'

Since *tvis* marks nominals in the functions illustrated in both (14) and (15), (16) is ambiguous between these two uses. Only in questions does the word order unambiguously reflect constituent structure.

I have shown here that the *tvis*-nominal is a dependent of the matrix clause in derived structure. If it had originated as the subject of the embedded clause, it should have remained a dependent of the infinitive, as did *visgan* and *vistvis* in (13) and (14). In ch. 11 an additional argument is given that the *tvis*-nominal must have originated in the matrix clause. This argument is based on the fact that this nominal does not have the properties of a retired subject.

6 Object Raising as a test of direct-objecthood

In Georgian, only the direct object may undergo Object Raising. In (*17b) an indirect object raises, in (*18b) the object of a postposition, and in (*19b) the subject of an intransitive; all the resulting sentences are ungrammatical. (17d) and (18d), however, show that the direct object from those same sentential subjects can raise. The (*b) and (*c) sentences differ from one another only in that the latter the direct object has been omitted, as is possible in English.

(17) (a) *ʒnelia anzoristvis sačukris micema.*
hard-it-is-I-2 Anzor-for gift-GEN giving-NOM
'Giving gifts to Anzor is difficult.'
(b) **anzori ʒnelia sačukris misacemad.*
Anzor-NOM to-give
('Anzor is hard to give gifts to.')
(c) **anzori ʒnelia misacemad.*
('Anzor is hard to give to.')
(d) *sačukari ʒnelia anzoristvis misacemad.*
gift-NOM
'A gift is hard to give to Anzor.'

(18) (a) *advilia, ninostvis šarvlis šeḳerva.*
easy-it-is-I-2 Nino-for trousers-GEN sewing-NOM
'Sewing trousers for Nino is easy.'
(b) **nino advilia šarvlis šesaḳeravad.*
Nino-NOM to-sew
('Nino is easy to sew trousers for.')
(c) **nino advilia šesaḳeravad.*
('Nino is easy to sew for.')
(d) *šarvali advilia ninostvis šesaḳeravad.*
trousers-NOM
'Trousers are easy for Nino to sew.'
'Trousers are easy to sew for Nino.'

(See §5 above on the ambiguity of (17–18d).)

(19) (a) *damtknareba sasiamovnoa gočastvis.*
yawning pleasant-it-is-I-2 Gocha-for
'To Gocha, it is pleasant to yawn./ To Gocha, yawning is nice.'
(b) **goča sasiamovnoa dasamtknareblad.*
Gocha-NOM to-yawn
*'Gocha is pleasant to yawn.'

(19) is included just to show that this rule applies, not to absolutives, but to direct objects. In (17) and (18), indirect objects and objects of a postposition have raised like direct objects, but the result is ungrammatical. These data show that this rule applies only to direct objects. Notice that in English the comparable rule applies to any non-subject. Because of its restriction in Georgian, this rule will serve as a test for direct objects.

Object Raising is the first of the rules examined that change grammatical relations. The main purpose in coming chapters will be to examine the nature of other rules that change grammatical relations. A major concern will be the case marking of terms and the marking of retired terms, both processes differing in Georgian from the equivalent ones in other languages.

5 *Causative Clause Union*

Recent studies of causatives have focused on a type of causative formation that is important among the languages of the world (Aissen 1974a, b; Comrie 1975, 1976c; Xolodovich 1969; Shibatani 1976, etc.). This type can be characterized as having a complex (two-clause) initial structure and a simplex (single-clause) final structure. Georgian has a causative of this type. I will refer to this as the 'organic causative',[1] since Georgian also has a causative with a complex (two-clause) final structure. The organic causative is illustrated in (1).

(1) *masçavlebelma gadaatargmnina gelas aḳaḳis*
teacher-ERG he-caused-translate-him-it-II-1 Gela-DAT Akaki-GEN
leksi.
poem-NOM
'The teacher made Gela translate Akaki's poem.'

I will have nothing to say here about the periphrastic causative.

The Georgian data are important for the analysis of causatives because of the particularly strong evidence they bring to bear on the simplex nature of the final structure. Because of the case differential described in ch. 2, an analysis of Georgian that simply assigned the object cases to the nominal dependents of the embedded clause, instead of making them terms of the matrix verb, would be inadequate. Object Agreement and Object Camouflage offer further evidence of a kind not found in more familiar languages. The organic causative provides a particularly strong argument in favor of relational grammar, since the relevant generalizations cannot be simply stated on the basis of linear order and dominance or on the basis of case.

1 An analysis of organic causatives

In the studies cited above, it is shown that in this type of causative the following is generally true across languages:

The initial matrix subject is derived subject of the causative.

In the causative of an intransitive, the initial subject of the embedded verb is realized as direct object of the causative.

In the causative of a transitive,
(A) the initial embedded subject is derived indirect object
the initial embedded direct object is derived direct object
the initial embedded indirect object is a derived non-term

or

(B) the initial embedded subject is a final non-term
the initial embedded direct object is derived direct object
the initial embedded indirect object is derived indirect object.

Georgian exemplifies type (A). In (1) above, the initial matrix subject, *masçavlebeli* 'teacher', is the final subject of the organic causative; the initial embedded subject, *gela*, is the indirect object; and the initial embedded direct object, *aḳaḳis leksi* 'Akaki's poem', is the direct object. This can be seen immediately in the case pattern and will be supported by other evidence in §3.

French has causatives of type (B), as well as type (A). Consider (2) from Aissen (1974a).

(2) Jean a fait chanter l'hymne par les gendarmes.
'Jean had the anthem sung by the policemen.'

Aissen shows that in (2) the initial matrix subject, *Jean*, is also the final subject of the causative; the initial embedded direct object, *l'hymne*, is the final direct object; and the initial embedded subject, *les gendarmes*, is finally a non-term.

Postal & Perlmutter (1974) argue that the Georgian type is basic and that the French pattern in (2) is to be explained by the application of Passivization in the embedded clause. They propose that there is a general rule of Clause Union, partially specified as (3).[2]

(3) *Causative Clause Union*
The complement clause unites with the matrix clause to form a single clause in the following way:
a. The initial subject of an embedded intransitive becomes the direct object of the matrix verb.
b. The initial subject of an embedded transitive becomes the indirect object of the matrix verb.

c. The initial direct object of the complement clause becomes the direct object of the matrix verb.
d. The complement verb becomes a *retired verb.*
e. Other dependents of the complement clause become *emeritus dependents* of the united clause.

There are still a number of open questions concerning (3), including the following:

(i) Is (3b) part of the derivation of type (B) causatives, as claimed by Perlmutter & Postal?

Some linguists have argued that the rule of Clause Union itself has a variant output, and that (3) is not an adequate description for all languages (cf. Comrie 1976e; Cole & Sridhar 1976).

(ii) What is the nature of the complement verb finally?

This problem is touched upon in ch. 10.

(iii) Are there language-particular conditions that affect (3e)?

Georgian, with type (A) organic causatives only, is accurately described by (3). But while it supports (3), it offers no evidence as to whether this analysis is adequate for Causative Clause Union in all languages. Georgian does provide especially strong evidence that an initial indirect object of the complement clause may behave as a non-term dependent of the united clause. Since an emeritus dependent of a clause is not a term of that clause, this behavior would follow from its being emeritus indirect object of the matrix verb under Clause Union. The evidence that I present here does not distinguish between types of retired indirect object; it can be interpreted as evidence that the initial complement indirect object is emeritus dependent of the matrix verb as stated in (3e). I will also present evidence for (3a, b, and c) in Georgian.

In Georgian, the matrix verb and the retired verb fuse to form a single word; the matrix verb is realized morphologically as the causative circumfix (cf. n. 1). The same is true in Turkish and Japanese (cf. Aissen 1974a, b; Kuno 1973), but not in French, where the matrix and retired verbs are distinct words (cf. Kayne 1975), or German, where the matrix and retired verbs are not even necessarily contiguous in the clause (cf. Reis 1973; and Harbert 1977). In Georgian all causatives are in Class 1; this may be attributed to the membership of the matrix verb in Class 1.

I propose that (3) is a part of the grammar of Georgian. It relates initial structures like (5) and (8) to complete networks (6) and (9), respectively.

(4) *direkṭorma* *asṭumra* *vanos*
director-ERG he-caused-visit-him-it-II-1 Vano-DAT
ḳomisia.
commission-NOM
'The director had the commission visit Vano.'

(5)

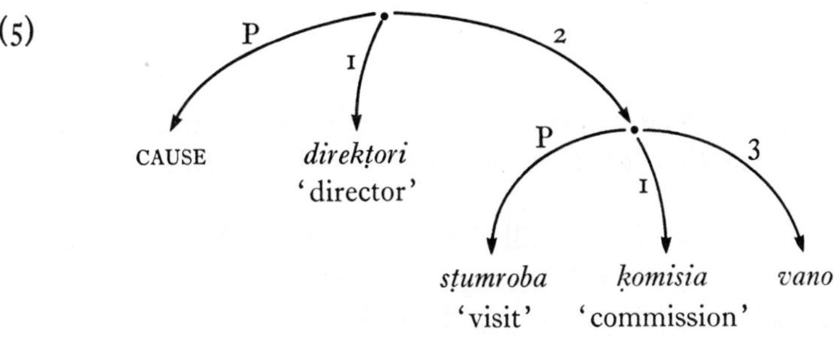

(6)

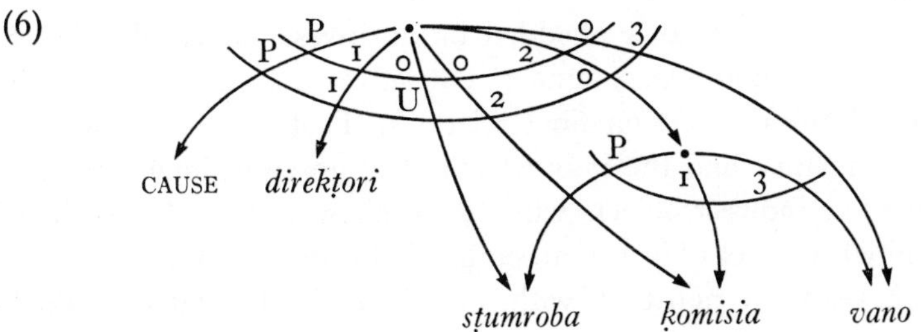

(7) *mamam* *mimacemina* *vardebi* *dedistvis.*
father-ERG he-caused-give-me-it-II-1 roses-NOM mother-for
'Father had me give roses to Mother.'

(8)

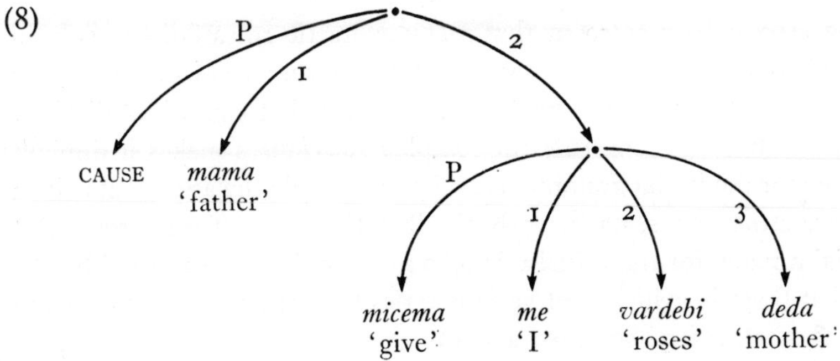

(9)

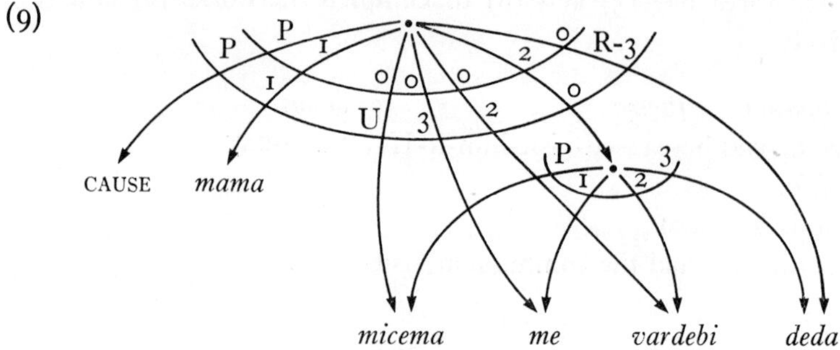

(The principles of diagramming used here are briefly explained in the Notes on Presentation, §3. Here 'U' marks a retired verb.)

In the next two sections I will show that the initial structure of an organic causative has as its direct object a clause, and that the relations that nominals bear to the clause are the same as the relations borne in a simple clause. I will show that the direct objects of embedded transitives and the subjects of embedded intransitives behave like direct objects of the united clause under Causative Clause Union, with respect to all rules stated on final relations. That the subject of an embedded transitive and the indirect object of an embedded intransitive behave like indirect objects will also be shown. In §4 I will show that the initial indirect object of an embedded transitive, under Clause Union, behaves like a non-term with respect to all rules stated on final relations.

2 Initial grammatical relations

Aissen (1974a, b) points out that many syntactic rules fail to apply in the embedded clauses of causatives. She proposes ways of accounting for this, but there remain problems. The fact that causatives disallow the application of many rules in complement clauses makes it difficult to argue for the initial grammatical relations. While the arguments given here are strong ones, particularly the last, they are not numerous. But the claim made for the initial relations in Georgian is supported by the fact that there is evidence of various types for such structures in many languages (cf. references cited above).

2.1 *Lexical entries*

If we do not derive causative sentences from structures like (5) and (8), then we must complicate the lexical entry for each verb in at least the following ways: (i) In addition to the inventory of initial grammatical relations for each non-causative verb, we must list an inventory for each causative verb. The verb *gadaçqveṭa* 'decide', for example, has a subject and direct object in its inventory of initial grammatical relations; its causative has subject, direct object, and indirect object. The verb *šeʒinva* 'sleep' has only a subject in its inventory; its causative has a subject and direct object. The verb *tamašoba* 'play' has a subject and optional direct object in its inventory of initial grammatical relations; the corresponding causative, however, has a subject, direct object, and optional indirect object (cf. ch. 12, §2). All of these facts about causatives are predictable from the analysis given in §1.

(ii) In addition to the selection restrictions on each non-causative verb, we would have to list selection restrictions on each causative. The verb *çevs* 'lies', for example, takes only animate subjects, as shown in (10).

(10) (a) *gela* *çevs* *ṭaxṭze.*
Gela-NOM he-lies-I-2 couch-on
'Gela is lying on the couch.'
(b) **çigni* *çevs* *ṭaxṭze.*
book-NOM it-lies-I-2 couch-on
('The book is lying on the couch.')

The same constraint governs the direct object of the corresponding causative, as shown in (11).

(11) (a) *mama* *gelas* *açvens* *ṭaxṭze.*
father-NOM Gela-DAT he-causes-lie-him-I-1 couch-on
'Father makes Gela lie on the couch.'/'Father lays Gela on the couch.'
(b) **mama çigns* *açvens ṭaxṭze.*
book-DAT
('Father lays the book on the couch.')

These facts are predictable if we derive (11a) from a structure like (5), where the verb *çola* 'lie' is embedded under CAUSE, since the subject of *çevs* 'lies' is the direct object of *açvens* 'causes to lie'.

(iii) The rules that relate syntactic structures to semantic representations would have to be complicated, since, in (10a), for example, it is the subject that lies, but in (11a) the direct object.

A complex structure analysis makes the correct generalizations about the language and predicts the regular relations which exist between every verb and its causative. These regularities could also be accounted for by lexical redundancy rules. In the following section we will see, however, that the facts of *Tav*-Reflexivization force us to choose the complex structure analysis over the redundancy rule analysis.

2.2 Tav-*Reflexivization*[3]

In ch. 1, §1 I showed that *Tav*-Reflexivization can be triggered only by subjects. In an organic causative, *tav-* can be coreferential either with the matrix subject, or with the final indirect object in causatives of transitives, or with the final direct object in causatives of intransitives.

In (12), the causative of an intransitive, *tav-* may be coreferential to *ekimma* 'doctor' or to *vano*, the final subject and direct object, respectively. In (13), the causative of a transitive, *tav-* may be coreferential to *genom* or *rezos*, the final subject and indirect object, respectively.

(12) *ekimma vano alap̣araḳa tavis tavze*
doctor-ERG Vano-NOM he-caused-talk-him-II-1 self's self-on
'The doctor$_i$ got Vano$_j$ to talk about himself$_{i,\ j}$.'

(13) *genom miaṭanina rezos c̣ignebi*
Geno-ERG he-caused-take-him-it-II-1 Rezo-DAT books-NOM
tavistan.
self-at
'Geno$_i$ got Rezo$_j$ to take the books to his$_{i,\ j}$ place.'

Only if *vano* (in (12)) and *rezo* (in (13)) are initial subjects, and *Tav*-Reflexivization is stated on initial terms, are these sentences consistent with the facts of *Tav*-Reflexivization established in ch. 1.[4]

2.3 *Summary*

I conclude that causatives like (4) and (7) must have complex initial structures like (5) and (8). This analysis will account for the lexical correspondences between causatives and the corresponding non-causatives in a simple and elegant way. This is the only analysis that can account in a straightforward way for the fact that the final indirect object can trigger *Tav*-Reflexivization. The arguments to support the initial structure proposed here are not numerous, because, as is known, causatives generally disallow the application of many syntactic rules in the embedded clause. The conclusion reached here is consistent with conclusions other researchers have drawn for other languages based on similar evidence.

3 Derived grammatical relations

We will find that Georgian gives particularly strong evidence for the derived relations proposed in §1.

3.1 *Case Assignment*

In this section I will show that the initial embedded direct object and the initial embedded subject of an intransitive have the case marking of a direct object, dative in Series I and nominative in Series II. I will show that the initial embedded subject of a transitive and the initial embedded indirect object of an intransitive have the case marking of an indirect object, regardless of Series. This is very strong evidence that the case marking of nominals in organic causatives is not arbitrary; rather, the nominals actually become direct or indirect objects.

Below I give an inventory of organic causatives in order to show the case marking of each kind of nominal. Because of the case differential, each example of an organic causative will be given in a Series I tense and in a Series II tense. In each instance, the syntax of a causative verb form will be compared with that of the non-causative corresponding to it.

In Georgian all organic causatives are Class 1 forms, regardless of the Class of the corresponding non-causative verb form.

3.1.1 *The causative of an intransitive.* Intransitive verbs may be in Class 1, 2, or 3.

(14) (a) *bavšvi ʒinebs.*
child-NOM he-sleeps-I-1
'The child is sleeping.'

(b) *ubeduri šemtxveva xdeba baɣši.*
unfortunate accident-NOM it-happens-I-2 garden-in
'An unfortunate accident happens in the garden.'

(c) *sporṭsmeni varjišobs.*
athlete-NOM he-exercises-I-3
'The athlete is exercising, training.'

The causatives in (15) and (16) should be compared with the non-causative verbs of (14); (14a) contains a Class 1 verb, (14b) a Class 2, and (14c) a Class 3 verb. In (14) and (15) the verbs are in Series I, and in (16) in Series II. In (14) the nominative-nominal is the subject of each verb. In (15) and (16) this nominal has the case marking of the direct object: dative in Series I (examples (15)), nominative in Series II (examples (16)). In each causative example, the final subject is marked nominative in Series I, ergative in Series II.

(15) (a) *deda bavšvs aʒinebs.*
mother-NOM child-DAT she-causes-sleep-him-I-1
'The mother is getting the child to sleep.'

(b) *paṭara biči axdens ubedur*
little boy-NOM he-causes-happen-it-I-1 unfortunate
šemtxvevas baɣši.
accident-DAT garden-in
'The little boy is causing an unfortunate accident to happen in the garden.'

(c) *mc̣vrtneli sporṭsmens avarjišebs.*
coach-NOM athlete-DAT he-causes-exercise-him-I-1
'The coach is making the athlete exercise./The coach is training the athlete.'

(16) (a) *dedam bavšvi daaʒina.*
mother-ERG child-NOM she-caused-sleep-him-II-1
'The mother got the child to sleep.'

(b) *paṭarma bičma moaxdina ubeduri*
little boy-ERG he-caused-happen-it-II-1 unfortunate
šemtxveva baɣši.
accident-NOM garden-in
'The little boy caused an unfortunate accident to happen in the garden.'

(c) *mc̣vrtnelma sporṭsmeni avarjiša.*
coach-ERG athlete-NOM he-caused-exercise-him-II-1
'The coach made the athlete exercise./The coach trained the athlete.'

Thus, with an intransitive verb of any Class in the embedded clause, the nominal which corresponds to the subject of the non-causative is, in the corresponding causative, in the case of the direct object; that is, it is in the dative in Series I and the nominative in Series II.

3.1.2 *The causative of a transitive.* While there are transitive verbs in Class 2, they present problems with respect to identifying grammatical relations (cf. ch. 16, Appendix B). Class 1 and 3 transitives are illustrated here. In §4 examples of Class 2 transitives with indirect objects are given, and we will see that their causatives behave like those of Class 1 and 3 verbs.

(17) (a) *mziam cecxli daanto.*
Mzia-ERG fire-NOM she-lit-it-II-1
'Mzia lit the fire.'
(b) *mziam itamaša nardi.*
she-played-II-3 backgammon-NOM
'Mzia played backgammon.'

Compare the non-causatives of (17), which are in Series II, with the causatives of (18) and (19), which are in Series I and II, respectively. In each of the non-causatives, the subject is *mzia*; in the corresponding causatives, *mzia* is in the indirect object case, dative in both Series. The direct objects of the non-causatives, *cecxli* 'fire' and *nardi* 'backgammon', are in the case appropriate to the direct object in each causative: dative in Series I (examples (18)), nominative in Series II (examples (19)). The subject of each causative is in the subject case: nominative in Series I, ergative in Series II.

(18) (a) *mama mzias antebinebs cecxls.*
father-NOM Mzia-DAT he-causes-light-her-it-I-1 fire-DAT
'Father makes Mzia light the fire.'
(b) *mzias vatamašeb nards.*
I-cause-play-her-it-I-1 backgammon-DAT
'I am getting Mzia to play backgammon.'

(19) (a) *mamam mzias daantebina cecxli.*
father-ERG he-caused-light-her-it-II-1 fire-NOM
'Father made Mzia light the fire.'
(b) *mzias vatamaše nardi.*
I-caused-play-her-it-II-1 backgammon-NOM
'I got Mzia to play backgammon.'

Thus, the nominal which corresponds to the subject of the non-causative transitive verb is, in the causative, in the case of the indirect object; that is, it is dative in both Series. The nominal which corresponds to the direct object of the non-causative is in the case of the direct object in the causative construction.

3.1.3 *The causative of an intransitive with indirect object.* There is a group of intransitive predicates that take indirect objects; e.g. *esalmeba* 'he greets him', *etamašeba* 'he plays with him', *elaparaḳeba* 'he talks to him'. These forms are in Class 2; they are illustrated in (20) for Series II.

(20) (a) *bavšvi miesalma deidas.*
child-NOM he-greeted-her-II-2 aunt-DAT
'The child greeted (his) aunt.'
(b) *ḳomisia esṭumra vanos.*
commission-NOM it-visited-him-II-2 Vanos-DAT
'The commission visited Vano.'

The non-causatives in (20) should be compared with the causatives in (21) and (22), which are in Series I and II tenses, respectively. The subject of each of the non-causatives – *bavšvi* 'child' and *ḳomisia* 'commission' – in the causative bears the case of the direct object; that is, it is dative in Series I and nominative in Series II. The indirect objects of (20) also bear the case of the indirect object in causatives, that is, the dative case in both Series.

(21) (a) *deda asalmebs bavšvs deidas.*
mother-NOM she-causes-greet-her-him-I-1 child-DAT aunt-DAT
'The mother is making the child greet (his) aunt.'
(b) *direḳtori ḳomisias asṭumrebs*
director-NOM commission-DAT he-causes-visit-him-it-I-1
vanos.
Vano-DAT.
'The director is having the commission visit Vano.'

(22) (a) *dedam miasalma bavšvi*
mother-ERG she-caused-greet-her-him-II-1 child-NOM
deidas.
aunt-DAT
'The mother made the child greet (his) aunt.'
(b) *direḳtorma ḳomisia asṭumra*
director-ERG commission-NOM he-caused-visit-him-it-II-1
vanos.
Vano-DAT
'The director had the commission visit Vano.'

On the basis of the data discussed in §3.1.1 and these data, we can draw the following conclusion about the case pattern in the causative of intransitives: The subject of the non-causative corresponds to the direct object of the causative, and the indirect object, if there is one, to the indirect object.

An analysis that did not treat the nominals being discussed here as terms of the united clause would have to complicate the case marking rules. In particular, such an analysis would have to repeat the facts of direct object marking for Class 1 verbs: under causative formation, initial direct objects are marked with the dative case in Series I and the nominative in Series II. In addition, such an analysis would claim that the direct object of a Class 2 verb in Series II is marked with the nominative, a case not otherwise used for the direct object of a Class 2 verb (cf. (2–3) in the Introduction). The analysis proposed here considers all causative verbs to be Class 1 verbs, and it is therefore natural and predictable that their direct objects will be in the nominative in Series II. The Class 1 status of these verbs is not determined by the case marking they govern, but by their morphology (cf. ch. 16, Appendix A); the case marking is predictable from their status as Class 1 verbs.

3.2 Tav-*Reflexivization*

The rule of *Tav*-Reflexivization is governed by a clausemate constraint (cf. ch. 1, §1.3); *tav-* has as its antecedent the subject of its own clause. But in an organic causative, *tav-* may be coreferential to a nominal which is, in initial structure, in another clause. Consider again (12) and (13), which are repeated here for the convenience of the reader.

(12) *ekimma* *vano* *alaparaḳa* *tavis* *tavze.*
doctor-ERG Vano-NOM he-caused-talk-him-II-1 self's self-on.
'The doctor$_i$ got Vano$_j$ to talk about himself$_{i,j}$.'

(13) *genom* *miaṭanina* *rezos* *çignebi*
Geno-ERG he-caused-take-him-it-II-1 Rezo-DAT books-NOM
tavistan.
self-at
'Geno$_i$ got Rezo$_j$ to take the books to his$_{i,j}$ place.'

The reading 'The doctor got Vano to talk about the doctor' for (12) is consistent with the clausemate constraint on *Tav*-Reflexivization only if *ekimma* 'doctor' and *tav-* are final dependents of the same clause.

Similarly, in (13) the reading 'Geno made Rezo take the books to Geno's place' is consistent only with a simple final structure.

3.3 *Person Agreement*

In ch. 1 it was shown that only terms trigger Person Agreement; in chs. 3–4 it was established that this rule is stated on final terms.

The initial embedded subject does not trigger Subject Person Agreement in organic clauses; it does trigger Direct Object Person Agreement or Indirect Object Person Agreement, depending upon whether it is the initial subject of an intransitive or transitive verb. That this is so is shown by (23), which illustrates the causative of a transitive. The (*a) sentences have first person Subject Person Agreement *v*-, the (b) sentences, first person Object Person Agreement *m*- (cf. paradigms in ch. 1, §3).

(23) (a) **tamadam* **v***amɣera.*
toastmaster-ERG **I**-caused-sing-him-II-1
('The toastmaster made me sing.')
(b) *tamadam* **m***amɣera.*
he-caused-sing-**me**-II-1
'The toastmaster made me sing.'

(24) (a) **ninom* *ga***v***aç̣mendina* *saxli.*
Nino-ERG **I**-caused-clean-her-it-II-1 house-NOM
('Nino made me clean the house.')
(b) *ninom ga***m***aç̣mendina* *saxli.*
she-caused-clean-**me**-it-II-1
'Nino made me clean the house.'

The Person Agreement in (23–24) is explained by (a) the fact that Person Agreement is stated on final terms, and (b) the first person in (23–24), while being initial subject, is final object, as described in §1 above.

3.4 *Unemphatic Pronoun Drop*

I showed in ch. 1, §4 that this rule operates only on terms; in ch. 3 I suggested that it is stated on final terms. Some examples have already been given in this chapter which show that those nominals which are terms on the proposed analysis may be dropped. (7) illustrates the dropping of the initial subject of an embedded transitive. (18–19b) illustrate the dropping of the initial matrix subject. (25) and (26) below show that the initial direct object and the initial subject of an intransitive can also drop; the sentences are used naturally when the reference of the dropped nominals has already been established in discourse.

(25) *mamam* *mimacemina* *dedistvis.*
father-ERG he-caused-give-me-it-II-1 mother-for
'Father made me give it to Mother.'

(26) *ʒaγli* *aṭirebs.*
dog-NOM he-causes-cry-him-I-1
'The dog makes him cry.'

The fact that an initial matrix subject, an initial embedded subject of a transitive or intransitive, and an initial embedded direct object can all be dropped is consistent with the analysis in §1 and with the proposal that Unemphatic Pronoun Drop is stated on final terms.

3.5 *Question Formation*

As shown in §4.2 of the Introduction, Q-words must occur immediately before the verbs which govern them. Consider the sentences below. They show that all the nominals under discussion here must occur immediately before the clause-united verb.

(27) (a) *vin* *migacemina* *ṭorṭi* *dedistvis?*
who-ERG he-caused-give-you-it-II-1 cake-NOM mother-for
'Who made you give the cake to Mother?'
**vin ṭorṭi migacemina dedistvis?*
**vin dedistvis migacemina ṭorṭi?*

(b) *mamam* *vis* *miacemina* *ṭorṭi dedistvis?*
father-ERG who-DAT he-caused-give-him-it-II-1
'Who did Father make give the cake to Mother?'
**vis mamam miacemina dedistvis ṭorṭi?*
**mamam miacemina vis dedistvis ṭorṭi?*

(c) *mamam ra* *migacemina* *dedistvis?*
what-NOM he-caused-give-you-it-II-1
'What did Father make you give to Mother?'
**ra mamam migacemina dedistvis?*
**mama migacemina ra dedistvis?*

The proposed analysis correctly predicts that the nominative-, ergative-, and dative-nominals are final dependents of the united clause and will therefore immediately precede the causative verb in questions.

3.6 *Object Camouflage*

This rule provides additional evidence that in final structure organic causatives are simple clauses. It will be remembered that the rule substitutes a possessive pronoun + *tavi* for a first or second person direct object when there is an indirect object in the same clause. In organic causatives the rule applies to final direct objects if there is in the same clause a final indirect object (= initial embedded transitive subject or initial embedded intransitive indirect object). This is shown in (28); in (*28b) the rule has failed to apply.

(28) (a) *anzorma gaalanʒγvina vanos*
Anzor-ERG he-caused-insult-him-him-II-1 Vano-DAT
čemi tavi.
my self-NOM
'Anzor made Vano insult me.'
(b) **anzorma gamalanʒγvina vanos (me).*
he-caused-insult-him-me-II-1 me-NOM
('Anzor made Vano insult me.')

In ch. 3 I showed that Object Camouflage applies only if there is an indirect object in the same clause. In (28) the only indirect object is the derived one, *vanos*, which is an initial subject; (28) thus confirms that *vanos* is an indirect object. Since the rule has only direct objects as its targets, it confirms that *me* is the direct object. It also shows that Object Camouflage must be stated on the output of Causative Clause Union, not on its input, since the absence of an initial indirect object in (28) is inconsequential to the application of the rule.[5]

3.7 *Summary*

In this section and the preceding one I have argued that the initial structure of an organic causative must be complex, and that its final structure must be simplex. It has been shown that the initial structure of an organic causative has as its direct object a clause in which the relations that nominals bear are the same as the relations borne in a simple clause. Furthermore, the direct objects of embedded transitives and the subjects of embedded intransitives behave like direct objects under Causative Clause Union, with respect to all rules stated on final relations. The subject of an embedded transitive and the indirect object of an embedded intransitive behave like indirect objects under these conditions.

4 The tvis-nominal

In the causative of a transitive, the indirect object of the embedded clause is marked with the postposition *tvis* in all Series. (29a) illustrates this for Series I, and (29b) for Series II.

(29) (a) *mama* *maceminebs* *ṭorṭs* *dedistvis.*
father-NOM he-causes-give-me-it-I-1 cake-DAT mother-for
'Father is making me give the cake to Mother.'
(b) *mamam* *mimacemina* *ṭorṭi* *dedistvis.*
father-ERG he-caused-give-me-it-II-1 cake-NOM mother-for
'Father made me give the cake to Mother.'

Micems 'gives', the non-causative corresponding to the verb form of (29), is a Class 1 verb. The causatives of Class 2 verbs show the same pattern of case marking; (30a) illustrates the causative of a Class 2 verb in Series I, (30b) in Series II.

(30) (a) *anzori* *vanos* *daapirebinebs*
Anzor-NOM Vano-DAT he-will-cause-promise-him-it-I-1
sabeč̣d *mankanas* *ninostvis.*
printing machine-DAT Nino-for
'Anzor will make Vano promise Nino a typewriter.'
(b) *anzorma* *vanos* *daapirebina* *sabeč̣di*
Anzor-ERG he-caused-promise-him-it-II-1
mankana *ninostvis.*
machine-NOM
'Anzor made Vano promise Nino a typewriter.'

In all of the sentences of (29) and (30) the initial indirect object of the embedded clause is marked with *tvis* 'for'. The marking of this nominal in causatives in Series III is discussed in ch. 11, §2.4.

(3), the rule of Clause Union in §1 above, predicts that the initial indirect object of an embedded transitive will be a derived non-term.

4.1 *The* tvis-*nominal as a non-term governed by the organic causative*

4.1.1 *Question Formation.* I have shown previously that Question Formation is a test for clause constituency, since just those nominals governed by a verb immediately precede it when they are questioned. (31) shows that the *tvis*-nominal, when questioned, must immediately precede the organic causative.

(31) *mamam vistvis migacemina torṭi?*
father-ERG who-for he-caused-give-you-it-II-1 cake-NOM
'Who did Father make you give the cake to?'
**vistvis mamam migacemina torṭi?*
**mamam migacemina torṭi vistvis?*

Hence, the *tvis*-nominal must be governed by the clause-united verb.

4.1.2 *Case Assignment.* In previous chapters I showed that all final terms are marked with the nominative, ergative, or dative case in Series I and II. The *tvis*-nominal is not marked with one of these cases. It follows that it is not a final term.

4.1.3 *Unemphatic Pronoun Drop.* In chs. 1 and 3 it was shown that Unemphatic Pronoun Drop applies to all and only unemphatic final term pronouns. If the *tvis*-nominal were a final term, it should undergo this rule.

(32) shows that the *tvis*-nominal cannot be dropped without changing the meaning of the sentence. Compare (32a), where the initial indirect object is also final indirect object, to (32b), where the initial indirect object is a final non-term. Only the former may be the target of Unemphatic Pronoun Drop.

(32) (a) *genom mo***m***ca torṭi.*
Geno-ERG he-gave-**me**-it-II-1 cake-NOM
'Geno gave me a cake.'
(b) *mamam genos miacemina torṭi*
father-ERG Geno-DAT he-caused-give-him-it-II-1 cake-NOM
čemtvis.
me-for
'Father made Geno give me a cake.'
(c) *?mamam genos miacemina torṭi.*
'Father made Geno give the cake (to someone).'

The fact that this pronoun is not droppable confirms that it is a final non-term.

4.1.4 *Person Agreement.* The rules of Person Agreement also provide evidence that the *tvis*-nominal in organic causatives is not a final term. This nominal triggers none of the agreement rules; this is shown in

(33), where the person of the *tvis*-nominal changes, but the verb form does not.

(33) (a) *mamam ṭorṭi miacemina čemtvis.*
father-ERG cake-NOM he-caused-give-him-it-II-1 me-for
'Father had a cake given to me.'
(b) *mamam ṭorṭi miacemina šentvis.*
you-SG-for
'Father had a cake given to you (SG).'
(c) *mamam ṭorṭi miacemina genostvis.*
Geno-for
'Father had a cake given to Geno.'

Since only final terms trigger Person Agreement (cf. chs. 3 and 4), the lack of agreement in (33) is explained by the proposed analysis, according to which the initial indirect object of a transitive verb is not a final term in the corresponding organic causative.

4.1.5 *Summary*. Question formation provides a test of clause constituency and shows that the *tvis*-nominal is a final dependent of the simplex clause, not of the embedded clause in which it originated. Other syntactic rules also show that the *tvis*-nominal is a final non-term, a retired term.[6] Additional support for this position may be found in ch. 11.

4.2 *On so-called 'four-person causatives'*

Traditional analyses have discussed causatives of transitives in which the initial embedded indirect object is in the dative case (cf. Kiknadze 1937; Shanidze 1973: §431; Vogt 1971: §2.75). (34) illustrates this construction.

(34) '*da kals ar migaceminebt teimurazsa.*'
and woman-DAT not I-cause-give-you-her-I-1 Teimuraz-DAT
'... and I do not permit you to give the woman to Teimuraz.'[7]

In the embedded clause, the initial grammatical relations are the following: subject – *tkven* 'you'; direct object – *kali* 'woman'; indirect object – *teimuraz*. Each of these is in the dative, though *tkven* 'you' gets dropped by Unemphatic Pronoun Drop, having triggered Object Person Agreement in the organic causative. The existence of such sentences makes causative formation in Georgian seem unsystematic and throws doubt on the accuracy of rule (3), since *teimuraz* seems to be a final indirect object, in contrast to the analysis proposed above.

In the remainder of this section, I will make the following points about examples like (34). (i) They are taken from earlier periods of Georgian or from non-standard modern dialects, not from the dialect being described in this work. (ii) There are certain idioms where the same case pattern is found in the standard modern dialect. (iii) These idioms are limited to the first and second persons. (iv) In those dialects where examples like (34) are to be found, one of the dative-nominals is a retired term, not an indirect object as has been claimed.

Sentences like (34) are unacceptable in Standard Modern (Tbilisi) Georgian, though they are grammatical both in older Georgian, and in some modern dialects. Kiknadze, Shanidze, and Vogt cover a broad period of Georgian and a range of dialects, without always noting the historical and geographical contexts of various facts. My informants rejected examples of this type quoted in the works cited, though they observed that they could understand the sentences.

There are, however, at least two idioms in which this construction remains in the standard modern dialect. These are *šemaçmevina* 'he$_i$ made me feed him$_j$ it' and *damalevina* 'he$_i$ made me give it to him$_j$ to drink'.[8] These idioms in Modern Georgian, and apparently also in the construction illustrated in (34), are limited to instances where the initial embedded subject is first or second person, as shown in (35) and (*36). (35) contains a grammatical sentence with the idiom for 'cause-feed', where the initial embedded subject is first person. (*36) is exactly parallel to (35), but the initial embedded subject is third person.

(35) *dedam bavšvs papa šemaçmevina.*
mother-ERG child-DAT gruel-NOM she-caused-feed-me-it-II-1
'The mother made me feed gruel to the child.'

(36) **dedam kals bavšvs papa šeaçmevina.*
woman-DAT she-caused-feed-her-it-II-1
('The mother made the woman feed gruel to the child.')

While the double-dative idiom can be used with an initial embedded first or second person subject, it cannot be used with a third person, as the ungrammaticality of (*36) shows.

Comrie (1976e) discusses this construction in Georgian, based on the examples quoted by Vogt. Comrie states that there are two indirect objects, a claim he apparently bases on case marking. Notice, however, that the embedded initial indirect object has no characteristics of final indirect objects, apart from case. In particular, it cannot trigger Person Agreement, Number Agreement (cf. ch. 15), or Unemphatic Pronoun Drop.[9] Nor is it productive; in Standard Modern Georgian it is limited to a very few idioms, and to first and second person initial embedded subjects. I suggest that the dative-nominal which is an initial embedded indirect object is finally a retired indirect object, just like the *tvis*-nominal in (29). This proposal is not inconsistent with the case marking, since case marking alone does not define termhood. Postal & Perlmutter (1974) have shown that in other languages retired terms often bear the case marking of the relation they formerly held.[10]

Since *bavšvs* 'child' in (35) and *kals* 'woman' in (34) have none of the properties of final indirect objects, save case, and since there is independent evidence that retired terms in some languages bear the case marking of terms, I conclude that these nominals, like the *tvis*-nominal in (36b), are retired indirect objects. Causative formation in Standard Modern Georgian is not unsystematic; rather rule (3) represents the system, to which there are a very few idiomatic exceptions, such as (35).

5 Theoretical implications

Georgian provides very strong arguments in favor of an analysis of single-clause causatives on which initial dependents of both clauses become dependents of the matrix clause. An analysis on which initial dependents of the complement are not final dependents of the matrix clause would be inadequate in Georgian because (i) the derived term dependents are marked, not with one case, but with whatever case is appropriate to the derived term relation it holds; (ii) the derived term dependents have the morphological (Person Agreement) characteristics of final terms; and (iii) the derived terms have the syntactic characteristics of final terms (triggers of *Tav*-Reflexivization, Unemphatic Pronoun Drop, and Object Camouflage).

Georgian provides evidence in favor of the formulation of Clause Union given in (3), in that it shows clearly that the *tvis*-nominal (initial embedded indirect object) is finally a non-term. It has also been shown that what some grammarians have considered a double indirect object is really one derived indirect object and a retired indirect object.

Causative formation provides strong evidence in favor of relational grammar, since the cross-language regularities of causatives with simplex derived structures cannot be stated in a simple way on the basis of linear order and dominance relations. The fact that the theory of relational grammar makes the correct predictions for Georgian provides confirmation for this theory.

6 *Version: rules that create indirect objects*

In Georgian there are syntactic rules that create indirect objects; these phenomena are traditionally referred to as *kceva* or 'version'.[1] Three types are illustrated in (1–3); in the (b) sentences there is an indirect object; in the (a) sentences there is none.

(1) *Benefactive Version*

(a) *gelam šeḳera axali šarvali šentvis.*
Gela-ERG he-sewed-it-II-1 new trousers-NOM you-for
'Gela made new trousers for you.'

(b) *gelam šegiḳera axali šarvali* (*šen*).
he-sewed-you-it-II-1 you-DAT
'Gela made new trousers for you.'

(2) *Possessive Version*

(a) *mzia çmends dis pexsacmlebs.*
Mzia-NOM she-cleans-it-I-1 sister-GEN shoes-DAT
'Mzia is cleaning her sister's shoes.'

(b) *mzia uçmends das pexsacmlebs.*
she-cleans-her-it-I-1 sister-DAT
'Mzia is cleaning her sister's shoes.'

(3) *Superessive Version*

(a) *gelam surati daxaṭa ḳedelze.*
Gela-ERG picture-NOM he-painted-it-II-1 wall-on
'Gela painted a picture on the wall.'

(b) *gelam surati daaxaṭa ḳedels.*
he-painted-it-it-II-1 wall-DAT
'Gela painted a picture on the wall.'

There are the following significant differences between the (a) and (b) sentences in each pair:

(i) In the (b) sentences there is a dative-nominal; in the (a) sentences this nominal (henceforth the 'version nominal') is marked with a postposition (*-tvis* or *-ze*) and/or the genitive case.
(ii) In the (b) sentences, but not the (a) sentences, a version marker has been added to the verb form (*i-* in (1), *u-* in (2), and *a-* in (3)).
(iii) In the (b) sentences, but not the (a) sentences, the verb agrees with the version nominal in person (*g-* in (1), *u-* in (2), ø in (3)).
(iv) In the (b) sentences, but not the (a) sentences, the version nominal is deletable by Unemphatic Pronoun Drop.

In this chapter it is argued that in the (b) sentences of (1–3) a version rule has applied to create an indirect object.

1 An analysis

The pair of sentences in (1) can be explained by a rule of Benefactive Version (Benefactive Advancement), which advances a benefactive non-term nominal to indirect-objecthood.

(4) *Benefactive Version*
A benefactive nominal may advance to indirect object.
SIDE EFFECT: Add *i-* as a prefix to the root of the verb which governs the version nominal.

(1b) may be represented as network (5).

(5)

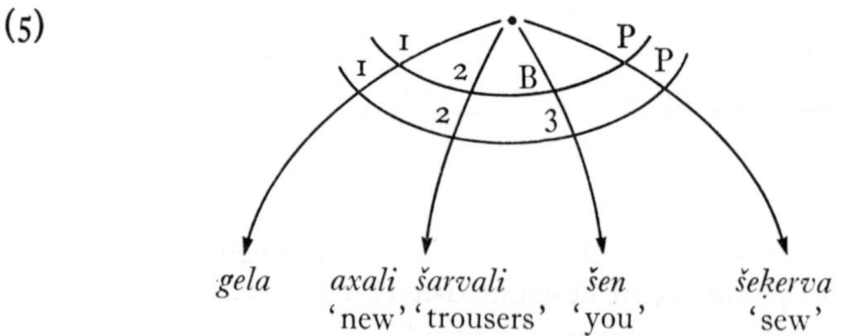

Possessive Version, illustrated in (2b), is like Benefactive Version in that it creates an indirect object and in that the side effect of the rule is the same. (The morphological difference between (1b) and (2b) is the result of Person Agreement, which is discussed in §2.1 below.) Possessive Version, however, may belong to a different rule-type, the ascension (cf. Aissen 1980; Perlmutter, to appear c); it will not be discussed in detail here.

Superessive Version, like Benefactive Version, is an advancement of an initial non-term nominal to indirect-objecthood. Its side effect is the prefixation of the version vowel *a*-. It is also not discussed in detail here.

The indirect objects created by Possessive Version, Superessive Version, Locative Version, and Comitative Version behave like those created by Benefactive Version in all significant respects (cf. Boeder 1968; and Harris 1976: ch. 6); they present no known counter examples to the analysis presented here.

2 Benefactive Version

In this section I show that the analysis proposed in (4–5) makes the correct predictions with respect to rules previously considered.

2.1 *Person Agreement*

The basic facts of Person Agreement were presented in ch. 1, §3. It was shown in succeeding chapters that Person Agreement is stated on final terms. The proposed analysis predicts, then, that the derived indirect object triggers Indirect Object Person Agreement. This is correct, though not necessarily immediately obvious to the reader who does not know Georgian, since the markers differ somewhat from those described in ch. 1, for reasons explained below.

Earlier I noted the following paradigm, which represents an intersection of person and number.

(6) *Indirect Object Person Agreement*

	singular	plural
1. person	*m*—	*gv*—
2. person	*g*—	*g*—*t*
3. person	*s*/*h*/*ø*—	*s*/*h*/*ø*—*t*

(7) illustrates the use of these markers in sentences corresponding to (1b).

(7) (a) *še*-**m-i**-*ḳera*.
'He sewed it for me.'

(b) *še*-**g-i**-*ḳera*.
'He sewed it for you (SG).'

(c) *še-***u***-ḳera.*
'He$_i$ sewed it for him$_j$.'

The object markers occur together with a 'version vowel' or 'version marker', which is introduced by the rule of Benefactive Version, (4). In (7a, b) we can clearly distinguish the first and second person markers.[2] But in (7c) the object marker that is elsewhere realized as *s*-, *h*-, or ø has combined with the *i*-marker by a synchronic morphophonemic rule to give *u*. An *i*- prefix occurs in Georgian (i) as a marker of Benefactive or Possessive Version, (ii) as part of the marker of future, aorist, etc. for Class 3 verbs (cf. ch. 16, §1), (iii) as part of the marker of the first evidential for Class 1 and 3 verbs, and (iv) as an empty morpheme with a few verbs. In any one of these functions it may combine with the third person indirect object marker as the fusional morpheme *u*-.

(8) $+h+i+ \rightarrow +u+$

The morpheme *h*- and a following morpheme *i*- combine to *u*-. One example of this rule occurs in (9c), where *i*- functions as part of the future marker for a Class 3 verb.

(9) (a) **m***iqvirebs.*
he-will-yell-**me**-I-3
'He will yell to me.'
(b) **g***iqvirebs.*
he-will-yell-**you**-I-3
'He will yell to you.'
(c) **u***qvirebs.*
he-will-yell-**him**-I-3
'He will yell to him.'

Another example may be found in ch. 8, n. 5 illustrating the second evidential. Thus, in spite of the occurrence of the *u*- variant in the third person, we can see that (7) contains regular indirect object markers. The fact that the dative-nominal in sentences like (1b) triggers Indirect Object Person Agreement, while the object of the postposition *tvis* in sentences like (1a) does not trigger any Person Agreement, supports the analysis of the former as an indirect object and the latter as a (benefactive) non-term.

2.2 *Case*

In ch. 2 it was shown that the indirect object is marked with the dative case in both Series I and Series II. In (10b) *merab* is in the dative in

Series II; this is good evidence that *merab* is the indirect object in that sentence. In (10a), on the other hand, *merab* is not in the case of the indirect object, but in the genitive with a postposition; this is good evidence that *merab* is not the indirect object in that sentence.

(10) (a) *gelam šeḳera axali šarvali merabisatvis.*
Gela-ERG he-sewed-it-II-1 new trousers-NOM Merab-for
'Gela made new trousers for Merab.'
(b) *gelam šeuḳera axali šarvali merabs.*
he-sewed-him-it-II-1 Merab-DAT
'Gela made new trousers for Merab.'

(11) corresponds to (10), but is in a Series I tense.

(11) (a) *gela ḳeravs axal šarvals merabisatvis.*
Gela-NOM he-sews-it-I-1 new trousers-DAT
'Gela is making new trousers for Merab.'
(b) *gela uḳeravs axal šarvals merabs.*
he-sews-him-it-I-1
'Gela is making new trousers for Merab.'

In (11a) *merab* is the genitive object of the postposition *-tvis*, in (11b) it is in the dative. This is consistent with the latter, but not the former, being an indirect object.

2.3 *Unemphatic Pronoun Drop*

It has been shown that the rule of Unemphatic Pronoun Drop drops all and only unemphatic pronouns that are final terms. As indicated above, *šen* 'you' can be dropped from (1b), but not from (1a). This is consistent with the analysis of this nominal as a benefactive non-term in (a)-type sentences and as an indirect object in (b)-type sentences.

2.4 *Object Camouflage*

The rule of Object Camouflage replaces a first or second person direct object with a possessive pronoun + *tavi* if there is an indirect object in the clause. (12) shows that this rule applies when there is a version indirect object in the clause. In (12a) neither Benefactive Version nor Object Camouflage has applied. In (*12b), Benefactive Version has created an indirect object, but Object Camouflage has failed to apply. In (12c) Benefactive Version and Object Camouflage have both applied.

(12) (a) *važam* *dagxaṭa* (*šen*) *čemtvis.*
Vazha-ERG he-painted-you-II-1 you-NOM me-for.
'Vazha painted you for me.'
(b) **važam damixaṭa* (*šen*) (*me*).
he-painted-me-it-II-1 I-DAT
('Vazha painted you for me.')
(c) *važam damixaṭa šeni tavi* (*me*).
your self-NOM
'Vazha painted you for me.'

In (12c) *tavi* can have its more concrete meaning 'head', in addition to 'self' (cf. ch. 1, §1). For this reason, another expression, such as *šeni parṭreṭi* 'your portrait' is preferred by some speakers for the more general meaning. But the fact that (*12b), without Object Camouflage, is ungrammatical, while (12c), with Object Camouflage, is grammatical shows that this rule must apply here. Since Object Camouflage applies only when there is an indirect object in the clause, *me* 'me' must be an indirect object.

2.5 *Summary*

The four phenomena discussed above show that the version nominal, when it is in the dative case, is the indirect object, which supports the *final* grammatical relations proposed in §1. The *initial* grammatical relations are discussed in the following section.

3 Stative verbs

Holisky (1978) shows that true stative verbs in Georgian consistently do not occur with benefactive nominals, as illustrated in (*13).

(13) (a) **pasuxi* *vicodi* *masçavleblisatvis.*
answer-NOM I-knew-it-II-3 teacher-for[3]
('I knew the answer for the teacher.')
(b) **mcioda* *dedisatvis.*
I-cold-I-4 mother-for
('I was cold for my mother.')

The same set of verbs do not occur with version objects, as (*14) shows.

(14) (a) **pasuxi masçavlebels vucodi.*
teacher-DAT I-knew-him-it-II-3
('I knew the answer for the teacher.')
(b) **skeli dedas vuqavi.*
fat mother-DAT I-was-her-II-2
('I was fat for Mother.')

If version objects are derived from non-term benefactive nominals, as proposed in §1, the ungrammaticality of (*14) follows automatically from that of (*13).

4 Why not generate version objects directly?

Since some verbs have initial indirect objects, it does not seem unreasonable to propose generating all indirect objects in the same way.

Consider the sets of sentences below. They show a correlation between the presence of a character vowel (here *u-*), the occurrence of an indirect object, and the meaning attached to that indirect object. What is especially interesting is that the pattern for the verb *miçera* 'write' is different from that for the verb *daçera* 'write' (cf. also ch. 1, §4).

(15) (a) *çerili misçera ʒmas.*
letter-NOM he-wrote-him-it-II-1 brother-DAT
'He wrote a letter to (his) brother.'
(b) *çerili misçera ʒmistvis.*
brother-for
'He$_i$ wrote a letter to him$_j$ for his brother$_k$.'
(c) **çerili miuçera ʒmas.*
he-wrote-him-it-II-1
('He wrote a letter to him for his brother.'/'He wrote a letter to his brother.')

(16) (a) **çerili dasçera ʒmas.*
letter-NOM he-wrote-him-it-II-1 brother-DAT
('He wrote a letter to (his) brother.')
(b) *çerili daçera ʒmistvis.*
he-wrote-it-II-1 brother-for
'He wrote a letter for his brother.'
(c) *çerili dauçera ʒmas.*
he-wrote-him-it-II-1
'He wrote a letter for his brother.'

I propose to account for the different patterns exhibited by these two verbs in the following way. *Miçera* obligatorily takes an initial indirect object in what we may loosely describe as the '*to*-relation'. *Daçera* may not take an initial indirect object. As in (6) above, third person indirect objects trigger the *s/h/ø*-prefix, which is realized as *s* before *ç*. These facts account for the (a) sentences of (15–16). Both *miçera* and *daçera* may take a benefactive-nominal; as non-terms, such nominals do not trigger agreement. This accounts for the (b) sentences above; in (15b) the initial indirect object is dropped by Unemphatic Pronoun Drop, as shown in the gloss. The rule of Benefactive Version may advance the benefactive-nominal in (16), where there is no initial indirect object, but not in (15), where there is an initial indirect object.[4] The different meanings of (15a) and (16c) are attributable to their different initial structures. The difference between the meanings of (15b) and (16b) is also to be attributed to the fact that the former, but not the latter, has an initial indirect object.

Consider now a different analysis, on which version objects are not derived from non-term nominals. Such a grammar would state that *miçera* takes an indirect object obligatorily, while *daçera* takes one optionally. Instead of a rule of Benefactive Version, it will have rules relating the benefactive relation to the occurrence of *i*- in the verb form and the '*to*-relation' to the occurrence of ø in the verb form. This direct-generation analysis thus requires one rule more than the analysis proposed here.

In addition, that analysis fails to capture the fact that indirect objects in the '*to*-relation' exist in all languages, while those in the benefactive relation do not. The fact that the '*to*-relation' is morphologically unmarked must be treated as an accident by that grammar. The analysis proposed here, on the other hand, embodies the claim that the '*to*-relation' for indirect objects is basic and unmarked, while the benefactive relation for indirect objects is derivative and marked.

The importance of this difference is even more obvious when we consider Superessive Version, illustrated in (3). The direct-generation analysis, if extended to Superessive Version, would require that the superessive indirect object in (3b) be associated by rule with the occurrence of the *a*-prefix in the verb form. According to the analysis proposed here, the superessive indirect object is derived by Superessive Version, the side effect of which is the insertion of *a*-. Again, only the latter analysis captures the fact that indirect objects in the superessive relation do not exist in all languages, are derivative, and are marked.

5 Coreferential Version Object Deletion

In (17) the version nominal is coreferential to the subject of its clause. In (17a), *Tav*-Reflexivization has applied; in (*17b) both Benefactive Version and *Tav*-Reflexivization have applied, according to the rules as stated.

(17) (a) *gela tavistvis ḳeravs axal šarvals.*
Gela-NOM self-for he-sews-it-I-1 new trousers-DAT
'Gela is making new trousers for himself.'

(b) **gela (tavis) tavs uḳeravs axal šarvals.*[5]
self's self-DAT he-sews-him-it-I-1
('Gela is making new trousers for himself.')

(c) *gela iḳeravs axal šarvals.*[6]
he-sews-self-it-I-1
'Gela is making new trousers for himself.'

In (17c) the benefactive nominal is not overt. It is like the examples of Benefactive Version considered earlier, in that benefaction is included in the meaning, and the marker of Benefactive Version, *i-*, is present in the verb form. (17c) differs from (11b) in the following significant respects:

A. In (17c) the subject and the benefactive nominal are coreferential; in (11b) they are not.
B. In (11b) there is third person Indirect Object Person Agreement (cf. §2.1); in (17c) there is no Indirect Object Person Agreement.
C. In (11b) the version object is overt; in (17c) it is not.

In the remainder of this section, I will discuss the treatment of (17) in the grammar of Georgian.

5.1 *Analysis*

I propose that (17) be accounted for in the following way. The rule of Benefactive Version, as proposed in §1, does not refer to coreference. A rule of Coreferential Version Object Deletion obligatorily deletes reflexive version objects. (A similar analysis is proposed for Tzotzil, a Mayan language (Aissen ms.).) There are two obvious ways to state this condition: (i) An object created by the application of a version rule deletes under the conditions specified. (ii) An initial non-term (of any verb) that is a derived indirect object deletes under the conditions specified. I know of no reason to prefer one of these over the other; the rule below is stated on the basis of a 'version object', which could be defined in either of these ways.

(18) *Coreferential Version Object Deletion*
A reflexive version object deletes.[7]

5.2 *Deletion of indirect objects*

Indirect objects coreferential to the subjects of their clauses do not generally delete in Georgian. (19) illustrates a transitive verb which takes an obligatory indirect object. In (19a) the indirect object coreferential to the subject has been reflexivized; this should be compared with (*17b). (19b) is superficially similar to (17c), in that the indirect object does not appear; but (19b), unlike (17c), must be interpreted with a non-coreferential indirect object.

(19) (a) *çerili mivçere (čems) tavs.*
letter-NOM I-wrote-him-it-II-1 my self-DAT
'I wrote a letter to myself.'
(b) *çerili mivçere.*
'I wrote a letter to him.'

(20) and (21) illustrate other verbs with indirect objects; they pattern like (19), not like (17).

(20) (a) *merabi elaparaka tavis tavs.*
Merab-NOM he-talked-him-II-2 self's self-DAT
'Merab talked to himself.'
(b) *merabi elaparaka.*
'Merab talked to him.'

(21) (a) *merabi umγeris tavis tavs.*
he-sings-him-I-3 self's self-DAT
'Merab is singing to himself.'
(b) *merabi umγeris.*[8]
'Merab is singing to him.'

(22) shows that derived indirect objects, too, may not delete under the stated coreferentiality conditions. It contains a causative in which

the derived indirect object is coreferential to the final subject. In (22a), which is comparable to (*17b), *Tav*-Reflexivization has applied. In (22b), which is superficially similar to (17c), there is no overt indirect object. But in (22b), unlike (17c), the deleted indirect object is interpreted as an unspecified (non-coreferential) nominal.

(22) (a) *gelam* *gaaçmendina* *tavis tavs*
Gela-ERG he-caused-clean-him-it-II-1 self's self-DAT
sasaxle.
palace-NOM.
'Gela forced himself to clean the palace.'
(b) *gelam gaaçmendina sasaxle.*[9]
'Gela had the palace cleaned./Gela had him clean the palace.'

Sentences (19–22) show that indirect objects coreferential to the subjects of their clauses do not necessarily delete in Georgian. Rather, just those indirect objects that are derived by the application of a version rule are subject to deletion, as in (17).

5.3 *Other possible analyses*

Traditional grammars analyze Georgian mainly on the basis of morphology or final relations. Since (17c) is formally quite different from (11b), as pointed out in the introduction to this section, these verb forms are traditionally considered quite different. The former is called *sataviso kceva* 'the version for the self', the latter *sasxviso kceva* 'the version for another'(cf. Chikobava 1950; Fähnrich 1965; Schmidt 1965; Shanidze 1973; Tschenkéli 1958; and Vogt 1971).[10] The *extension* of that approach is that these two form-types are derived by two distinct, unrelated rules. While I do not know of anyone extending the traditional point of view to a grammar stated in terms of precise rules, I would like to argue that such an extension would be inadequate.

Consider what each analysis would require to account for the examples in (11) and (17).

The proposed analysis (Grammar A):
a. Coreferential Version Object Deletion, rule (18).
b. Rule (18) is obligatory.
c. Rule (18) is stated on non-final terms.

Description: The optionality of Benefactive Version accounts for the grammaticality of both (11a) and (11b) and of both (17a) and (17c). The obligatoriness of rule (18) accounts for the ungrammaticality of (*17b). Since rule (18) is stated on non-final grammatical relations, the deleted version nominal does not trigger rules like Person Agreement, which are stated on final termhood. This accounts for the difference between the morphology of (11b) and that of (17c) (cf. §2.1).

The extended traditional analysis (Grammar B):

a. Rule (23): *Coreferential Benefactive Deletion*
   A reflexive non-term benefactive nominal deletes.
b. Side Effect of rule (23): Add *i-* as a prefix to the root of the verb which governs the deleted nominal.
c. Rule (23) is optional.
d. Rule (23) is stated on initial terms.
e. Constraint (24): Version may not apply to nominals coreferential to the subjects of their clauses.

Description: (11a, b) are accounted for as above. Rule (23), unlike (18), applies directly to initial structures, to grammatical relations that have not been changed by Benefactive Version. The optionality of (23) accounts for the grammaticality of (17a). Rule (23) and its side effect, applying to initial terms, account for the grammaticality of (17c). (*17b) is derived by the application of Benefactive Version and *Tav*-Reflexivization, which must be included in any grammar of Georgian. In order to block (*17b), constraint (24) is added to the grammar.
Evaluation. Both grammars must include Benefactive Version, a statement of its side effect, and a statement of its optionality. Rules (18) and (23) are of equal complexity. But the Extended Traditional Analysis is significantly more complex and fails to capture two important generalizations.

(i) The Extended Traditional Analysis requires the extra statement B(b). It fails to capture the generalization that the side effect of rules (4) and (23) are the same. The proposed analysis, on the other hand, does not repeat this side effect; it captures this important generalization by deriving (11) and (17) through the application of Benefactive Version, with one side effect.

(ii) The Extended Traditional Analysis requires the extra condition (24) in order to block (*17b). On the analysis proposed here, the non-occurrence of such sentences is an automatic consequence of two rules that are independently needed, Benefactive Version and Coreferential Version Object Deletion. But on the Extended Traditional Analysis, an entirely *ad hoc* condition must be introduced.

It is clear that the analysis proposed here must be preferred over the extension of the traditional point of view, since it explains the grammatical status of the sentences of (17) and establishes the relatedness between (11b) and (17c).[11]

The discussion above raises the possibility of a third type of grammar: *Grammar* C. Description: No additional rule is needed. Benefactive Version applies freely, and the version object is dropped by the rule of Unemphatic Pronoun Drop.

This grammar is obviously simpler than the proposed analysis, but it is shown below that Grammar C makes the wrong predictions.

Arguments against Grammar C. (i) According to the rule of Unemphatic Pronoun Drop, a pronoun is dropped only if it is unemphatic; an emphatic pronoun is retained. But the benefactive indirect object coreferential with the subject cannot be retained, even as an emphatic pronoun, as shown in (*17b).

(ii) In no other situation does Unemphatic Pronoun Drop apply to reflexives (cf. ch. 3, §3.2).

(iii) Nominals dropped by Unemphatic Pronoun Drop trigger Person Agreement; that this is so is shown in ch. 1, §4. Nominals deleted by Coreferential Version Object Deletion do not trigger Person Agreement; this is shown by example (17c) above.

I conclude that the analysis proposed in §5.1 is the preferred grammar and that (17c) is derived by the application of Benefactive Version and Coreferential Version Object Deletion.

6 On so-called four-person verbs

Kiknadze (1937) and Shanidze (1973) give examples of sentences with two datives in Series II and three in Series I, stating that such sentences have two indirect objects. One such sentence is repeated here as example (25).

(25) '... *švilebs* *qeli* *damiçra.*'
children-DAT throat-NOM he-cut-me-it II-1
'... He cut my children's throats.' (Shanidze 1973: §402)

Sentences of this type are generally not acceptable in the dialect described here, the modern Tbilisi dialect. But in the dialects where they are acceptable, such sentences pose a problem for the Stratal Uniqueness Law, the claim that there can be at most one subject, one direct object, and one indirect object in a clause (cf. Introduction, §2).

The verb *dač̣ra* 'cut' does not take an initial indirect object; I assume that the two dative-nominals (*švilebs* and *me* 'me') were derived by successive applications of Possessive Version, from a structure containing the direct object *čemi švilebis qel(eb)i* 'my children's throat(s)'. When *me* becomes an indirect object, *švilebs* becomes an indirect object chomeur.[12]

The only evidence that could be cited to show that *švilebs* 'children' is an indirect object in (25) is the fact that it is in the dative case in Series II. But this is not sufficient evidence, for in natural languages, a nominal may become a retired $term_i$, while still bearing the case marking of a $term_i$ (cf. Perlmutter & Postal 1974). This does not occur in Standard Modern Georgian, but it did occur in Old Georgian (cf. Harris 1979) and apparently in the dialect represented by (25).

Notice that *me* 'me', but not *švilebs* 'children', has the following additional properties of an indirect object. (i) It triggers Indirect Object Person Agreement (*m*-marker). (ii) In the first and second persons, it triggers Number Agreement.[13] (iii) It can be dropped by Unemphatic Pronoun Drop, as shown by (25). That *švilebs* cannot be dropped is shown by the fact that *qeli damič̣ra* means 'he cut my throat', not 'he cut my someone's throat' (cf. Shanidze 1973:§402). I have been unable to test additional aspects of this construction, as I have had no informant who spoke this dialect.

Since *švilebs* does not have the other characteristics of an indirect object, I conclude that it is not an indirect object. The principal difference between this dialect and the standard one is that in the non-standard dialect, some former terms carry the case marking of the term relation which they last bore. As shown in ch. 11, this is not true in the standard dialect.

7 Version as relation-changing rules

I have proposed that the Version rules are formulated on the basis of the relations benefactive, possessor, and superessive. A theory of grammar according to which rules were based on linear order and dominance relations would be forced to formulate Version on the basis of the postposition or case with which the nominals concerned occurred, or on the basis of their position with respect to some other constituent. But both alternatives present enormous difficulties, as I will show below.

Consider, for example, a formulation of Possessive Version on the basis of the case of the possessor: 'Genitive nominals may become indirect objects.' (26a) illustrates a grammatical sentence with a genitive; the ungrammaticality of (*26b) shows that this nominal cannot be an indirect object in this sentence.

(26) (a) *kvis saxli avašene.*
stone-GEN house-NOM I-built-it-II-1
'I built a stone house.'
(b) **saxli avušene kvas.*
I-built-it-it-II-1 stone-DAT
('I built a stone house.')

As shown by (26), some genitive nominals cannot become indirect objects; it is only those that bear the possessor relation that may undergo this rule.

Similarly, only those *tvis*-nominals which bear the benefactive relation can undergo Benefactive Version. (27a) illustrates a non-benefactive *tvis*-nominal; (*27b) shows that it may not be an indirect object.

(27) (a) *moçapeebma unda moamzadon es gaḳvetili*
pupils-ERG should they-prepare-it-II-1 this lesson-NOM
xvalistvis.
tomorrow-for
'The pupils should prepare this lesson for tomorrow.'
(b) **moçapeebma unda moumzadon es gaḳvetili*
they-prepare-it-it-II-1
xvals.
tomorrow-DAT
('The pupils should prepare this lesson for tomorrow.')

Notice that an analysis that referred to the possessor by its position with respect to a head nominal would also be unable to account for the ungrammaticality of (*26b), since the unmarked position of *kva* is exactly the same as the unmarked position of *gela* in the grammatical pair (28).

(28) (a) *gelas* *saxli* *avašene.*
Gelas-GEN house-NOM I-built-it-II-1
'I built Gela's house.'
(b) *saxli avušene* *gelas.*
I-built-him-it-II-1 Gela-DAT
'I built Gela's house.'

Since a grammar based on linear order cannot refer in a straightforward way to the correct set of nominals, it cannot account for the sentences in a natural and simple manner. Relational grammar, on the other hand, refers to exactly the set of nominals involved, those that bear the relations possessor, benefactive, or superessive.

8 Summary

In Georgian there are rules that create indirect objects; the derived indirect objects have all of the syntactic characteristics of superficial indirect objects. A grammar that derives version objects from nominals bearing non-term relations is simpler than one which generates all indirect objects directly. A grammar which includes a rule of Coreferential Version Object Deletion is simpler than one that deletes non-term benefactives directly. It has been shown that the so-called second indirect object which is acceptable in some dialects does not have the properties of an indirect object, aside from the case marking. Thus, the Stratal Uniqueness Law and the Chomeur Law have been upheld in this set of data.[14]

7 *Passivization*

The (b) sentences below illustrate the Georgian passive construction, the (a) sentences the corresponding 'direct construction'.[1]

(1) (a) *vašls* *miscems* *masçavlebels.*
apple-DAT he-gives-him-it-I-1 teacher-DAT
'He will give an apple to the teacher.'
(b) *vašli* *micemulia* *masçavleblistvis.*
apple-NOM given-it-is-I-2 teacher-for
'The apple is given to the teacher.'

(2) (a) *ʒaɣli* *ukbens* *bavšvs.*
dog-NOM he-bites-it-I-1 child-DAT
'The dog is biting a child.'
(b) *bavšvi* *dakbenilia* *ʒaɣlis mier.*
child-NOM bitten-it-is-I-2 dog by
'The child is bitten by a dog.'

The passive is composed of the past passive participle plus an inflected form of the verb *qopna* 'be'. In (1–2b) the auxiliary *aris* 'is' has cliticized to the participle as *-a* (cf. '*Aris*-Cliticization' in the Introduction, §4.1). Although in each instance the full form, *aris*, could be used, the enclitic is more natural. The past passive participle is invariant for person, number, tense, Series, etc. Like the verb *qopna* 'be', all passives are Class 2 verbs and govern Pattern B in all Series;[2] the passive subject is therefore always in the nominative case.

It is necessary to show that the construction illustrated in (1–2b) is really a passive because little attention has been devoted to this construction[3] and because a different construction has been called a 'passive'. The latter is discussed in ch. 13 (see also appendix to ch. 13 and Harris, to appear b). The indirect object in the passive poses a problem; in (1b), the nominal which corresponds to the indirect object of (1a) is not treated as an indirect object. It is shown below that this nominal is a retired indirect object, and theoretical issues relating to it are discussed.

1 The passive from the viewpoint of language universals

In Comrie (1977), Keenan (1975), Perlmutter (1978), and Perlmutter & Postal (1974, 1977), it is shown that a clause in which an initial direct object becomes subject and in which an initial subject is a final non-term is a passive construction.[4] For Georgian, I will argue that the nominative-nominals of (1–2b) are initial direct objects, while the *mier*-nominal of (2b) is the initial subject, and that the nominative-nominals are final subjects and the *mier*-nominal is a final non-term. Since the nominative-nominal is an initial direct object and final subject, and the *mier*-nominal is an initial subject and final non-term, this construction is a passive with the characteristics stated above.

1.1 *Arguments for initial relations*

1.1.1 *Suppletion for number of direct object.* The verb *gadagdeba/gadaqra* 'throw' is suppletive for the number of its direct object, such that the former is used with singulars and the latter only with plurals (cf. Introduction, §4.3.2). This same constraint governs the nominative-nominals of passives. That this is so is shown in (3–4b); (3–4a) give the corresponding direct constructions.

(3) (a) **bavšvma gadaqara kva panjridan.*
child-ERG he-threw-it-II-1 stone-NOM window-from
('The child threw a stone from the window.')
(b) **es kva gadaqrilia panjridan.*
this stone-NOM thrown-it-is-I-2
('This stone was thrown from the window.')

(4) (a) *bavšvma gadaqara kvebi panjridan.*
stones-NOM
'The child threw stones from the window.'
(b) *es kvebi gadaqrilia panjridan.*
'These stones were thrown from the window.'

(*3) is ungrammatical because the initial direct object of the form *gadaqra* 'throw' must be plural.

The grammatical status of (*3) and (4) can be accounted for simply, if the nominative-nominal of the (b) sentences is treated as the initial direct object.

1.1.2 *Suppletion for animacy of direct object.* The verb *miṭana/ç̣aqvana* 'take' is suppletive for the animacy of the direct object, such that the former is used only with inanimate direct objects, and the latter only with animates. The constraint that governs the direct objects of the direct constructions also governs the nominative-nominal of the passives. (5–6b) below illustrate passives of both verb forms, with the nominative-nominal *gela*, a man's name; (5–6a) give the corresponding direct forms.

(5) (a) **gelas* *miiṭans* *mcxetaši.*
Gela-DAT he-takes-him-I-1 Mtsxeta-in
('He will take Gela to Mtsxeta.')
(b) **gela* *miṭanilia* *mcxetaši.*
Gela-NOM taken-he-is-I-2
('Gela is taken to Mtsxeta.')

(6) (a) *gelas* *ç̣aiqvans* *mcxetaši.*
he-takes-him-I-1
'He will take Gela to Mtsxeta.'
(b) *gela* *ç̣aqvanilia* *mcxetaši.*
taken-he-is-I-2
'Gela is taken to Mtsxeta.'

(*5) is ungrammatical because an animate nominal occurs with the form that takes only inanimate direct objects. This is good evidence that in the (b) sentences *gela* is the initial direct object.

1.1.3 Tav-*Reflexivization.* In ch. 1 it was shown that *tav-* can be coreferential only to the subject of its clause. In ch. 5 it is further established that this constraint on reflexivization is stated on initial termhood; that is, initial subjects may trigger *Tav*-Reflexivization even though they are not final subjects.

In passives, *tav-* may not be coreferential to the nominative-nominal, as (7) shows.

(7) (a) *gelam* *daxaṭa* *vano* *tavistvis.*
Gela-ERG he-painted-him-II-1 Vano-NOM self-for
'Gela$_i$ painted Vano$_j$ for himself$_i$.'

(b) **vano daxaṭulia* *tavistvis.*
painted-he-is-I-2
('Vano is painted for himself.')

In (7a), *tav-* cannot be triggered by *vano* because the latter is the direct object.

The ungrammaticality of (*7b) is consistent with the facts of *Tav*-Reflexivization previously established if (i) the nominative-nominal is not the initial subject, and (ii) *tav-* triggers are limited to initial subjects, as stated in (8).

(8) Only initial subjects trigger *Tav*-Reflexivization.

Rule (8) makes the correct predictions for (7) and for examples considered in previous chapters, but it fails to account for the ungrammaticality of (*9), where the *mier*-nominal (= initial subject) has triggered *Tav*-Reflexivization.

(9) **vano daxaṭulia cnobili mxaṭvris mier tavistvis.*
famous painter by
('Vano is painted by a famous painter$_i$ for himself$_i$.')

In ch. 14 I will reconsider the formulation of *Tav*-Reflexivization and show that (8) is essentially correct, but that an additional clause must be appended to account for (*9). Nevertheless the ungrammaticality of (*7b) is evidence that the nominative-nominal of a passive is not its initial subject.

1.2 *Arguments for final relations*

1.2.1 *Person Agreement.* The nominative-nominals (= initial direct objects) in (1–2b) trigger Subject Person Agreement. This will not be immediately apparent, since it is the irregular auxiliary *qopna* 'be' that registers agreement. The agreement will be more apparent from a comparison of the following two paradigms. (10) illustrates the verb 'be' as an independent verb, varying here for the person of its subject. (11) shows the verb 'be' as an auxiliary in the passive construction, varying for the person of the nominative-nominal.

(10) (a) *pexšisveli var.*
barefoot I-am-I-2
'I am barefoot.'

(b) *pexšišveli xar.*
you(SG)-are-I-2
'You(SG) are barefoot.'
(c) *pexšišvelia.*
he-is-I-2
'He is barefoot.'

(11) (a) *darçmunebuli var.*
convinced I-am-I-2
'I am convinced.'
(b) *darçmunebuli xar.*
you(SG)-are-I-2
'You(SG) are convinced.'
(c) *darçmunebulia.*
he-is-I-2
'He is convinced.'

(10–11c) are derived from *pexšišveli aris* and *darçmunebuli aris* by *Aris*-Cliticization, which is described in the Introduction, §4.1.

I have shown in previous chapters that Person Agreement is stated on final terms. The fact that the nominative-nominal (= initial direct object) triggers Subject Agreement shows that this nominal is the final subject.

The *mier*-nominal fails to trigger any rule of Person Agreement, as shown by the invariance of the verb in (12). If the *mier*-nominal triggered Person Agreement, the verb would vary with the person of the nominal.

(12) (a) *saxli gaqidulia čems mier.*[5]
house-NOM sold-it-is-I-2 me by
'The house is sold by me.'
(b) *saxli gaqidulia šens mier.*
you by
'The house is sold by you.'
(c) *saxli gaqidulia mis mier.*
him by
'The house is sold by him.'

In ch. 1, §3, it was shown that terms trigger Person Agreement; in chs. 3–6, evidence was given that Person Agreement is stated on final terms. The fact that the *mier*-nominal fails to trigger any Person Agreement therefore supports the view that it is a final non-term.

1.2.2 *Unemphatic Pronoun Drop*. I showed above that all and only unemphatic pronominal final terms may be dropped. (13) is parallel to (2b) and differs from it only in that the nominative-nominal has been pronominalized. (13a) has an emphatic pronoun as final subject; (13b) has an unemphatic pronoun as final subject.

(13) (a) *is* *daḳbenilia* *ʒaɣlis mier.*
he-NOM bitten-he-is-I-2 dog by
'He is bitten by a dog.'
(b) *daḳbenilia ʒaɣlis mier.*
'He is bitten by a dog.'

This confirms that the nominative-nominal is a final term.

The *mier*-nominal cannot be dropped in the same way. In (12) we see the pronoun and postposition remaining. (*14) is parallel, but the pronoun has been dropped.

(14) **saxli* *gaqidulia* *mier.*
house-NOM sold-it-is-I-2 by
('The house was sold by him.')

If the entire postpositional phrase were omitted, the resulting sentence would be grammatical, but the meaning would not be that of (12); *saxli gaqidulia* means 'the house is sold', not 'the house is sold by him'. Since these pronominal initial terms cannot undergo Unemphatic Pronoun Drop, and since terms can undergo this rule, these must not be final terms. This is consistent with the conclusion drawn in earlier chapters that Unemphatic Pronoun Drop is stated on final terms.

1.2.3 *Case Marking*. As noted above, the verb *qopna* 'be', which is the auxiliary used with passives, is a Class 2 verb according to the morphological criteria that define this Class (cf. ch. 16, Appendix A). In all tense Series, Class 2 verbs govern Case Pattern B, which requires that the subject be in the nominative case. This is evidence that the nominative-nominal of passives is the subject.

The *mier*-nominal is not in a case associated with terms, but is marked with a postposition. Since Case Marking is stated on final termhood (cf. chs. 4–6), and since the *mier*-nominal is the initial subject, it must be finally a retired subject.

1.2.4 *Object Camouflage*. Object Camouflage acts on direct objects in the presence of an indirect object; it applies to the output of rules that change grammatical relations (cf. chs. 5 and 6). If I am correct, then, in claiming that the initial direct object is a derived subject, then the target conditions for Object Camouflage are not met in a passive, and the rule should not apply. In (15a) Object Camouflage has correctly applied in a direct construction. But in the corresponding passive, (16b), Object Camouflage must not apply, as shown by the ungrammaticality of (*16a).

(15) (a) *masçavlebels gaugzavnes* *čemi tavi.*
teacher-DAT they-sent-him-him-II-1 my self-NOM
'They sent me to the teacher.'
(b) **masçavlebels gam(i)gzavnes* (*me*).
they-sent-him-me-II-1 I-NOM
('They sent me to the teacher.')

(16) (a) **čemi tavi* *gagzavnilia* *masçavleblistvis/masçavlebels.*
my self-NOM sent-he-is-I-2 teacher-for /teacher-DAT
('I am sent to the teacher.')
(b) (*me*) *gagzavnili var* *masçavleblistvis.*
I-NOM sent I-am-I-2
'I am sent to the teacher.'

The proposed analysis correctly predicts the ungrammaticality of (*16a). If 'I' is the derived subject of the passive sentence, there is no final direct object; since Object Camouflage is stated on derived termhood, the rule cannot apply in this sentence.

1.3 *Summary*

The nominative-nominal has been shown to be both initial direct object and final subject, while the *mier*-nominal is initial subject and final non-term. On these grounds I conclude that the construction considered here is a passive in the general linguistic use of that notion. The arguments presented in this section imply no particular analysis beyond the initial and derived grammatical relations of each nominal involved.

The data given above also confirm conclusions drawn in earlier chapters with respect to rule interaction and rule statement: *Tav*-Reflexivization must be stated on initial terms, and the rules of Person Agreement, Case Marking, and Unemphatic Pronoun Drop on final terms. §1.2.4 confirms that Object Camouflage applies to the output of rules that change grammatical relations.

2 Indirect objects in passives

In (1a) *masçavlebels* 'teacher' is an indirect object, initially and finally; in (1b) its grammatical relations are less clear. In this section I will discuss the syntactic characteristics of this nominal.

2.1 *Initial indirect object*

In ch. 1, §4, I showed that *miçera* 'write', but not *daçera* 'write', takes an initial indirect object. The same constraint that governs the occurrence of an indirect object in direct forms of these two verbs also governs the occurrence of the *tvis*-nominal in passives. The postposition *-tvis* means 'for' and can occur in that meaning with *daçera*, in its direct or passive constructions. While *miçera* may also have a *tvis*-nominal in its clause in the direct construction, if a *tvis*-nominal occurs with the passive of this verb, it is interpreted as a 'to' indirect object. (*18b) below is grammatical, but not in the meaning glossed for it.

(17) (a) *çerili* *misçera* *ʒmas.*
letter-NOM he-wrote-him-it-II-1 brother-DAT
'He wrote a letter to his brother.'
(b) **çerili da(s)çera* *ʒmas*
he-wrote-(him)-it-II-1
('He wrote a letter to his brother.')

(18) (a) *çerili miçerilia* *ʒmistvis.*
written-it-is-I-2 brother-for
'The letter is written to his/my brother.'
(b) **çerili daçerilia* *ʒmistvis.*
written-it-is-I-2
'(The letter is written to his/my brother.')

The last example is grammatical only in the meaning 'The letter is written *for* his/my brother'. This is predictable from the restrictions independently placed on the inventories of initial terms of these two verbs if the *tvis*-nominal is the initial indirect object of the passive sentences.

2.2 *Final non-term*

The *tvis*-nominal of the passive construction does not have the characteristics of final terms. It can be seen in (1b) that this nominal does not trigger Person Agreement. Nor does it bear the case marking of a final subject, direct object, or indirect object, but rather that of a final non-term (cf. ch. 11). This nominal cannot undergo Unemphatic Pronoun Drop. If the pronoun is dropped, leaving the postposition, the result is ungrammatical, as in (*19a).

(19) (a) **vašli* *micemulia* *tvis.*
apple-NOM given-it-is-I-2 for
('The apple is given to him.')
(b) *vašli micemulia.*
'The apple is given.'

(19b), while grammatical, can only be interpreted as having an unspecified indirect object, not a pronominalized indirect object. Thus, the *tvis*-nominal lacks the ability to undergo Unemphatic Pronoun Drop and the other characteristics of final terms. It must therefore be a final non-term.

2.3 *Variations in the marking of the initial indirect object*

The status of *masçavleblistvis* 'to the teacher' in (1b) is confusing for several reasons. First, there are at least two dialects in Standard Modern Georgian with respect to such sentences. For some speakers, (1b) is grammatical. But for some, Passivization is blocked when there is an initial indirect object; these speakers find (1b) unacceptable. Second, with the passive of certain verbs, the initial indirect object is in the dative, not marked with *tvis.*[6] We therefore find the following contrasts:

Dialect A

(20) (a) *viγacam* *ačvena* *vanos* *surati.*
someone-ERG he-showed-him-it-II-1 Vano-DAT picture-NOM
'Someone showed the picture to Vano.'
(b) **surati iqo* *načvenebi vanos.*
it-was-II-2 shown
('The picture was shown to Vano.')
(c) *surati iqo načvenebi vanostvis.*
Vano-for
'The picture was shown to Vano.'
(d) *surati iqo načvenebi.*
'The picture was shown.'

Dialect B

(20′) (a)
(b)*
(c)*
(d)

Dialects A and B

(21) (a) *es ḳacebi mivačviet mušaobas.*
these men-NOM I-accustomed-it-them-II-1 work-DAT
'I accustomed these men to work.'
(b) *es ḳacebi arian čveuli mušaobas.*
they-are-I-2 accustomed
'These men are accustomed to work.'
(c) **es ḳacebi arian čveuli mušaobistvis.*
work-for
('These men are accustomed to work.')

In Dialect A the verb 'show' is grammatical in the direct construction, (20a), and in the passive, with or without an initial indirect object, which is marked with *tvis* ((20c), (20d), respectively). In Dialect B, the direct construction is grammatical, but the passive is possible only if it has no initial indirect object (contrast (20′d) with (*20′b, c)). In both dialects, the verb 'accustom', unlike 'show', is grammatical with a dative indirect object (example (21)).

3 Theoretical issues

With respect to the behavior of the initial subject and direct object, the Georgian passive is in no way remarkable, as shown in §1. But the behavior of the initial indirect object is puzzling. At issue is the motivation of the final non-term status of at least some initial indirect objects. Some linguists claim that 'spontaneous chomage' is possible in language (Comrie 1977; Keenan 1975). If such rules must indeed be countenanced, we can simply add a rule to the grammar of Georgian describing what happens in passives. But Perlmutter and Postal, attempting to characterize possible variations among languages, have proposed the Motivated Chomage Law, a constraint on the class of possible grammars (Perlmutter 1978; Perlmutter & Postal 1977, to appear c). This law, formally stated in Perlmutter & Postal (to appear c), claims in effect that nominals bear the chomeur relation only under the conditions specified in the Chomeur Law (cf. Introduction, §2). This means that the conditions for the existence of chomeurs are completely determined by universal principles. In the instance of *tvis*-nominals of the Georgian passive, it is not obvious how the indirect object might be put *en chomage*. If Perlmutter and Postal's claim is correct, either the *tvis*-nominals are not chomeurs or the conditions of their *chomage* have yet to be discovered.

Relational grammar defines two classes of initial terms that are final non-terms – chomeurs and emeritus terms (Perlmutter & Postal, to appear c). Together these are called 'retired terms'. Chomeurs are governed by the Chomeur Law and the Motivated Chomage Law, and their behavior has been studied in some detail.[7] Much less is understood about nominals bearing the emeritus relations. They are known to exist in causatives (cf. ch. 5 and works cited there). In ch. 11 it is suggested that emeritus terms also exist in nominalizations and infinitive constructions. If Georgian indicated clearly the difference between chomeurs and emeritus terms, the *tvis*-nominal of the passive construction would be an empirical test of the validity of the Motivated Chomage Law. However, as shown in ch. 11, Georgian marks chomeurs and emeritus terms in the same way, and they have the same behavior with respect to the superficial syntactic properties investigated here. It is therefore impossible to determine at present whether the *tvis*-nominal is an indirect object chomeur or an indirect object emeritus. Therefore, it is impossible to give a complete analysis of the construction. From §1 it is clear that the initial direct object is a final subject and that the initial subject is a final retired subject. I therefore propose that (2b) is correctly described by the relational network (22) and that Passivization in Georgian is at least *partially* stated as the universal rule (23).

(22)

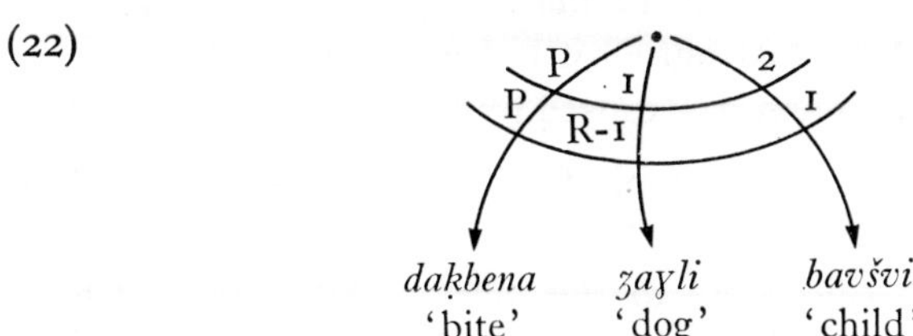

(23) *Passivization*

In the presence of a subject, a direct object may advance to subject.

Neither (22) nor (23) describes the fate of the initial indirect object, but there is not sufficient evidence for doing so at present, for the reasons stated above.

4 Interaction with other rules

In this section I will consider the rules we have previously dealt with and show that this analysis makes the correct predictions in each case.

4.1 *Object Raising*

Object Raising and Passivization can never apply in a single clause. (24a) is grammatical without Passivization; but (*24b), where Passivization has applied in the embedded clause, is ungrammatical.

(24) (a) *es motxroba advilia çasaķitxavad.*
this story-NOM easy-it-is-I-2 to-read
'This story is easy to read.'
(b) **es motxroba advilia çaķitxuli (sa)qopnad.*
read to-be
('This story is easy to be read.')

This is predicted by the proposed analysis. Since the input conditions to each rule require a direct object, and since the output of each contains no direct object, they are mutually exclusive in a clause.

4.2 *Causative Clause Union*

This analysis correctly predicts that Passivization can apply to the output of Causative Clause Union, since the output of that rule contains a direct object. (25) exemplifies that situation (cf. example (15b) of ch. 5).

(25) *ubeduri šemtxveva moxdenilia paṭara biçis mier.*
unfortunate accident-NOM caused-it-is-I-2 little boy by
'An unfortunate accident was caused by the little boy.'

Passivization does not, however, apply freely to a causative with three terms.

While Passivization can apply to the output of Causative Clause Union, the latter cannot apply to the output of the former. This is not automatically predicted from our analysis, but the same is true in other languages, such as French, Turkish, etc. (cf. Aissen 1974a, b). The inability of rules to apply in the complement of causatives is discussed above in ch. 5.

4.3 *Version*

The Version rules cannot apply to the output of Passivization. This may be due to the fact that the finite verb of passives is *qopna* 'be', which cannot take a version object, as shown in (26) and (27).

(26) (a) *es vašli aris šentvis.*
this apple-NOM it-it-I-2 you-for
'This apple is for you.'
(b) **es vašli garis.*
it-is-you-I-2
('This apple is for you.')

(27) (a) *es aris šeni otaxi.*
this it-is-I-2 your room-NOM
'This is your room.'
(b) **es garis otaxi.*
it-is-you-I-2
('This is your room.')

Since *qopna* never takes Version, we may conjecture that this also blocks the application of Version to a passive sentence.

Passivization cannot apply to the output of Version. In (28a), neither rule has applied. In (28b), Possessive Version has applied, making *zurab* the indirect object. In (*28c, d), both Possessive Version and Passivization have applied. Since Version makes *zurab* the indirect object, and Passivization causes it to retire (cf. §2 and 3), we would expect it to be marked with *tvis* or the dative case, as in (*28c) and (*28d), respectively.

(28) (a) *zurabis das çoraven.*
Zurab-GEN sister-DAT they-gossip-her-I-1
'They are gossiping about Zurab's sister.'
(b) *das uçoraven zurabs.*
they-gossip-him-her-I-1 Zurab-DAT
'They are gossiping about Zurab's sister.'
(c) **da gaçorilia zurabistvis*
sister-NOM gossiped-she-is-I-2 Zurab-for
('Zurab's sister is being gossiped about.')
(d) **da gaçorilia zurabs.*
('Zurab's sister is being gossiped about.')
(e) *zurabis da gaçorilia.*
'Zurab's sister is being gossiped about.'

(28e) establishes that Passivization can apply with this verb, as long as Version does not apply. Thus, (28) documents the inability of Possessive Version and Passivization to interact.

We cannot determine whether Passivization can apply to the output of Benefactive Version. Since the initial indirect object in a passive construction and the non-term benefactive are both marked with *tvis*, it is impossible to tell whether or not Benefactive Version has applied in the derivation of

(29) *axali šarvali šeḳerilia šentvis.*
new trousers-NOM sewn-it-is-I-2 you-for
'New trousers are made for you.'

The inability of Version to apply in passives does not follow automatically from any rule previously proposed.[8]

5 Conclusion

The construction illustrated in (1–2b) has been shown to be a passive, according to accepted definitions of passive. Peculiarities of the initial indirect object in a passive construction have been discussed; it has been shown that that nominal is a final non-term, but no proposal has been made concerning its precise derivation. Finally, the interaction of Passivization and other rules of the grammar has been discussed.

8 *Inversion*

In ch. 2 I described the different correlations between grammatical relations and case markings as they exist in Series I and II. There is also a Series III, in which a third set of correspondences apparently holds. This chapter will describe and account for that case marking differential.

1 The problem: the case marking differential in Series III

The sentences in (1) are in the present tense, which belongs to Series I; (1a) contains a Class 1 verb, (1b) a Class 2 verb, and (1c) a Class 3 verb. In each, the subject is in the nominative, the direct and indirect objects are in the dative.

(1) (a) *rezo* *samajurs* *ačukebs* *dedas.*
Rezo-NOM bracelet-DAT he-gives-her-it-I-1 mother-DAT
'Rezo is giving mother a bracelet.'
(b) *gelodebi* (*me*) (*šen*).
I-await-you-I-2 I-NOM you-DAT
'I am waiting for you.'
(c) *deida* *mɣeris* *naninas.*
aunt-NOM she-sings-I-3 lullaby-DAT
'Aunt is singing a lullaby.'

(2) gives the same sentences in the so-called perfect or first evidential, which belongs to Series III. Notice that, for verbs of Classes 1 and 3, the cases differ from those of Series I, though the meaning remains essentially the same. For verbs of Class 2, the subject remains in the nominative, and the object in the dative.

(2) (a) *turme* *rezos* *samajuri* *učukebia* *dedistvis.*
apparently Rezo-DAT bracelet-NOM he-gave-it-III-1 mother-for
'Apparently Rezo gave a bracelet to his mother.'

(b) *turme daglodebivar* (*me*) (*šen*).
I-awaited-you-III-2 I-NOM you-DAT
'Apparently I (have) waited for you.'

(c) *turme deidas umɣeria nanina.*
aunt-DAT she-sang-it-III-3 lullaby-NOM
'Apparently Aunt has sung a lullaby.'

Traditionally, Georgianists have called the construction illustrated by (2a, c) 'inversion', and this name has been adopted in relational grammar. Inversion is illustrated here in the evidential mode, a verb form used to remove the speaker, in some sense, from the statement.[1] The evidential occurs felicitously with the word *turme* 'apparently', and examples from Series III may be translated this way in English even when *turme* does not actually occur in the Georgian example.

The correspondences illustrated in (2), as well as those discussed in earlier chapters for Series I and II, are summarized in (3–4), which may be compared with (13–14) of ch. 2.

(3)

	Subject	*Direct Object*	*Indirect Object*
Pattern A	ERGATIVE	NOMINATIVE	DATIVE
B	NOMINATIVE	DATIVE	DATIVE
C	DATIVE	NOMINATIVE	*tvis*

(4)

Series	I	II	III
Class 1	B	A	C
2	B	B	B
3	B	A	C

In this chapter it is argued that (3–4) represent an analysis that is unnecessarily complex. In particular, it is shown that Pattern C is reducible to a special instance of Pattern B by the application of two rules, Inversion and Unaccusative, which change grammatical relations, as described below in §2.

Traditional treatments have observed that Object Camouflage does not apply in Series III tenses; this has been treated as an idiosyncratic fact (cf. Shanidze 1973; Tschenkéli 1958; Vogt 1971). The failure of Object Camouflage to apply follows from the analysis presented here, with no additional device.

2 The proposal: a rule of inversion

I propose that the initial grammatical relations of (2a) are as listed in (5), while the final grammatical relations are as listed in (6).

(5) *Initial grammatical relations*

rezo	subject
samajuri 'bracelet'	direct object
deda 'mother'	indirect object

(6) *Final grammatical relations*

rezo	indirect object
samajuri	subject
deda	indirect object chomeur.[2]

I propose, further, that the grammatical relations in (5) are related to those in (6) in the following way. The rule of Inversion applies, making the subject an indirect object. According to the Chomeur Law, this makes the initial indirect object a chomeur. The initial direct object becomes subject by the rule Postal and Perlmutter have called Unaccusative. In Georgian this rule applies to a direct object at any level where it does not co-occur with a subject, making the direct object a subject. This may all be schematized as (7), where the top stratum represents initial grammatical relations, the second represents grammatical relations resulting from the application of Inversion, and the third represents grammatical relations resulting from the application of Unaccusative.

(7)

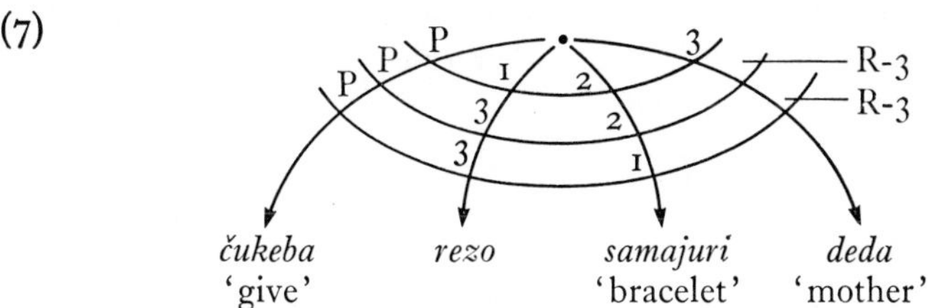

Inversion is triggered by a Class 1 or 3 verb in a Series III form; the rule must apply if this trigger condition is met.

Traditionally, some Georgianists have considered the dative-nominal to be the subject in Series III on the basis of the intuitive notion of 'subject'; others have considered the nominative-nominal to be the subject in this construction on the basis of the case and person agreement facts. But the question has been argued on the basis of these facts alone.[3] Only by recognizing distinct levels of derivation and by considering a number of criteria, including syntactic as well as morphological ones, can we give an adequate analysis of the 'subject' in this construction.

Most of this chapter is devoted to arguments that in inversion constructions, such as (2a, c), the initial and final grammatical relations are as stated above. The arguments will establish that in inversion the dative-nominal, which corresponds to the syntactic subject in the indicative (Series I and II), has the syntactic properties of initial subjects and the syntactic properties of final indirect objects. Similarly, the nominative-nominal of inversion will be shown to have the syntactic properties of initial direct objects and those of final subjects. For expository reasons, the arguments will not be grouped in this way, however. Rather, the first group of arguments (§3) presents evidence for both initial and final relations and is based on the simplest type of inversion only, as illustrated in (2). I will then introduce an inversion construction that is not, like (2), limited to the evidential mode (§4); two properties of this type of construction are used as the basis for additional arguments. In §5, some further arguments, based on both types of inversion are given. A total of five arguments to support the proposed initial grammatical relations are presented – in §3.3, 3.4, 4.1, and 5.1. Five arguments to support the final grammatical relations proposed are given in §3.1, 3.2, 4.2, and 5.1. Additional evidence to support this rule is given in chs. 11, 15 and 16.

The arguments in §3–5 concern the initial and derived grammatical relations only; a discussion of the specific rules proposed is in §6. The interaction of Inversion with some other rules of syntax is described in §7.

3 Preliminary arguments

The form of the argument will be the same for both initial and final grammatical relations: I will show how one of the phenomena whose general characteristics in Georgian syntax have already been established operates in sentences like (2a, c). If the grammatical relations are as I have proposed, the phenomenon can be treated in a general manner throughout the grammar. If not, special *ad hoc* rules will be needed to account for each of these phenomena in inversion constructions. Final grammatical relations are discussed first.

3.1 *Person Agreement*

Paradigm (8) represents the intersection of the categories of person and number for Subject Person Agreement, first introduced in ch. 1.

(8) *Subject Person Agreement*

	singular	plural
1. person	*v—*	*v—t*
2. person	ø	*—t*
3. person	*—s/a/o*	*—en/es/nen, etc.*

The dash represents the position of the verb stem, which includes the root and certain formants. The alternations in the third person are determined by the tense and Class of the verb.

The markers in (8) indicate Subject Person Agreement generally in Georgian, as shown in ch. 1, §3.1. In subsequent chapters it was shown that Person Agreement is stated on final termhood (cf. chs. 4, 5, 6, and 7).

In Series III, it is the nominative-nominal which triggers Subject Person Agreement. (9) gives a paradigm of the singular with the markers of (8) in heavy type.

(9) (a) *mas undoda, (rom) (me) ga**v**egzavne kalakši.*
that I-NOM he-sent-**me**-III-1 city-in
'He wanted to send me into the city.'

(b) *mas undoda, (rom) (šen) gaegzavne kalakši.* (zero
you-NOM he-sent-**you**-III-1 marker)
'He wanted to send you into the city.'

(c) *mas undoda, (rom) (is) gaegzavn**a** kalakši.*
he-NOM he-sent-**him**-III-1
'He$_i$ wanted to send him$_j$ into the city.'

(9) establishes that the nominative-nominal triggers Subject Person Agreement in Series III.[4] From this and the fact established in earlier chapters that final subjects trigger Subject Agreement, we must conclude that the nominative-nominal in the inversion construction in Series III is a final subject.

Now let us turn to Indirect Object Person Agreement; the markers are given in paradigm (10).

(10) *Indirect Object Person Agreement*

	singular	plural
1. person	*m—*	*gv—*
2. person	*g—*	*g—t*
3. person	*s/h/ø—*	*s/h/ø—t*

Here the alternation in the third person markers is phonologically determined.

The markers in (10) indicate Indirect Object Agreement generally in Georgian, as shown in ch. 1, §3.1. In subsequent chapters it was shown that Indirect Object Person Agreement is stated on final termhood (cf. chs. 5 and 6).

In Series III, the dative-nominal triggers Indirect Object Person Agreement. (11) presents a paradigm of the singular, with the markers of (10) in heavy type.

(11) (a) *mas undoda, (rom) (me) da**m**etesa simindi.*
I-DAT **I**-sowed-it-III-1 corn-NOM
'He wanted me to sow corn.'

(b) *mas undoda, (rom) (šen) da**g**etesa simindi.*
you-DAT **you**-sowed-it-III-1
'He wanted you to sow corn.'

(c) *mas undoda, (rom) gelas daetesa simindi.*
Gela-DAT **he**-sowed-it-III-1 (zero marker)
'He wanted Gela to sow corn.'

Since final indirect objects trigger Indirect Object Person Agreement in Georgian, and the dative-nominal of the evidential (Series III) triggers Indirect Object Person Agreement, as established in (11),[5] the dative-nominal must be a final indirect object.

According to this analysis, as a consequence of the Chomeur Law, the *tvis*-nominal is an indirect object chomeur. Since Person Agreement is stated on final termhood, the *tvis*-nominal, not being a final term, should not trigger Person Agreement. I will show now that this prediction is borne out. In the indicative, illustrated with Series II in (12), the indirect object triggers Indirect Object Person Agreement, which is realized as *m-* in (a) for the first person, and as *g-* in (b) for the second person. By comparing the sentences of (12) with their counterparts in the evidential, given in (13), we can see that the nominal which in the indicative triggers Indirect Object Agreement, in the evidential triggers no agreement at all.

(12) (a) *rezom **m**ačuka samajuri.*
Rezo-ERG he-gave-**me**-it-II-1 bracelet-NOM
'Rezo gave me a bracelet.'

(b) *rezom* **ga***čuka* *samajuri.*
he-gave-**you**-it-II-1
'Rezo gave you a bracelet.'
(c) *rezom ačuka* *samajuri.*
he-gave-**him**-it-II-1 (zero marker)
'Rezo gave him a bracelet.'

(13) (a) *turme rezos učukebia samajuri čemtvis.*
apparently Rezo-DAT he-gave-it-III-1 me-for
'Apparently Rezo has given me a bracelet.'
(b) *turme rezos učukebia samajuri šentvis.*
you-for
'Apparently Rezo has given you a bracelet.'
(c) *turme rezos učukebia samajuri mistvis.*
him-for
'Apparently Rezo has given him a bracelet.'

(13) shows that the *tvis*-nominal of the evidential (Series III) fails to trigger any Person Agreement, thus supporting the view that it is not a final term.

3.2 *Object Camouflage*

In ch. 3 I showed that Object Camouflage applies obligatorily to first and second person direct objects in the presence of an indirect object, as illustrated in (14).

(14) (a) **deda (šen) gabarebs masçavlebels.*
mother-NOM you-DAT she-renders-him-you-I-1 teacher-DAT
('Mother is turning you over to the teacher.')
(b) *deda abarebs masçavlebels šens tavs.*
she-renders-him-him-I-1 your self-DAT
'Mother is turning you over to the teacher.'

(*14a) is ungrammatical because the input conditions for Object Camouflage are met, but the rule has failed to apply; in (14b) the initial direct object has been camouflaged. Both sentences of (14) are in Series I.

In Series III Object Camouflage never applies. (15) is exactly parallel to (14), but is in Series III. In (15a) Object Camouflage has not applied; in (*15b) it has.

(15) (a) *turme* *dedas* *čaubarebixar*
apparently mother-DAT she-rendered-you-III-1
masçavleblistvis.
teacher-for
'Apparently Mother (has) turned you over to the teacher.'
(b) **turme dedas čaubarebia* *šeni tavi*
she-rendered-him-III-1 your self-NOM
masçavleblistvis.
('Apparently Mother (has) turned you over to the teacher.')

(14) and (15) show that Object Camouflage must apply in Series I and must not apply in Series III.

I have shown in previous chapters that Object Camouflage applies to the output of rules that change grammatical relations (chs. 5, 6, 7). Inversion and Unaccusative are relation-changing rules. From this it follows that Object Camouflage applies to the output of these two rules. But Object Camouflage is a rule that affects direct objects; there is no direct object in the output of the obligatory rule of Unaccusative. The input conditions for Object Camouflage are therefore not met wherever Inversion and Unaccusative have applied (cf. network (16)).

(16)

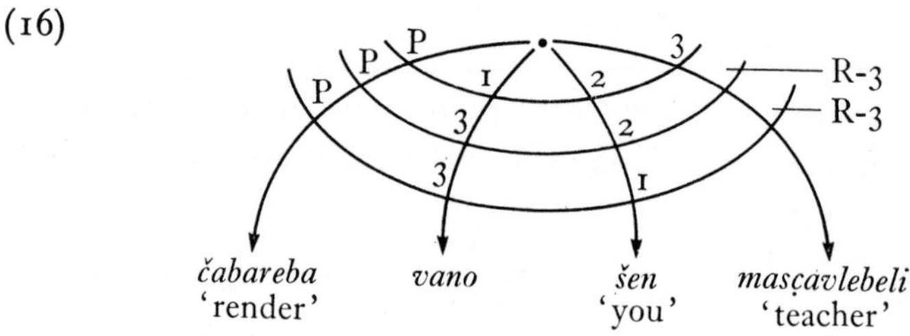

Thus, on my analysis, the fact that Object Camouflage never applies with Series III is accounted for automatically.[6] An analysis on which the nominals have the relations listed in (5) at *all* levels of derivation must treat Series III as an exception to Object Camouflage.

3.3 Tav-*Reflexivization*

Tav-Reflexivization is triggered only by subjects (cf. ch. 1), and the subject-trigger condition on this rule is stated on initial termhood (cf. ch. 5, §2.2, and ch. 7, §1.1.3).

In inversion constructions in Series III, only the dative-nominal can trigger *Tav*-Reflexivization. In (17a) the nominative subject of a verb in Series I triggers *tav-*; in (17b) the same nominal is the trigger, though its case is different in the inversion construction.

(17) (a) *gela* *irçmunebs* *tavis tavs.*
Gela-NOM he-convinces-him-I-1 self's self-DAT
'Gela is convincing himself.'
(b) *gelas* *turme* *daurçmunebia* *tavisi tavi.*
Gela-DAT apparently he-convinced-him-III-1 self's self-NOM
'Gela apparently (has) convinced himself.'
(c) **tavis tavs* *turme daurçmunebia gela.*
self's self-DAT Gela-NOM
('Apparently Gela (has) convinced himself.')
(d) **gela turme daurçmunebia tavis tavs.*

(*17c) shows that the nominative-nominal of the inversion construction cannot trigger *Tav*-Reflexivization in the dative-nominal. (*17d) is identical to (*17c) except for word order; it establishes that the ungrammaticality of (*17c) is not due to word order.

The fact that it is the dative-nominal that can trigger *tav-* in (17) is consistent with the fact that only initial subjects can trigger *Tav*-Reflexivization (cf. ch. 7, §1.1.3), since on the proposed analysis the dative-nominal is the initial subject of the inversion construction. An analysis that claimed the relations of (6) for all levels of derivation would render this construction an exception to *Tav*-Reflexivization.

3.4 *Suppletion*

It has been established that there are verbs in Georgian that are suppletive for the number or animacy of their subjects or objects. Each of those verbs supplies arguments in support of the analysis proposed in §2; two will be discussed here.

3.4.1 *Suppletion for number of the direct object.* The verb 'throw' is suppletive for the number of its direct object; *gadagdeba* is used with singular direct objects, *gadaqra* with plurals (cf. Introduction, §4.3.2).

This number condition is governed by the nominative-nominal in inversion sentences in Series III. The sentences in (18) have singular nominative-nominals; those in (19) have plurals.

(18) (a) *turme bavšvs* *gadaugdia* *kva.*
child-DAT he-threw-it-III-1 stone-NOM
'Apparently the child threw a stone.'

(b) **turme bavšvs gadauqria kva.*
he-threw-it-III-1
('Apparently the child threw a stone.')

(19) (a) **turme bavšvs gadaugdia kvebi.*
stones-NOM
('Apparently the child threw stones.')
(b) *turme bavšvs gadauqria kvebi.*
'Apparently the child threw stones.'

On the analysis proposed above in §2, *kva/kvebi* 'stone/stones' is the initial direct object in (18–19). These sentences are therefore accounted for with the same condition needed for sentences of Series I and II, stating that condition on initial termhood (cf. ch. 4, §3.1.1 and ch. 7, §1.1.1). An analysis on which *kva/kvebi* were not initial direct objects would have to complicate the rule governing the suppletion of 'throw', just when it occurred in a Series III form.

3.4.2 *Suppletion for animacy of the direct object.* The verb 'bring' is suppletive for the animacy of its direct object; *moiṭana* 'he brought it' is used only with inanimate direct objects, *moiqvana* 'he brought him' only with animate direct objects. It has been shown in earlier chapters that this constraint is stated on initial termhood.

The same condition on animacy governs the nominative-nominal in Series III; on the proposed analysis, these are initial direct objects. The direct objects in (20) are inanimate, those in (21) animate.

(20) (a) *gelas mouṭania ɣvino supraze.*
Gela-DAT he-brought-it-III-1 wine-NOM table-on
'Gela has apparently brought wine to the party.'
(b) **gelas mouqvania ɣvino supraze.*
he-brought-him-III-1
('Gela has apparently brought wine to the party.')

(21) (a) **gelas mouṭania megobari supraze.*
friend-NOM
('Gela has apparently brought a friend to the party.')
(b) *gelas mouqvania megobari supraze.*
'Gela has apparently brought a friend to the party.'

(20) and (21) show that the nominative-nominal of the inversion con-

struction must meet the animacy requirements on the direct object of the suppletive verb 'bring'.

On the proposed analysis, *γvino* 'wine' and *megobari* 'friend' are initial direct objects in (20–21). They are therefore accounted for with the same condition needed to account for suppletion in Series I and II. An analysis that did not derive (20–21) from initial structures in which *γvino* and *megobari* were direct objects would have to complicate the condition governing suppletion in the verb 'bring', just when it occurred in the inversion construction.

We have seen that the dative-nominal of the inversion construction has the characteristics of a final indirect object with respect to the rules of Indirect Object Agreement and the characteristics of an initial subject with respect to the rules of *Tav*-Reflexivization. The nominative-nominal of the inversion construction has been shown to have the characteristics of a final subject with respect to the rule of Subject Agreement and the characteristics of an initial direct object with respect to two verbs suppletive for properties of their direct objects. In addition, we have seen that this nominal does not have the characteristics of a final direct object with respect to the rule of Object Camouflage, or the characteristics of an initial subject with respect to the rule of *Tav*-Reflexivization. The *tvis*-nominal of the inversion construction, while it corresponds to the indirect object of Series I and II, has been shown to have the characteristics of a final non-term. Thus arguments have been given for both the initial and final relations of each nominal, as proposed in §2.

4 Inversion verbs

Georgian has a group of so-called 'affective' predicates, including verbs like *miqvarxar* 'I love you', *uxaria* 'he is pleased, happy', and *segiʒlia* 'you can'. These verbs have many of the same syntactic properties that the inversion construction of Series III has. Appendix A to this chapter provides evidence that sentences like (22) are like inversion in Series

(22) *gelas uqvars nino.*
Gela-DAT he-loves-her-I-4 Nino-NOM
'Gela loves Nino.'

III (e.g. (2a, c)) with respect to all of the applicable rules discussed in §3. Specifically, it shows that the dative-nominal has the syntactic properties of a final indirect object and of an initial subject, while the nominative-nominal has the syntactic properties of a final subject and of an initial non-subject.

The construction illustrated in (22) differs from the inversion construction of (2a, c) in one important respect: 'affective' verbs like that in (22) govern this construction not only in Series III, but in all Series. This means that the alternation illustrated by (1a, c)/(2a, c) does not exist for affective verbs. Because of this difference, the question arises, are these constructions the same?

I will argue below that sentences like (22) involve Inversion and Unaccusative, the same rules that are involved in the derivations of (2a and c). I am claiming that the 'experiencer' is the initial subject and final indirect object, and that the 'stimulus' is the initial direct object and final subject, as stated in (23) and (24).

(23) *Initial grammatical relations*
gela subject
nino direct object

(24) *Final grammatical relations*
gela indirect object
nino subject

When Inversion applies in the derivation of (22), it makes the initial subject, *gela*, the indirect object. Unaccusative then makes the initial direct object, *nino*, the subject. There are no verbs of this type – henceforth 'Class 4' or 'inversion verbs' – with an initial indirect object; thus there is never an indirect object chomeur, as there may be with inversion in the evidential. The derivation of (22) may be represented as (25).

(25)

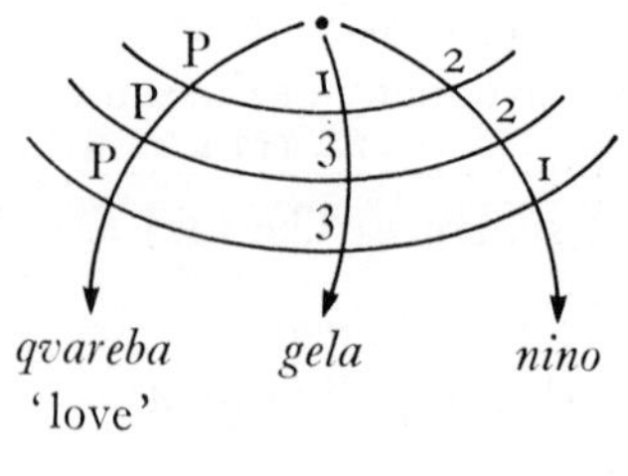

P 1 2
P 3 2
P 3 1

qvareba *gela* *nino*
'love'

Preliminary arguments that this construction is the same as inversion in Series III are given in Appendix A to this chapter. In the remainder of this section I will give two additional arguments for an Inversion analysis. The first is based on suppletion and is relevant to inversion verbs alone. This is an argument against a solution where each nominal has its *final* termhood at all levels of derivation. The second argument is based on case marking; it is an argument for an Inversion analysis for both inversion verbs and Series III forms and considers the verbal system of the language as a whole. This set of facts argues against a solution where each nominal has its *initial* termhood at all levels of derivation. Since these two constructions behave the same with respect to all syntactic rules that interact with them, I conclude that the derivations of both types involve the application of Inversion and Unaccusative.[7] The two types differ in that inversion verbs trigger Inversion in all finite forms, while with other verbs, the evidential mode (Series III) alone triggers Inversion.

4.1 *Suppletion for tense*

In §4.3.4 of the Introduction I showed that the verb 'take' is multiply suppletive in Georgian – for animacy of the direct object, and for tense. In this section I will argue on the basis of the latter suppletion that Inversion applies with Class 4 verbs. To simplify the situation, I will cite only those forms used with inanimate direct objects.

Consider the pair of sentences in (26). The first is in the present tense (Series I), formed on the root *kv*; the second is in the aorist (Series II) and formed on the root *ṭan*. These are in a suppletive relation to one another; the first root cannot occur in the aorist, the second cannot occur in the present. What is of particular interest here is the difference in case marking.

(26) (a) *gelas çignebi miakvs samḳitxvelośi.*
Gela-DAT books-NOM he-takes-it-I-4 reading-room-in
'Gela is taking the books into the reading room.'

(b) *gelam çignebi miiṭana samḳitxvelośi.*
Gela-ERG he-took-it-II-1
'Gela took the books into the reading room.'

The verb form in (26a), *miakvs*, is in Class 4 and governs Pattern C case marking in all Series. The verb form in (26b), *miiṭana*, is in Class 1, which in Series II governs the case Pattern A, as we saw in ch. 2. The meaning of the two sentences is the same; only the tense – and for this verb, that involves also the root – is different.

If *miakvs* is not treated as an inversion verb and does not undergo the rule of Inversion, the rules that relate syntax to semantic interpretation must be complicated to account for the pair of sentences in (26). On the inversion analysis proposed here, on the other hand, the initial subject of the inversion verb form is the same as the (initial and final) subject of the non-inversion verb form. Therefore the semantic interpretation of both sentences can naturally be related to their initial term dependents.

4.2 *Case Marking*

In §1 of this chapter, I gave a summary of the Class–Series–case correlations for Georgian. (27) repeats (3); (28) repeats (4), with the addition of Class 4 (inversion) verbs.

(27)

	Subject	*Direct Object*	*Indirect Object*
Pattern A	ERGATIVE	NOMINATIVE	DATIVE
B	NOMINATIVE	DATIVE	DATIVE
C	DATIVE	NOMINATIVE	*tvis*

(28)

	Series I	II	III
Class 1, 3	B	A	C
2	B	B	B
4	C	C	C

(27) and (28) summarize in chart form a traditional description of case marking in Georgian.[8] It is based on an analysis of the inversion construction where the dative-nominal is the subject; thus (28) indicates Pattern C across the board for inversion verbs. Similarly, it shows Pattern C (dative subject) for Class I and 3 verbs, which govern Inversion in Series III.

However, given the analysis of the inversion construction proposed above, it is not necessary to have Pattern C at all; it reduces to a special instance of Pattern B. According to the proposed analysis, the dative-nominal in an inversion construction is not only the initial subject, but also the final indirect object. If case marking in Series III is stated on final termhood, then this nominal will be correctly marked by Pattern B, the most general pattern in the language. Similarly, according to the Inversion analysis, the nominative-nominal is not only the initial direct object, but also the final subject. If case marking in Series III is stated on final termhood, then this nominal will also be correctly marked by Pattern B. There is independent evidence that case marking is stated on final termhood (cf. chs. 3, 4, 5, 6, 7 and 16). For (27) and (28), then, we can substitute (27′) and (28′):

(27′)

	Final Subject	*Final Direct Object*	*Final Indirect Object*
Pattern A	ERGATIVE	NOMINATIVE	DATIVE
B	NOMINATIVE	DATIVE	DATIVE

(28′)

	Series I	II	III
Class 1, 3	B	A	B
2, 4	B	B	B

This correctly represents case marking in relation to final termhood, showing that Pattern B is general for Georgian, Class 1 and 3 verbs in Series II being an exception to the general rule. The traditional statement, (27–28), is misleading in the sense that it represents case marking in relation to initial termhood, while case marking rules are, in fact, based on final termhood.[9] The facts summarized in (27′–28′) show that if one accepts the final termhood proposed above for the inversion construction, significant simplifications can be achieved in the rules of case marking.

The marking of the *tvis*-nominal is also accounted for naturally on the proposal outlined above. Since case marking in Series III is based on final termhood, if the initial indirect object of a sentence like (2a) is finally an indirect object chomeur as proposed, it should have marking appropriate to a non-term. *Tvis* is used to mark non-term benefactives (cf. ch. 6) and delegatives, as well as certain retired terms (cf. chs. 5 and 7). The systematic nature of the latter will be established in ch. 11.

4.3 *Summary*

Inversion verbs, predicates that trigger Inversion in all finite verbal categories, and inversion in Series III have been shown to involve the same two rules – Inversion and Unaccusative. One argument, based on suppletion, has been offered for the initial grammatical relations claimed in (23), while a second argument provides support for the final grammatical relations claimed in (6) for Series III and in (24) for inversion verbs. This is based on the fact that the Inversion analysis effects a significant simplification in the case marking rules: once inversion is incorporated into the grammar of Georgian, the need for Pattern C disappears.

5 Additional arguments

5.1 *Causative Clause Union*

In ch. 5 I showed that the subject of an intransitive is realized as the direct object of the causative of that verb. In the causative of an intransitive inversion verb, the initial subject is also realized as the direct object of the causative. (29a) contains an intransitive inversion verb; (29b) contains the corresponding causative.

(29) (a) *ṭusaɣs šioda.*
prisoner-DAT he-hungered-I-4
'The prisoner was hungry.'
(b) (*mat*) *ṭusaɣi moašives.*[10]
they-ERG prisoner-NOM they-caused-hunger-him-II-1
'They let the prisoner go hungry./They starved the prisoner.'

On the Inversion analysis, *tusaɣ-* is the initial subject of *-šiv-* in both sentences of (29). Inversion, like other rules that change grammatical relations, does not apply in the complement clause of a causative (cf. ch. 5). Since Inversion does not apply to *tusaɣ-* in (29b), it is treated like the subjects of other intransitive verbs under Clause Union. It therefore becomes the direct object of the causative, just as other intransitive subjects do. This is shown by case marking (Pattern A), Person Agreement, etc. The fact that the experiencer of an intransitive inversion verb is treated like other intransitive subjects argues against an analysis of inversion constructions where the experiencer has its final grammatical relation, indirect object, at all levels of derivation.[11]

Clause Union and Inversion also interact in the Series III forms of organic causatives. I have stated above that all causatives are Class 1 verbs, and that all Class 1 verbs undergo Inversion in Series III. (30a) illustrates a complex causative in Series II; (30b) shows the Series III form of the same sentence.

(30) (a) *mepem gagaçmendina sasaxle.*
king-ERG he-caused-clean-you-it-II-1 palace-NOM
'The king made you clean the palace.'
(b) *turme mepes šentvis gauçmendinebia sasaxle.*[12]
apparently king-DAT you-for he-caused-clean-it-III-1
'Apparently the king (has) made you clean the palace.'

My analysis makes the correct predictions concerning the application of Inversion to the output of Causative Clause Union. First, the subject of the causative, *mepe* 'king', should be the final indirect object (by Inversion). Second, the direct object of the causative, *sasaxle* 'palace', should be the final subject of the inversion construction (by Unaccusative). Third, the indirect object of the causative should be an indirect object chomeur (by the Chomeur Condition). Each of these predictions of derived termhood is borne out in (30b), as shown by the case marking and agreement facts.

5.2 *Summary and Extension*

Arguments based on a variety of different syntactic and morphological phenomena have been given for both the initial and final grammatical relations claimed, and for Inversion both with inversion verbs and with Series III forms.[13] In chs. 11 and 15 it will be shown that the rules of Number Agreement and Retired Term Marking cannot be stated simply without an Inversion analysis. Other analyses cannot account for the fact that the dative-nominal of inversion has the syntactic characteristics of initial subjects and final indirect objects, or for the fact that the nominative-nominal of inversion has the syntactic characteristics of initial direct objects and of final subjects. I conclude that we must posit rules of Inversion and Unaccusative in Georgian, to relate the initial grammatical relations of (5) and (23) to the final grammatical relations of (6) and (24), respectively.

6 The form of the rule

Arguments presented above concern only the initial and final grammatical relations in the inversion construction, without respect to the form of the rules involved. We must consider in more detail what kind of rule or rules relate the initial grammatical relations to the final ones.

Treatments of inversion phenomena written within the framework of transformational grammar have generally proposed a rule that would switch the relative linear order of the subject and direct object (cf. Rosenbaum 1967; R. Lakoff 1968; G. Lakoff 1970; Postal 1970 & 1971). This proposal has the problem that a single rule cannot be used for languages with different basic word orders. In addition, it makes the wrong predictions about the word order of many languages, including Hindi (Davison 1969), Kannada (Sridhar 1976a, b), and Georgian, where the initial subject of inversion constructions and the subject of non-inversion constructions occupy the same position in unmarked order. Further, this treatment fails to account for the fact that the initial subject becomes indirect object, not direct object, as the difference between these is, in many languages, not predictable merely from the position of the nominal. One could, however, propose a relational counterpart to this, which would obviate these problems. According to such a proposal, two processes form a single rule:

A. *Inversion*
(i) Subject → Indirect Object
(ii) Direct Object → Subject

As an alternative to this, it might be proposed that Inversion is the advancement of a direct object to subject, the initial subject becoming a chomeur. The subject chomeur would then advance to indirect object. According to this proposal, there are two different rules that often apply together.

B. *Inversion*
(i) Direct Object → Subject
(ii) Subject Chomeur → Indirect Object

A third proposal is the one outlined in §1 above and is due to Postal and Perlmutter. According to this hypothesis, Inversion is a single process:

C. *Inversion*
Subject → Indirect Object

The initial indirect object is put *en chomage*, according to the Chomeur Condition. The direct object advances to subject, by Unaccusative. Inversion proper is just the process of a subject becoming an indirect object.

Each of these proposals makes different predictions about the range of data to be found in natural languages. Proposal A predicts that the two processes will always be found together in all examples. The second predicts that each process will be found in some languages without the other. The third predicts that the rule may be found without Unaccusative, and that the latter will operate in sentences that lack a subject for reasons other than the application of Inversion.

In addition, each of these proposals raises theoretical questions. Can a single rule have two parts, as in A? (Is there any other rule that has two parts?) Can a chomeur advance, as in B? (Is there any other rule that advances chomeurs?) Can a term be demoted, as in C? None of these questions can be answered here. Nor is it possible at this time to test the predictions outlined above against the facts of many natural languages. We can choose between these three proposals only by taking into account the properties of many languages. However, Georgian does shed some light on the problem; these data too must be taken into account in determining the correct approach.

All of the hypotheses outlined above can account equally well for inversion with transitive verbs. In Georgian, Inversion can also apply with intransitive verbs, as shown by the examples that follow. (31) contains intransitive non-inversion verbs in the indicative; (32) gives their counterparts in the evidential (Series III). (33) contains intransitive inversion verbs.

(31) (a) *merabi amtknarebs.*
Merab-NOM he-yawns-I-1
'Merab is yawning.'
(b) *merabi mušaobs.*
he-works-I-3
'Merab is working.'
(c) *merabi ṭiris*
he-cries-I-3
'Merab is crying.'
(d) *merabi cekvavs.*
he-dances-I-3
'Merab is dancing.'

(32) (a) *merabs turme daumtknarebia.*
Merab-DAT apparently he-yawned-III-1
'Merab apparently (has) yawned.'
(b) *merabs turme umušavnia.*
he-worked-III-3
'Merab apparently (has) worked.'
(c) *merabs uṭiria.*
he-cried-III-3
'Merab apparently (has) cried.'

(d) *merabs uceḳvia.*
he-danced-III-3
'Merab apparently (has) danced.'

(33) (a) *bavšvs šia.*
child-DAT he-hungers-I-4
'The child is hungry.'
(b) *bavšvs sciva.*
he-cold-I-4
'The child finds it cold./The child is cold.'
(c) *bavšvs uxaria.*
he-happy-I-4
'The child is happy, pleased.'

It is clear from (32) that intransitive verbs in the Classes that govern Inversion in the evidential must undergo the rule, just as transitive verbs do. Intransitive inversion verbs must also undergo Inversion in all finite verbal categories.

In sentences of this sort, there appears to be no direct object to undergo the first component of Inversion according to proposals A and B above. Both proposals could be altered to accommodate the additional data. On hypothesis A, we could make the direct object optional. That is, if there is a direct object, it must undergo its part of the rule; but if there is no direct object, the second component of the rule could still apply. On hypothesis B, part (ii) can apply only if the nominal has been put *en chomage* (by the Motivated Chomage Law). A dummy could be introduced to undergo the first rule, putting the subject *en chomage* and thus implementing the application of part (ii).

Hypothesis C, on the other hand, can account for the intransitive cases with no additional devices. Because it treats Inversion as just the process of a subject becoming an indirect object, it is able to account for (31–33) in a natural and simple way. Unaccusative will never be involved in the derivation of sentences like these, since there is no direct object. (31–33), then, would have no derived subject.[14]

(31–33) establish that Inversion applies independently of Unaccusative in Georgian. In ch. 13 it is shown that Unaccusative also applies independently of Inversion. Unaccusative differs from Passivization in that, while the latter applies only at a level of derivation where there is a subject, the former applies only at a level of derivation where there is no subject (cf. Perlmutter 1978). This difference may be represented by the partial networks below.

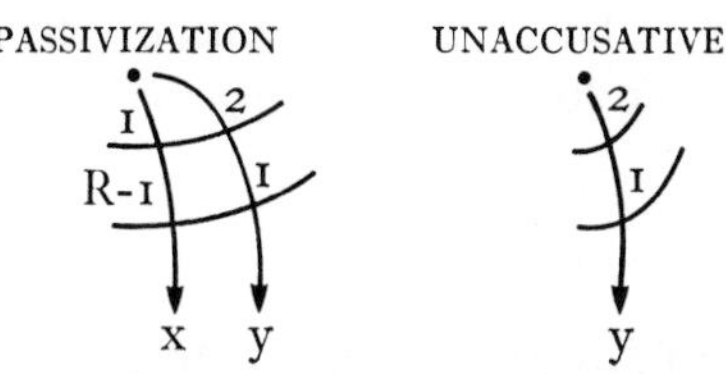

Unaccusative thus never creates a chomeur. The fact that Unaccusative applies only in the absence of a subject correctly prevents its applying before Inversion with a Class 1 or 3 verb in Series III or with a Class 4 verb.

In Georgian, Unaccusative applies obligatorily whenever its input conditions are met. It is this property that blocks the derivation of a sentence like (*34),

(34) **gelas* *uqvars* *ninos.*
Gela-DAT he-loves-her-I-4 Nino-DAT
('Gela loves Nino.')

where Inversion has correctly demoted *gela* to indirect object, but Unaccusative has failed to advance *nino*, leaving it as direct object, marked with the dative according to Pattern B.

Hypothesis C handles the Georgian data more elegantly than the other two proposals considered because it allows for the fact that Inversion applies independently of Unaccusatives, as established in (31–33), as well as the fact that Unaccusative applies independently of Inversion, as established in ch. 13. It is for this reason that I have adopted it in the analysis proposed here. It is proposed that the universal part of these rules is, informally stated,

(35) *Inversion*
A subject demotes to indirect object.

(36) *Unaccusative*
In the absence of a subject, a direct object advances to subject.

Inversion in Georgian is triggered by

(37) (a) Class 4 verbs
(b) Series III forms.

Trigger condition (b) must be further restricted:

(38) Class 1 and 3 verbs trigger Inversion, Class 2 does not.

In ch. 16 it is shown that trigger condition (38) follows from other facts and that it is therefore unnecessary to state it in a grammar of Georgian.

7 The interaction of Inversion with other rules of syntax

I have not yet described the interaction of Inversion with three rules – Passivization, Object Raising, and Inversion itself. Since there are two distinct triggers of Inversion, there are two distinct ways in which Passivization and Object Raising could each interact with Inversion; this means a total of five potential syntactic environments for interaction. In each of these five environments only one of the rules can apply in a given clause.

7.1 *Passivization and Series III*

A passive sentence may, of course, be in the evidential; but Inversion does not apply with passives in Series III. (39a) illustrates a passive in Series I, (39b) its counterpart in Series III.

(39) (a) *puli damalulia ujraši.*
money-NOM hidden-it-is-I-2 drawer-in
'The money is hidden in a drawer.'
(b) *puli damaluli qopila ujraši.*
hidden it-is-III-2
'The money is apparently hidden in a drawer.'

It is apparent from case marking, agreement, and other verbal morphology that Inversion has not applied in (39b). (40) illustrates direct forms of the verb in (39), 'hide'. (40b) shows that this form of the verb does trigger Inversion in Series III.

(40) (a) *merabma damala puli ujraši.*
Merab-ERG he-hid-it-II-1
'Merab hid money in a drawer.'
(b) *turme merabs daumalavs puli ujraši.*
apparently Merab-DAT he-hid-it-III-1
'Apparently Merab hid money in a drawer.'

These sentences establish the failure of Inversion to apply to the output of Passivization.[15] Although (39a) has a subject, *puli* 'money', this nominal does not undergo Inversion in Series III.

7.2 *Passivization and Class* 4
Inversion does not apply in clauses containing Class 4 verbs if they have undergone Passivization. (41) illustrates the passive associated with an Inversion verb.

(41) *direkṭori šeʒulebulia.*
director-NOM hated-he-is-I-2
'The director is hated.'

Case marking, agreement, and other verbal morphology show that Inversion does not apply to the derived subject, *direkṭori*. (42) illustrates the non-passive form of the verb in (41), showing that it is a Class 4 verb and an Inversion trigger.

(42) *vanos sʒuls direkṭori.*
Vano-DAT he-hates-him-I-4
'Vano hates the director.'

The examples establish the inability of Inversion, triggered by a Class 4 form, and Passivization to apply in a single clause.

7.3 *Object Raising and Series III*
When an object-raised sentence is in the evidential, Inversion does not apply. (43b) illustrates the Series III counterpart of (43a).

(43) (a) *ḳargi magalitebi ʒnelia mosaʒebnad.*
good examples-NOM hard-it-is-I-2 to-find
'Good examples are hard to find.'
(b) *ḳargi magalitebi ʒneli qopila mosaʒebnad.*
hard it-is-III-2
'Apparently good examples are hard to find.'

Case marking, agreement, and other verbal morphology show that Inversion has not applied in (43b). (44) shows that the verb of (43) triggers Inversion in Series III, if Object Raising has not applied.

(44) *turme rezos mouʒebnia satvale.*
Rezo-DAT he-found-it-III-1 glasses-NOM
'Apparently Rezo (has) found his glasses.'

7.4 *Object Raising and Class* 4

Inversion does not apply in clauses containing Class 4 verbs, if they have undergone Object Raising. (45) illustrates an object-raised sentence; (42) shows that other forms of this verb undergo Inversion.

(45) *direkṭori advilia vanostvis šesaʒuleblad.*
easy-he-is-I-2 Vano-for to-hate
'The director is easy for Vano to hate.'

(45) is a simple object-raised sentence of the kind discussed in ch. 4. If Inversion had applied to the output of Object Raising, *direkṭori* would be an indirect object. Case marking, agreement, and other verbal morphology show it instead to be the final subject. Thus, Inversion does not apply to the output of Object Raising.

7.5 *Class* 4 *and Series III*

Both Class 4 and Series III trigger Inversion. But a Series III form of a Class 4 verb undergoes Inversion once, not twice, as shown by (46); (42) gives the corresponding clause in Series I.

(46) *turme vanos sʒulebia direkṭori.*
Vano-DAT he-hates-him-III-4 director-NOM
'Apparently Vano hates the director.'

The input conditions for Inversion are met initially and again after Inversion and Unaccusative have applied. (47) represents a theoretically possible network for such a clause; (48) represents the clause as it actually occurs.

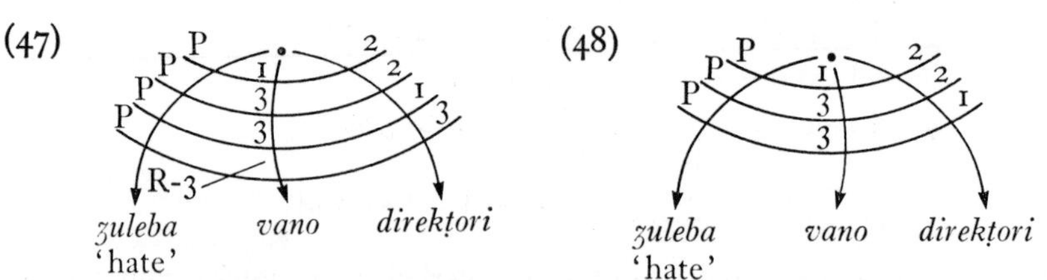

The non-occurrence of (*47) has not yet been accounted for.

7.6 *Summary*

We have seen that Inversion – triggered by a Series III or a Class 4 form – fails to apply to certain structures that meet the input conditions that have been specified thus far. In ch. 16, §3 it is shown that this is part of a more general, and perfectly regular, phenomenon.

8 Summary

This chapter has established that the initial grammatical relations of (5) and (23) are realized as (6) and (24), respectively, and that Inversion with inversion verbs and in Series III is essentially the same. In addition, evidence has been adduced to support the form of the rules of Inversion and Unaccusative proposed here, and the interaction of Inversion with other rules considered in this work has been described.

This analysis solves two major problems of Georgian syntax. It shows why Object Camouflage does not apply in Series III. It shows that Georgian does not have three distinct case marking patterns, but only two. At the same time, the proposed analysis raises new questions. If Pattern C reduces to a special instance of Pattern B, cannot Pattern A be similarly reduced? In ch. 9 it is shown that Pattern A does not reduce to B. Why do Class 1 and 3 verbs, but not Class 2 verbs, govern Inversion in Series III? This question is answered in ch. 16.

Appendix A: Additional arguments for inversion verbs

This appendix contains data to show that the arguments made in §3 above are applicable, not only to Inversion in the evidential, but also to Inversion triggered by inversion verbs. There are no new arguments given here, only new data.

A. PERSON AGREEMENT

In §3.1, I showed that Person Agreement is stated on final termhood. The analysis proposed for inversion predicates in §4 therefore makes the prediction that the nominative-nominal (= final subject) will trigger Subject Person Agreement. It likewise predicts that the dative-nominal (= final indirect object) will trigger Indirect Object Person Agreement.

As (1) shows, it is indeed the nominative-nominal that triggers Subject Person Agreement with inversion verbs. The bold-type subject marker in (1a) is from paradigm (8) above; the example is in the aorist (Series II). In (1b), the bold-type agreement marker is from the set of secondary markers of subject agreement (cf. n. 4); the example is in the present tense (Series I).

(1) (a) *me mašinve momeçone***t** *tkven.*[16]
I-DAT then-immediately I-liked-**you**(PL)-II-4 you(PL)-NOM
'I liked you immediately.'
(b) *gelas uqvar***var** *(me).*
Gela-DAT he-loves-**me**-I-4 I-NOM
'Gela loves me.'

The second prediction is also borne out. (2) shows that the dative-nominal triggers Indirect Object Person Agreement with inversion verbs. The indirect object markers in heavy type in (2) are from paradigm (10) above; the sentences are in the present and aorist tenses.

(2) (a) *(me) mo***m***çons pelamuši.*
I-DAT **I**-like-it-I-4 pelamushi (a food)-NOM
'I like pelamushi.'
(b) *(šen) mo***g***eçona pelamuši.*
you-DAT **you**-liked-it-II-4
'You liked the pelamushi.'

From the fact that Person Agreement is stated entirely on final termhood and the fact that the nominative-nominal triggers Subject Person Agreement in this construction and the dative-nominal Indirect Object Person Agreement, it follows that the former is the final subject and the latter the final indirect object.

B. OBJECT CAMOUFLAGE

Object Camouflage never applies with inversion predicates. Compare (*3a) and (*3b), where Object Camouflage has applied, with (2a) and (1b), respectively, where the rule has not applied.

(3) (a) **čems tavs mosçons pelamuši.*
my self-DAT he-likes-it-I-4 pelamushi-NOM
('I like pelamushi.')
(b) **gelas uqvars čemi tavi.*
Gela-DAT he-loves-him-I-4 my self-NOM
('Gela loves me.')

In (*3a) Object Camouflage has applied to the dative-nominal, in (*3b) to the nominative-nominal.

The fact that Object Camouflage never applies with inversion verbs is correctly predicted by the proposed analysis in the following way. As shown in ch. 3, Object Camouflage applies only to direct objects. Further, the rule applies to the output of rules that change grammatical relations. But after the application of Inversion and Unaccusative, there is no direct object for the rule to apply to. Thus, the ungrammaticality of (*3) is accounted for with no special devices.

C. *Tav*-REFLEXIVIZATION

In support of the analysis proposed in §4 above, I will show that *tav-* can be coreferential only to the initial subject. It has been shown that *tav-* can be triggered only by the initial subject of its clause. In (4a) *tav-* is triggered by the dative-nominal, *temur*, confirming that the latter is initial subject. In (*4b), *tav-* is triggered by the nominative-nominal (= final subject); the ungrammaticality of this sentence shows that the final subject is not the initial subject. (*4c) is identical to (*4b) except that the order of dependents has been changed, showing that the relative order of pronoun and antecedent is not responsible for the ungrammaticality of (*4b).

(4) (a) *temurs* *uqvars* *tavisi tavi.*
Temur-DAT he-loves-him-I-4 self's self-NOM
'Temur loves himself.'
(b) **tavis tavs* *uqvars temuri.*
self's self-DAT Temur-NOM
('Temur loves himself.')
(c) **temuri uqvars tavis tavs.*

Thus, the dative-nominal of inversion verbs behaves like the dative-nominal (= initial subject) of inversion sentences in the evidential and like the initial subject of other verbs, in that it alone triggers *Tav*-Reflexivization. I conclude that the dative-nominal is the initial subject, as claimed in §4 above.

D. SUMMARY

In this appendix I have considered in turn each of the relevant arguments given in §3, which were based on Inversion in the evidential. The arguments presented in §3.4 are not applicable to Inversion with Class 4 verbs, but a different argument based on suppletion is given in §4.1. The data presented here lend further support to the analysis proposed in §4 for inversion verbs. Only an analysis of this type can account for both the initial subject and final indirect object properties of the dative-nominal and for both the initial direct object and final subject properties of the nominative-nominal.

Appendix B: Transitive inversion verbs with no overt subject

There is a small group of inversion verbs (Class 4 verbs) which pattern like *mešinia* 'I fear' in (1).[17]

(1) (a) **mešinia* *šen* /*ʒaɣli* /*tvitmprinavi.*
I-fear-it-I-4 you-NOM dog-NOM airplane-NOM
('I am afraid of you/of the dog/of an airplane.')
(b) *mešinia šeni* /*ʒaɣlisa* /*tvitmprinavisa.*
you-GEN dog-GEN airplane-GEN
'I am afraid of you/of the dog/of an airplane.'

Under certain circumstances,[18] verbs of this Class require that their initial direct objects be marked with the genitive case, instead of the nominative, which is usual for inversion verbs.

Consider the following hypothesis for accounting for (1):

(2) Verbs of the *šešineba* 'fear' class mark their final subjects with the genitive case.

I will show below that the genitive-nominal does not have the properties of a final subject, and that (2) is therefore inadequate.

The first argument is, of course, the case itself. In Georgian, final terms are never marked with a case other than the nominative, ergative, or dative. This set of verbs would provide the only counter-example to that generalization.

Second, the genitive-nominal in (1b) fails to trigger Person Agreement. When the genitive-nominal is second person, the verb cannot be marked for a second person (final) subject, as the ungrammaticality of (*3) shows. In (*3) the verb bears a second person subject affix, but otherwise is identical to (1b).

(3) **mešinixar* *šeni.*
I-fear-you-I-4
('I am afraid of you.')

Nor does the genitive-nominal trigger Object Person Agreement. For these reasons, I reject the analysis (2) for this sub-class of verbs.

A second possibility for accounting for sentences like (1) involves making the genitive-nominal the complement of a head noun, which then gets deleted or dropped. This would explain why these nominals are in the genitive, and not some other case. The complement of verbs like 'hear', 'fear', etc. have special case marking in many languages. This hypothesis fails to explain the fact that in languages like German and Turkish the special case marking used for the complements of such verbs is not genitive.

A third proposal involves the insertion of a dummy, putting the initial direct object *en chomage*. This insertion might apply before or after Unaccusative, the dummy being inserted as direct object or subject, respectively. Other analyses fail to explain why the complement of this sub-class of verbs is marked with the genitive and not some other case. But on the dummy-insertion analysis, their marking is predicted from a more general process. In ch. 11 I will show that all direct object chomeurs are marked with the genitive case. I conclude that the most reasonable way of accounting for sentences like (1) is by a dummy insertion rule. It is to be hoped that investigations of other languages will shed more light on the nature of such rules.

9 *Why Pattern A is not reducible to Pattern B*

It was shown in ch. 8 that the case marking chart represented here as (1) is unduly complicated and can be simplified to (1′).

(1)		Series I	II	III
	Class 1, 3	B	A	C
	2	B	B	B
	4	C	C	C
(1′)	Class 1, 3	B	A	B
	2, 4	B	B	B

(1) refers to the patterns as stated below in (2), while (1′) refers to the restatement in (2′).

(2)		*Subject*	*Direct Object*	*Indirect Object*
	Pattern A	ERGATIVE	NOMINATIVE	DATIVE
	B	NOMINATIVE	DATIVE	DATIVE
	C	DATIVE	NOMINATIVE	*tvis*-nominal

(2′)		*Final Subject*	*Final Direct Object*	*Final Indirect Object*
	Pattern A	ERGATIVE	NOMINATIVE	DATIVE
	B	NOMINATIVE	DATIVE	DATIVE

The simplification in (2′) is due to the fact that (2) was based on initial grammatical relations, which is inappropriate, since case marking in Series III is stated on final grammatical relations. Once this is realized, and the rule of Inversion is incorporated in the grammar, C is reduced to a special instance of B, and need not be included in the case marking rules at all, as shown in ch. 8, §4.2.

It seems natural, then, to ask, 'Is not Pattern A of (2′) reducible in a similar way to a special instance of Pattern B?' The answer, unfortunately for the simplicity of our grammar, must be 'no'. The reasons for this are given below.

1 An analysis of A as a special instance of B

The most natural way of reducing Pattern A to Pattern B would be to consider that the nominative-nominal in Pattern A is the final subject. That would require that verbs of Class 1 and 3 undergo a rule that advances direct objects to subjecthood, thus putting the initial subject *en chomage*, and giving it special chomeur marking with the so-called ergative case.

(3) Direct objects advance to subjecthood.
Subject chomeurs are marked with the ergative case.

This is not an unreasonable analysis.[1] It would require verbs of Class 1 and 3 to undergo an obligatory change of grammatical relations triggered by Series II tenses, just as they undergo the change of grammatical relations called Inversion, which is triggered by Series III tenses. The change from Series I forms to Series II is primarily a change of tense and aspect, while that from Series I or II to Series III is primarily a change of mood.

According to this analysis, sentence (4b), which is in Series II, differs from (4a), which is in Series I, in that the former has undergone rule (3), and the final subject is *simindi* 'corn'.

(4) (a) *glexi* *tesavs* *siminds.*
farmer-NOM he-sows-it-I-1 corn-DAT
'The farmer is sowing corn.'
(b) *glexma* *datesa* *simindi.*
farmer-ERG he-sowed-it-II-1 corn-NOM
'The farmer sowed corn.'

Although this seems to be a reasonable analysis, I will show below that it cannot be right.

2 Arguments against the proposed analysis

2.1 *Person Agreement*

It has been shown that final subjects trigger Subject Person Agreement. According to (3), the nominative-nominal, being final subject, should trigger this rule. It does not, as shown in (5).

(5) (a) *(me) ga**m**gzavnes skolaši.*
I-NOM they-sent-**me**-II-1 school-in
'They sent me to the school.'
(b) *amanati miiɣo.*
packet-NOM he-received-**it**-II-1 (zero marker)
'He received a package.'

In (5) the nominative-nominal triggers object markers, not subject markers.

Further, the ergative-nominal, being a chomeur on this analysis, should not be able to trigger Person Agreement at all; in ch. 1, §3, and subsequent chapters it was established that final non-terms never trigger Person Agreement in Georgian. Yet the ergative-nominal triggers Subject Person Agreement, as shown in examples (6).

(6) (a) *namcxvari gamo**v**acxve (me).*
pastry-NOM **I**-baked-it-II-1 I-ERG
'I baked pastry.'
(b) *istvene (šen)?*
you-whistled-II-3 you-ERG (zero marker)
'Did you whistle?'

Direct objects trigger Direct Object Person Agreement, which must be stated on final terms (ch. 1). According to the analysis proposed above in this chapter, no nominal should trigger this rule, there being no final direct object, in Series II with Class 1 or 3 verbs. However, the nominative-nominal triggers Direct Object Person Agreement, as shown in ch. 2 and example (5b) above.

The fact that the nominative-nominal triggers Direct Object Person Agreement and the ergative-nominal triggers Subject Person Agreement, when coupled with the fact established in chs. 3–8 that Person Agreement is stated simply on final termhood, indicates that these nominals could not possibly bear the grammatical relations assigned to them by rule (3).

2.2 *Object Camouflage*

In ch. 3 it was shown that a first or second person direct object is obligatorily replaced by a *tav*-nominal if there is an indirect object in the clause. It has been shown further that this rule is stated on the output of rules that change grammatical relations. The analysis proposed above would thus predict that Object Camouflage never applies with Class 1 or 3 verbs in Series II, since (3) obviates the direct object. (7) shows that Object Camouflage does apply.

(7) (a) **gelam šemadara šen.*
Gela-ERG he-compared-me-him-II-1 you-NOM
('Gela compared you to me.')
(b) *gelam šemadara šeni tavi.*
your self-NOM
'Gela compared you to me.'

The fact that the nominative-nominal is *tav-* shows that it must be the final direct object. (3) makes incorrect predictions in this respect.

2.3 *Unemphatic Pronoun Drop*

In ch. 1, §4, I showed that terms can undergo Unemphatic Pronoun Drop, while non-terms do not undergo this rule. In later chapters, especially 5, 7, and 8, it was shown that Unemphatic Pronoun Drop is stated on final termhood. In particular, it has been shown several times that retired terms do not undergo this rule.

According to the analysis proposed in §1, the ergative-nominal is a subject chomeur; it therefore should not undergo Unemphatic Pronoun Drop. But in ch. 2, §2.5 it was established that the ergative-nominals in clauses containing Class 1 and 3 verbs in Series II do undergo this rule. Thus, (3) makes incorrect predictions with respect to the rule of Unemphatic Pronoun Drop.

2.4 *Number Agreement*

In ch. 15 it is shown that only final terms can trigger Number Agreement in Georgian. While the trigger conditions on Number Agreement are much more complex than this, this single facet of the rule provides the basis for an additional argument against rule (3).

(8) shows that a plural ergative-nominal in Series II triggers Number Agreement. The plurality is marked with the fusional suffix *-es*.

(8) *durglebma gaaḳet***es** *ḳarada.*
carpenters-ERG **they**-made-it-II-1 bookcase-NOM
'The carpenters made a bookcase.'

According to (3), the ergative-nominal is an initial subject, but not a final term, and therefore not an eligible trigger for Number Agreement.

Thus, the fact that ergative-nominals trigger Number Agreement is not consistent with (3); it is consistent with their being final subjects.

3 Conclusion

We have seen that the ergative-nominal behaves like a subject with respect to all rules stated on final termhood; rules that change grammatical relations provide no evidence relevant to the proposal made in §1. It is important to note that the ergative-nominal does not lack any characteristics of subjects – initial or final. Only in case marking does it differ from the nominative-nominal of Series I; these two nominals behave in exactly the same way with respect to all other rules. This is in marked contrast to Series III, where it is the dative-nominal that behaves like the nominative-nominal of Series I in many respects.

If (3) were incorporated into the grammar in order to simplify the rules of case marking, all of the following rules would have to be complicated: Subject Person Agreement, Direct Object Person Agreement, Object Camouflage, Unemphatic Pronoun Drop, and Number Agreement. I conclude that (3) must be rejected and that a complex set of case marking rules must be incorporated into the grammar.

10 *Non-finite verb forms*

In Georgian there are at least three types of non-finite verb forms: the so-called 'masdar'[1] or nominalization, the infinitive, and the participle, including so-called 'future (passive) participles', 'past passive participles', and 'active participles' (cf. Chikobava 1950; Shanidze 1973; Tschenkéli 1958; Vogt 1971 for details). The foci of this chapter are the masdar and the infinitive, but most of the remarks made in §3–5 apply equally to the participles. Space prevents my considering them in detail.

Non-finite verb forms are not well understood from the point of view of linguistic theory or language universals. In particular, I know of no theory that accounts adequately for the initial and final grammatical relations borne by the nominals governed by non-finite verb forms. Nor is there a theory that can predict when a subordinate clause will be realized as a non-finite construction. Is a verb realized as a non-finite form because of the application of a relation-changing rule or of some other rule of syntax? Or is the occurrence of a non-finite form predictable from universal principles such as those that predict the occurrence of a chomeur (cf. Introduction, §2)? These questions will not be answered here. I hope, however, that the data presented will help to clarify the nature of non-finite verb forms and contribute to solving some of those problems.

In this chapter, I wish to make the following points about non-finite verb forms: (§1) So-called 'masdars' are derived nominals, not gerundives; (§2) forms characterized by the morphology *sa—elad* are synchronically infinitives, not participles; (§3) nominals governed by non-finite verb forms are marked in ways that are predictable on the basis of the initial grammatical relations they bear; (§4) although these nominals bear term relations initially, they are final non-terms. While I am not proposing a complete analysis of non-finite verb forms in Georgian, the facts presented here will have to be accounted for by any analysis that might be proposed in the future.

This chapter and the one that follows are intimately related. On the basis of material presented in §3 and elsewhere, I will propose in ch. 11 a general system of retired term marking. That, in turn, provides evidence for a clausal source for non-finite verb forms. This explains some of the facts presented in §4 and at the same time represents a new kind of argument for a clausal source for 'derived nominals', which masdars are shown to exemplify in §1.

1 Masdars: gerundives or 'derived nominals'?

Chomsky (1970) observes that gerundives and so-called derived nominals differ in at least three ways. I will show below that according to each of these criteria, masdars are derived nominals.

First, there are a number of constructions to which Masdar Formation cannot apply. Compare the sentences of (1) with the ungrammatical nominalizations in (2).

(1) (a) *ḳargi magalitebi* *ʒnelia* *mosaʒebnad.*
good examples-NOM hard-it-is-I-2 to-find
'Good examples are hard to find.'

(b) *mepem* *gaaçmendina* *sasaxle.*
king-ERG he-caused-clean-him-it-II-1 palace-NOM
'The king had the palace cleaned.'

(2) (a) **ḳargi magalitebis* *ʒneli qopna mosaʒebnad...*
examples-GEN hard being
('Good examples' being hard to find...')

(b) **sasaxlis* *gaçmendineba* *mepis mier...*
palace-GEN cause-cleaning king by
('The king's causing the palace to be cleaned...')

Second, the relationship between the masdar and the associated proposition is often idiosyncratic. Compare the verbs and nominalizations of (3) in form and meaning. The formant of the masdar is in heavy type in each.

(3) *dapaṭižebs* 'he will invite him' *dapaṭižeb***a** 'invitation'
daḳargavs 'he will lose it' *daḳargv***a** 'loss'
mospobs 'he will destroy it' *mospob***a** 'destruction'
stxovs 'he asks him for it' *txov***na** 'request'
unda 'he wants it' *nd***oma** 'desire'

icinis 'he laughs'	**si***c***ili** 'laughter'
ibrʒvis 'he fights'	*brʒ***ola** 'battle'
ṭquis 'he lies'	*ṭqu***ili** 'lie'
ḳaḳanebs 'it clucks'	*ḳaḳan***i** 'cluck'
saubrobs 'he converses'[2]	*saubar***i** 'conversation'
ċava 'he will go'	*ċa***s***v***la** 'going'

Though there are tendencies toward regular correspondences, the use of the affixes *-a*, *-oma*, *-ila*, *si—ila*, etc. is not completely predictable from other facts about the verb. For example, *ṭiris* 'he cries', *icinis* 'he laughs', and *kris* 'it blows' are verbs of the same morphological type. There is nothing to tell us that their masdars will be formed with the affixes *-ili*, *si—ili*, and *-ola*, respectively. Further, some roots undergo a change that is not predictable by regular phonological rule; for example, the root *cin* is reduced to *c* in *sicili* 'laughter'.

There is also variation in the meaning. Although in general masdars have the 'factive' and 'action' meanings, they have additional ones as well.[3] For example, *rċmena* means both 'the act/fact of believing' and 'belief'. *Ṭquili* means both 'lying' and 'lie'. *Dapaṭižeba* means 'invitation' in the abstract sense, but not in the sense of something that can be held in the hand; there is a distinct expression for that. *Šoba* means both 'birth' and 'Christmas'.

Third, masdars have the internal structure of a noun phrase. Masdars have the following noun-like properties:

(a) They decline.
rċmena 'belief-NOM', *rċmenis* 'belief-GEN',
rċmenas 'belief-DAT', *rċmenit* 'belief-INST', etc.

(b) They have number, when they are concrete and not mass-nouns.
mogoneba 'remembering, memory'
mogonebebi 'memories'[4]

(c) They may have quantifiers and adjectives.
erti txovna 'one request'
sašineli ṭquili 'terrible lie'

(d) They may be possessed.
givis ṭquili 'Givi's lie'

(e) They may co-occur with positionals (postpositions).
ṭquilis šesaxeb 'about lying/the lie'

(f) They may have relative clauses.
čxubi, romelic vnaxe 'the fight which I saw'

In addition, masdars occur in the full range of nominal functions:

(4) (a) *miqvars* *saubari.*
I-love-it-I-4 conversation-NOM
'I love conversation.' / 'I love to talk.'
(b) *vilaparaḳet* *kalakis* *mospobis* *šesaxeb.*
we-talked-II-3 city-GEN destruction about
'We talked about the destruction of the city.'

Thus, according to the criteria outlined in Chomsky (1970), Georgian masdars belong to the type of nominalization there called a 'derived nominal'.[5] (They are glossed with English *-ing* forms in order to standardize them.)

2 Infinitive or 'future participle in the adverbial case'?

Non-finite verb forms like *gasaḳeteblad* 'to make, do' are traditionally called 'future participles in the adverbial case'. In this section I will argue that, while that name may be descriptive of their origin diachronically, it does not accurately represent their use synchronically. I will argue that they are infinitives. This is important for two reasons. First, in Georgian we can predict that an infinitive will occur when the subject of the verb it represents is deleted by Equi. Second, by using terminology consistently, we can compare constructions across languages; the Georgian infinitive is comparable to infinitives in other languages.

True future participles are used as modifiers, as illustrated in (5). The participle is in the dative case in (5a) because it modifies the head noun *indaurs* 'turkey', which is the direct object of the verb in Series I, and therefore in the dative. In (5b) the verb is in Series II, and the direct object and its modifying participle are accordingly in the nominative.

(5) (a) *vqidulob* *dasaḳlav* *indaurs.*
I-buy-it-I-3 killing-DAT turkey-DAT
'I buy a turkey to kill./I buy a turkey for killing.'
(b) *viqide* *dasaḳlavi* *indauri.*[6]
I-bought-it-II-3 killing-NOM turkey-NOM
'I bought a turkey to kill./I bought a turkey for killing.'

The future participle in this use precedes its head noun and agrees with it in case. I will show below that the so-called 'future participle in the adverbial case' does not have these properties.

There is no doubt that the infinitive in Georgian bears the morphology of the future participle (*sa—el*) and that of the adverbial case (*-ad*). I suggest, however, that synchronically there is a circumfix *sa—elad*, which is probably derived diachronically from the conjoining of the other two; I shall argue that forms so constructed are infinitives, not participles.[7]

First, observe that the future participle in the adverbial case occurs in two of the same uses as the infinitive in English. In (6) it is the chomeur of the sentential subject in an object-raised sentence. In (7) it represents a purpose clause.

(6) *kargi magalitebi ʒnelia mosaʒebnad.*
good examples-NOM hard-it-is-I-2 to-find
'Good examples are hard to find.'

(7) *ċavedi ṭqeši datvis mosaḳlavad.*[8]
I-went-II-2 woods-in bear-GEN to-kill
'I went into the woods to kill a bear.'

As far as I am aware, these are the only uses of this form in Georgian.[9] It cannot be used in all situations where an infinitive would be used in English; for example (*8) is ungrammatical.

(8) **minda (misi) gasaḳeteblad.*[10]
I-want-it-I-4 it-GEN to-do
('I want to do it.')

Second, notice that the forms in (6–7) do not have the characteristics of the participle in (5):

a. In (5) the participle modifies a head noun; in (6–7) the infinitive does not.

b. In (5) the participle precedes its head noun; in (6–7) the infinitive is the head noun and in (7) is preceded by other words with which it forms a constituent.[11]

c. In (5) the participle shows case concord with its head noun; the case of the head noun itself is determined by its grammatical relation to the governing verb. In (6–7) the form of the infinitive is invariant.

Third, the uses of the infinitive in (6–7) are not covered by any of the regular uses of the adverbial case.[12] That is, it is not predictable on any independent grounds that the adverbial, rather than some other case, would be used in (6) or in (7). Therefore, if it is treated as a 'future participle in the adverbial case', the grammar must add distinct rules for these uses of that case.

Fourth, this verb form can never have a final subject, though it may govern other term nominals. That this form can have other initial terms is shown below in §4. (9) shows that it cannot have a final subject.

(9) (a) **gela* *ak* *movida* *saatis* *gasaḳeteblad čems mier.*
Gela-NOM here he-came-II-2 clock-GEN to-fix me by.
('Gela came here for me to fix the clock.')
(b) **gelam* *ak moiṭana* *saati* *čemi* /*cemtvis*
Gela-ERG he-brought-it-II-1 clock-NOM me-GEN/me-for
gasaḳeteblad.
to-fix
('Gela brought the watch here for me to fix (it).')

The grammaticality of (10) shows that the ungrammaticality of (9) is due to the fact that the initial subjects have not been deleted, or are not coreferential to the matrix subjects.

(10) (a) *gela ak movida saatis gasaḳeteblad.*
'Gela came here to fix the clock.'
(b) *gela ak moiṭana saati gasaḳeteblad.*
'Gela brought the clock to fix (it).'

An infinitive is often, though not exclusively, used in other languages when the subject of the verb it represents has been deleted or raised out of its clause, as in the English equivalents of (6–8).

I conclude that this verb form is synchronically a true infinitive, not a future participle in the adverbial case. I suggest that the infinitive occurs in Georgian if and only if the subject of the verb it represents has been deleted by Equi. Equi applies in Object Raising, as discussed in ch. 4, and in purpose clauses, as illustrated in (7) and in n. 8. In many of the situations where Equi applies in English, Unemphatic Pronoun Drop applies instead in Georgian, as in example (8) and (vi) of n. 10.

3 The marking of nominals governed by non-finite verb forms

In this section I will note the correspondences between the initial grammatical relation that a nominal bears to a finite verb and the marking it receives in a masdar or infinitive construction. Arguments to support the grammatical relations are given in §4.1.

3.1 *Direct object*

The nominal that corresponds to the initial direct object of a finite verb is, in construction with a masdar or infinitive, in the genitive case. This is so whether it is the only overt term, as in (11), is with an overt subject, as in (12), or is with both an overt subject and indirect object, as in (13).

(11) *datvis mokvla am tqeši akrʒalulia.*
bear-GEN killing-NOM this woods-in forbidden-it-is-I-2
'Killing bears in these woods is forbidden.'

(12) *monadiris mier datvis mokvla akrʒalulia.*
hunter by
'The killing of bears by hunters is forbidden.'

(13) *mamas unda qvavilebis micema mziastvis*
father-DAT he-wants-it-I-4 flowers-GEN giving-NOM Mzia-for
vanos mier.
Vano by
'Father wants Vano to give flowers to Mzia.'

While (13) is grammatical, such a sentence would rarely occur; a finite verb form would be more likely to be used.

Examples (7), (10a), and (i) of n. 8 illustrate an infinitive's direct object in the genitive case. A direct object cannot occur with the infinitive that is the chomeur of the sentential subject of an object-raised sentence, since the direct object is raised out of its clause (cf. ch. 4).

3.2 *Subject of an intransitive*

The nominal that corresponds to the subject of the finite form of an intransitive verb is, with a non-finite verb form, in the genitive case. In (14–15) the intransitive subject is the only nominal governed by the masdar; in (16) an indirect object is also present.

(14) *tamadis damtknareba supraze uzrdelobaa.*
tamada-GEN yawning-NOM table-on rudeness-it-is-I-2
'It is rude for the *tamada* to yawn at the table.'

(15) *cxenosnis ak šesvla akrʒalulia.*
horseman-GEN here entering-NOM forbidden-it-is-I-2
'It is forbidden for horsemen to enter here.'

(16) *čemtvis bavšvis salami sasixaruloa.*
me-for child-GEN greeting-NOM pleasant-it-is-I-2
'It is nice for the child to call me.'

As noted in §2, infinitives do not have overt subjects.

3.3 *Subject of a transitive*

The nominal that corresponds to the subject of a transitive finite verb is, with the masdar, marked with the postposition *mier* 'by', which governs the genitive case.[13] This has been illustrated in (12) and (13), where the subject co-occurs with a direct object. (17) shows that the same marking is used when the direct object is not overt.

(17) *monadiris mier mokvla akrʒalulia.*
hunter by killing-NOM forbidden-it-is-I-2
'It is forbidden for hunters to kill.'

The subject of a transitive verb (cf. ch. 13) can never be assigned the marking appropriate to the subject of an intransitive, the genitive case; for this reason (*18) is ungrammatical in the meaning of (17).

(18) **monadiris mokvla akrʒalulia.*
hunter-GEN
('It is forbidden for hunters to kill.')

(*18) is grammatical, however, in the meaning 'It is forbidden to kill hunters', where 'hunter' is the initial direct object.

The subject of an intransitive similarly cannot be marked with the postposition *mier*, which is appropriate only to the subject of a transitive. (*19) and (*20) are parallel to (14) and (15), with the difference that their subjects are marked with *mier*.

(19) **tamadis mier damtknareba supraze uzrdelobaa.*
('It is rude for the *tamada* to yawn at the table.')

(20) **cxenosnis mier ak šesvla akrʒalulia.*
('It is forbidden for horsemen to enter here.')

As observed above, infinitives do not co-occur with their initial subjects.

3.4 *Indirect objects*

Those nominals that correspond to the indirect objects of finite verbs are, in construction with non-finite verbs, marked with the postposition *-tvis*; they are not marked with a dative in Standard Modern Georgian (cf. Harris 1979 on the use of the dative in this function in Old Georgian). The use of *-tvis* is illustrated with masdars governing a variety of nominals in (13), (16), and (21). An initial indirect object with an infinitive is illustrated in (22), (34b), and (42a).

(21) *ristvis iqide es qvavilebi? minda deidistvis micema.*
I-want-it-I-4 aunt-for giving-NOM
'Why did you buy these flowers? I want to give them to Aunt.'

(22) *es qvavilebi viqide masp̣inʒlistvis misacemad.*
this flowers-NOM I-bought-it-II-3 host-for to-give
'I bought these flowers to give to the host.'

The indirect object can never be marked with just the genitive case. (*23), (*24), and (*25) correspond to (21), (22), and (16), respectively. In the ungrammatical examples, the genitive case alone marks the initial indirect object.

(23) *minda deidis micema.*
aunt-GEN
('I want to give them to Aunt.')

(24) *es qvavilebi viqide masp̣inʒlis misacemad.*
host-GEN
('I bought these flowers to give to the host.')

(25) *čemi salami sasiamovnoa.*
me-GEN
('The greeting to me was pleasant.')

(23) and (25) are possible if the genitive-nominal is interpreted, not as initial indirect object, but as initial direct object or intransitive subject; that is 'I want to give away Aunt. . .' and 'My greeting was pleasant.'

3.5 *Summary*

Nominals corresponding to initial direct objects and subjects of intransitives are marked with the genitive case when they occur in construction with masdars or infinitives. Similarly, initial transitive subjects are marked with the postposition *mier*, and initial indirect objects with the postposition -*tvis*. This marking is independent of what other nominals also occur in construction with the non-finite verb form.

4 The nature of the nominals governed by non-finite verb forms

The nominals governed by masdars and infinitives are shown to be related to the initial terms of corresponding finite verb forms (§4.1), but these nominals do not behave like final terms with respect to the rules that are tests for final termhood (§4.2). The nature of these constructions is not well understood from the point of view of language universals. An adequate analysis of the Georgian data cannot be made outside a theory of the universal nature of such constructions – a theory that does not exist at this time.

4.1 *Facts concerning initial grammatical relations*

4.1.1 *Suppletion for number of direct object.* The verb 'throw' is suppletive for the number of its direct object, such that forms of *gadagdeba* (root *gd*) occur with singular objects, while forms of *gadaqra* (root *qr*) occur only with plurals (cf. Introduction, §4.3.2).

The suppletion that is governed by the number of the direct object is also governed by the genitive-nominal associated with the masdars and infinitives of this verb. This is established for the masdar in (26) and (27). In the (a) examples, the genitive-nominal is singular, in the (b) examples plural. The sentence containing the masdar form *gadagdeba* is grammatical only in example (a), that containing the masdar *gadaqra* is good only in (b).

(26) (a) *kvis gadagdeba akrʒalulia.*
stone-GEN throwing-NOM forbidden-it-is-I-2
'Throwing a stone is forbidden.'
(b) **kvebis gadagdeba akrʒalulia.*
stones-GEN
('Throwing stones is forbidden.')

(27) (a) **kvis gadaqra akrʒalulia.*
throwing-NOM
('Throwing a stone is forbidden.')
(b) *kvebis gadaqra akrʒalulia.*
'Throwing stones is forbidden.'

The same suppletion is established for infinitives of this verb in (28).

In these examples, the preverb *ča-* 'down' has been substituted for *gada-*. As the example shows, the same suppletion holds.

(28) (a) **ak amovedi didi kvis časaqrelad.*
here I-came-up-II-2 big stone-GEN to-throw
('I came up here to throw a big stone.')
(b) *ak amovedi didi kvebis časaqrelad.*
stones-GEN
'I came up here to throw big stones.'

An additional example is given as (8) in ch. 4.

An analysis that relates the genitive-nominal to the initial direct object can account for the grammatical status of (26–28) with the same rule needed independently to account for sentences with 'throw' that have undergone no change of grammatical relations.

4.1.2 *Suppletion for number of subject.* As noted in the Introduction, the verb *dajdoma/dasxdoma* 'sit' is suppletive for the number of its subject, such that the first occurs with singular subjects, the second with plurals. This same constraint holds with respect to the genitive-nominal of these masdars. (Since these are intransitive verbs, their subject is in the genitive, cf. §3.2.)

(29) (a) *im bavšvis ik dajdoma šeuʒlebelia.*
that child-GEN there sitting-NOM impossible-it-is-I-2
'It is impossible for that child to sit there.'
(b) **im bavšvebis ik dajdoma šeuʒlebelia.*
children-GEN
('It is impossible for those children to sit there.')

(30) (a) **im bavšvis ik dasxdoma šeuʒlebelia.*
sitting-NOM
('It is impossible for that child to sit there.')
(b) *im bavšvebis ik dasxdoma šeuʒlebelia.*
'It is impossible for those children to sit there.'

In the (a) sentences the genitive-nominal is singular, in the (b) sentences plural. Only when *dajdoma* occurs with a singular and *dasxdoma* with a plural, are the sentences grammatical. This can be accounted for by the same rule that accounts for the grammaticality of sentences with the finite verb 'sit', if *bavš(eb)i* 'child(ren)' is the initial subject of *dajdoma/dasxdoma*.

4.1.3 *Idioms.* Idioms retain their idiomatic meanings in non-finite forms. The collocation *xels ušlis* (literally 'he disturbs his hand') has the idiomatic reading 'he distracts/bothers him'. The idiom retains its meaning in the masdar construction in (31) and in the infinitive of purpose in (32).

(31) *xelis šešla magižebs.*
hand-GEN disturbing-NOM it-crazes-me-I-1
'Distraction drives me crazy.'

(32) *aval gelastan xelis šesašlelad.*
I-will-go-I-2 Gela-to hand-GEN to-disturb
'I will go up to Gela's to bother him.'

The meanings of (31–32) can be accounted for simply with the rule independently needed to account for the finite forms of this idiom, if *xeli* 'hand' is analyzed as the initial direct object of the masdar and of the infinitive.

4.1.4 *Restrictions on the inventory of initial terms.* The root *ç̣er* 'write' occurs with a variety of preverbs. When it occurs with the preverb *da-*, the verb takes an initial subject and initial direct object; it may have an indirect object only derivatively. When it occurs with the preverb *mi-* or *mo-*, on the other hand, the verb takes an initial subject, direct object, and indirect object. This has been discussed in previous chapters, especially ch. 1, §4, and ch. 6, §4.

The same distribution of nominals holds with respect to the masdars and infinitives corresponding to the finite verb forms, except that, as noted above, the subject does not appear overtly with an infinitive. This distribution of initial terms is exemplified for infinitives in (33–34).

(33) (a) *avedi čems ḳabineṭši ç̣erilis dasaç̣erad.*
I-went-up-II-2 my study-in letter-GEN to-write
'I went up to my study to write a letter.'

(b) *avedi čems ḳabineṭši ç̣erilis dasaç̣erad uprosisṭvis*
boss-for
'I went up to my study to write a letter for the boss.'

(34) (a) *avedi čems ḳabineṭši ç̣erilis misaç̣erad.*
to-write
'I went up to my study to write a letter to him.'

(b) *avedi čems ḳabineṭši çerilis misaçerad uprosistvis.*
'I went up to my study to write a letter to the boss.'

The different inventories of initial relations of these two different verbs result in two differences between (33) and (34). First, (34a) is interpreted as having an initial indirect object that has been dropped; this is reflected in the different translations of (33a) and (34a). Second, the *tvis*-nominal of (33b) is interpreted as a benefactive (*tvis* means 'for'), since this verb form cannot take an initial indirect object. But the identical *tvis*-nominal in (34b) is interpreted as an indirect object, since this form of the verb requires an initial indirect object, which has the meaning 'to'.

(35–36) show that the same distribution holds for masdars and the nominals they govern.

(35) (a) *çerilis dačera...*
letter-GEN writing-NOM
'The writing of the letter...'
(b) *çerilis dačera uprosistvis...*
boss-for
'The writing of the letter for the boss...'

(36) (a) *çerilis mičera...*
writing-NOM
'The writing of the letter to him...'
(b) *çerilis mičera uprosistvis...*
'The writing of the letter to the boss...'

The facts established in (33–36) can be accounted for with no additional statement in the grammar, if each nominal governed by the non-finite verb forms bears to the verb the same initial grammatical relation it would bear to the corresponding finite verb form.

4.1.5 *Selection restrictions.* The verb *çevs* 'he is lying' requires that its subject be animate, as shown in (37).

(37) (a) *gela çevs ṭaxṭze.*
Gela-NOM he-lies-I-2 couch-on
'Gela is lying on the couch.'
(b) **çigni çevs ṭaxṭze.*
book-NOM
('The book is lying on the couch.')

The same constraint governs the genitive-nominal of the corresponding masdar, *ḉola*, as shown in (38).

(38) (a) *gelas* *ḉola* *ṭaxṭze...*
Gela-GEN lying-NOM
'Gela's lying on the couch...'
(b) **ḉignis* *ḉola ṭaxṭze...*
book-GEN
('The book's lying on the couch...')

This can be accounted for with the same statement independently needed to account for (37), if *ḉigni* 'book' and *gela* are the initial subjects of the masdars in (38), as in (37).

4.2 *Facts concerning derived grammatical relations*

In this section I will show that the nominals governed by non-finite verb forms are final non-terms.

4.2.1 *Case Marking.* The nominals governed by masdars and infinitives are not marked like terms in Modern Georgian. The marking they are assigned has been given in detail in §3 and may be compared with that listed in (2′) of the preceding chapter.

4.2.2 *Person Agreement.* It has been shown that Person Agreement is stated on final relations. The nominals governed by non-finite verb forms differ from those governed by finite verb forms, in that the former cannot trigger Person Agreement. This is shown for the subject of masdars in (39) and for the direct object of infinitives in (40), where the nominal in question varies for person, but the verb form does not change.

(39) (a) *gadaḉera* *čems mier...*
copying-NOM me by
'My copying over...'
(b) *gadaḉera* *šens mier...*
you
'Your copying over...'
(c) *gadaḉera imis mier...*
him
'His copying over...'

(40) (a) *čemi megobari movida čems sanaxavad.*
my friend-NOM he-came-II-2 me-GEN to-see
'My friend came to see me.'
(b) *čemi megobari movida šens sanaxavad.*
you-GEN
'My friend came to see you.'
(c) *čemi megobari movida gelas sanaxavad.*
Gela-GEN
'My friend came to see Gela.'

It can be seen in (39) and (40) that there is no variation in the form of the non-finite verbs for person of subject or object.

4.2.3 *Object Camouflage.* Direct objects that are first or second person are camouflaged if there is an indirect object in their clause (ch. 3); this rule applies to the output of rules that change grammatical relations.

Object Camouflage does not apply to nominals governed by non-finite verb forms, as shown for masdars in (41) and for infinitives in (42). In the (a) sentences the rule has not applied, in the (*b) sentences it has.

(41) (a) *šeni čabareba masçavleblistvis...*
you-GEN rendering-NOM teacher-for
'Turning you over to the teacher...'
(b) **šeni tavis čabareba masçavleblistvis...*
self-GEN
('Turning you over to the teacher...')

(42) (a) *gela movida šens časabareblad*
Gela-NOM he-came-II-2 you-GEN to-render
masçavleblistvis.[14]
teacher-for
'Gela came to turn you over to the teacher.'
(b) **gela movida šeni tavis časabareblad masçavleblistvis.*
you-GEN self-GEN
('Gela came to turn you over to the teacher.')

These sentences show that the genitive-nominal and *tvis*-nominal do not behave like final direct and indirect objects, respectively, in relation to the rule of Object Camouflage.

4.2.4 *Question Formation.* As shown in §4.2.4 of the Introduction, nominals governed by an embedded finite verb cannot be questioned, when Question Formation is governed by the matrix verb. But the dependents of non-finite verb forms can be questioned, as shown in the examples below.

(43) *risi moḳvla aris aḳrʒaluli?*
what-GEN killing-NOM it-is-I-2 forbidden
'What is it forbidden to kill?'

(44) *visi šesvla aris aḳrʒaluli?*
who-GEN entering-NOM
'For whom is it forbidden to enter?'

(45) *risi gadasatargmnad movida gela?*
what-GEN to-translate he-came-II-2 Gela-NOM
'What did Gela come to translate?'

(46) *risi mosaḳlavad c̣axvedi ṭqeši.*
to-kill you-went-II-2 woods-in
'What did you go into the woods to kill?'

Additional examples involving infinitives can be found in ch. 4, §4.2.

These sentences illustrate a second difference between final terms and the nominals governed by non-finite verb forms. When a nominal governed by a finite form is questioned, the question-word immediately precedes the verb (cf. Introduction, §4.2). But when a nominal governed by a masdar or infinitive is questioned, as in (43–46), the Q-word precedes the non-finite verb form, which in turn precedes the finite verb form. Other orders are not possible, as (*47) and (*48) show. In the (a) sentences, the Q-word holds the place that would normally be held by the Q-word governed by a finite verb; in the (b) sentences, the non-finite form fails to fall immediately before the finite verb.

(47) (a) **risi aris moḳvla aḳrʒaluli?*
risi aris aḳrʒaluli moḳvla?
(b) **risi moḳvla aḳrʒalulia?*
**aḳrʒalulia risi moḳvla?*

(48) (a) **risi movida gadasatargmnad gela?*
**risi movida gela gadasatargmnad?*
(b) **risi gadasatargmnad gela movida?*

In (*47b) *Aris*-Cliticization has applied. Another grammatical order for (45) is (49).

(49) *gela risi gadasatargmnad movida?*

Thus, nominals governed by non-finite verb forms differ from final terms in two ways with respect to Question Formation.

4.3 *Conclusion*

The evidence amassed above leads me to conclude that (i) a $term_i$ of a finite verb form corresponds to an initial $term_i$ of a masdar and infinitive, but (ii) the initial $term_i$ of a masdar or infinitive differs superficially from the $term_i$ of the corresponding finite verb. The facts presented here can be handled by an initial clausal source to which syntactic rules apply or by a lexical analysis with redundancy rules. In ch. 11 I will argue for a clausal source.

11 *Retired Term Marking*

The theory of relational grammar advanced by Postal and Perlmutter (Perlmutter & Postal 1974, 1977, to appear c, and elsewhere) defines a set of retired terms. In preceding chapters we have seen six constructions where retired terms may occur. In this chapter I will propose that in Georgian there must be a set of general rules that mark retired terms on the basis of the last term relation they bear, without reference to the rule that retires them.

1 Motivating retired termhood

Relational grammar defines a class of retired terms. A retired term is a nominal which bears a term relation in some stratum and which does not bear any term relation in the final stratum. A retired subject, for example, is a nominal which bears the subject relation as its last term relation, and which is a final non-term.

Postal and Perlmutter suggest that there are two types of retired terms – chomeurs and emeritus terms (Perlmutter & Postal 1977, to appear c). The former are relatively well understood (cf. references cited in ch. 7, n. 7); their occurrence is entirely predicted by the Chomeur Law and the Motivated Chomage Law (cf. discussion in ch. 7, §3). A term becomes a chomeur if and only if another nominal assumes the grammatical relation borne by it. Emeritus terms are relatively poorly understood. In theory, their occurrence, too follows from universal principles; but there are problems concerning their occurrence in causatives (cf. ch. 5, §1 and references cited there), and the possibility of their occurrence elsewhere remains relatively unstudied.

In chs. 4 to 10, a class of retired terms has been identified in Georgian. They are recognized by the fact that (i) they behave like terms with respect to phenomena like suppletion and *Tav*-Reflexivization, which are stated on initial termhood, and (ii) they behave like non-terms with respect to rules like Person Agreement and Object Camouflage, which are stated on the output of rules that change grammatical relations. In Standard Modern Georgian, final terms and final non-terms are clearly distinguished by a number of phenomena considered in previous chapters.

However, while linguistic theory defines two types of retired terms, Georgian grammar does not distinguish between them in any way I have discovered. All retired terms behave the same with respect to rules stated on final grammatical relations. The marking they are assigned does not distinguish between chomeurs and emeritus terms, as shown below.

I suggest that only those retired terms are chomeurs, whose occurrence is predicted by the Chomeur Law and the Motivated Chomage Law. Which nominals are chomeurs, then, is completely determined by the analyses given in previous chapters. There are at least two chomeurs in Georgian. The *mier*-nominal in the passive is a subject chomeur; it is put *en chomage* by the advancement of the direct object to subjecthood (cf. ch. 7, §3). The *tvis*-nominal in the inversion construction is an indirect object chomeur; it is made a chomeur by the demotion of the subject to indirect-objecthood (cf. ch. 8, §2 and 6). In §4.2 I will argue that the genitive-nominal that occurs with certain inversion verbs represents a third chomeur, a direct object chomeur (cf. ch. 8, Appendix B).

Perlmutter and Postal analyze as an indirect object emeritus the initial indirect object that is, under Causative Clause Union, a final non-term (cf. ch. 5, §1). I suggest that those retired terms in Georgian that have not been identified as chomeurs are also emeritus terms. It is to be hoped that by studying the occurrence of these in Georgian and other languages linguists can discover the universal principles that govern their occurrence. In Georgian there are a number of retired terms that are not chomeurs in the sense defined above. The *tvis*-nominal in the organic causative is an indirect object emeritus. In the passive, the initial indirect object is a final non-term.

In Object Raising, the direct object of a sentential subject is raised to matrix subject; the embedded subject is deleted on identity with the *tvis*-nominal of the matrix clause. The entire sentential subject is put *en chomage* by the raising of the direct object; an indirect object dependent of that clause is a retired indirect object (cf. ch. 4). There is no absolute way in Georgian to determine what kind of retired term this represents.

Initial subjects of infinitives of purpose are deleted. As shown in the preceding chapter, all other nominals bearing initial term relations to verbs realized as infinitives of purpose or masdars are themselves realized as retired terms.

In the remainder of this chapter I shall not distinguish between chomeurs and emeritus terms, but shall refer to both as retired terms.

2 Correlations between grammatical relations and final marking

In this section I will review in turn the various retired grammatical relations and show that each is consistently marked, regardless of the construction in which it occurs and regardless of whether it is a chomeur or an emeritus term. I am claiming that the set of rules that marks retired terms is sensitive to the last term relation that a nominal holds and to whether it is a final term or non-term. In each instance, the discussion is limited to specified nominals; unspecified retired terms do not appear on the surface.

2.1 *Retired direct object*

A retired direct object is marked with the genitive case. We have seen at least two examples of this. (1) illustrates an initial direct object in a masdar, (2) in an infinitive of purpose.

(1) *datvis mok̦vla am ṭqeši ak̦rʒalulia.*
bear-GEN killing-NOM this woods-in forbidden-it-is-I-2
'It is forbidden to kill bears in these woods.'

(2) *çavedi ṭqeši datvis mosak̦lavad.*
I-went-II-2 to-kill
'I went into the woods to kill a bear.'

The genitive case is also used to mark the initial direct object in a subset of inversion verbs. (3) illustrates such a verb with the initial direct object *tkven* 'you(PL)'.

(3) *mesmis tkveni.*
I-understand-it-I-4 you-GEN
'I understand you.'

It is argued in ch. 8, Appendix B that these genitive-nominals are retired direct objects.

2.2 *Retired intransitive subject*

A retired intransitive subject is marked with the genitive case. I know of only one construction in Georgian that has retired intransitive subjects. (4) illustrates genitive case marking of intransitive initial subjects of masdars of verbs of Classes 2 (*ç̣asvla*) and 3 (*mušaoba*).

(4) (a) *ḳargia ḳacebis ç̣asvla.*
good-it-is-I-2 men-GEN going-NOM
'It is good that the men go.'
(b) *ḳargia ḳacebis mušaoba.*
working-NOM
'It is good that the men work.'

2.3 *Retired transitive subject*

A retired transitive subject is marked with the postposition *mier*, which governs the genitive case. This occurs in at least two constructions.

In passives the initial subject is realized as a *mier*-nominal. This is illustrated in (5), where *ʒaɣli* 'dog' is the retired subject.

(5) *bavšvi daḳbenilia ʒaɣlis mier.*
child-NOM bitten-he-is-I-2 dog by
'The child is bitten by a dog.'

With masdars, the initial transitive subject is also realized as a *mier*-nominal, as illustrated by (6).

(6) *monadiris mier nadiris moḳvla aḳrʒalulia.*
hunter by game-GEN killing-NOM forbidden-it-is-I-2
'It is forbidden for hunters to kill game.'

Thus, retired transitive subjects are marked generally with *mier*.[1]

2.4 *Retired indirect object*

A retired indirect object is marked with the postposition *tvis*, which governs the genitive case. There are at least seven situations in which this occurs.

In a clause in which Inversion applies, an initial indirect object is put *en chomage* by the demotion of the initial subject. This is illustrated in (7).

(7) *rezos turme učukebia samajuri šentvis.*
Rezo-DAT apparently he-gave-it-III-I bracelet-NOM you-for
'Rezo has apparently given you a bracelet.'

In Causative Clause Union, the initial indirect object of an embedded transitive verb becomes the retired indirect object of the causative verb and is marked with *tvis*, as in (8).

(8) *mamam mimacemina vardebi dedistvis.*
father-ERG he-caused-give-me-it-II-I roses-NOM mother-for
'Father had me give the roses to Mother.'

In the causative of a transitive, the initial embedded subject is the derived indirect object of the organic causative. In Series I and II, this is marked with the dative case, like other indirect objects. In Series III all causatives, being Class I verbs, undergo Inversion; the indirect object of the input to Inversion is put *en chomage* by the demotion of the initial matrix subject. Like the indirect object chomeur in (7), this one is marked with *tvis*. (9a) is the causative of a transitive in Series I; (9b) is the Series III counterpart of (9a).

(9) (a) *masçavlebeli atargmninebs gelas*
teacher-NOM he-causes-translate-him-it-I-I Gela-DAT
akakis lekss.
Akaki-GEN poem-DAT
'The teacher had Gela translate Akaki's poem.'

(b) *turme masçavlebels gelastvis gadautargmninebia*
apparently teacher-DAT Gela-for he-caused-translate-it-III-I
akakis leksi.
poem-NOM
'Apparently the teacher had Gela translate Akaki's poem.'

In both sentences, the embedded clause has the initial subject *gela* and the initial direct object *akakis leksi* 'Akaki's poem'; Causative Clause Union makes the former the derived indirect object. Under Inversion, the initial matrix subject becomes indirect object, putting *gela en chomage*; the causative direct object, *akakis leksi*, becomes subject. (9) differs from (7) in that the retired indirect object in (9) is an initial subject, not an initial indirect object, as in (7). Yet the two retired indirect objects are marked in the same way. This shows that the final marking of retired terms depends on the last held term grammatical relation.

Retired indirect objects also occur in passives; these too are marked with *tvis*, as illustrated in (10).

(10) *vašli micemulia masçavleblistvis.*
apple-NOM given-it-is-I-2 teacher-for
'An apple is given to the teacher.'

(11) illustrates the marking of the retired indirect object of a masdar with *tvis*.

(11) *vašlis micema masçavleblistvis...*
apple-GEN giving-NOM
'Giving an apple to the teacher...'

With infinitives of purpose, too, retired indirect objects are marked with *tvis*, as in (12).

(12) *vašli viqide masçavleblistvis misacemad.*
apple-NOM I-bought-it-II-3 teacher-for to-give
'I bought an apple to give to the teacher.'

Finally, in object-raised sentences, an initial indirect object of the embedded clause is marked with *tvis*. Here the initial indirect object is a retired dependent of the infinitive.

(13) *sačukari ʒnelia anzoristvis misacemad.*
gift-NOM hard-it-is-I-2 Anzor-for to-give
'Gifts are difficult to give to Anzor.'

Thus, *tvis* is used in a wide variety of constructions to mark retired indirect objects.

2.5 *Summary*

The examples above are drawn from chs. 4 to 10; additional examples are given in each of the relevant chapters. In each instance, evidence has already been given that the nominals marked with the genitive case, or with *mier*, or with *tvis* are term nominals that have been retired by the application of some rule.

In Modern Georgian retired terms are marked regularly according to the last term grammatical relation they bear. Georgian does not distinguish between chomeurs and emeritus terms by marking: it assigns retired term marking on the basis of the last term relation held, not on the basis of the rule that retires the nominal. One can imagine a number of other principles upon which final non-term marking might be assigned; in §3 some of these will be explored.

2.6 *Overview of the proposed grammar*

Rules of the type investigated in this work, rules that change grammatical relations, might be viewed as consisting of four parts: (i) the statement of the change of grammatical relation itself, (ii) the accompanying morphological changes in the verb form, (iii) the accompanying changes in nominal marking, (iv) conditions on the application of the rule. (i) is generalized by relational grammar, so that the grammar of a language need only register the fact that it has a particular rule and need not itself state this part of the rule. Part (iv) of the rule may also be partially universal, but languages also impose their own constraints. Parts (ii) and (iii) must be language particular, since languages do not generally share morphemes; (ii) and (iii) may, of course, have certain things in common across languages.

The grammar that I believe to be possible for Georgian would require that rules that change grammatical relations state only the following: (i′) a registration of the fact that the grammar of Georgian contains a particular rule, which is characterized in universal grammar, (ii) the accompanying morphological changes in verb forms, and (iv′) conditions on the application of the rule, where necessary. The retirement of terms is specified by general principles, as described in §1 of this chapter. Once the retirement of terms has been specified by universal principles, Georgian will mark them with a set of general marking rules used for all retired terms. These are stated below.

(14) (a) A retired direct object is marked with the genitive case.
(b) A retired intransitive subject is marked with the genitive case.
(c) A retired transitive subject is marked with the postposition *mier*.
(d) A retired indirect object is marked with the postposition *tvis*.[2]

The definition given for *retired term* in §1 is assumed in (14). Rules (14a) and (14b) can be simplified as (14ab).

(14ab) A retired absolutive is marked with the genitive case,

where *absolutive* is defined universally as a direct object or intransitive subject.

The generalizations made by (14ab, c, and d) can be made only with a theory which, like relational grammar, specifies a set of retired terms. Any other approach would require more than these three statements and would fail to show, for example, why some nominal is marked with *mier* rather than with some other case or postposition. This is discussed in detail in §3.

3 Alternative analyses

Below I will discuss some other principled bases for marking retired terms but in each instance I will show that this is not the best analysis of Georgian.

Without further data, we might assume that at least the following language types exist:

A. Retired terms are individually marked by the rule that retires them.
B. Retired terms are marked by a general set of rules on the basis of the last term relation borne by the nominal.
C. Retired terms are marked by a general set of rules on the basis of the initial term relation borne by the nominal.
D. Retired terms bear the same marking as the term relation they last bore.
E. Retired terms are marked semantically.

Most analyses – of Georgian, as well as of other languages – have assumed that principle A is the best to describe the data. Perhaps the most familiar example of this kind of analysis is the rule of Passivization usually stated for English; one feature of it is the marking of the initial subject with the preposition *by*. This approach is possible for Georgian, but it fails to draw the significant generalizations embodied in the rules (14). One could, for example, make *tvis*-assignment part of the rules of Inversion, Causative Clause Union, Masdar Formation, Passivization, Object Raising, and the rule that forms infinitives of purpose. But that analysis would miss the generalization that *all* retired indirect objects are marked with *tvis*, regardless of which rule retires them.

Data from a few of my Georgian informants suggest that C is a possible language type. Instead of (14c, d), they seem to apply rules (15c, d).

(15) (c) An initial transitive subject that is a final non-term is marked with the postposition *mier*.

(d) An initial indirect object that is a final non-term is marked with the postposition *tvis*.

The evidence for this is a single type of example (cf. 9b):

(16) *turme* *masçavlebels gadautargmninebia* *akakis*
apparently teacher-DAT he-caused-translate-it-III-1 Akaki-GEN
leksi *gelas mier.*[3]
poem-NOW Gela by
'Apparently the teacher had Gela translate Akaki's poem.'

The nominal in question, *gela*, is an initial subject, made indirect object by Causative Clause Union and retired by Inversion. I found the following judgements: *in Georgia* none of my informants accepted (16), only (9b). Among my three informants *in the United States*, who are older and emigrated from Georgia some time ago, two accepted (16) and rejected (9b); the third accepted only (9b). I assume that (16) represents a real dialect, and hence possible language type, but that (9b) represents the standard current in Georgia.

In theory there are other constructions that would also test the difference between (14c, d) and (15c, d): (i) In the passive of the causative of a transitive verb, the initial embedded subject would become the causative indirect object and be retired by Passivization. But Passivization applies to causatives only in a very limited way, and never to a causative with an indirect object (cf. ch. 7). (ii) In a double causative of a transitive verb, such as 'The boss made me make the secretary write a letter', the initial subject of the most deeply embedded verb would become indirect object, then be retired. Shanidze (1973) describes the occurrence of double causative verb forms, such as *açerinebinebs* 'he causes him to cause him to write it'. Some of my informants say that such forms exist, but none will use them in complete sentences with case-marked nominals. Further, they reject all reasonable translations of the English sentence above using the form *açerinebinebs*. Hence, the inverted form of a causative is the only construction I know of that will test the difference between the two hypotheses represented by (14) and (15).

There are facts that suggest that type D is relatively frequent (cf. Perlmutter & Postal 1974; Chung 1976a, b). In this system, a retired $term_i$ is marked with the same case or positional used to mark a final $term_i$. Such a system was used in Old Georgian for retired indirect objects (Harris 1979) and there are some petrified forms in Modern Georgian that still mark on this basis (cf. ch. 5, §4.2; ch. 6, §6). But Standard Modern Georgian does not use this marking system productively (but cf. ch. 7, §2.3).

The putative type E language would mark former terms, not on the basis of their termhood, but on the basis of semantics.[4] This would mean, for example, that agents are marked with *mier*. This can be shown to make the wrong predictions for Georgian. Agents are generally limited to animate or personified nominals (Fillmore 1968). But (17) illustrates the use of *mier* with nominals that are neither animate nor personified.

(17) (a) *Nazmnari saxelis mier saxelta martva udur*
deverbal noun by nouns-GEN governing-NOM Udi
enaši
language-in
'The governing of nouns by deverbal nouns in the Udi language.'
Title of Panchvidze (1960)

(b) . . .*p̣rocesi* **eb***iani mravlobitis mier zmnis šetanxmebisa.*
process-NOM plural by verb-GEN agreeing-GEN
'. . .the process of the *eb*-plural agreeing with the verb.'
Imnaishvili (1957: 664)

(c) . . .*inp̣inịtivis mier p̣irdap̣iri obiekṭis martvis*
infinitive by direct object-GEN governing-GEN
šemtxvevebi . . .
instances-NOM
'. . .instances of the governing of the direct object by the infinitive. . .'
Chxubianishvili (1972: 78)

There is evidence of another kind, too, that *mier* is not just an agent marker. The initial subject of 'affective' (inversion) verbs is an experiencer, not an agent. Yet this experiencer is marked with *mier* in masdars, as shown in (18).

(18) (a) *tkveni megobris daviçqeba čems mier didi*
your friend-GEN forgetting-NOM me by big
uzrdelobaa.
rudeness-it-is-I-2
'It was very rude of me to forget your friend.'

(b) *čemtvis gaugebaria tkven mier čemi*
me-for not-understandable-it-is-I-2 you by my
megobris šezuleba.
friend-GEN hating-NOM
'For me it is incomprehensible that you would hate my friend.'

I conclude from the evidence in (17) and (18) that *mier* does not mark only agents, but rather marks retired subjects. More generally, I conclude that the markers of retired terms are assigned, not on the basis of semantics, but on the basis of grammatical relations.[5]

In addition to the five possible language types discussed above, there are many possible mixed systems; for example, a language might choose to mark all chomeurs with one case or positional and mark all emeritus terms with another case or positional. But to use *any* mixed system to describe Standard Modern Georgian would be to miss the generalizations made in §2 above.

It has been shown here that type B above represents one possible language type. It is hoped that further research in other languages will reveal more about what types of marking exist and more about the nature of retired terms, especially about the poorly understood emeritus relations.

4 Implications of this analysis

4.1 *Object Raising*

In ch. 4 I proposed an analysis of Object Raising according to which the *tvis*-nominal of (19) originates in the matrix clause, not as the subject of the embedded clause. At that time I discussed evidence for this position from other languages, and evidence from Question Formation in Georgian, which shows that the *tvis*-nominal is not a constituent of the embedded clause.

(19) *ḳargi magalitebi ʒnelia gelastvis mosaʒebnad.*
good examples-NOM hard-it-is-I-2 Gela-for to-find
'Good examples are hard for Gela to find.'

The system of former term marking proposed above gives additional evidence for the analysis of Object Raising proposed in ch. 4. Retired transitive subjects are marked with *mier* (§2.3), so that if the *tvis*-

nominal in (19) were the retired subject of the embedded clause, it should be marked by *mier*. This therefore provides another argument that this nominal is a dependent of the matrix verb.[6]

4.2 *Transitive inversion verbs without final subjects*

In ch. 8, Appendix B I discussed possible analyses for sentences like (20), where the nominal that is apparently the initial direct object is not final subject, as expected for inversion verbs.

(20) *mešinia* *ʒaɣlisa.*
I-fear-it-I-4 dog-GEN
'I am afraid of the dog.'

I argued there for an analysis involving the insertion of a dummy. We can now see that Retired Term Marking provides additional evidence in favor of this analysis. If a dummy is inserted, the term it replaces becomes a chomeur (*ʒaɣli* 'dog' in (20)). There are two possibilities: (i) The dummy is inserted as direct object, making *ʒaɣli* a direct object chomeur; the dummy then undergoes Unaccusative, triggers Subject Person Agreement (third person singular), but does not show up on the surface. (ii) The initial direct object, *ʒaɣli*, undergoes Unaccusative; the dummy is inserted as subject, making *ʒaɣli* an intransitive subject chomeur. Since direct object chomeurs and intransitive subject chomeurs have the same marking in Modern Georgian (cf. §2.1 and 2.2), there is no way to decide between these two analyses. In either case, the genitive marking of this nominal constitutes an argument for a dummy analysis, since such an analysis would not need an additional rule to mark this nominal with the genitive case. Further, this analysis explains why the genitive is used in this construction in Georgian instead of some other case.

4.3 *Masdar Formation*

The generalizations concerning the marking of retired terms also provide a very strong argument in favor of a clausal source for masdars (derived nominals). If masdars are derived from full clauses, no further statement need be made concerning the marking of the dependents of masdars. But if masdars are lexically inserted as nominals, the grammar will have to state the generalizations concerning marking of retired terms for the retired terms created by Object Raising, Clause Union,

Version, Passive, and Inversion; it will have to state the same set of generalizations a second time as redundancy rules in the lexicon for masdars. Thus, a grammar that inserts masdars lexically as nominals will miss the generalization that the retired terms of masdars are marked like the retired terms of other verbs.

12 *Transitivity*

The verbs *çers* 'he is writing it' (Class 1) and *tamašobs* 'he is playing' (Class 3) are alike in that Series II counterparts of both govern ergative case subjects, and Series III counterparts of both govern Inversion. In this chapter I will discuss some syntactic differences between these two verbs. This short chapter has three purposes: (i) to show that some verbs have an initial direct object obligatorily, while others have an initial direct object optionally or not at all, (ii) to relate this difference in inventories of initial terms to the difference between Classes 1 and 3, and (iii) to discuss and define the notions 'transitive' and 'intransitive', which will be important in later chapters.

1 Analysis

I suggest that inventories of initial terms are lexically determined, and that a given verb may govern a particular term relation either obligatorily, optionally, or not at all. In Georgian, a 'verb' in this sense must be understood as a verb root with a specific preverb, if that root takes preverbs. In ch. 1 it was shown that the verb *daçera* 'write' takes an initial subject and direct object, while the verb *miçera* 'write' takes an initial indirect object, as well as an initial subject and direct object. Thus, for the purposes of stating initial term inventories, *daçera* and *miçera* must be considered different verbs, even though they share the root *çer*.[1]

I propose the following specific requirements for some verbs in Georgian:

(1)

VERB	GOVERNS AN INITIAL DIRECT OBJECT
daçera 'write'	obligatorily
miçera 'write'	obligatorily
datesva 'sow'	obligatorily

VERB	GOVERNS AN INITIAL DIRECT OBJECT
daxrčoba 'drown'	obligatorily
gašroba 'dry'	obligatorily
gamocxoba 'bake'	obligatorily
tamaši 'play'	optionally
laparaḳi 'talk'	optionally
ceḳva 'dance'	optionally
qiqini 'croak'	not at all
xitxiti 'giggle'	not at all

I am claiming, then, that some verbs have an obligatory initial direct object (e.g., *daçera*, *daxrčoba*), some verbs have an optional direct object (e.g., *tamaši*), and some do not permit an initial direct object (e.g., *qiqini*).[2]

2 Causative Clause Union

In causatives, the subject of an intransitive is realized as the direct object of the causative (ch. 5). The embedded subject of a transitive is realized as the indirect object of the causative. This provides us with a test for transitivity of the embedded verb.

With the verb *daçera* 'write' and others of its type, the initial subject corresponds to the indirect object of the corresponding organic causative, regardless of whether the initial direct object of *daçera* is overtly expressed. Example (4) gives the causatives corresponding to the simple sentences (3).

(3) (a) *vanom daçera.*
Vano-ERG he-wrote-it-II-1
'Vano wrote it.'
(b) *vanom daçera çerili.*
letter-NOM
'Vano wrote the letter.'

(4) (a) *vanos davaçerine.*
Vano-DAT I-caused-write-him-it-II-1
'I got Vano to write it.'
(b) *vanos davaçerine çerili.*
'I got Vano to write the letter.'

Case marking and Person Agreement show at a glance that *vano* is the final indirect object in the causatives, (4). (*5) shows that the causative would be ungrammatical if *vano* were instead the direct object; (*5) is identical to (4a), except that *vano* is case-marked as the direct object.[3]

(5) **vano* *davaçerine.*[4]
Vano-NOM
('I got Vano to write.')

With the verb *tamaši* 'play' and other verbs of its type, on the other hand, the derived termhood of the initial subject in an organic causative depends upon whether or not an initial direct object of *tamaši* is overtly expressed. The causatives in (7) correspond to the simple sentences in (6). In the (a) sentences, no initial direct object of *tamaši* is overtly expressed; in the (b) sentences, the initial direct object *sami parṭia* 'three rounds' is expressed.

(6) (a) *vanom* *itamaša.*
Vano-ERG he-played-II-3
'Vano played.'
(b) *vitamašet* *sami parṭia.*
we-played-II-3 three rounds-NOM
'We played three rounds.'

(7) (a) *vano* *vatamaše.*
Vano-NOM I-caused-play-him-II-1
'I got Vano to play.'
(b) *bebiam* (*čven*) *gvatamaša*
grandmother-ERG we-DAT she-caused-play-us-it-II-1
sami parṭia.
'Grandmother got us to play three rounds.'

Case marking and Person Agreement reveal that here *vano* is the final direct object in (7a), that 'us' is the final indirect object in (7b), and that *sami parṭia* is the direct object. (8) shows that it would be ungrammatical for *vano* to be instead the final indirect object of the causative in (7a).

(8) **vanos* *vatamaše.*[3]
Vano-DAT I-caused-play-him-II-1
('I got Vano to play.')

The simple sentences in (3) and (6) are apparently alike; the causatives in (4b) and (7b) are apparently alike. But the causatives in (4a) and (7a) are different. The initial subject of *daçera* 'write' is the final indirect object of the corresponding organic causative, regardless of whether an initial direct object of *daçera* is overtly expressed. The initial subject of *tamaši* 'play', on the other hand, is the final indirect object of the corresponding causative if an initial direct object of *tamaši* is overtly expressed – (7b); the initial subject is the final direct object of the causative if no initial direct object of *tamaši* is expressed – (7a).

This difference between *daçera* and *tamaši* can be handled most simply by (i) assigning to these verbs initial direct objects as specified in (1), and (ii) recognizing that Unemphatic Pronoun Drop does not apply to nominals which are optional in the inventory of initial terms.[5]

3 Retired Term Marking

Retired subjects of transitive verbs are marked with the postposition *mier*, while retired subjects of intransitive verbs are marked with the genitive case (ch. 11). The marking given to retired terms therefore provides an additional test for transitivity.

With the verbs *daçera* 'write' and *miγeba* 'receive', the retired subject is marked with *mier*, regardless of whether a direct object is overtly expressed. In the nominalizations of (9), the retired direct object is expressed; in (10) it is not. In both, *mier* is required.

(9) (a) *vanos mier çerilis daçera...*
Vano by letter-GEN writing
'Vano's writing (of) the letter...'

(b) *glexis mier simindis datesva...*
peasant by corn-GEN sowing
'The peasant's sowing (of) corn...'

(c) *rezos daxrčoba vanos mier...*
Rezo-GEN drowning Vano by
'Vano's drowning (of) Rezo...'

(d) *bičis mier čurčelis gašroba...*
boy by crockery-GEN drying
'The boy's drying (of) the crockery...'

(10) (a) *vanos mier daçera...*
'Vano's writing [something]...'

(b) *glexis mier datesva...*
'The peasant's sowing [something]...'

(c) *vanos mier daxrčoba...*
'Vano's drowning [someone]...'
(d) *bičis mier gašroba...*
'The boy's drying [something/someone]...'

With the verbs *tamaši* 'play' and *laparaki* 'speak', on the other hand, the marking of the retired subject depends upon the overt expression of a direct object. If the initial direct object is overtly expressed, as in (11), the retired subject is marked with *mier*. If the retired direct object is not expressed, as in (12), the retired subject is marked with the genitive case.

(11) (a) *givis mier pexburtis tamaši...*
Givi by soccer-GEN playing
'Givi's playing soccer...'
(b) *bavšvis mier sisulelis laparaki...*
child by nonsense-GEN speaking
'The child's talking nonsense...'

(12) (a) *givis tamaši...*
Givi-GEN
'Givi's playing...'
(b) *bavšvis laparaki inglisurad...*
child-GEN English-ADV
'The child's speaking English ...'

The marking noted above is not optional. (*13) shows that the retired subject of *daçera* may not be marked with the genitive instead of the postposition *mier*. (*13) differs from (10a) only in this respect.

(13) **vanos daçera...*
Vano-GEN
('Vano's writing...')

Similarly, (*14) shows that the retired subject of *tamaši* may not optionally be marked with *mier* when there is no expressed initial direct object.

(14) **givis mier tamaši...*
Givi by
('Givi's playing...')

These sentences show that *daçera*, but not *tamaši*, is treated as a transitive verb by the rules of Retired Term Marking, regardless of whether an initial direct object is overtly expressed. These facts can be handled in a simple way according to the proposal made in §2 above.

4 Conclusion and extension

In §2 and 3 I have argued that some verbs have initial direct objects obligatorily and some optionally. Verbs like *qiqini* 'croak' and *xitxiti* 'giggle' never occur with a direct object, and there is no reason to believe that they ever permit one.

It is important to observe that *daçers* 'he will write it' is typical of Class 1 verbs in that it takes an obligatory initial direct object. *Tamašobs* 'he plays' and *qiqinebs* 'he croaks' are typical of Class 3 in that they take an initial direct object optionally or not at all. It is not the case, however, that *all* Class 1 verb forms take an obligatory direct object. Nor is it the case that *all* Class 3 verb forms take a direct object optionally or not at all. Nevertheless, this characteristic is widespread enough for us to state the following generalization: *Most Class 1 verb forms take an obligatory initial direct object*; *most Class 3 verb forms take an initial direct object optionally or not at all.*

5 Transitive and intransitive

In this work, a transitive verb is understood to be one which has a subject and a direct object; an intransitive is one which does not satisfy those criteria. The notions 'subject' and 'direct object' in Georgian are clarified in chs. 1–8.

The transitivity of a verb form must be stated with respect to a particular level of derivation. Certain verb forms (or clauses) may be transitive initially but not finally. For example, *bavšvi daḳbenilia ʒaɣlis mier* 'the child is bitten by a dog', is a final intransitive (subject, but no direct object) derived by Passivization from an initial transitive (cf. ch. 7). Similarly, *givis uqvars nino* 'Givi (DAT) loves Nino (NOM)' is a final intransitive (subject, but no direct object) derived by Inversion and Unaccusative from an initially transitive structure (cf. ch. 8). Logically, a clause could be intransitive initially and transitive finally. However, I know of no rules in Georgian that create the grammatical relations that would be an example of such a possibility.

As shown in this chapter, the verb *daçera* always has an initial direct object. The verb *tamaši*, on the other hand, is transitive initially (and finally) in *tamašobs burts* 'he is playing ball', but intransitive (initially and finally) in *tamašobs* 'he is playing'.

Appendix: Real and apparent exceptions to transitivity

This appendix gives examples of verbs that are real or apparent exceptions to the generalization that Class 1 verbs are transitive and Class 3 intransitive. §1 deals with intransitive and apparently intransitive Class 1 verbs; §2 discusses transitive Class 3 verbs.

A. SPECIAL CLASS I VERBS

One sub-class of Class 1 verbs never takes a direct object; this group includes *šeiçqiṭa* 'he peeked', *daaboqina* 'he burped', *daaxvela* 'he coughed', and *gakusla* 'he hurried away'.

Another small group of verbs take a direct object optionally. When they have a direct object they are Class 1 verbs; when they lack a direct object, they are irregularly members of Class 2. For example, *šeagina* 'he cursed him' (Class 1), but *šeigina* 'he cursed' (Class 2); *ḳbens* 'he bites it' (Class 1), *iḳbineba* 'he bites' (Class 2).

A handful of verbs occur with a direct or indirect object, but not with both. For example, the case marking in the sentences below shows that for this verb, persons are indirect objects, while inanimates are direct objects.[6]

(1) (a) **vano gavige.*
Vano-NOM I-heard-him-II-1
(b) *vanos (*vano) gavuge.*
Vano-DAT I-heard-him-it-II-1
'I heard, understood Vano.'

(2) *vanos ambavi /*ambavs gavige.*
Vano-GEN news-NOM/news-DAT I-heard-it-II-1
'I heard, understood Vano's news.'

A verb with similar characteristics is *dareḳva* 'ring', although for this verb the indirect object is derived by Locative Version.[7] For both of these verbs, additional examples show that the inanimate behaves as direct object and the animate as indirect object with respect to Passivization (3–4), Inversion (5–6), Retired Term Marking (7–8) and Causative Clause Union (9).

(3) *zari dareḳilia.*
bell-NOM rung-it-is-I-2
'The bell was rung.'

(4) **deda* *darekilia.*
Mother-NOM
('Mother was rung (up).')

(5) *vanos* *turme* *daurekia* *zari.*
Vano-DAT apparently he-rang-it-III-1 bell-NOM
'Vano apparently rang the bell.'

(6) *vanos turme daurekia dedistvis* /**deda.*
mother-for mother-NOM
'Vano apparently rang (up) his mother.'

(7) *vanos mier zaris* *darekva*
Vano by bell-GEN ringing
'Vano's ringing the bell'

(8) *vanos mier dedistvis* /**dedis* *darekva*
mother-for mother-GEN
'Vano's ringing (up) his mother'

(9) *vanom* *damarekina* *dedastvis.*
Vano-ERG he-caused-ring-me-it-II-1 mother-for
'Vano made me ring (up) Mother.'

Examples (8) and (9) show in addition that even though no direct object occurs, the verb is treated as a transitive with respect to Retired Term Marking and Causative Clause Union. *Darekva* and *gageba* thus differ from *daçera* and other regular Class 1 verbs only in that the direct object is not expressed when there is an indirect object.

The Class 1 verb *šecodva* 'sin' is similar to *darekva* and *gageba* except that it never has an expressed direct object in Modern Georgian. In Old Georgian it had both a direct and an indirect object.

Another small group of Class 1 verbs takes an initial direct object which is idiosyncratically demoted to indirect object. The examples below show that the objects of *kocna* 'kiss' and *mibaʒva* 'imitate' are case marked as indirect objects.

(10) *dedam* *akoca* *švils.*
mother-ERG she-kissed-him-II-1 child-DAT
'The mother kissed her child.'

(11) *maimunma* *mibaʒa* *bavšvis* *mokmedebas.*
monkey-ERG he-imitated-it-II-1 child-GEN action-DAT
'The monkey imitated the child's action.'

The initial direct-objecthood of these objects is supported by their behavior with respect to Masdar Formation (12), Object Raising (13), and Inversion (14).

(12) *advilia šeni xelis mibaӡva.*
easy-it-is-I-2 your hand-GEN imitating-NOM
'Imitating your handwriting is easy.'

(13) *šeni xeli advilia misabaӡavad.*
your hand-NOM easy-it-is-I-2 to imitate
'Your handwriting is easy to imitate.'

(14) *bavšvs ar uḳocnia deida.*
child-DAT NEG he-kissed-her-III-1 aunt-NOM
'The child didn't kiss his aunt.'

It appears that speakers are somewhat confused about the grammatical relations borne by the objects of the verbs of this small sub-class. First, passives of verbs of this class are avoided, but not considered ungrammatical. The use of retired terms is also avoided. Second, there is more than usual variation in grammaticality judgements among speakers, and among various verbs of this group. This confusion on the part of speakers is not surprising once we recognize that direct object demotion applies to the objects of only a tiny group of verbs. Other verbs in this class are *sӡlia* 'he overcame it' and *miaɣc̣ia* 'he achieved, reached it'.

B. SPECIAL CLASS 3 VERBS

One subclass of Class 3 verbs takes an obligatory initial direct object; this group includes *ipovna* 'he found it', *išova* 'he got it', *iqida* 'he bought it', *itxova* 'he borrowed it', *isesxa* 'he borrowed it'. The initial direct objects of these verbs behave regularly with respect to case marking, agreement, Passivization (16), Inversion (17), Retired Term Marking (18), and all other rules.

(15) *ipove satvale?*
you-found-it-II-3 glasses-NOM
'Have you found your glasses?'

(16) *čemi satvale sanagve qutši nap̣ovni iqo.*
my glasses-NOM trash can-in found it-was-II-2
'My glasses were found in the trash can.'

(17) *turme gip̣ovnia satvale.*
apparently you-found-it-III-3 glasses-NOM
'Apparently you have found your glasses.'

(18) *satvalis p̣ovna*
glasses-GEN finding
'Finding the glasses'

This class of verbs behaves like Class 1 verbs syntactically, but like Class 3 verbs morphologically. As discussed in Holisky (1980a), these verbs are intrinsically perfective in aspect and are characterized by the suffix *-ulob* in Series I.

Another small group of Class 3 verbs also take an obligatory initial direct object. Examples are *upasuxa* 'he answered it to him' and *uqvira* 'he yelled it to him'. The examples below show that *upasuxa* behaves like *miçera*, and that its initial objects are regular with respect to case marking and agreement (19), Passivization (20), Retired Term Marking (21) and (22), and Inversion (23) and (24).

(19) *vupasuxe gaḳvetili masçavlebels.*
I-answered-him-it-II-3 lesson-NOM teacher-DAT
'I answered the lesson to the teacher.'

(20) *gaḳvetili napasuxebia.*
answered-it-is-I-2
'The lesson is answered.'

(21) *šens mier gaḳvetilis pasuxi*[8]
you by lesson-GEN answering
'Your answering the lesson'

(22) *masçavleblistvis pasuxi*
teacher-for
'Answering the teacher'

(23) *vanos sçorad upasuxia gaḳvetili /*gaḳvetilistvis.*
Vano-DAT correctly he-answered-it-III-3 lesson-NOM lesson-for
'Vano apparently answered the lesson correctly.'

(24) *vanos sçorad upasuxia masçavleblistvis /*masçavlebeli.*
teacher-for teacher-NOM
'Vano apparently answered the teacher correctly.'

This appendix contains facts relating to verbs which are exceptions or apparent exceptions to the generalizations made in this chapter. It is important to keep in mind, however, that the vast majority of Class 1 verbs behave like *daçera* and *miçera*, taking an obligatory initial direct object. The vast majority of Class 3 verbs behave either like *tamaši*, taking an optional initial direct object, or like *qiqini*, taking no direct object. Examples of regular verbs are listed in ch. 16, Appendix A.

13 *Synthetic passives*

In ch. 12 it was shown that some verbs, such as *daçera* 'write' and *daxrčoba* 'drown', have an obligatory initial direct object; even when the direct object is not overtly expressed, it must be posited as an initial relation because of the meaning and because of the syntax of organic causatives and the marking of retired terms. In this chapter it will be shown that a subset of such verbs, while they have an initial direct object obligatorily, take an initial subject optionally.

When verbs of this type lack an initial subject, their (obligatory) initial direct object becomes the subject. This is illustrated in (1b).

(1) (a) *vano* *axrčobs* *rezos.*
Vano-NOM he-drowns-him-I-1 Rezo-DAT
'Vano is drowning Rezo.'

(b) *rezo* *ixrčoba.*
Rezo-NOM he-drowns-I-2
'Rezo is drowning.'

Verb forms like that in (1b) have traditionally been called 'passives' by Georgianists. I have argued elsewhere (Harris, to appear b) that forms of this type must be sharply distinguished from true passives, those of the type discussed in ch. 7. However, because of the traditional name and the similarities between the two, I will refer to forms like that in (1b) as 'synthetic passives'; true passives, those discussed in ch. 7, will henceforth be referred to as 'analytic passives'.

The purposes of this chapter are to distinguish between the direct construction, the analytic passive, and the synthetic passive in Georgian and to relate them to those notions in general linguistics.

1 Identification of direct, analytic passive, and synthetic passive constructions

The notions 'direct construction', 'analytic passive' and 'synthetic passive' cannot be defined independently of the initial and final grammatical relations that characterize them and the rules that derive them. These are discussed in §3. In this section, the three constructions are illustrated and delimited.

1.1 *Examples*

All three constructions are illustrated in (2–6). Additional examples of direct forms, analytic passives, and synthetic passives are given in ch. 16, Appendix A as group A of Class 1, and groups D and E of Class 2, respectively. In each example below, the direct (a) and (b) sentences have undergone no rule that changes grammatical relations. In the (b) sentences, the subject and direct object are coreferential; in the (a) sentences they are not. The (c) sentences are synthetic passives, and the (d) sentences analytic passives.

(2) (a) *vano axrčobs rezos.*
Vano-NOM he-drowns-him-I-1 Rezo-DAT
'Vano is drowning Rezo.'
(b) *vano ixrčobs tavs.*
he-drowns-self-him-I-1 self-DAT
'Vano is drowning himself.'
(c) *rezo ixrčoba.*
Rezo-NOM he-drowns-I-2
'Rezo is drowning.'
(d) *rezo damxrčvalia vanos mier.*
drowned-he-is-I-2 Vano by
'Rezo is drowned by Vano./Rezo has been drowned by Vano.'

(3) (a) *vanom gamozarda ʒma.*
Vano-ERG he-raised-him-II-1 brother-NOM
'Vano brought up his brother.'
(b) *vanom gamozarda (tavisi) tavi*
self's self-NOM
'Vano brought himself up.'
(c) *vano gamoizarda.*
Vano-NOM he-raised-II-2
'Vano grew up.'
(d) *ʒma gamozrdilia vanos mier.*
brother-NOM raised-he-is-I-2 Vano by
'Vano's$_i$ brother was brought up by him$_i$.'

(4) (a) *paṭroni atbobs otaxs.*
landlord-NOM he-warms-it-I-1 room-DAT
'The landlord heats the room.'
(c) *otaxi tbeba.*
room-NOM it-warms-I-2
'The room is warming up.'
(d) *otaxi gamtbaria paṭronis mier*
heated-it-is-I-2 landlord by
'The room is heated by the landlord.'

(5) (a) *bičma č̣urč̣eli gaašro.*
boy-ERG crockery-NOM he-dried-it-II-1
'The boy dried the crockery.'
(c) *č̣urč̣eli gašra.*
it-dried-II-2
'The crockery dried.'
(d) *č̣urč̣eli gamšralia bičis mier.*
dried-it-is-I-2 boy by
'The crockery is dried/has been dried by the boy.'

(6) (a) *deda xač̣apurs acxobs.*
mother-NOM cheese-bread-DAT she-bakes-it-I-1
'Mother is baking cheese-bread.'
(c) *xač̣apuri cxveba.*
cheese-bread-NOM it-bakes-I-2
'The cheese-bread is baking.'
(d) *xač̣apuri gamomcxvaria dedis mier.*
baked-it-is-I-2 mother by
'The cheese-bread is baked/has been baked by mother.'

The English glosses have been selected to correspond precisely to the Georgian. (2a) would be interpreted as 'Vano is drowning someone else', even if the direct object were unspecified; this form of the verb is used only in this way. (2b) contains a verb form used only where the subject and object are coreferential. Here *Tav*-Reflexivization, Possessive Version, and Coreferential Version Object Deletion have applied.[1] (2b) means unambiguously that Vano is committing suicide by drowning; it cannot be used to describe an accidental drowning. (2c) is used when the action is accidental. (2d) states that Rezo has drowned through Vano's direct intervention. Parallel meanings are associated with the sentences in (3–6). (3b) is normally used only if Vano has no family.

1.2 *Morphological identification*

In Georgian, the forms to which the labels 'direct', 'analytic passive', and 'synthetic passive' apply can be identified – at least in part – by morphological criteria. Analytic passives are formed from a past passive participle (cf. Chikobava 1950; Shanidze 1973; Tschenkéli 1958; and Vogt 1971) and the auxiliary *qopna* 'be'; the form of these is discussed in somewhat more detail in ch. 7, in the appendix to this chapter, and in Harris (to appear b).

Synthetic passives are a subset of the forms characterized in the present tense by one of the circumfixes *i—ebi*, *e—ebi*, or *ø—ebi*: the use of these different circumfixes is discussed in Chikobava (1950), Shanidze (1973), Tschenkéli (1958), Vogt (1971), and in many other works. Here I consider as synthetic passives only those forms which are related to direct forms, in the sense that they are formed from the same abstract verb. Verb forms which share the morphological characteristics of the synthetic passive, but which are not related to direct forms in this sense are discussed in ch. 16. These include forms like *ikneba* 'he will be', *xdeba* 'he becomes', and *vardeba* 'he is falling'. Synthetic passives must also be separated from certain verb forms that share their morphology, but which do not share all of the syntactic–semantic characteristics which are discussed below.[2] Thus, the claims made in this chapter for synthetic passives are limited to the examples given here and the additional forms listed as group E of Class 2 in ch. 16, Appendix A.

'Direct construction' is used here only to contrast with 'analytic passive' and with 'synthetic passive', and it relates only to verbs which make such a distinction. Verbs like *qopna* 'be' and *mušaoba* 'work' do not participate in these distinctions. In this sense, 'direct' designates only constructions which are initially and finally transitive.[3]

1.3 *Identification in general linguistics*

The three constructions discussed here correspond to voice distinctions.[4] The direct construction corresponds to the active, and the analytic passive to the passive; the synthetic passive partially corresponds to the middle voice. The traditional names are eschewed here for several reasons. First, the labels 'middle' and 'passive' have been used in traditional Georgian linguistics in a way that does not correspond to their use in general linguistics (cf. ch. 16, §1 and Harris (to appear b)). To apply the same labels differently here would therefore be confusing to Georgianists. Second, the label 'active' has been used to refer to many different things in linguistics, and it is used for a different purpose in ch. 16. Third, the synthetic passive as defined here corresponds to only a sub-class of the middle voice of Indo-European (cf. Benveniste 1950; Gonda 1960; Kuryłowicz 1964; and many other works).[5]

'Direct form', 'analytic passive', and 'synthetic passive' are used here just for different forms of a single abstract verb (cf. ch. 12, n. 1). Verbs which have no voice distinctions cannot be said to belong to any one of these three types.

2 Some syntactic-semantic characteristics

In this section I will establish some syntactic and semantic distinctions between the direct, analytic passive, and synthetic passive constructions.

2.1 *Agent is final subject of direct form*

In a recent paper, Holisky shows that certain universal characteristics of agentive subjects are associated with specific syntactic properties in Georgian (Holisky 1978, section III). For example, adverbs expressing the notion 'intentionally, deliberately' occur with sentences where the semantic agent is final subject. Similarly, the command imperative may be used only in sentences where the semantic agent is the final subject. These properties serve to show one syntactic difference between the direct form on the one hand, and the analytic and synthetic passives on the other; they show at the same time that only in the direct form is the agent the final subject. (7) shows that direct forms, but not analytic passives or synthetic passives, co-occur with the adverb *ganzrax* 'intentionally'.[6] (8) shows that the direct construction, but not the analytic or synthetic passive, may be in the imperative.

(7) (a) *vanom ganzrax daaxrčo rezo.*
Vano-ERG intentionally he-drowned-him-II-1 Rezo-NOM
'Vano drowned Rezo on purpose.'

(b) *vanom ganzrax daixrčo tavi.*
he-drowned-self-him-II-1 self-NOM
'Vano drowned himself on purpose.'

(c) **rezo ganzrax daixrčo.*
he-drowned-II-2
('Rezo drowned on purpose.')

(d) ?**rezo ganzrax damxrčvali iqo.*
drowned-he-is-II-2
('Rezo was drowned on purpose.')

(8) (a) *vano! rezo daaxrčve!*
Vano-VOC Rezo-NOM you-drown-him-IMP-II-1
'Vano, drown Rezo!'
(b) *vano! tavi daixrčve!*
self-NOM you-drown-self-him-IMP-II-1
'Vano, drown yourself!'
(c) **rezo! ixrčve!*
Rezo-VOC you-drown-IMP-II-2
('Rezo, drown!')
(d) **rezo! damxrčvali iqavi!*
drowned you-be-IMP-II-2
('Rezo, be drowned!')

(7) and (8) show two of the ways that the direct construction differs syntactically from the analytic and synthetic passives. These differences are due to the single fact that only in the direct construction is the final subject an agent.

2.2 *Passive has an initial subject*

One syntactic property that distinguishes analytic from synthetic passives is that the former, but not the latter, co-occur freely with a *mier*-nominal. This difference can be seen by comparing (*9) with (2–6d).

(9) (a) **rezo daixrčo vanos mier*
Rezo-NOM he-drowned-II-2 Vano by
(*'Rezo drowned by Vano.')
(b) **ʒma gamoizarda vanos mier.*
brother-NOM he-raised-II-2 Vano by
(*'Vano's$_i$ brother grew up by him$_i$.')
(c) **otaxi tbeba patronis mier.*
room-NOM it-warms-I-2 landlord by
(*'The room is warming up by the landlord.')
(d) **čurčeli gašra bičis mier.*
crockery-NOM it-dried-II-2 boy by
(*'The crockery dried by the boy.')

(e) **xačapuri cxveba dedis mier.*
cheese-bread-NOM it-bakes-I-2 mother by
(*'The cheese-bread bakes by mother.')

The sentences of (2–6c) are identical to those of (*9), except that the former lack the *mier*-nominal. The grammaticality of (2–6c) shows that the ungrammaticality of (*9) is caused by the presence of the *mier*-nominal.

The sentences of (2–6d) could, of course, occur without an expressed *mier*-nominal; in that case the nominal is *unspecified* (cf. ch. 1, n. 14). The sentences cited above show that the analytic passive differs from the synthetic passive in that the former may have a *mier*-nominal.

In this section I have pointed out some of the ways in which these three constructions differ semantically and syntactically.

3 A proposal that accounts for the differences

Analyses of direct constructions and analytic passives have been discussed in ch. 7 and other previous chapters. I propose that synthetic passives are characterized by having an initial direct object and no initial subject. (Some may also take an initial indirect object.) The initial grammatical relations of all three types are compared in (10), where indirect objects are not considered.

(10) *Initial grammatical relations*

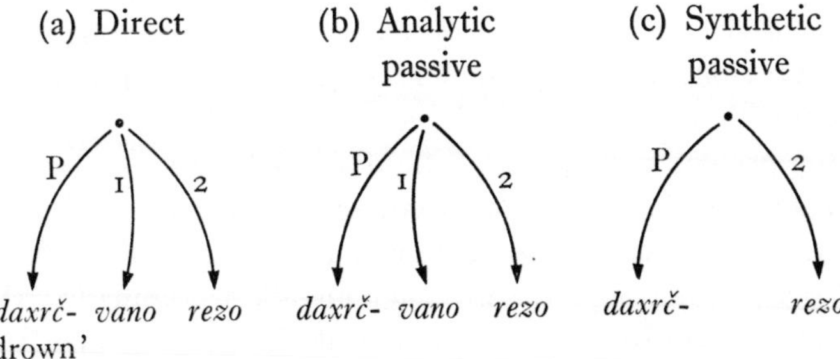

(Any of the nominals may, of course, be unspecified, in any of the forms.) I propose further that synthetic passives are characterized by a final subject. Initial and final levels are represented in (11).

(11) *Initial and final grammatical relations*

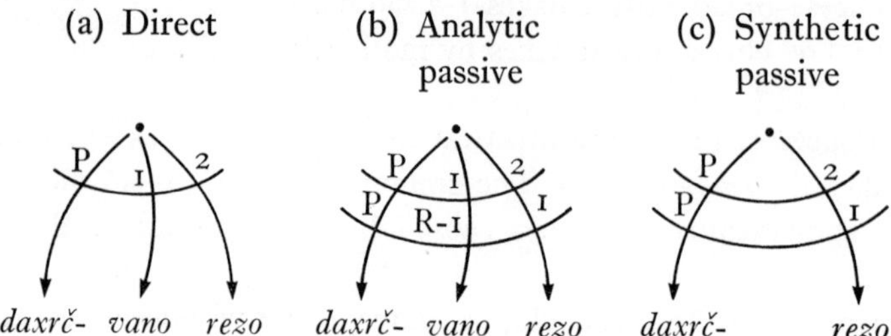

Analytic passives are derived by Passivization; in ch. 7 it was shown that this rule may apply optionally when there are a subject and a direct object at a single level of derivation. Synthetic passives do not have these characteristics. First, (10–11c) does not meet the input conditions for Passivization, since there is no initial subject. Second, the rule which makes the initial direct object of a synthetic passive its subject applies obligatorily wherever there exists a direct object and no subject. That is, there are no grammatical sentences in Georgian in which there is a final direct object and no final subject. The rule which derives synthetic passives is not Passivization, but Unaccusative, the rule which also applies in the derivation of transitive inversion verbs (cf. ch. 8, §6). Unaccusative, it will be remembered, is an obligatory rule which applies in the absence of a subject to promote a direct object to subjecthood. This proposed analysis of Georgian synthetic passives may be related to a general phenomenon in languages, referred to by Postal and Perlmutter as the 'Unaccusative Hypothesis' (cf. Perlmutter 1978 and Perlmutter & Postal (to appear a)).

This analysis accounts automatically for the characteristics observed in §2 above. Holisky's (1978) examples show that *ganzrax* 'intentionally' may occur with sentences in which the agent is the final subject. According to the present analysis, synthetic passives have no semantic agent (initial subject), while in analytic passives the agent is finally a subject chomeur.[7] This analysis thus accounts for the fact that (7a–b) are grammatical, while (*7c–d) are ungrammatical. Similarly, Holisky shows that imperatives may occur only if the agent is final subject. According to the analyses presented in (11), this condition is met only in (a), the direct form. This accounts for the grammaticality judgements indicated in (8).

In ch. 11 it was shown that *mier* marks retired subjects of transitive verbs. According to (11), the analytic passive, but not the synthetic passive, has such a nominal. This accounts for the fact that analytic passives occur with a *mier*-nominal, as in (2–6d), while synthetic passives do not, as shown in (*9).

Additional arguments to support the initial and final grammatical relations proposed in (11) are presented in §4 and 5, respectively.

4 Arguments for the initial grammatical relations proposed for synthetic passives

The arguments given in this section support the proposed initial grammatical relation, direct object. They argue against an analysis on which *rezo* in (2c) is subject at all levels of derivation.[8]

4.1 *Suppletion*

Shanidze observes that the verb 'kill' is suppletive for the number of its direct object, such that *moḳvla* is used for the singular and *daxoca* for the plural (Shanidze 1973:504). He cites the examples (12); the glosses are added.

(12) (a) *mgeli* *movḳali.*
wolf-NOM I-killed-it-II-1
'I killed the wolf.'
(b) *mglebi* *davxoce.*
wolves-NOM I-killed-it-II-1[9]
'I killed the wolves.'

From his exposition we can infer that this alternation is obligatory.

In the corresponding synthetic passive, the same suppletion is governed by the nominative-nominal. Shanidze cites these examples:

(13) (a) *ʒma* *momiḳvda.*[10]
brother-NOM he-died-me-II-2
'My brother died (on me).'
(b) *ʒmebi* *damexoca.*
brothers-NOM he-died-me-II-2
'My brothers died (on me).'

If the nominative-nominal of the synthetic passive is its initial direct object, and if suppletion is stated on initial termhood as proposed in previous chapters, we can account for the suppletion in (13) with the same rule independently required for (12). This argues against an analysis on which the nominative-nominal is subject at all levels, requiring distinct rules to account for (12) and (13).

4.2 *Preverb alternation*

Schmidt (1957) observes that one of the uses of the preverb *da-* in Georgian is to indicate plurality of the 'goal'.[11] He cites a large number of verbs which regularly use the preverb *ga-* or some other preverb with singular 'goals' and *da-* with plural 'goals'. He shows that for transitive verbs of this type, the use of *da-* is triggered by a plural (direct) object; while for intransitive forms derived from the same root, the same preverb is triggered by a plural subject. The forms below are from Tschenkéli (1960–73); the glosses are added.

(14)	*Direct Form*	*Synthetic Passive*
Singular	*gamovzrdi* (*mas*)	(*is*) *gamoizrdeba*
	'I will raise him'	'He will grow up'
Plural	*davzrdi* (*mat*)	(*isini*) *daizrdebian*
	'I will raise them'	'They will grow up'

We must add a rule to the grammar to account for the use of the preverb *da-* with plural direct objects. The same rule will account for the use of *da-* with plural subjects of intransitives if (i) final subjects (nominative-nominals) of synthetic passives are initial direct objects, and (ii) the *da-* rule is stated on initial termhood. If the nominative-nominal of the synthetic passive were not its initial direct object, two syntactic rules would have to be stated, missing the relevant generalization.

4.3 *Restrictions on the inventory of initial terms*

In ch. 12 it was shown that certain verbs, such as *daxrčoba* 'drown' and *gašroba* 'dry', have an obligatory direct object in their initial term inventory. In the synthetic passive, only the nominative-nominal is obligatory, as shown by (2–6c). On the analysis proposed in §3, *rezo* is the initial direct object in (2c). The sentence therefore satisfies the requirement that verbs of this type have an initial direct object. An analysis that recognized only the subjecthood of this nominal would render the synthetic passive an exception to the generalization that this verb requires an initial direct object.

5 Arguments for the final grammatical relations proposed for synthetic passives

5.1 *Person Agreement*

The markers of Subject Person Agreement, Direct Object Person Agreement, and Indirect Object Person Agreement were introduced in ch. 1. In subsequent chapters it was shown that Person Agreement is stated on final termhood.

The nominative-nominal of the synthetic passive triggers Subject Person Agreement, as shown in (15), where the subject markers are in heavy type.

(15) (a) *sakartvelos̆i da**v**ibade.*
Georgia-in **I**-born-II-2
'I was born in Georgia.'
(b) *sakartvelos̆i daibade.*
you-born-II-2 (zero marker)
'You were born in Georgia.'
(c) *sakartvelos̆i daibad**a**.*
he-born-II-2
'He was born in Georgia.'

The nominative-nominal triggers Subject Person Agreement, not Object Person Agreement. This supports the final grammatical relations proposed above.

5.2 *Case marking*

Synthetic passives can be identified as Class 2 verbs by the morphological criteria stated in ch. 16, Appendix A. The following facts of case marking, among others, have been established in the preceding chapters:

(i) Class 2 verbs govern Pattern B in all Series (chs. 1, 2, and 8).
(ii) Pattern B marks the subject with the nominative case.
(iii) Case marking is sensitive to final termhood (chs. 4–8, 10).

From these facts it follows that the nominative-nominal of the synthetic passive is the final subject, as proposed above.

5.3 *Object Camouflage*

Final first and second person direct objects obligatorily undergo Object

Camouflage in the presence of an indirect object (ch. 3). Object Camouflage does not apply with synthetic passives, as shown in (16).

(16) (a) *daebade* (*šen*) *čḳvian kals.*
you-born-her-II-2 you-NOM clever woman-DAT
'You were born to a clever woman.'
(b) **šeni tavi daebada čḳvian kals.*
your self-NOM he-born-her-II-2
('You were born to a clever woman.')

(17) (a) *avejit savse otaxši daveḳarge mšoblebs.*
furniture-INST full room-in I-lost-him-II-1 parents-DAT
'In the room full of furniture, I got lost to my parents.'
(b) **avejit savse otaxši čemi tavi daeḳarga mšoblebs.*
my self-NOM he-lost-him-II-1
('In the room full of furniture, I got lost to my parents.')

If 'you' were the final direct object in (16), being a second person nominal in the presence of the indirect object *čḳvian kals* 'clever woman', it would obligatorily undergo Object Camouflage. (16) shows that the synthetic passive must not undergo this rule. This argues against an analysis on which the nominative-nominal is the direct object at all levels.

In this section, it has been shown that the nominative-nominal has the characteristics of a final subject with respect to three rules stated on final termhood – Person Agreement, Case Marking, and Object Camouflage. Most of the syntactic rules discussed in earlier chapters do not interact with this construction.[12]

6 Conclusion and extension

Sentences like (2–6c), which may be called 'synthetic passives', are characterized by an initial direct object which is the final subject. The synthetic passive, which differs from the analytic (or true) passive morphologically, also differs from it with respect to initial inventory of terms and deriving rule. The analytic passive is derived by Passivization, the synthetic by Unaccusative, the same rule which applies in the derivation of transitive inversion forms.

In ch. 12 it was established that some verbs, such as *daçera* 'write' and *daxrčoba* 'drown', take an obligatory initial direct object. In this chapter we have seen that some of these same verbs, such as those in

(2–6), take an initial subject optionally. From the arguments presented in these two chapters, we can conclude that verbs like those illustrated in (2–6) *have an obligatory initial direct object and an optional initial subject*. Direct forms of these verbs are all Class 1 verbs and are typical of that Class. It is not the case, however, that all Class 1 verbs are direct forms, as defined here. Synthetic passives are all Class 2 forms, though the converse is not true (cf. n. 2).

Appendix: On four 'passives' in Georgian

In addition to the synthetic and analytic passives, two other constructions in Georgian have been called 'passive'. These are illustrated below.

(1) ikna-*Passive*
saxli ikna šeɣebili ċitlad.
house-NOM it-was-II-2 painted red
'The house got painted red.'

(2) *Zustandspassiv*
mṭveri aparia iaṭaḳze.
dust-NOM it-spreads-on-I-2 floor-on
'Dust is spread on the floor.'

The purpose of this appendix is briefly to compare the characteristics of these four constructions, so that the reader is more fully aware of the systematic nature of the verbal complex of the language. The claims made cannot be fully justified here.

The four 'passives' may be characterized as in table 1.

Table 1

A Analytic (*iqo*-) Passive	B Analytic (*ikna*-) Passive	C Zustandspassiv	D Synthetic Passive
Initial 1 & 2 Stative	Initial 1 & 2 Non-stative	Initial 2 Stative	Initial 2 Non-stative

The analytic *iqo*-passive (discussed in ch. 7 and in this chapter) and the analytic *ikna*-passive have the same initial inventories of terms; both are derived by Passivization.[13] The *Zustandspassiv* and synthetic passive, on the other hand, have initial direct objects, but no initial subjects; they are derived by Unaccusative.

The two analytic passives are alike formally, except in the auxiliary they use. The A-type above uses the verb *qopna* 'be', while the B-type uses the verb 'become'. The latter is generally used only in the aorist. The *ikna*-passive has not been discussed at length here because it is used only in the written language.

The *iqo*-passive differs from the *ikna*-passive in that the former is stative and the latter non-stative. This is shown by the fact that the *ikna*-, but not the *iqo*-passive, can co-occur with adverbs like *sam saatši* 'in three hours', which limit the duration of the action, as illustrated in (3).[14]

(3) (a) *saxli* *sam* *saatši* *ikna* *šeɣebili.*
house-NOM three hour-in it-was-II-2 painted
'The house was painted in three hours.'
(b) **saxli sam saatši iqo* *šeɣebili.*
it-was-II-2
('The house was painted in three hours.')

Note that *saxli iqo šeɣebili* 'the house was painted' is grammatical without the limiting phrase *sam saatši.*

The synthetic passive and the *Zustandspassiv* also differ from one another in stativity, as stated above.

Finally, the analytic (*iqo*- and *ikna*-) passive is necessarily perfective. It cannot be used to express the dynamic and necessarily imperfective passive of English, such as *the house is being painted.* The participle, which constitutes a part of the analytic passive, must always occur with a preverb, which is in general an indication of perfectivity in Georgian. The synthetic passive, on the other hand, may be either perfective or imperfective; that is, it has forms both with and without a preverb.

14 *Reflexivization*

In this chapter I will show that *Tav*-Reflexivization in Georgian can be stated simply and in such a way that there are few exceptions or problems. The rule, first stated in ch. 1 and refined in later chapters, will here be stated on the basis of grammatical relations and levels of derivation, but without extrinsic rule ordering.

1 A review of the facts

The pronoun *tav-* must be coreferential with the subject of its clause (cf. ch. 1). The *Tav*-Reflexivization rule is stated on initial terms; that is, the rule can be triggered only by initial subjects (cf. ch. 5, §2.2; ch. 7, §1.1.3; and ch. 8, §3.3). But some facts have been left unaccounted for. In object-raised sentences, there cannot be coreference between the derived subject and the matrix *tvis*-nominal. (*1a, b) show that coreference is not possible between these two nominals if either is reflexivized; (*1c, d) show that coreference is also impossible if neither nominal is reflexivized. (*1c, d) are grammatical on the non-coreferent reading.

(1) (a) *(*tavisi*) *tavi* *ʒnelia* *gelastvis* *gasatavisupleblad.*
self's self-NOM hard-it-is-I-2 Gela-for to-free
cf. *'Himself is hard for Gela to set free.'

(b) **gela* *ʒnelia* *tavistvis* *gasatavisupleblad.*
Gela-NOM self-for
cf. *'Gela is hard for himself to set free.'

(c) **is*$_i$ *ʒnelia* *gelastvis*$_i$ *gasatavisupleblad.*
he-NOM
cf. *'He$_i$ is hard for Gela$_i$ to set free.'

(d) **Gela*$_i$ *ʒnelia* *mistvis*$_i$ *gasatavisupleblad.*
him-for
cf. *'Gela$_i$ is hard for him$_i$ to set free.'

The grammaticality of (2), where the derived subject and the matrix *tvis*-nominal are not coreferent, shows that the ungrammaticality of (*1) must be due to coreferentiality.

(2) *merabi ʒnelia gelastvis gasatavisupleblad.*
Merab-NOM
'Merab is hard for Gela to set free.'

In analytic passives, there cannot be coreference between the derived subject and the *mier*-nominal (= initial subject). In (*3a, b), one of the coreferent nominals is reflexivized; in (*3c, d), neither is.

(3) (a) **vano iqo mokluli tavis mier*
Vano-NOM he-was-II-2 killed self by
cf. *'Vano was killed by himself.'
(b) **tavi iqo mokluli vanos mier.*
self-NOM Vano by
cf. *'Himself was killed by Vano.'
(c) **vano*$_i$ *iqo mokluli mis*$_i$ *mier.*
him
cf. *'Vano$_i$ was killed by him$_i$.'
(d) **is*$_i$ *iqo mokluli vanos*$_i$ *mier.*
he-NOM
cf. *'He$_i$ was killed by Vano$_i$.'

But the active sentence (4) is fully grammatical, even though there is coreference.

(4) *vanom moikla tavi.*
Vano-ERG he-killed-him-II-1 self-NOM
'Vano committed suicide.'

(5) shows that there is no constraint against passivizing this verb.

(5) *datvi iqo mokluli vanos mier.*
bear-NOM it-was-II-2 killed Vano by.
'The bear was killed by Vano.'

Therefore, the ungrammaticality of (*3) must be the result of the coreference between these two nominals in a passive.

The *mier*-nominal of a passive cannot trigger *Tav*-Reflexivization, as (*6) shows.[1]

(6) (a) **es çigni naqidia ninos mier tavistvis.*
this book-NOM bought-it-is-I-2 Nino by self-for
('This book was bought by Nino for herself.')
(b) **es çigni naqidia tavistvis ninos mier.*
('This book was bought by Nino for herself.')

In (*6) the initial subject is coreferential with *tav-*. Yet in the corresponding direct construction, (7), the initial subject can trigger *Tav*-Reflexivization.

(7) *ninom tavistvis iqida es çigni.*
Nino-ERG she-bought-it-II-3
'Nino bought this book for herself.'

Example (8) shows that this verb is compatible with Passivization.

(8) *es çigni naqidia ninos mier gelastvis.*
Gela-for
'This book was bought by Nino for Gela.'

The ungrammaticality of (*6) must therefore arise from the *mier*-nominal being the antecedent of *tav-*.

The derived subject is also unable to trigger *Tav*-Reflexivization in passives, as established by the ungrammaticality of (*9).

(9) **vano daxaṭulia (cnobili mxaṭvris mier) tavistvis.*
Vano-NOM painted-he-is-I-2 famous painter by self-for
('Vano was painted (by a famous painter) for himself.')

(*9) has no grammatical reading, whether or not the *mier*-nominal is included. Yet without *tav-*, the sentence would be grammatical.

(10) *vano daxaṭulia (cnobili mxaṭvris mier).*
'Vano was painted (by a famous painter).'

Thus, the ungrammaticality of (*9) must be due to the fact that the derived subject triggers *Tav*-Reflexivization.

In ch. 6 we saw that either the initial embedded subject or the initial matrix subject can trigger *tav-* in an organic causative. This accounts for the ambiguity of (11), where *vano* and *ekimi* 'doctor' are the initial embedded subject (=final direct object) and initial matrix subject, respectively.

(11) *ekimma alaparaḳa vano tavis tavze.*
doctor-ERG he-caused-talk-him-II-1 Vano-NOM self's self-on
'The doctor$_i$ got Vano$_j$ to talk about himself$_{i,j}$.'

In ch. 8 we saw that under Inversion only the initial subject, not the final subject, can trigger *Tav*-Reflexivization, as in (12–13). (12) illustrates inversion in Series III, (13) inversion with an inversion verb. In the (a) sentences the reflexive pronoun is coreferent to the initial subject (= final indirect object). In the (*b) and (*c) sentences it is coreferential with the final subject (= initial direct object).

(12) (a) *turme gelas daurçmunebia tavisi tavi.*
apparently Gela-DAT he-convinced-him-III-1 self's self-NOM
'Apparently Gela has convinced himself.'
(b) **turme tavis tavs daurçmunebia gela.*
self's self-DAT Gela-NOM
('Apparently Gela has convinced himself.')
(c) **turme gela daurçmunebia tavis tavs.*

(13) (a) *vanos uqvars tavisi tavi.*
Vano-DAT he-loves-him-I-4 self's self-NOM
'Vano loves himself.'
(b) **tavis tavs uqvars vano.*
self's self-DAT Vano-NOM
('Vano loves himself.')
(c) **vano uqvars tavis tavs.*

While I have accounted for the grammatical status of many of the sentences in (1–13), some have been left unaccounted for. We must refine the rule of *Tav*-Reflexivization stated above or add constraints to the grammar. The former course is taken in the next section.

2 A proposal

I propose the following restatement of *Tav*-Reflexivization to account for all the facts enumerated above:

(14) The antecedent of *tav-* must be
a. the initial subject of a clause of which *tav-* is a dependent,
and
b. a final term.

I will show below how (14) correctly predicts the facts of *Tav*-Reflexivization.

In object-raised sentences, the initial embedded subject is deleted on coreference to the matrix *tvis*-nominal (cf. ch. 4 and ch. 11, §4.1). Since it is deleted, it is not a final term, and therefore cannot be an antecedent of *tav*-.[2] The derived subject cannot trigger *tav*-, as shown in (*1b), since it is not an initial subject, which (14) requires an antecedent to be.

(14) also correctly predicts the ungrammaticality of (*2a), and (*9) where the derived subject of a passive triggers *tav*-. The initial subject of a passive cannot be the antecedent, as shown in (*2b) and (*6), since it is not a final term.

(14) permits both readings of (11). The pronoun *tav*- is an initial dependent of the embedded clause and final dependent of the matrix clause. Both of the nominals *ekimi* 'doctor' and *vano* satisfy the trigger conditions in (14), since both are initial subjects of clauses of which *tav*- is a dependent, and both are final terms – subject and direct object, respectively.

At the same time, the rule also accounts for the Inversion data. In (12a) and (13a) the dative-nominal is the initial subject and a final term (indirect object). In (*12b, c) and (*13b, c) the nominative nominals, *gela* and *vano*, cannot trigger *tav*-, since they are derived subjects, and are not initial subjects.

I have not yet accounted for the ungrammaticality of (*1c, d) and (*3c, d). We can see from the grammaticality of (4) that there is no initial-structure constraint blocking (*3). The grammaticality of (15) shows that (*1c, d) also break no constraint on initial structures; (15) is derived from the same initial structure as (*1) (cf. ch. 10).

(15) *tavis* *tavisupleba* *ʒnelia* *gelastvis.*
self-GEN freeing-NOM hard-it-is-I-2 Gela-for
'It is hard for Gela to set himself free.'

We can therefore not account for the ungrammaticality of (*1c, d) and (*3c, d) in terms of an initial-structure constraint. We can account for them correctly with a convention, (16).

(16) Coreference involving an initial subject that is a clausemate of the nominal coreferential to it must be resolved by reflexivization.[3]

Examples (*1c, d) and (*3c, d) break this convention. The grammatical sentences above, (4), (7), (11), (12a), and (13a), do not violate (16).

Coreference not satisfying the conditions of (16) may be resolved with ordinary personal pronominalization, as in (17a). Here the coreferential nominals are not clausemates at any level, and there is therefore no violation of (16).

(17) (a) *vano* *pikrobs,* *rom* (*is*) *didi sporṭsmeni*
Vano-NOM he-thinks-I-3 that he-NOM big athlete
ikneba.
will-be-I-2
'Vano thinks that he will be a great athlete.'

(b) **vano pikrobs, rom* (*tavisi*) *tavi* *didi sporṭsmeni ikneba.*
self's self-NOM
('Vano thinks that he will be a great athlete.')

Thus, there is no general convention that *all* coreference must be resolved by reflexivization.

3 An alternative proposal

Postal (1971) proposes to account for sentences in English similar to the ones we have been discussing in Georgian with a Crossover Constraint. He proposes that coreferent nominals cannot cross one another in a derivation.[4]

A crossover approach makes sense only with respect to ordered strings. If we adopt a linear order analysis, instead of the relational analysis proposed in this work, the Crossover Constraint will correctly predict the ungrammaticality of the object-raised sentences (*1a, b) and the passive sentences (*3a, b). But it could not account for the grammaticality of the inversion sentences (12a) and (13a). In order to state that under Inversion the initial subject becomes the final indirect object and that the direct object becomes the final subject, any grammar in which rules operate on structures in which constituents are linearly ordered must have a rule in which these two nominals cross one another in the course of derivation. The Crossover Constraint would then predict incorrectly that (12a) and (13a) are ungrammatical.

In order to save Crossover, we might propose to account for inversion sentences without a crossing rule. But it would greatly complicate the statement of the rules of Case Marking, Subject Person Agreement, Indirect Object Person Agreement, and Object Camouflage in such a grammar not to have these nominals cross in Inversion.

I conclude that a Crossover approach is inadequate for Georgian because it misses the generalizations captured simply in (14) and (16).

15 *Number Agreement*

In this chapter I will consider the rule of Number Agreement and the conditions under which it applies.[1] It will be shown that certain facts can be accounted for best with a rule sensitive to both initial and final grammatical relations. The primary purpose of the chapter is to provide an example of the relevance of initial grammatical relations to agreement. Until recently it has generally been assumed that all agreement rules are stated on final grammatical relations. This chapter contributes an example of a process in which initial grammatical relations are one of several determining factors in agreement.

The approach will be this: I will give data and make a generalization that describes it, then give more data and revise the generalization to account for the additional facts. Several increments of this sort will be necessary. It is first established that any term grammatical relation can trigger Number Agreement in Modern Georgian. Then it is shown that third person nominals trigger Number Agreement only if they are subjects. Third, it is final termhood that is relevant to the trigger condition among third person nominals. Fourth, it is shown that among final third person terms, that nominal which is the first subject triggers Number Agreement. This correctly excludes initial subjects that are not final terms, includes derived subjects of passivization, and includes the initial subject of the inversion construction. As a last refinement, it is shown that this condition holds unless the third person nominal is outranked (on the relational hierarchy) by a first or second person nominal in final structure. It will be shown that this rule accounts for a wide variety of constructions in Modern Georgian. In §7 some alternative analyses will be considered and shown to be inadequate.

1 Polypersonalism

In Georgian, any term grammatical relation can trigger Number

Agreement. The plural morphemes themselves are either markers of subject plurality or of object plurality, as summarized in charts (1), (2), and (3). These paradigms show an intersection of the categories of person and number, since for fusional morphemes these cannot be separated. (1a–3) repeat (15–17) of ch. 1; (1b) is first introduced in ch. 8, n. 4, (ii).

(1) *Subject markers*

(a) *Primary*

	singular	plural
1. person	*v—*	*v—t*
2. person	ø	*—t*
3. person	*—s/a/o*	*—en/es/nen, etc.*

(b) *Secondary*

	singular	plural
1. person	(*v*)*—var*	(*v*)*—vart*
2. person	*—xar*	*—xart*
3. person	*—a/s*	*—a/s*

(2) *Direct object markers*

	singular	plural
1. person	*m—*	*gv—*
2. person	*g—*	*g—t*
3. person	ø	ø

(3) *Indirect object markers*

	singular	plural
1. person	*m—*	*gv—*
2. person	*g—*	*g—t*
3. person	*s/h/ø—*	*s/h/ø—t*[2]

As shown in previous chapters, the primary subject markers are used for most verb forms, the secondary for a few. The agglutinating plural affix, *-t*, overlaps (1–3). But those persons (first and third) that have some fusional morphology in their paradigms distinguish clearly between subject and object markers; for example, plurality in a first person subject is marked by the agglutinating *-t*, but plurality in a first person object is marked by the fusional affix *gv-*.

A term, if it is singular, triggers singular agreement; if it is plural, it triggers plural agreement. But singular agreement is realized as ø in some persons, namely where it is marked with an agglutinative affix, e.g., in first and second person subjects. The ø-marker can also occur for other reasons, as shown in some of the examples below. For this reason, examples of number agreement in this chapter will always illustrate plural agreement, which necessarily has an overt marker.[3]

The examples in (5) show that Number Agreement can be triggered by any term relation. In (5a) the plural morpheme is triggered by the subject, in (5b) by the direct object, in (5c) by the indirect object. Each sentence in (5) corresponds to a sentence in (4), with the difference that in (5) the appropriate term has been pluralized for contrast with (4). Throughout, markers of agreement are set off by hyphens and plural markers are in heavy type.

(4) (a) *imušav-a.*
he-worked-II-3
'He worked.'
(b) *g-icnob-s.*
he-knows-you-I-1
'He knows you(SG).'
(c) *m-ačukeb-s* *am çigns.*
he-gives-me-it-I-1 this book-DAT
'He is giving me this book.'

(5) (a) *imušav*-**es**.
they-worked-II-3
'They worked.'
(b) *g-icnob*-**t**.[4]
he-knows-**you**(PL)-I-1
'He knows you(PL).'
(c) **gv**-*ačukeb-s* *am çigns.*
he-gives-**us**-it-I-1
'He is giving us this book.'

From (5) we see that any term can trigger Number Agreement.

2 First refinement: failure of third person to trigger Number Agreement

As the examples in (6) show, there are instances in which Number Agreement fails to apply. When Number Agreement does not apply, a singular form occurs. There are no plurality markers in the verbs of (6).

(6) (a) *icnob-s* *čems sṭudenṭebs.*
he-knows-it-I-1 my students-DAT
'He knows my students.'

(b) *ačukeb-s tavis çigns čems sṭudenṭebs.*
he-gives-him-it-I-1 self's book-DAT my students-DAT
'He is giving his book to my students.'

Although it was shown in (5b) that direct objects trigger Number Agreement, in (6a) the direct object fails to do so. Although it was shown in (5c) that indirect objects trigger Number Agreement, in (6b) an indirect object fails to trigger this rule.[5] The objects that trigger agreement in (5) are first and second person; those that fail to trigger agreement in (6) are third person. On the basis of this and similar data, I conclude that

(7) (a) First and second person nominals trigger Number Agreement in the verbs of which they are terms.
(b) Third person subjects trigger Number Agreement in the verb which governs them, but third person objects do not.

Part (b) of this statement is supported by (5a) and (6). The first clause of (7) is supported by (5b, c), which show that second person direct objects and first person indirect objects trigger Number Agreement. (8) confirms that second person subjects trigger Number Agreement, (9) that second person indirect objects trigger this rule. (10) confirms the same for first person subjects and (11) for first person direct objects. In each example, the (a) sentence is singular, and the (b) sentence differs from it only in having the appropriate term in the plural.

(8) (a) *imušave?*
you-worked-II-3 (zero marker)
'Did you(SG) work?'
(b) *imušave-***t***?*
you(PL)-worked-II-3
'Did you(PL) work?'

(9) (a) *g-ačukeb-s am çigns.*
he-gives-you-it-I-1 this book-DAT
'He is giving you(SG) this book.'
(b) *g-ačukeb-***t** *am çigns.*
he-gives-**you**(PL)-it-I-1
'He is giving you(PL) this book.'

(10) (a) *v-imušave.*
I-worked-II-3
'I worked.'

(b) *v-imušave-***t.**
we-worked-II-3
'We worked.'

(11) (a) *m-icnob?*
you-know-me-I-1
'Do you know me?'
(b) **gv**-*icnob?*
you-know-**us**-I-1
'Do you know us?'

3 Second refinement: statement on final termhood

In the examples above, the sentences have undergone no rule that would change the grammatical relations in them. When we look at analytic or synthetic passives or at object-raised sentences, we find that (7) must be stated with respect to final termhood.

Analytic passives are derived by Passivization, which promotes direct objects to subjecthood; the nominal which bore the subject relation becomes a chomeur, according to the Chomeur Condition (cf. chs. 7 and 13). In (12), the verb agrees with the derived subject, not with the initial subject.

(12) *Analytic Passives*
(a) *kurdebi dačerili ari-***an** *policielis mier.*
thieves-NOM caught **they**-are-I-2 policeman by
'The thieves are caught by the policeman.'
(b) *dačerili v-ar-***t.**
we-are-I-2
'We are caught.'
(c) *kurdi dačerili-a policielebis mier*
thief-NOM caught-he-is-I-2 policemen by
'The thief is caught by the policemen.'

The verb agrees in number with its third person final subject. The derived subject was the initial direct object and, being third person, could not trigger Number Agreement according to (7); only in its derived capacity as subject could the third person nominal trigger Number Agreement according to (7). Further, in (12c), the initial subject, *policieleb-* 'policemen', fails to trigger Number Agreement; only in final structure, where this nominal is a chomeur, is this fact consistent with (7).

Synthetic passives are also derived by promoting a direct object to subjecthood (cf. ch. 13). (13) shows that in synthetic passives, too, it is the final subject that triggers Number Agreement.

(13) *Synthetic passives*
 (a) *bičebi daixrč*-**nen**.
 boys-NOM **they**-drowned-II-2
 'The boys drowned.'
 (b) *da-v-ixrče*-**t**.
 we-drowned-II-2
 'We drowned.'

Since the nominal in (13a) is third person, according to (7) it must have been in its capacity as derived subject that it triggered Number Agreement.

Object-raised sentences are derived by promoting the direct object of a sentential subject to subjecthood of the matrix clause. (14) shows that the verb agrees with the derived subject.

(14) *Object-raised sentences*
 (a) *bavšvebi advili ari*-**an** *dasačerad.*
 children-NOM easy **they**-are-I-2 to-catch.
 'The children are easy to catch.'
 (b) *advili v-ar*-**t** *dasačerad.*
 we-are-I-2
 'We are easy to catch.'

As in the other examples, third person final subjects trigger Number Agreement. From these facts, I conclude that (7) is stated with respect to final termhood.

(7′) (a) First and second person nominals tıigger Number Agreement in the verb of which they are final terms.
 (b) Third person final subjects trigger Number Agreement, but third person final objects do not.

4 Third refinement: first subjects

With (7′) in mind, consider the sentences of (15), which are in the evidential mode.

(15) (a) *turme studenṭebs gamo-u-gzavni-a-***t** *gela.*
apparently students-DAT **they**-sent-him-III-1 Gela-NOM[6]
'Apparently the students (have) sent Gela.'
(b) *turme gelas gamo-u-gzavni-a studenṭebi.*
Gela-DAT he-sent-him-III-1 students-NOM
'Apparently Gela (has) sent the students.'

These sentences reveal the need for a further revision of (7b′). (15) shows that in the inversion construction, third person *final* subjects do not trigger Number Agreement, but third person *initial* subjects do. Yet (12–14) showed clearly that in three other constructions, third person final subjects trigger Number Agreement, while third person initial subjects do not. Further, it has been shown in example (6b) that third person final indirect objects do not, in general, trigger Number Agreement; yet in (15) the Number Agreement trigger is a third person final indirect object.

To understand the apparently anomalous position of (15), contrast these sentences with (16). In (15) and (16) the final grammatical relations are the same: there is a final subject, *bavšvi* 'child', and a final indirect object, *mšoblebs* 'parents'. Yet in (15) the final indirect object triggers Number Agreement, while in (16) the final subject does so.

(16) (a) *mšoblebs daeḳarg-a bavšvi.*
parents-DAT he-lost-him-II-2 child-NOM
'The child was lost to the parents./The parents' child was lost.'
(b) *mšoblebs daeḳarg-***nen** *bavšvebi.*
they-lost-him-II-2 children-NOM
'The children were lost to the parents./The parents' children were lost.'

The final indirect objects in (15) differ from those in (16) in one important respect: the former are initial subjects, while the latter are not.

Inversion constructions are like object-raised sentences and passives in that the initial direct object, if there is one, becomes subject. Inversion constructions differ from the others in that their initial subjects are final terms (indirect objects). In analytic passives and object-raised sentences, the initial subject is a chomeur, a final non-term. In synthetic passives, there is no initial subject. This difference between inversion sentences and the others lead us to a further revision of (7b′).

(7b″) A third person nominal triggers Number Agreement if it is the first subject that is a final term.

In sentences that undergo no change in grammatical relations, the initial subject is the first subject that is a final term, and it triggers Number Agreement in all persons, as stated in (7a′)/(7b″). In analytic passives, the initial subject is finally a chomeur, not a term. The first subject that is a final term is the derived subject; (7b″) correctly states that it will trigger Number Agreement. In synthetic passives, there is no initial subject; the first subject that is a final term is the derived subject. (7b″) makes the correct statements for this construction too. Similarly, in object-raised sentences, the object which is raised to subject is the first subject that is a final term, the sentential subject being a chomeur. In inversion constructions, the initial subject is a final indirect object, a final term; therefore it is the first subject that is a final term. Thus (7b″) captures a generalization that accounts for all of the data considered thus far.

(7b″) is complex, but it is not possible to account for all of the sentences of Modern Georgian with a simple rule of Number Agreement. The constraint on which third person nominals trigger Number Agreement is partially similar to the constraint on which nominals trigger *Tav*-Reflexivization (cf. ch. 14).[7]

5 Last refinement: relational hierarchy

The sentences of (17) show the need for a further condition on the statement of Number Agreement. (17) is analogous to (15). In (15) both nominals are third person; in (17) the initial direct object (= final subject) is second person.

(17) (a) *turme studenṭebs gamo-u-gzavni-xar (šen).*
apparently students-DAT he-sent-you(SG)-III-1 you(SG)-NOM
'Apparently the students (have) sent you(SG).'
(b) *turme sṭudenṭs gamo-u-gzavni-xar*-**t** *(tkven).*
student-DAT he-sent-**you**(PL)-III-1 you(PL)-NOM
'Apparently the student (has) sent you(PL).'

(17) differs from (15) only in the person of the final subject (= initial direct object) and in Number Agreement. In (17) *sṭudenṭ(eb)s* 'student(s)' does not trigger Number Agreement as it does in (15). In (17) the final subject does trigger Number Agreement, while in (15) it did not. In fact, if there is a first or second person term in a clause, a third person

nominal in that clause triggers Number Agreement only if it is subject at all levels of derivation. This generalization is expressed in a different form in (18), which incorporates (7a′) and a further-revised version of (7b″).

(18) (a) First and second person nominals trigger Number Agreement in the verb of which they are final terms.
(b) A third person nominal triggers Number Agreement in the verb of which it is a final term, if
(i) It is the first subject of that verb that is a final term,
and
(ii) It is not outranked finally by a first or second person nominal in its clause.[8]

Here 'outranking' refers to the hierarchy of grammatical relations, where subject ranks highest: subject—direct object—indirect object—non-terms. In (15a) the third person nominal *sṭudenṭ(eb)s* meets both criteria of (18b). As the initial subject, it is the first subject that is a final term. There is no first or second person nominal that could outrank it in its clause. In (17), on the other hand, this same nominal *is* outranked finally by the second person nominal, *šen/tkven* 'you'. *Šen/tkven* is the final subject and therefore higher on the relational hierarchy than *sṭudenṭ(eb)s*, the final indirect object.

Rule (18) accounts for the trigger of Number Agreement in all sentence types considered here. In a sentence which undergoes no change in grammatical relations, an initial third person subject is also the final subject and thus (i) is the first subject that is a final term, and (ii) is not outranked by any nominal finally. In a passive, the initial subject is not a final term. A third person direct object is (i) the first subject that is a final term and, as subject, is (ii) not outranked by any nominal finally. Thus, (18) makes the correct statements for the selection of the Number Agreement triggers for each of these constructions; the reader can confirm that it also makes the correct statements for synthetic passives and for object-raised sentences.

By (18), Number Agreement may be triggered by more than one term, but only if each satisfies either (18a) or both parts of (18b). Rule (18) could be stated in other ways, but only a complex rule referring to both initial and final grammatical relations can capture all of the linguistically significant generalizations and can resolve the apparent contradictions in the nature of Number Agreement in Georgian.[9]

6 The applicability of rule (18)

It was shown above that the rule proposed here as (18) accounts for a wide variety of constructions, including simple sentences (clauses in which no change of grammatical relations takes place), analytic and synthetic passives, object-raised sentences, and inversion constructions. In this section, I will discuss some additional constructions – causatives and version – which completes the list of major syntactic constructions of Modern Georgian. In each instance I will show that (18) correctly accounts for Number Agreement. I conclude that (18) accounts for Number Agreement generally in Modern Georgian.

6.1 *Causatives*

If an embedded clause is intransitive, its subject becomes the direct object of the corresponding causative; (19) illustrates this type.

(19) (a) *ekimma* **gv**-*alaparaḳ-a* (*čven*).
doctor-ERG he-caused-talk-**us**-II-1 we-NOM
'The doctor got us to talk.'
(b) *ekimma alaparaḳ-a* *bičebi.*
he-caused-talk-him-II-1 boys-NOM
'The doctor got the boys to talk.'

The initial grammatical relations in (19) are established in ch. 5. (i) *Ekimma* 'doctor' is the initial subject of the matrix clause. (ii) The predicate of this clause is 'cause'. (iii) Its direct object is the clause containing the verb *laparaḳ-* 'talk'. (iv) *Čven* is the initial subject of that clause in (19a), and *bičebi* 'boys' is in (19b).

According to (18a), the first person final direct object in (19a) should trigger Number Agreement. It does, and this is reflected in the first person plural direct object marker *gv-*. According to (18b), *ekimma* 'doctor' in (19a, b) should trigger Number Agreement, since it is the final subject of the causative and is (i) the first subject of that verb that is a final term, and (ii) not outranked finally by any nominal. The number of this nominal is reflected in the *-a* suffix, which is a marker of third person singular subjects. *Bičebi* 'boys' in (19b) does not satisfy criterion (18b–i) and is therefore not a Number Agreement trigger. It does not satisfy (18b–i) because, although it is a final term of the causative, it is never its subject. Although it is the initial subject of *laparaḳ-* 'talk', it is not a final term of that verb. As predicted by (18b), the number of *bičebi* is not reflected in the verb form.

The causative of a transitive is illustrated in (20).

(20) (a) *mepem* *ga-**gv**-açmendin-a* *sasaxle* (*čven*).
king-ERG he-caused-clean-**us**-it-II-1 palace-NOM we-DAT
'The king made us clean the palace.'
(b) *mepem gaaçmendin-a* *monebs* *sasaxle.*
he-caused-clean-him-it-II-1 slaves-DAT
'The king made the slaves clean the palace.'

The initial matrix subject, *mepem* 'king', is the final subject of the causative verb *ga-açmendin-* 'cause to clean'. The initial direct object of *ga-çmend-* 'clean', the nominal *sasaxle* 'palace', is the final direct object of the causative verb. The initial subjects of *ga-çmend* 'clean', the nominals *čven* 'we' and *monebs* 'slaves', are the final indirect objects of the causatives.

According to (18a), the first person final indirect object of (20a), being a final term of the causative, should trigger Number Agreement. Its plurality is indeed reflected in the first person plural indirect object marker, *gv-*. According to (18b), the third person final subject of (20a, b) should trigger Number Agreement, as in (19). Its singular number is reflected in the third person singular subject suffix *-a*. The third person final indirect object of (20b), *monebs* 'slaves', is not a qualified Number Agreement trigger according to (18b–i). Although it is the initial subject of the verb *ga-çmend-* 'clean', it is not a final term of this verb, rather of the causative verb, *ga-acmendin-* 'cause to clean'. Although it is a final term of the causative, it is never its subject. As predicted, its plurality is not reflected in the verb form. The third person final direct object, *sasaxle* 'palace', does not satisfy (18b–i); its number is not reflected in the verb form.

Thus, (18) accurately accounts for Number Agreement in causatives in Modern Georgian.

6.2 *Version*

Benefactive Version promotes a benefactive-nominal to indirect-objecthood. Number Agreement in this construction is illustrated in (21).

(21) (a) *jadosanma (tkven)* *ga-g-iķet-a-***t** *jadokruli*
witch-ERG you(PL)-DAT she-made-**you**(PL)-it-II-1 magic
sarķe?
mirror-NOM
'Did the witch make a magic mirror for you(PL)?'

(b) *jadosanma mepis ḳacebs ga-u-ḳet-a jadokruli*
king-GEN men-DAT she-made-him-it-II-1
sarḳe.
'The witch made a magic mirror for the king's men.'

The final indirect objects of (21), *tkven* 'you(PL)' and *mepis ḳacebs* 'king's men', are initially non-terms.

(18a) correctly predicts that the second person final indirect object in (21a) will trigger Number Agreement. Its plurality is reflected in the *-t* suffix in the verb form. (18b–i) correctly predicts that the third person final indirect object in (21b) will not trigger Number Agreement. Its person is reflected in the third person marker *-u-*, but its number is not reflected in the verb form.

(18) thus makes the correct statement of Number Agreement triggers for benefactive version, as well as for other version constructions in Modern Georgian.

6.3 *Object Camouflage*

Object Camouflage effects the substitution of *tav-* and a possessive pronoun for the former direct object. The possessive pronoun cannot trigger Number Agreement, since it is not a term. This is shown in (22), where the initial direct object (represented by the possessive pronoun) is singular in (a) and plural in (b).

(22) (a) *ga-g-acn-o čemi tavi.*
he-introduced-you-him-II-1 my self-NOM
'He introduced me to you(SG).'
(b) *ga-g-acn-o čveni tavi.*
our
'He introduced us to you(SG).'

The head of the final direct object is always singular; that is *čveni tavi* literally 'our self', not **čveni tavebi* 'our selves'. Since the marker of singularity is zero in third person objects, there is no overt indication of agreement.

6.4 *Conclusion: invariance*

It has been established in this section and the preceding sections that rule (18) correctly accounts for a wide variety of constructions in Modern Georgian. The generalization stated in (18) is invariant from one Class to another and from one Series to another. The Series III inversion forms are discussed in §4 and 5. In saying that Number Agreement does not vary from one Series to another, I mean that, stated on the basis of grammatical relations, as in (18), the same generalization is valid in Series I, II, and III. The fact that the correspondence between grammatical relations and the facts of Number Agreement is invariant supports the proposed analysis.

7 Some alternative analyses of Number Agreement

7.1 *A case-based analysis*

It might be proposed that the determination of the triggers of Number Agreement should be stated, not on grammatical relations, but on cases. Because of the peculiarly complex system of case marking in Modern Georgian, a solution of this kind would be particularly complicated. Stating Number Agreement on cases would entail incorporating the case marking differential ((1′–2′) of ch. 9) into the Number Agreement rules. It would require making at least the statements of (23).

(23) (a) First or second person nominative-, dative-, or ergative-nominals trigger Number Agreement.
(b) Third person nominative-nominals trigger Number Agreement in Series I, verbs of Class 1, 2, or 3.
(c) Third person nominative-nominals trigger Number Agreement in Series II or III, verbs of Class 2.
(d) Third person ergative-nominals trigger Number Agreement in Series II, verbs of Class 1 or 3.
(e) Third person dative-nominals trigger Number Agreement in Class 4 verbs in all Series and in Class 1 or 3 verbs in Series III, just in case the nominative-nominal is also third person.

This analysis fails to draw any relevant generalizations. (23) appears to be a random set of unrelated facts, while (18) presents general principles for determining Number Agreement triggers. Thus, (18), although complex, is more general than a case-based analysis.

7.2 *A morphology-based analysis*

To account for the failure of third person objects to trigger Number Agreement, an analysis might be proposed according to which a zero-marker was triggered by third person plural objects. In order to compare this hypothesis with that proposed in this chapter we must consider some additional aspects of Georgian morphology. With the convention that object agreement suffixes attach to the right of subject agreement suffixes,[10] the relevant morphophonemic rules may be stated as (24) and (25).

(24) +*s*+ ⟶ ø/ ___ +*t*+
The morpheme *s* deletes before the morpheme *t*.

(25) +*t*+ ⟶ ø/[PLURAL] ___
The morpheme *t* deletes after any plural marker.

The morpheme *t* in both rules is a plural marker (cf. paradigms (1–3/3′)). Rule (25) accounts for the non-occurrence of the following sequences, where 'V' represents the verb stem: *V-*en-t*, *V-*an-t*, *V-*es-t*, *V-*nen-t*, and *V-*t-t*. None of these sequences is ruled out by a phonological rule.

The morphology-based analysis would require the following statements to account for simple sentences: (1–2), (3′) to replace (3) of the proposed grammar, and the morphophonemic rules (24–25).

(3′) *Indirect object markers* (cf. (3))

	singular	plural
1. person	*m*—	*gv*—
2. person	*g*—	*g*—*t*
3. person	*s*/*h*/*ø*—	*s*/*h*/*ø*—

To account for (15) this analysis needs, in addition, rules (26–27).

(26) The third person plural object suffix is not ø, but rather -*t*, if and only if the sentence has undergone Inversion and the final subject is third person.

(27) The third person plural subject marker is not -*en*, -*es*, etc., but rather -*a* or -*s*, just in case the clause has undergone Inversion and the final object is third person.

Rules (26) and (27) are *ad hoc*, and this analysis fails to show that Number Agreement is based in part on non-final grammatical relations.

The hypothesis proposed in this chapter, on the other hand, needs statements (1–3), (24–25), and (18). While (18) is complex, it draws linguistically significant generalizations and avoids *ad hoc* rules.

7.3 *A rule- or construction-based analysis*

Traditional analyses assume (1–3) and (24–25), but replace (18) with statements equivalent to those in (28).

(28) I In the inversion construction:
- A. All first and second person final terms trigger Number Agreement.
- B. Third person initial subjects trigger Number Agreement, if there is no first or second person final term in the clause.

II In all other constructions:
- A. All first and second person final terms trigger Number Agreement.
- B. Third person final subjects trigger Number Agreement.

(28) could instead be formulated in terms of the application of rules; that is, 'I If Inversion has applied,... II If Inversion has not applied,...'

It is immediately clear that (28) is missing a generalization, since statement A is repeated in parts I and II. Aside from this, (28) fails to relate *third person initial subjects* in IB to *third person final subjects* in IIB. (18), on the other hand, does relate these through reference to the notion, 'first subject'. Thus (18) is to be preferred to a solution which gives different rules for inversion and non-inversion constructions.

7.4 *No-Inversion Analysis*

Finally, the complexity introduced by the inversion construction in §4 might be taken as an indication that the inversion analysis is incorrect. Since dative-nominals trigger Number Agreement in (15), as final subjects do elsewhere, it might be proposed that the dative-nominal is the final subject.[11] Like the other grammars considered, this one would need statements (1–3) and (24–25). In addition, it would need the following statements to account for (15–17):

(29) First and second person nominals trigger Number Agreement in the verb of which they are final terms (= 18a).

(30) Third person nominals trigger Number Agreement in the verb of which they are final subjects.

(31) Third person nominals do not trigger Number Agreement in the verb of which they are final subjects if:

(a) (i) the verb is in Series III
and
the verb is in Class 1 or 3
or
(ii) the verb is in Class 4 (in any Series)
and
(b) there is a first or second person nominal in the clause.

(29–31) would replace (18) of the grammar espoused here. While (29) and (30) are comparable to (18a) and (18b–i), respectively, (31) is a great deal more complex than (18b–ii). The complexity of (31), especially of part (a), is directly attributable to the fact that this grammar lacks Inversion.

A No-Inversion Analysis would be unable to account for the fact that the markers of Number Agreement are selected entirely on the basis of the *final* grammatical relations stated by the rules of Inversion and Unaccusative (cf. n. 8). That is, the final indirect object *sṭudenṭebs* 'students' in (15a) triggers an object plural marker *-t* from set (3), not a subject plural marker from set (1). The No-Inversion Analysis outlined above would have to have an additional *ad hoc* rule to account for this fact.

In addition, the No-Inversion Analysis would require giving up the economy in case marking effected by Inversion and would require complications in the rules of Subject Person Agreement, Indirect Object Person Agreement, Object Camouflage, *Tav*-Reflexivization, and suppletion of various types, as set out in ch. 8. Thus, while (18) is complex, a grammar that lacked Inversion would be still more complex.

Unlike the alternative analyses discussed in this section, rule (18) states a linguistically significant generalization. It avoids the entirely *ad hoc* rules (23), (26–27), (28), and (31) required by the other hypotheses. While (18) is a more complex rule than is usually needed in most languages for the statement of agreement phenomena, it presents an accurate account of the facts in the most succinct and general way possible.

8 Conclusions

Research on grammatical relations has revealed a hierarchy – subject, direct object, indirect object, other grammatical relations – such that subject is highest. The relevance of this hierarchy has been established in the accessibility of nominals to certain rules, including relativization (Keenan & Comrie 1977). It is also thought that the relational hierarchy affects verb agreement in the following way: If a language has agreement with direct objects, it will also have agreement with at least some subjects. If a language has agreement with indirect objects, it will have agreement with at least some subjects and direct objects. This chapter establishes a further relevance of the relational hierarchy in agreement phenomena. §5 shows that whether a particular nominal triggers agreement may be determined by whether it is outranked on the relational hierarchy by certain types of nominals (in Modern Georgian, by first or second person nominals). On the basis of our present understanding of the relational hierarchy and facts like those presented in (15) and (17), we can hypothesize that the presence of a nominal bearing a grammatical relation *lower* on the relational hierarchy would never be relevant to the selection of an agreement trigger. In Modern Georgian, the presence of a (first or second person) nominal bearing a grammatical relation *higher* on the relational hierarchy is relevant, as expressed in (18b–ii); but we may hypothesize that the converse of this would never occur in a natural language.

In §4, it is established that in Modern Georgian the determination of the triggers of Number Agreement is based on both final and non-final grammatical relations. The determination of the triggers of Person Agreement, on the other hand, is based on final grammatical relations alone (cf. chs. 1–8, 10, 13). It is also interesting that in Old Georgian, the determination of Number Agreement triggers was based on final grammatical relations alone (cf. Aronson 1976; Chikobava 1941; Shanidze 1976; Zorrell 1930). The fact that non-final grammatical relations are relevant to agreement in Modern Georgian is of interest to universal grammar, since it has been widely assumed that only final termhood is relevant in these phenomena.

16 *The nature of the Georgian verb classes*

In previous chapters we have examined several aspects of the distribution of cases in Georgian. In chs. 2 and 8, it was established that there are two case marking Patterns in Modern Georgian, Patterns A and B; in ch. 9, it was shown that Pattern A cannot synchronically be reduced to Pattern B. I have shown that the Patterns are correlated with grammatical relations in the following way:

(1) (a) *Distribution of cases in terms of Patterns*

	Subject	*Direct object*	*Indirect object*
Pattern A	ERGATIVE	NOMINATIVE	DATIVE
B	NOMINATIVE	DATIVE	DATIVE

The distribution of cases has been precisely stated in terms of the Class and Series of the governing verb form:

(b) *Distribution of cases in terms of Series and Class*

	Series I	II	III
Class 1	B	A	B
2	B	B	B
3	B	A	B
4	B	B	B,

but it has not yet been determined what kinds of verbs constitute each Class. I have not yet stated what characteristic of a verb form determines which Pattern it will govern. Thus, I must still address the following problem within the context of both general linguistics and Georgian grammar: *How can it be predicted which verbs govern Pattern A in Series II, and which Pattern B?*

In this chapter I will present in detail two solutions to this central problem of Georgian syntax. The first hypothesis (§1) represents the approach taken by most Georgianists today; they analyze the case marking system of Series II as ergative. The second hypothesis (§2) represents a new proposal based on the initial and final termhood of the nominal dependents, rather than their final termhood alone. This analysis draws on the important notion of initial intransitive direct objects (defined below). In §3 and 4, I will discuss Inversion and the semantics of Class, respectively. In §5, I will compare the two hypotheses, showing that the analysis proposed here is simpler with respect to case marking, Inversion, and predicting the Class membership of productive derivational types introduced in §4 and in earlier chapters. §6 is a brief discussion of the theoretical contributions of these aspects of Georgian to the study of language universals. Sample lists of each Class of verbs are included for reference, as Appendix A to this chapter. Appendix B deals with a few types that are irregularly ambivalent with respect to Class membership, discussing some verbs that are exceptions to both hypotheses.

Traditional analyses of Georgian have observed that Class 2 verbs do not undergo Inversion in Series III; this has been treated as an idiosyncratic fact. The failure of Class 2 verbs to undergo Inversion follows automatically from the analysis proposed here, with no additional *ad hoc* device.

1 Hypothesis A: The Ergative Hypothesis

Nearly all of the recent full-scale analyses of Georgian have claimed that the language has ergative case marking in Series II: Chikobava (1948, 1950, 1961, 1968), Klimov (1973), Nebieridze (to appear), Schmidt (1973), Shanidze (1973), Tschenkéli (1958), Vogt (1971), etc. A prominent exception is the work of Aronson, who specifically argues that Georgian is not ergative (cf. especially Aronson 1970). The tradition of the ergative analysis is embodied in the use of the traditional name, 'ergative', for the case that marks subjects in Pattern A.

1.1 *What is ergative case marking?*

Anderson (1976) states that 'In [ergative] languages, the morphological category to which the subject NP of an intransitive verb belongs is shared not with the NP we expect to be subject of a transitive verb, but rather with the NP we expect to be object of that verb'. In terms of case marking, in an ergative system, the case which marks the subject of an intransitive verb is shared, not with the nominal which is the subject of a transitive verb, but with the nominal which is the object of that verb. In an ergative system of case marking, one case marks the subject of an intransitive verb and the direct object of a transitive verb, while another case marks the subject of a transitive verb. Similar definitions are given in other recent discussions of general ergativity (Catford 1976; Chikobava 1961; Comrie 1973, 1978; Dixon 1979; Johnson (to appear), Klimov 1973; Kuryłowicz 1946; Sapir 1917; Silverstein 1976; and Troubetskoj 1939). According to all of these definitions, an ergative system is predicated upon a division of verbs into transitive and intransitive. The terms 'transitive' and 'intransitive' are used here in their general linguistic meaning, which is discussed in ch. 12, §5.

1.2 *What are the implications of the Ergative Hypothesis for Georgian?* We have established the existence of two case marking Patterns in Modern Georgian, as shown in (1a). A large amount of evidence has been amassed to support the correlations between the cases and the grammatical relations stated in (1a); this evidence is presented particularly in chs. 2–9 and 13–16. In particular, these data show that nominals marked with the ergative in Pattern A and with the nominative in Pattern B are subjects, while those marked with the nominative in Pattern A and with the dative in Pattern B are direct objects.

The ergative analysis of Georgian Series II identifies the 'ergative'-marked subject with transitive verbs and the 'nominative'-marked subject with intransitive verbs. According to the Ergative Hypothesis, in Series II, transitives govern Pattern A and intransitives govern Pattern B. We have seen the following distribution of Patterns A and B with respect to different Classes in Series II.

(2) *Distribution of Patterns in Series II*

Class 1	Pattern A
Class 2	Pattern B
Class 3	Pattern A
Class 4	Pattern B

Grammarians writing within the framework of the Ergative Hypothesis have made the following statements about these verb Classes:

(3) Class 1 is transitive and governs Pattern A.
Class 2 is intransitive and governs Pattern B.
Class 3 is neither transitive nor intransitive and governs Pattern A.[1]

1.3 *Insights of this analysis*

Historically, the Ergative Hypothesis was proposed for Series II of Georgian as an attempt to distinguish it from the obviously very different systems found in most European languages. In the context of attempts to force all languages into the mold of the accusative construction, it was essential to recognize that case marking in Series II of Georgian is not accusative; and so it was grouped with the ergative type. It was observed that most Class 1 verbs are final transitives, most Class 2 verbs final intransitives, and that a large number of verbs in Georgian fall therefore into the pattern,

	Subject	*Direct Object*
Transitive	ERGATIVE	NOMINATIVE
Intransitive	NOMINATIVE	—

which defines an ergative case marking system. For example, there are a great many final transitive–intransitive pairs, like those listed in (4).

(4) *Transitive*	*Intransitive*
svams 'he drinks it'	*ismeba* 'it is drinkable'
ḳlavs 'he kills him'	*ḳvdeba* 'he dies'
zrdis 'he raises him'	*izrdeba* 'he grows up'
xerxavs 'he saws it'	*ixerxeba* 'it saws easily; it is being sawn'
ṭexavs 'he breaks it'	*ṭqdeba* 'it breaks' (cf. ch. 13)

All of the transitive verbs in (4) govern Pattern A in Series II, and all of the intransitive ones Pattern B. In addition to pairs like these, verb forms like *mivida* 'he went', *movida* 'he came', *iqo* 'he was', and *darča* 'he stayed, he remained', are intransitive and govern Pattern B. Further, as established in ch. 8, inverted verbs are finally intransitive, with Pattern B marking. Thus, the Ergative Hypothesis makes the correct predictions for a large number of verbs in Georgian.

1.4 *Inadequacies of this analysis*

A glance at (3) will show that Class 3 verbs present a problem for the ergative analysis. Class 3 contains a few verbs that may take a direct object, such as *tamaši* 'play' and *laparaḳi* 'talk' (cf. ch. 12); most verbs in this Class, however, never take a direct object: *qiqini* 'croak', *xitxiti* 'giggle'. In order to include Class 3 verbs in the system of case marking, traditional grammarians have given some rather interesting *apologiae* for this Class. In this section, those explanations will be examined.

(i) The first such explanation is embodied in (3), namely that Class 3 verbs are neither transitive nor intransitive. In the sense defined in ch. 12 for these notions, this claim has no apparent meaning. In the work of linguists who make this claim about Georgian, the terms 'transitive' and 'intransitive' have lost the meanings that they have in general linguistics and have become the names of particular verb Classes, regardless of the syntactic properties of the verbs. Thus, 'transitive' has become the name of Class 1, and 'intransitive' the name of Class 2. This nomenclature has led to calling Class 3 verbs 'neutral' and stating that they are neither transitive nor intransitive. Clearly this statement is meaningless if the notions 'transitive' and 'intransitive' are also to be used with reference to languages other than Georgian.

(ii) A second approach is to play down the importance of this large class of counterexamples by labeling it 'irregular'. Indeed, the Class has even been defined as the set of irregular verbs (cf. Holisky 1980a for a history of the analyses of this Class). The implication seems to be that if a group of verbs is morphologically irregular, it cannot be expected to be regular from the point of view of the case Pattern it governs. The label 'irregular' seems to have been applied on the grounds that verbs of Class 3 build their future/aorist forms[2] with a formant *different* from that used by verbs of Classes 1 and 2. This Class is, however, regular in the sense that its members *regularly* use one particular formant to build the tenses in question. (5) lists the formants regularly used to form these tenses by verbs of Class 1 and 2 on the one hand, and of Class 3 on the other.

(5)	*Classes* 1, 2	*Class* 3
Future	Preverb—	*i—eb*
Conditional	Preverb—*(o)d-i*	*i—eb-(o)d-i*
Future Subjunctive	Preverb—*(o)d-e*	*i—eb-(o)d-e*[3]
Aorist	Preverb—*e/i*	*i—e*
Optative	Preverb—*o/a*	*i—o*

In (5), dashes indicate the position of the verb root. The preverbs used by Classes 1 and 2 are chosen from a set which includes *mi-*, *mo-*, *a-*, *amo-*, *ča-*, *čamo-*, *da-*, *ga-*, *gamo-*, *ça-*, *çamo-*, etc. and are lexically determined. In the aorist and optative, respectively, most of the Class 1 and 2 verb forms use the *-e* and *-o* suffixes; some, however, use *-i* and *-a*, respectively. All of the Class 3 verbs on the other hand, use *-e* and *-o* regularly. In order to illustrate the striking regularity of this Class, I have listed the verbs in the future in Appendix A to this chapter. While there exist irregularities in this Class as in every other, the overwhelming majority of verbs in Class 3 show a consistent morphology. These verbs have 'irregular' morphology, then, only in the sense that their morphology is *different* from that of Class 1 and 2 verbs.[4]

The 'irregularity' of this Class has also been understood to mean that it is arbitrary, that is, that the verbs which constitute the Class are an arbitrary set.[5] Holisky (1980a) shows that Class 3 is semantically regular, as well, constituting the Class of dynamic verbs that are inherently of durative aspect (cf. n. 4). Even a glance at the representative list of Class 3 verbs in Appendix A will reveal that the verbs which constitute Class 3 are not an arbitrary set.

In earlier chapters we have seen that Class 3 verbs exhibit a high degree of syntactic regularity. In particular, all verbs which satisfy the morphological definition of Class 3 (cf. Appendix A), also have the following syntactic characteristics: (a) they trigger Inversion in Series III, and (b) they govern ergative case subjects (Pattern A) in Series II.

This Class of verbs is strikingly regular, then, in its morphology, syntax, and semantics. Labeling these verbs 'irregular' in no way accounts for the case Pattern they govern in Series II. Labeling them in this way simply disguises the fact that linguists have not been able to account for the case Patterns governed by a large and systematic Class of verbs in Georgian.

(iii) A third explanation that has been offered for the case marking of Class 3 verbs in Series II is that these verbs 'do not have their own Series II forms' and that the Series II forms used are 'borrowed from the corresponding' Class 1 verbs. (This entails that the future forms are also 'borrowed', since futures and aorists are similar morphologically for all regular verbs in Georgian; cf. (5) above.) Thus, for example, the aorist of *vbaṭonob* 'I reign' – *vibaṭone* 'I reigned' – is said to be 'borrowed' from the Class 1 transitive verb: *gavibaṭone čemi tavi* 'I made myself ruler'. Since the form is borrowed, it is implied, so is the case Pattern. Thus, an intransitive verb, *vbaṭonob* 'I reign', has an ergative case subject in Series II because the morphology of the verb is 'borrowed' from a transitive, which naturally governs an ergative subject.[6] Thus, by claiming that these verbs have 'no Series II forms of their own', linguists have tried to explain the fact that these intransitive verbs govern an ergative case subject in an ergative system of case marking.

There are at least two problems with such an explanation. The first is that this theory does not explain why syntactic characteristics should be 'borrowed' along with morphological ones. In a language with an ergative case system, case marking is determined by the transitivity of the verbs, rather than by the origin of their morphology. If a language has ergative case marking, it will apply the principles of that system to all verbs alike, whether or not they are derived or borrowed. Until the borrowing of morphological formants can be shown to be related systematically to the borrowing of syntactic characteristics, this explanation for the use of the ergative case by intransitive verbs is completely *ad hoc*.

A second fault of such a hypothesis is that it offers no explanation of why some verbs (Class 3) should 'borrow' their morphology while others (Class 1, 2) do not. Even if we accept the notion that 'borrowed' morphology entails 'borrowed' syntax, we still have no answer as to why Class 3 is different from Class 2.[7]

To summarize, neither the notion 'neither transitive nor intransitive', the label of 'irregular', nor the concept that Series II forms of Class 3 verbs are 'borrowed' offers a satisfactory explanation of the systematic use of Pattern A by many intransitive verbs in Series II. We must recognize that there is no way adequately to incorporate Class 3 verbs into the ergative analysis of Georgian.

There are other problems for the claims made in (3). Intransitive verbs in Class 1 include *daaboqina* 'he burped', *daamtknara* 'he yawned', and *daacxiḳva* 'he sneezed'. The transitive verbs in Class 2 are discussed in Appendix B to this chapter. While the existence of intransitives in Class 1 and transitives in Class 2 is contrary to the claims of (3), it does not pose a serious problem for the Ergative Hypothesis; these verbs are few in number and may be treated as simple exceptions. The existence of the large, systematic Class 3, however, shows the real inadequacy of the ergative analysis for Georgian.

At the beginning of this chapter I stated a problem for general linguistics and Georgian grammar, as it has traditionally been viewed by Georgian specialists. Looking at the distribution of cases in (2), we see that it is appropriate to pose this question in a different way as well:

Problems for general linguistics and Georgian grammar

1. How can we capture a generalization uniting Class 1 with Class 3 in Series II?
2. How can we predict which verbs govern Pattern A in Series II?

2 Hypothesis B: The Unaccusative Hypothesis

It will be shown that the notions 'active' and 'inactive' correlate with the morpho-syntactic divisions of Classes, such that Classes 1 and 3 constitute the set of active verbs, while Classes 2 and 4 constitute the set of inactive verbs. On this basis the case marking rules of Georgian can be stated.

2.1 *Language universals*

Sapir (1917) was perhaps the first to make a clear typological division of languages on the basis of case marking systems. He observed the existence of five distinct types. Of particular interest to us here is the clear distinction he made between ergative (transitive vs. intransitive) and active vs. inactive systems, deploring the usual inclusion of these two types under one rubric. He represents these two case systems schematically as in (8), which also includes his representation of an accusative language for comparison; the names given to the types of case systems are not used by Sapir (*op. cit.*).[8]

(8)

Object transitive	*Subject intransitive* Inactive	Active	*Subject transitive*	*Type of case system*
A	A		B	Ergative
A	A	B	B	Active/Inactive
A	B		B	Accusative

Although Sapir does not go into detail about the active/inactive type, we may infer something about its nature from Dakhota, the language he cites as its archetype. It has often been said that Dakhota and the other Siouan languages distinguish between stative verbs and dynamic verbs. In Lakhota, a Dakhota dialect, sentences like those below suggest that *wa* marks first person singular in dynamic verbs, while *ma* marks the same person and number in statives.

*wa*kte′ 'I kill it'.
tha*wa*′šoše 'I spit.'
*ma*hā′ske 'I am tall'.

However, examples like

*ma*hī′xpaye 'I fall down.' (Examples from Van Valin (1977))

show that *ma* is used not only by statives but also by intransitive dynamic verbs that are non-agentive, involuntary, or non-controllable.

Recent treatments of the syntax of Dakhota and other Siouan languages have observed that the *wa/ma* dichotomy is not dynamic/stative, but controllable/non-controllable (Matthews 1965:63; Van Valin 1977:10). A close examination of the verb classes in other languages reveals that a controllable vs. non-controllable distinction is not uncommon (e.g. Chafe 1970). Since the languages cited by Sapir distinguish controllable, voluntary, or agentive verbs on the one hand from non-controllable, involuntary, or non-agentive on the other, we may assume that it is this dichotomy he intended; it is this distinction, not a dynamic/stative distinction, that is here referred to as 'active/inactive'.

Postal and Perlmutter observe that there is evidence that the final subject of 'inactive' verbs is initially not a subject, but a direct object (cf. Perlmutter 1978; and Perlmutter & Postal, to appear a). They have proposed a theory of language which would recognize at least the following initial term inventories:

(9) *Initial term inventories*

Subject and direct object		(transitive)
Subject		(intransitive)
	Direct object	(intransitive)

The initial intransitive direct object becomes subject, as will be shown below.

Initial term inventories are determined by the semantics of the individual verb. Initial subjects include agents, cognizers, and other controlling nominals, as well as experiencers. Initial direct objects include patients and stimuli. Examples of verbs that take initial intransitive subjects include 'work', 'fight', 'talk', and 'growl'. Examples of verbs that take initial intransitive direct objects include 'exist', 'fall', 'remain', and 'grow up'.

Verbs which have an initial intransitive subject correspond to Sapir's 'active intransitives'; verbs which have an initial intransitive direct object correspond to his 'inactive intransitives'. Thus, languages in which transitive subjects are marked with one case, and intransitive subjects and transitive direct objects are marked with another, have 'ergative' case marking. Languages in which final subjects are marked with one case, and final direct objects with another, have 'accusative' case marking. And languages in which *initial* subjects are marked with one case, and initial direct objects with another, have what Sapir termed 'active/inactive' case marking.

Notice in (8) that there is only a relatively small difference between the ergative and the active/inactive systems; this difference is the marking assigned to the subjects of active intransitive verbs, verbs like 'work', 'play', 'fight', 'growl', and 'talk'. This is exactly the type of verb that constitutes Class 3 in Georgian, the Class that causes difficulties for the ergative hypothesis (cf. §1.4). According to Sapir, the subject of active intransitive verbs in an active/inactive system is marked with the same case as that used for the subject of a transitive verb. We shall see in §2.2 that this provides the key to case marking in Georgian.

Postal and Perlmutter have further observed that the distinction in (9) is used also as the basis for other processes in various languages. For example, in Mohawk it is a necessary, but not sufficient, condition on incorporation that the incorporated noun be the (final) subject of an inactive verb or direct object of a transitive verb (those nominals marked with case 'A' in the active/inactive system in Sapir's schema (8)) (Postal, personal communication). Perlmutter (to appear d) shows that this distinction accounts for a number of distinct phenomena in Italian, including the selection of auxiliaries and the rule of Partitive Ascension. The schema in (9) accounts for the fact that the same intransitive verbs which take case A in (8) also may allow incorporation in Mohawk and take the auxiliary *essere* in Italian.

2.2 *Specific proposal for Georgian*

I suggest that case marking in Series II is of the active/inactive type.[9] In general, verbs that take an initial intransitive subject are in Class 3 in Georgian, while those that take an initial intransitive direct object are in Class 2. The initial term inventory of each verb form is determined by its semantics, as specified in §2.1. Notice that the verbs listed above as exemplifying initial intransitive direct objects all belong to Class 2 in Georgian, while those illustrating initial intransitive subjects all belong to Class 3 in Georgian. In the discussion below, I will show in detail how each derivational type fits into a precise schema characterizing the Classes in terms of initial and final termhood. The reader is referred to Appendix A of this chapter for representative lists of verbs of the derivational types constituting each Class. Capital letters in parentheses in the text below refer to sub-lists under each Class in Appendix A.

2.2.1 *Class* 1. Class 1 contains two derivational types: basic verb forms (A)[10] and organic causatives (B).[11] *Daçers* 'he will write it' is a basic

Class 1 verb (direct construction) with initial subject and direct object, as established in ch. 13. The structure of this form is represented in network (10).

(10)

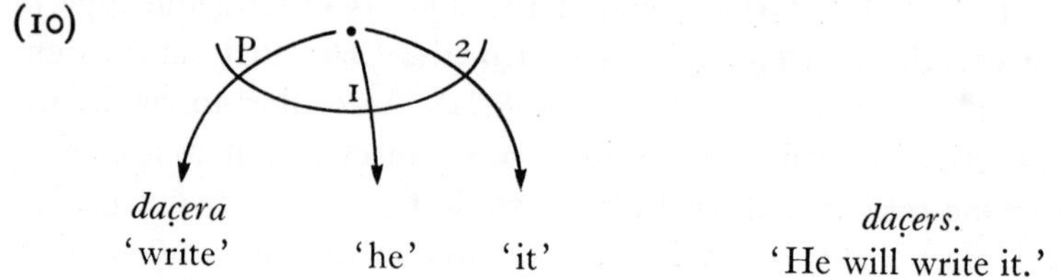

This Class includes a few verbs which take an initial intransitive subject; one is represented in (11).

(11)

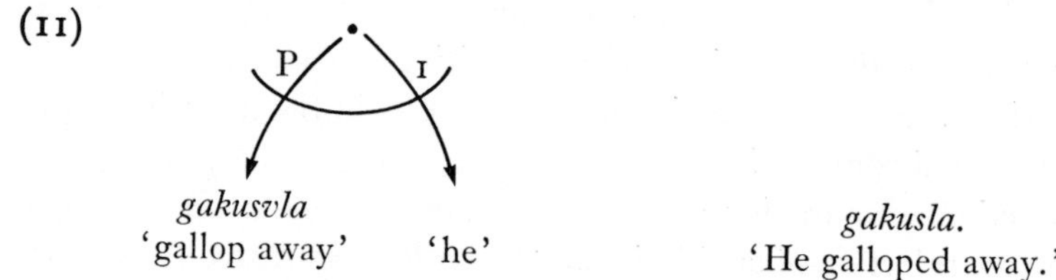

Daaçerina 'he caused him to write it' is the causative of a transitive; its derivation is represented in (12) (cf. ch. 5).

(12)

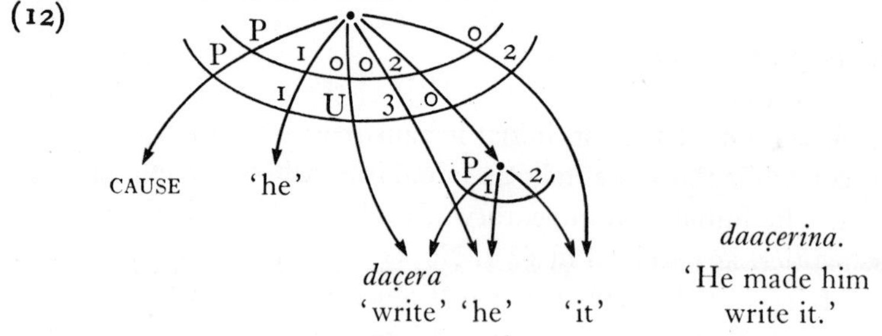

As observed in ch. 12, most Class 1 verbs are transitive. *All* Class 1 verbs are characterized by an initial subject, as illustrated in networks (10–12).

2.2.2 *Class* 3. Class 3 also contains two derivational types: basic verb forms (M) and denominals (N). *Tamašobs* 'he plays' is an example of the former. As established in ch. 12, it takes an optional initial direct object; (13) and (14) give the two constructions possible for this verb form.

(13)

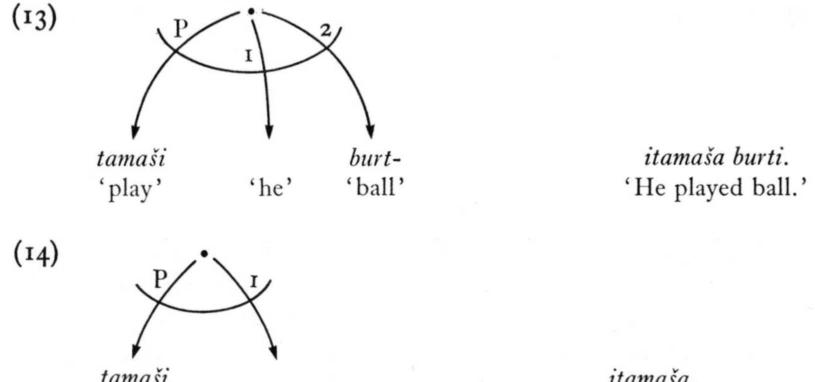

The construction in (13) is identical to that in (10), and (14) to (11). Class 3 verbs which never take a direct object, like *iqiqina* 'it croaked', have only constructions like (14).

Verbs like *gmirobs* 'he is taking on the characteristics of a hero, he is acting brave' are formed from nouns like *gmiri* 'hero'. They have a structure similar to (14).

Class 3 verbs are characterized by an initial subject. Class 3 differs from Class 1 only in that the latter are mostly transitive (initially and finally), while the former mostly take a direct object optionally or not at all (initially and finally).

2.2.3 *Class 2.* Class 2 contains the following derivational types: basic verb forms (C), analytic passives (D), synthetic passives (E), and inceptives (F). The *ikna*-passive (G) and Zustandspassiv (H) are discussed briefly in the appendix to ch. 13; derivationally, they do not differ from types D and E, respectively.

Network (15) represents an analytic passive (cf. ch. 7), and (16) a synthetic passive (ch. 13).

(15)

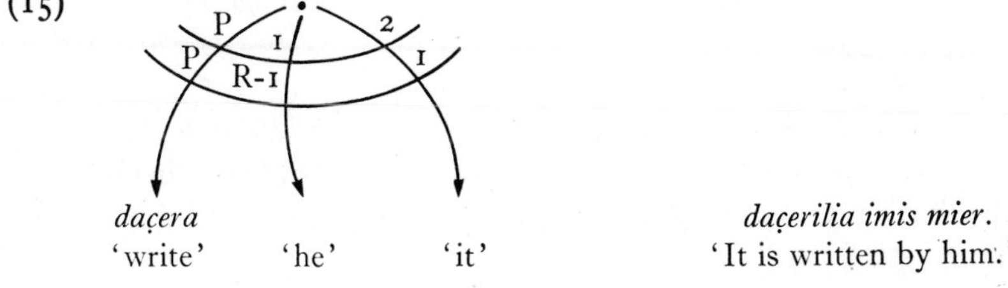

(16)

Passivization is responsible for the change in grammatical relations represented in (15). Unaccusative is responsible for the change in (16).

We know from preceding chapters (especially chs. 1 and 2) that in the clause *is iqo enatmecnieri* 'he was a linguist', *is* 'he' is a final subject; but we have no evidence concerning its initial termhood. I suggest that this verb, as well as other basic Class 2 verbs, is characterized by an initial intransitive direct object. The set of basic Class 2 verbs (C) is consonant with Sapir's 'intransitive inactives', with the set of intransitive verbs that may allow incorporation in Mohawk, and with the set of intransitive verbs that take the auxiliary *essere* in Italian. Semantically the term nominal associated with these verbs (the final subject) is always non-controlling, a patient. I suggest further that the initial direct object, *is* 'he' in the example above, becomes subject, and that this operation is performed by the rule Unaccusative (cf. chs. 8 and 13 for the characteristics of this rule). Unaccusative, it will be remembered, applies in the absence of a subject, and promotes direct objects to subjecthood. In Georgian, Unaccusative is obligatory; there are no verbs such that their initial term inventory includes a direct object, but no subject, and the direct object fails to undergo Unaccusative.[12] This clause is represented in (17).[13]

(17)

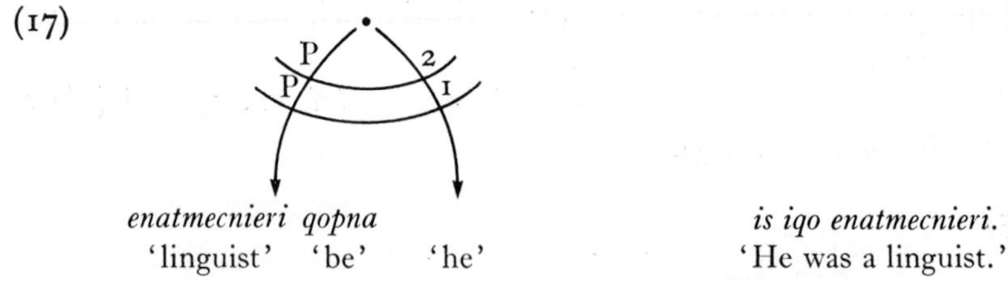

Inceptives in Georgian are discussed in Holisky (1980b). Inceptives may be formed on two types of predicates in Georgian: adjectives or verbs. Each is represented below. The predicate COME ABOUT is a basic Class 2 verb form (C).

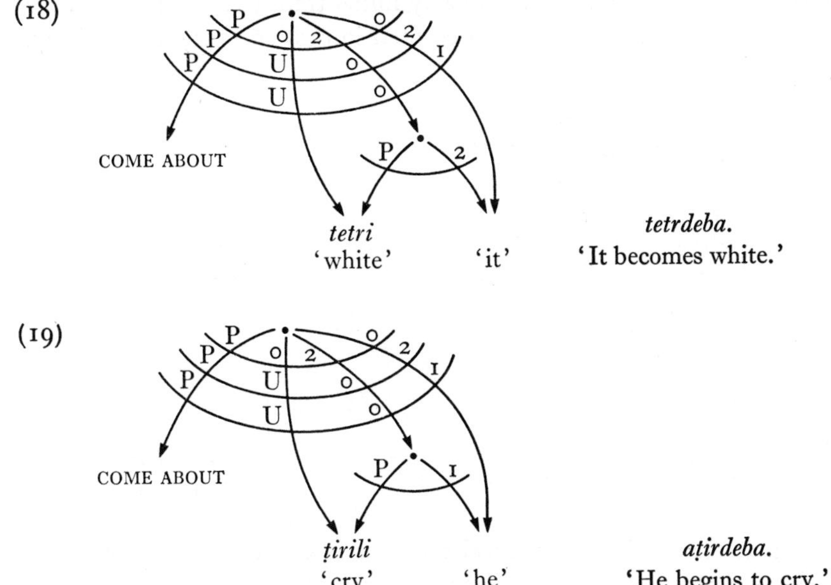

Clause Union applies in both (18) and (19). As discussed in ch. 5, it is predictable that direct objects and intransitive subjects of the embedded clause become direct objects of the united clause, as shown in (18) and (19). Since there is no subject at the output level of Clause Union, Unaccusative must apply, advancing the direct object to subject.[14]

Class 2 verbs like *darča* 'he remained', *iqo* 'he was', and *gaxda* 'he became' differ from Class 3 verbs like *imepa* 'he reigned', *itamaša* 'he played', and *iqiqina* 'it croaked' in the following way. The Class 3 intransitives have initial subjects, while the Class 2 intransitives have initial direct objects which become final subjects by the application of some rule (Passivization or Unaccusative).

Notice that synthetic passives (E) and basic Class 2 verbs (C) do not differ derivationally (cf. (16) and (17)), morphologically, or syntactically. They differ in only one respect. Synthetic passives are formed on verb roots which also form the base for basic Class 1 verbs; this is not true of basic Class 2 verbs.[15] Thus (C) and (E) constitute a natural sub-class of Class 2 verbs.

2.2.4 *Class* 4. Class 4 contains three derivational types: basic Class 4 verbs (P), desideratives (Q), and the type discussed in ch. 8, Appendix

B (R). Basic Class 4 verbs are mostly initial transitives, but there are a few intransitives. These are represented in (20) and (21), respectively.

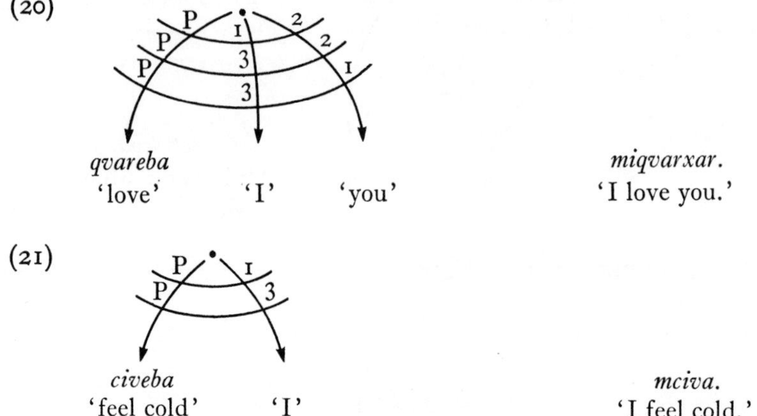

The first change in grammatical relations is due to the application of Inversion, the second ((20) only) to Unaccusative.

Desideratives may be formed on verbs or on nouns. No specific analysis will be proposed here, but it is clear that these verb forms involve Inversion. An example of a desiderative formed on a verb is *mecekveba* 'I feel like dancing, I want to dance', where *m–* is the first person singular indirect object agreement marker, *e—eb* is the circumfix for deriving desideratives, *cekv* is the root 'dance', and *-a* is the third person singular subject agreement marker. An example of a desiderative formed on a noun is *ar meɣvineba* 'I don't feel like any wine', where *ar* is the negative, and the root 'wine' is *ɣvino*.

Class 4 verbs are like Class 1 verbs in that they have an initial subject and most have an initial direct object. They are like Class 2 verbs in that their initial direct object, if they have one, is advanced to subject. Class 4 differs from both Class 1 and 2 in that it triggers Inversion in all Series.

I can now state my solution to Problem 1 posed at the end of the preceding section.

Generalization 1
In Series II, Class 1 and 3 verbs are those verbs which have an initial subject that is also their final subject.

By referring to networks (10–14), which characterize transitive and intransitive verbs of Classes 1 and 3, we can see that their initial subjects are also their final subjects. Class 2 verbs, on the other hand, either have no initial subject (networks (16–19)), or their initial subject is a final chomeur (passive network (15)). Verbs of Class 4 have an initial subject; but having obligatorily undergone Inversion, their initial subject is not a final subject, but a final indirect object (networks (20–21)). A solution to Problem 2 will be given in the following section.

Most of the derivations discussed here have been justified in detail in earlier chapters. The only new claims presented here are (a) initial termhood governed by basic Class 2 verbs (network (17)), (b) the derivation of the inceptive (networks (18–19)), and (c) the generalizations concerning the nature of each Class. The first two of these new claims are supported by the additional evidence which is presented in §3 and 4. The generalizations made in this section follow logically from all of the derivations which have been individually justified.

2.3 *The Term Case Marking rules of Georgian*

The framework outlined in §2.2 above enables us to make the following generalization, which corresponds to Problem 2 stated above in §1.4:

> *Generalization* 2
> In Series II, verbs with an initial subject that is also final subject govern Case Pattern A; other verbs govern Pattern B.

As shown above, the set of verbs with an initial subject that is also final subject exactly corresponds to the set of Class 1 and 3 verbs. Thus, the distinction between initial intransitive subjects and initial intransitive direct objects, which distinguishes Class 2 from Class 3, enables us to account correctly and succinctly for the facts summarized in (2) above.

Now it is possible to state the term case marking rules of Georgian. The rules for Series I and III are simple and, like those of most languages of the world, are based on final grammatical relations alone:

1 If the verb is in Series I or III,

   a. the final subject is marked with the nominative case.
   b. the final objects are marked with the dative case.

It was shown in earlier chapters, especially chs. 8 and 9, that case marking in Series I and III is based entirely on final grammatical relations. Initial subjects that undergo no change, subjects derived by Passivization, subjects derived by Object Raising, subjects derived by

Unaccusative – all are marked with the nominative case in Series I and III. All final objects – direct or indirect – are marked dative, whether they are initial objects that have undergone no change, were derived by Inversion, were derived by a Version rule, or were derived by Clause Union. Thus, the two parts of Rule I correctly account for the case marking of all term nominals in Series I and III.

For Series II, we must formulate a rule that marks with the 'ergative' case only the subjects of Class 1 and 3 verbs; these are the verbs whose initial subject is also final subject:

II If the verb is in Series II,

a. an initial subject which is also a final subject is marked with the ergative case.

This insures that retired subjects, subjects demoted by Inversion, and subjects whose grammatical relation is changed by Clause Union will not be marked with the 'ergative' case.

The nominative case marks the following nominals in Series II:

initial direct objects that undergo no change in grammatical relation
initial direct objects that advance to subject by Passivization
initial direct objects that advance to subject by Unaccusative
initial direct objects that become the subjects of object-raised constructions
initial direct objects that become the subjects of inceptives (*tetrdeba* and *šemiqvardeba* types)
initial direct objects that become the direct objects of organic causatives
initial subjects that become the direct objects, then the subjects, of inceptives (*aṭirdeba* type)
initial intransitive subjects that become the direct objects of organic causatives.

(Analyses of all the constructions referred to are found in preceding chapters, except inceptives, which are discussed in n. 14 and in Holisky (1980b).) A rule that includes all these nominals will be complex, and might be formulated in several ways; the simplest is

II If the verb is in Series II,

b. a direct object that is a final nuclear term is marked with the nominative case.

IIb correctly marks the nominals listed above and prevents retired direct objects from being marked with the nominative case.

In Series II the dative case marks indirect objects that have undergone no change, as well as indirect objects derived by Version or Inversion:

II If the verb is in Series II,

c. a final indirect object is marked with the dative case.

Unlike rules IIa and IIb, rule IIc need not refer to initial grammatical relations. Yet because of the rule inventory of Georgian, there is no overlap between the rules as stated. These five term case marking rules account for cases for *all* of the constructions of Georgian syntax.

These five rules could be written in a variety of other ways, some of them as succinct as those given here.[16] But the generalizations embodied in them must be preserved by any valid grammar of Georgian.

The five rules stated above do not refer to verb Classes as (1b) does. This means that *with respect to the rules of case marking, it is unnecessary to list Classes for each verb form in the lexicon.* Rather, we can predict case marking on the basis of rules I and II, together with the semantics of the verb. Thus, rules I and II effect an important simplification in the grammar, in terms of not requiring that Class be listed in the lexicon.

2.4 *Residual problems*

While the proposal made in §2.2 makes the correct predictions for the vast majority of verbs in Georgian, there remain a few verbs which it does not correctly account for. Both types of exception exist: semantically active verbs that are in Class 2 and govern Pattern B in Series II, and semantically inactive verbs that are in Class 3 and govern Pattern A in Series II. Three important points must be made about these exceptions: (a) All of them occur in synchronically non-productive morphological subclasses. (b) Some of them cause confusion for native speakers. (c) Some or all of them are regularized in the non-literary dialects.

Holisky (1980a) analyzes the morphological subclasses of Class 3 (medial) verbs, showing the formation process for each, distinguishing productive from non-productive types, and investigating the semantic characteristics of the subjects that are possible for each type. She shows that every Class 3 verb that is an exception to my proposal is in a frozen, non-productive subclass; most of the Class 3 verbs in the frozen subclasses and all those in productive subclasses are active verbs, in the sense of §2.1. Her data are an exhaustive list of the hundreds of Class 3 verbs, which she culled from standard dictionaries and tested with informants. Similarly, the semantically active verbs of Class 2 occur in closed subclasses; these include subclasses J and K (discussed in Appendix B to this chapter) and subclass L (discussed briefly in Harris (to appear b) and Harris 1976). The productive subclasses of Class 2 – inceptives, analytic passives, synthetic passives, object-raised constructions – are, without exception, inactive in the sense of §2.1.

A second important point about these exceptions is that some cause confusion among native speakers. (22) gives two variants for the verb *çvetva* 'drip' an inactive verb formally in Class 3. In the (a) sentence, Pattern A is used, in the (b) sentence, Pattern B.

(22) (a) *macivridan çqalma içveta.*
refrigerator-from water-ERG it-dripped-II-3
'Water dripped from the refrigerator.'
(b) *macivridan çqali içveta.*
water-NOM
'Water dripped from the refrigerator.'

Both Patterns are used for this verb, though (a) is considered more literary and is preferred by prescriptive norms.[17] Case marking, complex as it is in Georgian, does not generally cause any difficulty for the native speaker. The fact that it does cause a problem with this verb confirms its status as an exception, rather than a counterexample. Examples of confusion of case marking with active verbs formally in Class 2 are discussed in more detail in Appendix B.

Finally, although these frozen forms are retained as exceptions in the literary language of the metropolis, many or all of them are regularized in a number of dialects, including Gurian and Imerian (western Georgia), the mountain dialects (north central Georgia), and Pereidnian (Iran).[18] The examples most frequently cited in the literature on these dialects are of the type *ḳacma çavida* 'the man-ERG went' and *ḳacma adga* 'the man-ERG got up', where the subjects are in the ergative, as would be expected for active verbs; in the dialect of Tbilisi, these and several other very common verbs are irregular, taking Pattern B in Series II. It is well known in linguistics that a literary dialect tends to preserve irregularities, particularly with very common words.

3 Inversion and the Georgian verb classes

In earlier chapters it was noted that the Class of the governing verb determines two distinct syntactic phenomena – case marking in Series II and Inversion in Series III. In the preceding section it was shown that the rules of case marking do not need to refer to the notion of 'Class'. Rather, case marking can be predicted on the basis of the initial and final termhood of nominals, which is, in turn, determined by the semantics of the verb. If it were possible also to predict which verbs undergo Inversion in Series III without reference to Classes, then the notion 'Class' would not be needed in the syntax. In this section, I shall show that this is possible.

In ch. 8 it was shown that Inversion applies under two conditions:

(23) Inversion is triggered by
  (a) Class 4 (inversion) verbs
  (b) Series III (evidential) forms.

(23b) must be further restricted by (24).

(24) Class 1 and 3 verbs trigger Inversion,
  Class 2 does not.

Chapter 8, §7 describes five environments in which Inversion does not apply in a clause with some syntactic rule. Whether triggered by Class 4 or Series III forms, Inversion fails to apply to the output of Passivization, Object Raising, or Inversion and Unaccusative. Each of the impossible derivations discussed there involves the application of Inversion to a derived subject. If clauses of the types represented by networks (16–19) of the present chapter are put into Series III, they too fail to undergo Inversion. In each instance, Inversion fails to apply to a non-initial subject, just as was the case with the examples discussed in ch. 8. In fact, Inversion never applies to a non-initial subject; further, every clause to which Inversion fails to apply (if triggered by (23)) contains a non-initial subject. I therefore propose to replace the *ad hoc* statement (24) with

(24′) *The Initial Subject Constraint on Inversion*
  Inversion applies only to initial subjects.[19]

In the framework proposed here, (24′) prevents Inversion from applying to analytic passives (network (15)), synthetic passives (network (16)), basic Class 2 verbs (network (17)), inceptives of both sorts (18–19), basic inversion verbs (20–21), as well as with types G, H, Q, and R, which could not be discussed in detail above. In each of those derivational types, there is, according to my analysis, no initial subject which could undergo Inversion under the conditions imposed by (24′). It is entirely possible that (24′) is a part of the rule of Inversion universally. In the absence of sufficient evidence, I propose it as a language-particular constraint only.

Let us consider in greater detail some specific examples. Suppose that example (17) is in Series III, *is enatmecnieri qopila* 'he is apparently a linguist'. There is an initial direct object, but no initial subject. Inversion cannot apply, because its input conditions are not met (there is no subject). The input conditions for Unaccusative are met, and this rule obligatorily applies, making the direct object the subject. Now the input conditions for Inversion *are* met, since there is a subject. But the Initial Subject Constraint correctly prevents Inversion from applying to this non-initial subject. It remains subject, as shown by the case marking, verb agreement, etc.

Let us take as an example a verb root that occurs in both Class 1 and Class 2 forms. Consider (25) as an initial structure.

(25)

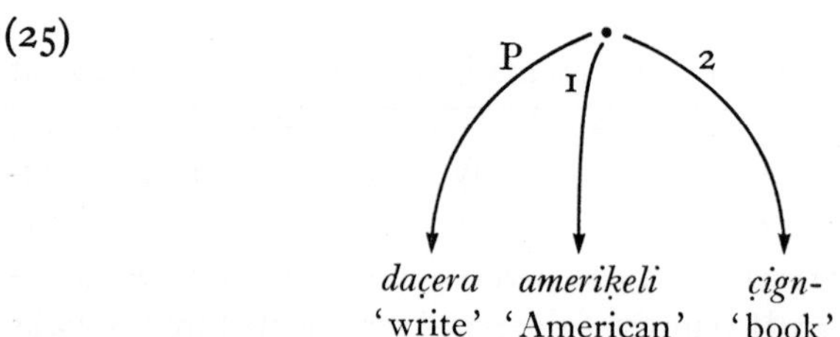

If no rule changes the grammatical relations, *daçera* will be realized as a transitive direct Class 1 verb. Then in Series III it will undergo Inversion as predicted, as well as Unaccusative.

(26)

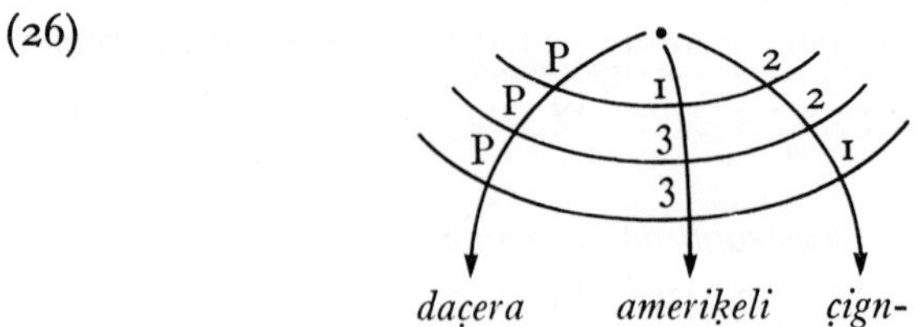

ameriḳels dauçeria es çigni.
American-DAT he-wrote-it-III-1 this book-NOM
'Apparently an American wrote this book.'

If, on the other hand, Passivization applies to (25), *daçera* will be realized as an analytic passive (Class 2 verb). In Series III, it will not be able to undergo Inversion, because this is blocked by the Initial Subject Constraint. The subject which satisfies the input conditions for Inversion (the derived subject) is not an initial subject. The resulting sentence will be (27), exactly as predicted.

(27)

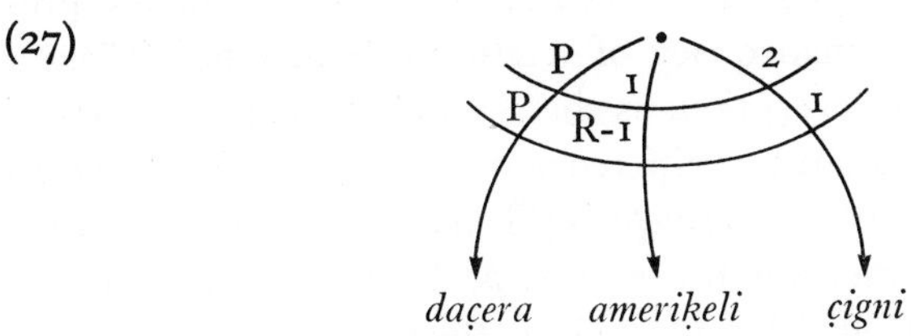

es çigni qopila daçerili amerikelis mier.
this book-NOM it-was-III-2 written American by
'This book was apparently written by an American.'

Thus, on the analysis proposed here for Class 2 verbs (crucially involving the notion of initial intransitive direct objects), the correct predictions are made for Series III by the rules of Inversion, Unaccusative, Passivization, (23) and the Initial Subject Constraint, all of which are independently necessary.

The proposal made in §2 enables us to effect three simplifications in the grammar: (i) the rules of case marking can be stated in a general way, (ii) a general statement can be made of which verbs govern Inversion in the evidential, and (iii) because neither case marking rules nor Inversion need refer to verb Class, the lexicon can be simplified.[20] In addition, the Initial Subject Constraint on Inversion, in the grammar proposed here, *explains* the otherwise arbitrary fact that Class 2 verbs do not undergo Inversion in Series III. These economies and this explanation can be made only with the analysis presented in §2.

4 The semantics of Class

In this section I will discuss two productive pairs of verb forms, where one member of the pair belongs to Class 2 and the other to Class 3. The purpose of this section is to show that in each instance the Unaccusative Hypothesis makes the correct predictions concerning Class membership. Or, differently stated, this hypothesis makes the correct predictions concerning case marking and Inversion. Other productive formations have already been discussed in detail elsewhere, including the analytic and synthetic passives. The two types discussed here particularly stand out because of the fact that in each pair both members are intransitive (finally and initially). This means that the Ergative Hypothesis will make the wrong predictions concerning the case marking and Inversion for one member of each pair. The fact that these formations are productive emphasizes the inadequacy of treating one member (Class 3 form) of each pair as an exception, as the Ergative Hypothesis does.

Holisky (1978) points out the difference between pairs like *tamarma imepa* 'Tamar reigned' and *tamari mepe iqo* 'Tamar was (a/the) monarch'. Both predicates are based on the root *mepe* 'monarch'. The first is deliberate, active, controlled by the subject; the second is stative, non-deliberate, and out of the control of the (final) subject. On the basis of the semantics of the verb, we know that the first takes an initial subject; the second takes an initial direct object, as *qopna* 'be' always does. The final subject of the first is its initial subject, and is correctly marked ergative by rule IIa. The final subject of the second is its initial direct object, and is correctly marked nominative by IIb. Derivations are represented in (28) and (29).

(28)

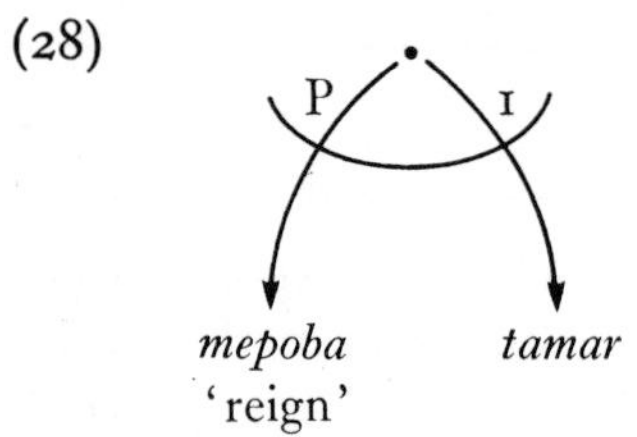

tamarma imepa.
tamar-ERG she-reigned
'Tamar reigned.'

(29)

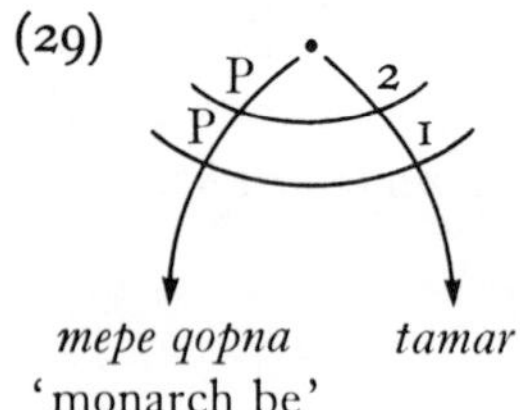

tamari iqo mepe.
tamar-NOM she-was monarch-NOM
'Tamar was the monarch.'

The Unaccusative Hypothesis also makes the correct predictions concerning Inversion in Series III. The Initial Subject Constraint correctly predicts that *tamar* can undergo Inversion in (28), but not in (29). These predictions are borne out in (30).

(30) (a) *tamars umepia.*
Tamar-DAT she-reigned-III-3
'Apparently Tamar reigned.'
(b) *tamari mepe qopila.*
Tamar-NOM monarch-NOM she-was-III-2
'Tamar was apparently the monarch.'
(c) **tamars mepe qopila.*
('Tamar was apparently the monarch.')

The initial subject in (30a), but not the derived subject in (30b), undergoes Inversion.

Thus, the Unaccusative Hypothesis makes the correct predictions concerning the case marking and Inversion of each member of this type of pair, without reference to Class, but rather on the basis of initial grammatical relations, which are predictable on the basis of the semantics of the verb. Since both predicates are intransitive, the Ergative Hypothesis cannot distinguish between them, except by treating them as exceptions and referring to a lexical listing of Class. Without referring to Class, the Ergative Hypothesis would incorrectly predict that both verb types govern nominative case subjects in Series II and fail to undergo Inversion in Series III.

A second productive type is illustrated in (31) and (32). (31) is formally an inceptive; it is inactive, and non-controllable.

(31) (a) *vano aɣiɣinda.*
Vano-NOM he-come-about-croon-II-2
'Vano began to croon/sing in a low voice.'
(b) *čaidani aɣiɣinda.*
teakettle-NOM
'The teakettle began to croon (i.e. whistle).'

The grammaticality of (31b) shows that the final subject of this verb is not semantically a controller, since an inanimate could not control this action. By the same token, (32) shows that the form of the verb illustrated there *is* controllable, since the inanimate subject is not grammatical.

(32) (a) *vanom ç̣aiɣiɣina.*
Vano-ERG he-crooned-II-3
'Vano began to croon.'

(32) (b) **čaidanma*/**čaidani* *ҫaiɣiɣina.*
teakettle-ERG/NOM
('The teakettle began to croon.')

The difference between (31) and (32) cannot be adequately glossed in English.[21] (31) and (32) represent non-controllable and controllable forms of the same verb.

As a semantic patient, the final subject of the verb in (31) must be an initial direct object. As a semantic agent, the final subject of the verb in (32) must be an initial subject. The final subject of (31) is correctly marked nominative by IIb. The final subject of (32) is correctly marked ergative by IIa.

Further, the Initial Subject Constraint correctly predicts that the subject in (32), being an initial subject, will undergo Inversion in Series III, while that in (31) will not. That this is correct is shown in (33), where the Class 3 verb, but not the Class 2 verb, has undergone Inversion, as indicated by case marking and agreement.

(33) (a) *vano* *aɣiɣinebula.*
Vano-NOM he-come-about-croon-III-2
'Vano apparently began to croon.'
(b) **vanos* *aɣiɣinebula.*
Vano-DAT
'Vano apparently began to croon.'
(c) *vanos* *ҫauɣiɣinia*
Vano-DAT he-crooned-III-3
'Vano apparently began to croon.'

The Unaccusative Hypothesis makes the correct predictions in each instance on the basis of initial and final termhood, which is predictable from the semantics of the verb and its dependents. The Ergative Hypothesis is unable to distinguish between these two intransitives without reference to a lexical listing of Class.[22]

Each of these pairs represents two productive derivational types. In each type there is a correlation between the semantics of the final subject and the syntax.

5 Comparison and conclusions

In §5.1 I shall summarize the most important aspects of the two theories considered in detail above. Comparing the grammars required of the two will reveal that the Unaccusative Hypothesis is more general, and therefore superior. In §5.2 I will briefly consider and dismiss the proposal that Georgian rather exhibits a low 'degree of ergativity'.

5.1 *Hypotheses A and B*

5.1.1 *Case Marking. Hypothesis A* (*The Ergative Hypothesis*). According to the Ergative Hypothesis, in Series II the case marking of nominals governed by verbs of Classes 1 and 2 is predictable on the basis of the transitivity of the verb. The grammar must, therefore, include the following rules of case marking.

II If the verb is in Series II.

a′. the subjects of transitive verbs are marked with the ergative case.

II If the verb is in Series II,

b′. the subjects of intransitive verbs and the direct objects of transitive verbs are marked with the nominative case.

In addition, it will include rules Ia and b and rule IIc, all stated above in §2.3. These rules (IIa′, b′) are inaccurate for the regular systematic group of Class 3 verbs, which are mostly intransitive, but do not fit the ergative generalization. For them, we must include another rule,

II If the verb is a Class 3 verb in Series II,

d. the subject is marked with the ergative case and the direct object with the nominative.

Few Class 3 verbs have direct objects, but the last clause must be included for those that do.

Hypothesis B (*The Unaccusative Hypothesis*). According to the proposal introduced here, in Series II, the case marking of nominals governed by verbs of all Classes is predictable on the basis of initial and final termhood. The transitivity of the verb and the secondary grammatical relations, ergative and absolutive, play no part in term case marking. The grammar must include rules I and II (five rules).

Conclusion. When we compare the statements (rules) which must be included in each grammar, we find that Hypothesis B is significantly more general. Hypothesis A is unable to include Class 3 in the generalization that covers the rest of the grammar; this is reflected in the inclusion of rule IId, which is unnecessary in Hypothesis B. There are exceptions to both proposals, including the verbs discussed in Appendix B. But while each has exceptions, Hypothesis B accounts for a significantly larger group of verbs. In this way it gives a general account of term case marking throughout the language.

5.1.2 *Inversion. Hypothesis A.* In Hypothesis A, no attempt is made to *explain* why Inversion fails to apply with Class 2 verbs in Series III. Proponents of the Ergative Hypothesis make statement (23) and add condition (34).

(34) Transitive verbs trigger Inversion; intransitive verbs do not.

Since Class 3 verbs are syntactically intransitive, but do not trigger Inversion, proponents of this theory must add,

(35) Class 3 verbs trigger Inversion,

which is treated as the statement of an irregularity.

Class 4 verbs must also be prevented from undergoing Inversion twice (cf. §3 and ch. 8, §7). But if (34) is interpreted as referring to transitivity at the level of input to the rule, an inversion verb will automatically be prevented from undergoing Inversion twice, since it will be intransitive after the first application of the rule. Hypothesis A therefore requires no additional statement for this purpose.

Hypothesis B. As stated above in §3, Hypothesis B requires rule (23) and the Initial Subject Constraint on Inversion. The latter accounts in a general way for both the fact that Class 2 does not undergo Inversion and the fact that Class 4 verbs do not undergo that process twice in Series III.

Conclusion. Hypothesis B requires fewer rules than Hypothesis A. In addition, Hypothesis B makes a linguistically significant generalization that is not made by A.

5.1.3 *Predictive power. Hypothesis A.* As pointed out in §4, Hypothesis A is unable to predict the difference between the members of the two types of productive pairs considered there: *imepa* 'he reigned'/*mepe iqo* 'he was monarch', and *ç̣aiɣiɣina* 'he deliberately began to croon'/*aɣiɣinda* 'he non-deliberately began to croon'. Since both members of each pair are intransitive, Hypothesis A predicts incorrectly that both members will govern the nominative case subject in Series II and will fail to undergo Inversion in Series III.

Hypothesis B. On the basis of the semantics of the verb, it is predictable on Hypothesis B that the final subject of the first member of each pair will also be its initial subject and will therefore be marked with the ergative case in Series II and undergo Inversion in Series III. Similarly, the semantics of the verb make it clear that the second member of each pair has an initial direct object, which is therefore marked with the nominative case in Series II and fails to undergo Inversion in Series III.

5.1.4 *Reference to Classes. Hypothesis A.* Since rules 11d and (35) refer specifically to Class 3, each verb of this Class must be indicated in the lexicon. In addition, exceptions must be indicated.

Hypothesis B. There are also exceptions to this theory and they must be listed in the lexicon. Class 3 is not referred to as such by any rule, and need not be indicated in the lexicon. Indeed, there is no need to make any special indication of the syntax of regular verbs discussed above.

5.1.5 *Interaction with other rules of grammar.* There is no significant difference between Hypothesis A and B with respect to the formulation of any rule discussed in earlier chapters. The difference between them is irrelevant to most rules of the grammar. Of the rules that have not already been discussed here, only *Tav*-Reflexivization, Number Agreement, and Causative Clause Union refer – directly or indirectly – to *specific initial* termhood. The last of these treats intransitive subjects and transitive and intransitive direct objects in the same way; therefore the new proposal does not practically affect the application of this rule. The reader can confirm that in earlier chapters, when any generalization was based on transitive vs. intransitive verbs, both types of intransitive were taken into consideration.

The Unaccusative Hypothesis does not alter the applicability of the statement of Number Agreement, since the same nominal is the 'first subject that is a final term' on both analyses. Number Agreement in the synthetic passive is discussed in ch. 15, and Number Agreement in other Class 2 verbs operates the same way.

Tav-Reflexivization is the only rule whose formulation could require alteration as a consequence of the analysis proposed here. I have not been able to find examples that would test this rule with Class 2 verbs. Further research could reveal a need to alter the statement of *Tav*-Reflexivization to

The antecedent of *tav-* must be
a. the first subject of a clause of which *tav-* is a dependent, and
b. a final term,

where 'initial subject' has been changed to 'first subject'. This formulation, if found to be correct, would not be more or less complex than that given in ch. 14 (cf. ch. 15, §4), and therefore would not affect the choice between Hypotheses A and B.

5.1.6 *Conclusion.* The grammar required by the Ergative Hypothesis is more complex than that required by the Unaccusative Hypothesis in the treatment of case marking, in the treatment of Inversion, and with respect to lexical listing of Class. Hypothesis A fails to capture the linguistically significant generalizations which are embodied in the approach of Hypothesis B. Hypothesis A is unable to make correct predictions concerning the syntactic behavior of at least two productive derivational types. Hypothesis B must be adopted.

5.2 *Ergativity in Georgian*

Because it is more general, we must prefer the Unaccusative Hypothesis over the Ergative Hypothesis. This means that case marking in Series II is not ergative, but belongs to the type Sapir described as active vs. inactive.

Nevertheless, some might suggest that Georgian is not a non-ergative language, but rather exhibits a low 'degree of ergativity'. In considering the usefulness of this idea in the description of Georgian, there are two points that must be made. First, labeling a language 'ergative' or stating that it has a high or low 'degree of ergativity' is an imprecise description and provides no insight into the nature of the language. A particular *rule* can be ergative, in the sense that it refers to transitive subjects on the one hand, or to direct objects and intransitive subjects on the other (cf. §1.1). Case marking and verb agreement are often cited as ergative rules in this sense, but other rules may also be ergative. The notion 'ergative language', on the other hand, has not been used in a consistent way. It has been used to refer to languages with ergative case marking only (e.g., Udi), languages with ergative verb agreement only (e.g., Abxaz), languages with both ergative case marking and ergative verb agreement (e.g., Avar), and languages with neither ergative case marking nor ergative verb agreement (e.g., Georgian). In order to give an accurate description of a language, it is better to avoid vague labels like 'ergative language' and use notions that can be precisely defined, such as 'ergative rule'.

Second, Georgian has, to the best of my knowledge, only two rules that might be considered ergative. Retired Term Marking is truly ergative; retired ergatives are marked one way (*mier*) and retired absolutives another (genitive case). Causative Clause Union is also ergative, in the sense that it treats ergatives one way, making them matrix indirect objects, and absolutives another way, making them matrix direct objects.[23] Interestingly, this type of causative occurs in languages that apparently have no other ergative rule, such as French, Turkish, and Japanese (cf. ch. 5, §1). As shown above, neither the term case marking rules, nor the agreement rules have anything to do with the secondary grammatical relations ergative and absolutive.[24]

Term case marking in Georgian might be mistaken for a 'partially ergative' rule because of the fact that marking in an active/inactive system differs from that in an ergative system only with respect to initial intransitive subjects. On the other hand, marking in an active/inactive system differs from that in an accusative system only with respect to initial intransitive direct objects.

Series II of Georgian belongs to a case marking type that was recognized at least as early as 1917. Sapir deplored the 'inclusion under one rubric of transitive *versus* intransitive, and active *versus* inactive' (Sapir 1917:85); yet sixty years later, the same fallacy is perpetuated in analyses of Georgian, and it is labeled an 'ergative language'. To maintain that Georgian is ergative or even 'partially ergative' would be to ignore the need for accurate description and to do violence to the integrity of the active/inactive system as a distinct type.

6 Theoretical implications

The Georgian data presented in this and earlier chapters are important for the study of universal aspects of active type rules. These data bring particularly strong evidence to bear on three interrelated questions: (a) What level of derivation is relevant to the active/inactive distinction? (b) Can active type rules be stated directly on semantic notions, rather than on syntactic relations? (c) Why is active distinguished from inactive in intransitive verbs, but not in transitive verbs, in (8)? The evidence from Georgian in each respect is summarized briefly below.

The many rules that change grammatical relations in Georgian make it clear that both initial and final levels of derivation must be taken into account in the following way:

(i) Initial grammatical relations are determined by semantic notions 'agent', 'experiencer', 'patient', etc. (cf. §2.1).
(ii) Syntactic rules may change grammatical relations.
(iii) Case marking in Series I and Inversion in Series III are sensitive to grammatical relations at more than one level (cf. §2.3 and 3).

Case marking in Series II cannot be stated directly on semantic notions, without the intervention of the syntactic relations, as stated above. Although agents in sentences like (10–14) are marked with the ergative case, it is not true that all and only agents are so marked. For example, the initial subject of a passive is a semantic agent but is not marked with the ergative. On the other hand, the subject of (34) below is non-agentive but is marked with the ergative.

Georgian also provides data that show why Sapir did not distinguish active from inactive in transitive verbs. Like intransitives, transitive verbs may be semantically active or inactive. The initial subjects of active transitives are agents, those of inactive transitives are experiencers. If inactive transitives undergo no change in grammatical relations, they will have a final subject and direct object, as in (34).

(34) (a) *kartulma* *dakarga* *'vin' da 'ra' kategoriata...*
Georgian-ERG it-lost-it-II-1 who and what categories-GEN
çarmoeba.
formation-NOM
'Georgian lost the formation of the human and neuter categories.'
(Example from text, Chikobava 1940:16.)

(b)

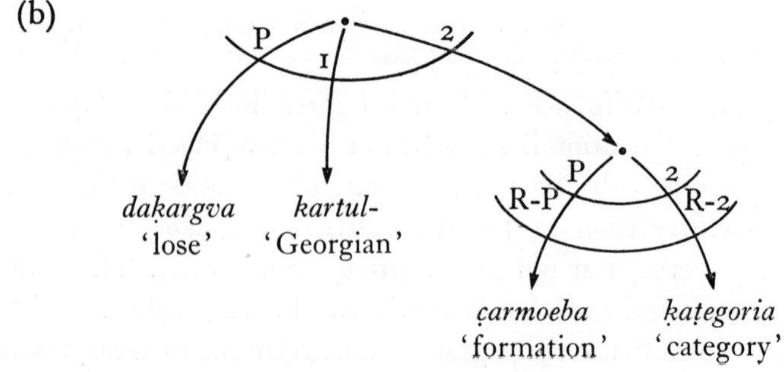

If, on the other hand, Inversion applies to an inactive transitive, it is a final intransitive, as in (35).

(35) (a) *evian* *zmnebs* **v** *eḳargebat. . . .*[25]
having-**v** verbs-DAT **v**-NOM they-lose-it-I-4
'Verbs in **v** lose **v**.'
(Example from text, Shanidze 1973:445.)

(b)

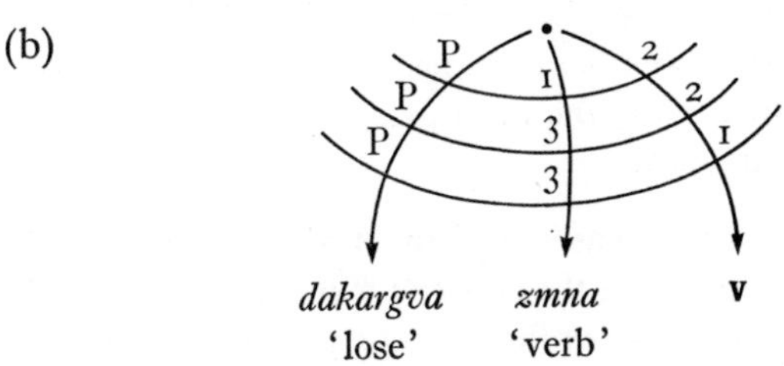

Because case marking and agreement are sensitive to grammatical relations, not to the semantic categories agent and experiencer, the inactive transitive in (34) does not differ in these respects from the active final transitive in (10). Similarly the inactive initial transitive that is a final intransitive in (35) does not differ in any apparent way from other inactive final intransitives discussed in §2.2.3. Thus (8) distinguishes only three types because inactive transitives coincide in the relevant respects with either active transitives or with inactive intransitives.

Appendix A: Sample lists of verb classes

The division of verbs into Classes 1 through 4 corresponds approximately to divisions made by traditional grammarians. However, because different criteria are used, the divisions differ slightly from traditional ones. The justification for this departure from tradition is the high degree of coincidence of morphological, syntactic, and semantic criteria in the system adopted here. Traditional labels are not used here because they are imprecise. For example, Class 1 verbs are traditionally called 'transitive verbs' (cf. §1 above); yet this Class includes some verbs which never take direct objects, such as *daamtknarebs* 'he will yawn'. Therefore a neutral name, 'Class 1', is used here.

Morphological criteria are taken here as the point of departure for defining Classes.[26] Morphologically, each Class can be characterized in the following way:

ASS 1: a. The future/aorist tenses are formed with a preverb.
b. In the future tense, the suffix *-s* marks third person singular subjects, the suffix *-en* third person plural subjects.
c. In the aorist tense, the third person plural subject is marked by the suffix *-es*.

CLASS 2: a. The future/aorist tenses are formed with a preverb or the character vowel *e-*.
b. In the future tense, the suffix *-a* marks third person singular subjects, the suffix *-an* third person plural subjects.
c. In the aorist tense, the third person plural subject is marked by the suffix *-nen*.

CLASS 3: a. The future/aorist tenses are formed with the circumfix *i—(eb)*.
b. In the future tense, the suffix *-s* marks third person singular subjects, the suffix *-en* third person plural subjects.
c. In the aorist tense, the third person plural subject is marked by the suffix *-es*.

CLASS 4: a. The future/aorist tenses are formed with the character vowel *e-*.
b. In the future tense, the suffix *-a* marks third person singular subjects.
c. In the aorist, the third person plural final subject is marked as a singular (cf. ch. 15).

Characteristic (a) sets apart Class 3. Characteristic (b) separates Classes 1 and 3 from 2 and 4. Characteristic (c) separates Classes 1, 3 from 2 and from 4.

For a few irregular verbs, one criterion or another may be inapplicable; in this case, the others will define the Class. For example, the verb *qopna* 'be' forms its future irregularly by root suppletion, so criterion (a) is inapplicable. But according to (b) and (c), this verb is in Class 2;

*ikneb***a** 'he will be'
*ikneb***ian** 'they will be'
*iqv***nen** 'they were'.

Syntactically, we may observe the following correlations (cf. chs. 2 and 8):

d. Verbs which fall into Class 1 or 3 by the above criteria govern Pattern A in Series II.
e. Verbs which fall into Class 1 or 3 by the above criteria trigger Inversion in Series III; verbs which fall into Class 2 by the above criteria do not trigger Inversion in Series III.
f. Verbs which fall into Class 4 by the above criteria trigger Inversion in all Series.[27]

The very few partial exceptions to these syntactic correlations are discussed in Appendix B and §2.4 above.

We may add one further syntactic correlation:

> g. Verbs which fall into Class 1 or 2 according to the above criteria take an initial direct object obligatorily; verbs which fall into Class 3 according to the above criteria take an initial direct object optionally or not at all.

The lists following show that (g), unlike (d–f), is a tendency, not an absolute correlation.

Some of the semantic correlates of Class are discussed in Holisky (1980a).

It must be noted that these are Classes of derivational forms, not of verb roots; a particular root may be represented in more than one derivational type. The root *c̣er*, for example, occurs as a basic Class 1 verb (A) *dac̣ers* 'he will write it', a causative (B) *daac̣erinebs* 'he will cause him to write it', an analytic passive (D) *dac̣erili ikneba* 'it will be written', an *ikna*-passive *dac̣erili ikna* 'it got written', a *Zustandspassiv* (H) *ec̣ereba* 'it will stand written'. The root *cur* 'swim' occurs as a basic Class 1 verb (A) *gacuravs* 'he will swim it', and as a basic Class 3 verb (M) *icuravebs* 'he will swim'. *Ceḳv* 'dance' occurs as a causative (B) *aceḳvebs* 'he will cause him to dance', as an inceptive (F) *aceḳvdeba* 'he will begin to dance', as a basic Class 3 verb (M) *iceḳvebs* 'he will dance', and as a desiderative (Q) *eceḳveba* 'he feels like dancing'. *Tetri* 'white' occurs as a causative (B) *gaatetrebs* 'he will make it white', and as an inceptive (F) *gatetrdeba* 'it will become white'. Each of these forms represents a regular, productive derivational category. Without exception, all causatives (B) belong to Class 1; all synthetic passives (E), analytic passives (D), inceptives (F), *ikna*-passives (G), and *Zustandspassivs* (H) to Class 2; and all desideratives (Q) to Class 4. Class 3 contains all the members of the *-ob* denominals (N) discussed in Holisky (1980a).

The lists are presented here to illustrate the verb types that constitute each Class and to illustrate the verbs which constitute each derivational type referred to in §2.2. The verbs selected are *typical*; they illustrate the *generalizations* made in the text above. At the same time, the lists contain examples of every kind of *exception* to the generalizations, both to the claims of traditional analyses and to the proposals made here.

SAMPLE LIST OF CLASS 1 VERBS

A. *gašlis* 'he will spread it (out)'
gaatbobs 'he will heat, warm it'
gamoacxobs 'he will bake it'
gazrdis 'he will raise him, grow it'

daiçqebs 'he will begin it'
gaxsnis 'he will open it up'
daxuravs 'he will close, shut it (up)'
aantebs 'he will light it, turn it on'
gaadnobs 'he will melt it'
daɣlis 'he will tire him out'
gaxdis 'it will reduce him (in weight)'
čaḳeṭavs 'he will lock it'
daxevs 'he will rip it'
čaʒiravs 'he will sink it'
moxaršavs 'he will cook it'
gaçqveṭs 'he will break it off'
gaašrobs 'he will dry it (off/out)'
modreḳs 'he will bend it'
čaakrobs 'he will put it (light) out'
çarmošobs 'he will engender it'
šobs 'she will bear/bears it'
dabadebs 'she will bear it'

daçers 'he will write it'
dač̣ris 'he will wound him'
garecxavs 'he will wash it'
gadatargmnis 'he will translate it'
daḳargavs 'he will lose it'
dagvis 'he will sweep it (out)'
daxarjavs 'he will spend it, use it up'
datesavs 'he will sow it'
šeḳeravs 'he will sew it'

gacuravs 'he will swim it (e.g., river)'
dausṭvens 'he will whistle it'

miscems 'he will give it to him'
ačukebs 'he will give it to him as a gift'
misçers 'he will write it to him'
arčevs 'he will select, prefer this over that'

daamtknarebs 'he will yawn'
amoaxvelebs 'he will cough'

B. *daaçerinebs* 'he will cause him to write it'
gaašlevinebs 'he will cause him to spread it (out)'

daačrevinebs 'he will cause him to wound him'
gaatbobinebs 'he will cause him to heat, warm it'

miaceminebs 'he will cause him to give it'

acekvebs 'he will cause him to dance'
amɣerebs 'he will cause him to sing'
atamašebs 'he will cause him to play'
varjišebs 'he will train him, cause him to exercise'

amepebs 'he will cause him to reign'
amušavebs 'he will cause him to work'
amecadinebs 'he will teach him, cause him to study'

gaatetrebs 'he will make it white'
gaamravlebs 'he will increase it, cause it to increase'
gaaʒvirebs 'he will make it more expensive'
gaagrʒelebs 'he will make it longer'

SAMPLE LIST OF CLASS 2 VERBS

C. *ikneba* 'he will be'
elodeba 'he will wait for him'
gatqdeba 'it will break'
šeesabameba 'it will correspond to s.t.'
šeesatqviseba 'it will agree with s.t., suit s.t.'
gaipotleba 'it will leaf'
čavardeba 'he will fall'
darčeba 'he will remain'
moxdeba 'it will happen'

D. *gašlili ikneba* 'it will be spread (out)'
gamtbari ikneba 'it will be heated, warmed'
gamomcxvari ikneba 'it will be baked'
gazrdili ikneba 'he will be raised'
daçqebuli ikneba 'it will be begun, started'
gaxsnili ikneba 'it will be opened up'
daxuruli ikneba 'it will be closed, shut (up)'
antebuli ikneba 'it will be lit, turned on'
gamdnari ikneba 'it will be melted'
daɣlili ikneba 'he will be tired out'
gamxdari ikneba 'he will be reduced (in weight)'
čaketili ikneba 'it will be locked'
daxeuli ikneba 'it will be ripped'

čaʒiruli ikneba 'it will be sunk'
moxaršuli ikneba 'it will be cooked'
gaçqveṭili ikneba 'it will will be broken off'
gamšrali ikneba 'it will be dried (off/out)'
modreḳili ikneba 'it will be bent'
čakrobili ikneba 'it will be put out (light)'
çarmošobili ikneba 'it will be engendered'
šobili ikneba 'it will be borne'
dabadebuli ikneba 'it will be borne'

daçerili ikneba 'it will be written'
dačrili ikneba 'he will be wounded'
garecxili ikneba 'it will be washed'
gadatargmnili ikneba 'it will be translated'
daḳarguli ikneba 'it will be lost'
dagvili ikneba 'it will be swept (out)'
daxarjuli ikneba 'it will be spent, used up'

E. *gaišleba* 'it will spread (out)'
gatbeba 'it will heat, warm up'
gamocxveba 'it will bake'
gaizrdeba 'it will grow (up)'
daiçqeba 'it will begin'
gaixsneba 'it will open (up)'
daixureba 'it will close, shut (up)'
ainteba 'it will light up, turn on'
gadneba 'it will melt'
daiγleba 'he will tire out'
gaxdeba 'he will reduce (in weight)'
čaiḳeṭeba 'it will lock'
daixeva 'it will rip'
čaiʒireba 'it will sink'
moixaršeba 'it will cook'
gaiçqviṭeba 'it will break off'
gašreba 'it will dry (out/off)'
moidriḳeba 'it will bend'
čakreba 'it (light) will go out'
çarmoišveba 'it will originate'
išveba 'it will be/is born'
daibadeba 'it will be born'

F. *gatetrdeba* 'it will become white'
gamravldeba 'it will become plentiful/multiply'

gaʒvirdeba 'it will become expensive'
gagrʒeldeba 'it will become long(er)'
gamepdeba 'he will become king'

acekvdeba 'he will begin to dance'
amɣerdeba 'he will begin to sing'
atamašdeba 'he will begin to play'

G. *daçerili ikna* 'it got written'
dačrili ikna 'he got wounded'
šeɣebili ikna 'it got painted'

H. *eçereba* 'it will stand written, be in a state of having been written'
exateba 'it will stand painted, be in a state of having been painted'
usxia 'it will be poured with respect to him, he will have a full glass of wine'

J. *etamašeba* 'he will play with him'
elaparakeba 'he will talk to him'
ečxubeba 'he will fight with him'
estumreba 'he will visit (with) him'

K. *mouqveba* 'he will tell it to him'
šepirdeba 'he will promise it to him'

L. *ikbineba* 'he bites'
ilanʒɣeba 'he abuses, curses'
igineba 'he curses, swears'

SAMPLE LIST OF CLASS 3 VERBS

M. *icekvebs* 'he will dance'
imɣerebs 'he will sing'
itamašebs 'he will play'
ivarjišebs 'he will exercise, train'
ičxubebs 'he will quarrel'
ibrʒvis 'he will fight'
isuntkebs 'he will breathe'
itirebs 'he will cry'
ixitxitebs 'he will giggle'
ikivlebs 'he will scream'
iqvirebs 'he will yell'
ibuzɣunebs 'he will grumble'
ilaparakebs 'he will talk'
isaubrebs 'he will converse'
ilaqbebs 'he will chatter'

iqbedebs 'he will chatter'
isṭvens 'he will whistle'
icinebs 'he will laugh'
ioxrebs 'he will sigh'
iḳvnesebs 'he will groan'
ixvnešebs 'he will moan'
ixvrinebs 'he will snore'
ipruṭunebs 'he will snort'
ibzuvlebs 'he will hum, buzz'
iqiqinebs 'he will croak'
izuzunebs 'he will hum, buzz'
iγuγunebs 'he will coo'
iciguravebs 'he will skate'
icuravebs 'he will swim'
irbens 'he will run'
igorebs 'he will roll'
icocebs 'he will crawl'
isrialebs 'he will slide'
iṭrialebs 'he will turn'
imoʒravebs 'he will move about in one place'
ipikrebs 'he will think'
upasuxebs 'he will answer him'

N. *imepebs* 'he will reign'
imušavebs 'he will work'
imecadinebs 'he will study'
iqaraulebs 'he will guard it'
ibavšvebs 'he will behave childishly'
ibebiavebs 'she will do midwifery'
igmirebs 'he will behave bravely'
iloṭebs 'he will carouse'
imgzavrebs 'he will travel'
imorigevebs 'he will be on duty as a doorman, concierge'
iparisevlebs 'he will flatter, play the hypocrite'
kartvelobs 'he behaves like a Georgian'

O. *iḳašḳašebs* 'it will glisten'
iḳrialebs 'it will shine'
iprialebs 'it will shine'
iduγebs 'it will boil'
içvetebs 'it will drip'
itkrialebs 'it will gush'
ičxrialebs 'it will jingle'

SAMPLE LIST OF CLASS 4 VERBS

P. *uqvars* 'he loves him'
sʒuls 'he hates him'
mosc̣ons 'he likes it'
aviç̣qdeba 'he forgets it'
axsovs 'he remembers it'
esmis 'he hears, understands it'
egemeba 'it tastes . . . to him, he tastes it'
eqnoseba 'it will smell . . . to him, he will smell it'
akvs 'he has it'
hqavs 'he has him'
šeuʒlia 'he can, is able to . . .'
unda 'he wants it, wants to . . .'
sč̣irs 'he needs it, needs to . . .'
uč̣irs 'he finds it difficult'
aklia 'he finds it lacking, necessary'
uḳvirs 'he finds it surprising, it surprises him'
surs 'he wants it, wishes for it'
sṭḳiva 'it hurts him'
uxaria 'he finds it pleasing, he is pleased, happy'
hgonia 'he finds it . . ., it seems . . . to him'
ešinia 'he is afraid of it'
rcxvenia 'he is embarrassed about it, he finds it embarrassing'
enaṭreba 'he misses him'
enaneba 'he regrets it'
hšia 'he is hungry'
sc̣quria 'he is thirsty'
sciva 'he is cold'
scxela 'he is hot'

Q. *eceḳveba* 'he feels like dancing'
emɣereba 'he feels like singing'
eɣvineba 'he feels like having wine'
eʒineba 'he feels sleepy'
esxvapereba 'it appears different to him'

R. *ešinia* 'he is afraid of it'
šurs 'he is shy of it'
esmis 'he understands it'

Appendix B: Ambivalent exceptions

The characteristics of Classes are of three types: morphological, syntactic, and semantic (cf. Appendix A). These three types of characteristics generally fall together, such that if a verb belongs to Class *n* according to morphological criteria, it will have also the syntactic characteristics of Class *n*. This is true of both the regular verbs and the few exceptions to the generalizations stated in §2 to 4 of this chapter. In this appendix, I will deal with three types of ambivalent verbs, giving the properties of their ambivalence and showing that their classification by normative grammarians does not always reflect the properties of the verbs, as they are actually used.

It is not at all typical for verbs in Georgian to be ambivalent about the case Pattern they govern or about undergoing Inversion. The only ambivalent verbs I know of belong to one of the very small non-productive groups discussed here, or to the type discussed briefly in §2.4.

Ambivalent verbs in Georgian have the following properties: (*i*) The Unaccusative Hypothesis predicts that they have the initial and final term inventories characteristic of Class X, but they belong formally (morphologically) to Class Y. (*ii*) Syntactically, they may have the characteristics (case Pattern, Inversion)of *either* Class X or Class Y. The ambivalence on the part of these exceptional verbs seems therefore to reflect on the one hand an adherence to the Class of which they are formally members, and on the other hand the behavior that would be regular for verbs of that semantic/syntactic type, as predicted by my analysis. Not surprisingly, normative grammar classifies them as belonging only to the Class which they fit formally. Three types are discussed below.

1 TRANSITIVE VERBS IN CLASS 2

This type has the following ambivalent properties: (i) My analysis predicts that they would belong to Class 1, since they have an initial subject and direct object, the initial subject being also the final subject. But they have the morphological characteristics of Class 2.[28] (ii) Syntactically, they behave either like Class 1 or Class 2 verbs. This group includes the following verbs: *mouqva* 'he told it to him', *šeeḳitxa* 'he asked him it', *šehṗirda* 'he promised it to him', *šeevedra* 'he begged him for it', and *šeexveca* 'he asked him for it'. An example of this group in Series I is provided in (1).

(1) *mama* *motxrobas uqveba* *ojaxs.*
father-NOM story-DAT he-tells-them-it-I-2 family-DAT
'Father is telling a story to the family.'

We can see that these verbs are transitive through their behavior under various rules. Under Causative Clause Union, for example, the nominals behave as we would predict for an embedded subject, direct object, and indirect object, respectively; that is, the embedded subject is the indirect object of the causative, the embedded direct object the direct object of the causative, and the embedded indirect object is the retired indirect object of the causative (cf. ch. 5):

INITIAL	Matrix 1	Embedded 1	Embedded 2	Embedded 3
CAUSATIVE	1	3	2	Retired 3

(2) illustrates the causative of (1) in Series II. Recall that all organic causatives are in Class 1 and thus govern Pattern A in Series II. (2) shows that in the causative of *qola* 'tell', each of the terms is case marked as expected for a causative according to the chart above.

(2) *ninom mamas moaqola motxroba ojaxisatvis.*
Nino-ERG father-DAT she-caused-tell-him-it-II-1 story-NOM family-for
'Nino got father to tell a story to the family.'

In (2), *motxroba* 'story' is clearly marked as the direct object of the causative, and *mama* 'father' as its indirect object. This confirms that the former is the direct object and the latter the initial subject of the verb *moqola* 'tell'.

A second argument that these verbs have a subject and direct object comes from the conventions of marking retired terms (cf. ch. 11). In masdars and other constructions that have retired terms, retired subjects of transitives are marked with *mier*. Retired direct objects are marked with the genitive case. Masdars of verbs of this group show clearly that the verbs are transitive.

(3) . . . *bečedis šepireba vanos mier* . . .
ring-GEN promising-NOM Vano by
'Vano's promising (of) a ring . . .'

The fact that the nominal *vano* is marked with *mier* in (3) shows that it is the retired subject of a transitive verb. The fact that *bečedi* 'ring' is marked with the genitive in (3) supports the view that it is the retired direct object.

A further argument that these are transitive verbs comes from Passivization. In ch. 7 it was shown that Passivization is a rule that promotes a direct object to subject. The fact that *moqola* 'tell' can undergo Passivization supports the view that it has a direct object initially and is a transitive verb. The passive of *qola* is illustrated in (4).

(4) *motxroba iqo moqolili myelvarebit.*
story-NOM it-was-II-2 told excitement-INST
'The story was told with excitement.'

[illegible] the verbs of this group can passivize, however. For example, there [illegible] Georgian sentence corresponding to '?Water was begged for'.[29]

Thus, causatives, masdars, and passives provide evidence that these verbs are transitive. My analysis predicts that their initial subject would undergo Inversion in Series III, and that in Series II the initial subject, being final subject, would be marked ergative. Yet these verbs unexpectedly have the morphology of Class 2. Sentences (5) and (6) show that *uqveba* 'he tells it to him' may have the syntactic characteristics of either Class 1 or 2.

(5) Class 1

(a) *mamam ojaxs motxroba mouqva.*
father-ERG family-DAT story-NOM he-told-them-it-II
'Father told the story to the family.'

(b) *turme bičs saxeli (še)ukitxia gogostvis.*
apparently boy-DAT name-NOM he-asked-it-III girl-for
'Apparently the boy (has) asked the girl her name.'

(6) Class 2

(a) *mama ojaxs motxrobas mouqva.*
father-NOM story-DAT
'Father told the story to the family.'

(b) *turme biči saxels šekitxia gogos.*
boy-NOM name-DAT he-asked-her-it-III girl-DAT
'Apparently the boy (has) asked the girl her name.'

In (5a) Pattern A is used, and in (6a) Pattern B. In (5b) the verb has undergone Inversion, in (6b) it has not. The difference in the verb forms in (5–6b) corresponds to the different morphology required for verbs that have undergone Inversion and verbs that have not.

I have shown that the verbs of this group are ambivalent in the following way: (i) On semantic grounds, they should belong to Class 1, but they have the morphological characteristics of Class 2. (ii) Syntactically, they may behave like Class 1 or 2 verbs ambivalently.

2 ACTIVE INTRANSITIVES IN CLASS 2

These verbs are ambivalent in the following way: (*i*) my analysis predicts that they all have an initial subject, some an optional initial direct object; that is, they are Class 3 verbs. Morphologically, they have some characteristics of Class 2 and some of Class 3. (*ii*) With respect to case marking in Series II, these verbs may have the characteristics of Class 2 or 3, under circumstances that are specified below. With respect to Inversion, they are strictly Class 3 verbs. Verbs of this group include *elaparakeba* 'he is talking to him', *etamašeba* 'he is playing with him', *esṭumreba* 'he is visiting him', *esaubreba* 'he is conversing with him', and others.

Each of the verbs in this group corresponds to a regular Class 3 verb:

(7) Class 3: *ob* form	Class 2 ?: *e—ebi* form
laparaḳobs 'he is talking'	*elaparaḳeba* 'he is talking to him'
tamašobs 'he is playing'	*etamašeba* 'he is playing with him'
sṭumrobs 'he is visiting'	*esṭumreba* 'he is visiting him'
saubrobs 'he is conversing'	*esaubreba* 'he is conversing with him'

Those verbs which, like *tamašobs*, take an optional initial direct object in the *ob* form (cf. ch. 12), may also take an optional initial direct object in the *e—ebi* form. The *e—ebi* type differs from its *ob* counterpart only in that the former, but not the latter, have an indirect object.[30] Based on the semantics of the verb, we would posit four possible inventories of final relations:

(8)

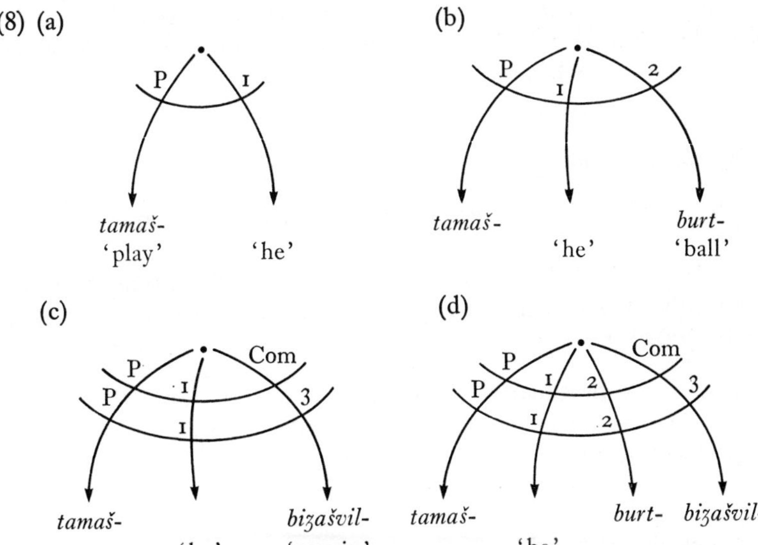

Based on the semantics of the verb, we would predict that each of the above types represents a Class 3 verb. However, the first two examples are expressed by *ob* forms, and the last two by *e—ebi* forms. It is not clear why the difference between having or not having a final indirect object should mean a difference in Class, especially as it does not elsewhere in the grammar (cf. ch. 6).

Although normative grammars indicate that *e—ebi* forms belong to Class 2, that does not tell the whole story. Let us consider each of the morphological characteristics of Class listed in Appendix A, with reference to these verb e first (a) is not applicable, since these forms have no future distinct neir present and form their aorists differently from any of the types sted in Appendix A. According to characteristic (b), these verbs are strictly in Class 2, since they use *-a*/*-an* as the third person markers in the future (=present):

(9) (a) *elaparaḳeba*
(b) **elaparaḳebs* } 'he will talk to him'

With respect to criterion (c), on the other hand, my informants accepted *-es* (typical of Class 3) or *-nen* (typical of Class 2) equally:

(10) (a) *elaparaḳes*
(b) *elaparaḳnen* } 'they talked to him'.

In addition to the morphological characteristics listed in Appendix A, the use of the morpheme *-od-* or *-d-* distinguishes roughly between Class 2 and 3 respectively (cf. n. 26). While the *ob* forms cited above use *-d-*, the *e—ebi* forms use only *-od-*, which is characteristic of Class 2:

(11) (a) **velaparaḳebdi*
(b) *velaparaḳebodi* } 'I was talking'.

Thus, the morphological characteristics are ambivalent, but mostly indicate membership in Class 2.

Syntactically, the balance swings the other way. With respect to case marking, either a nominative or ergative subject is possible in Series II, as shown by (12).[31]

(12) (a) *masçavlebeli dianas esaubra kartulad.*
teacher-NOM Dianne-DAT he-conversed-her-II-2 Georgian-ADV
'The teacher conversed with Dianne in Georgian.'
(b) *masçavlebelma dianas esaubra kartulad.*
teacher-ERG
'The teacher conversed with Dianne in Georgian.'

For some speakers, the ergative is used as subject case only when there is a direct object, and the nominative only when there is not:

(13) (a) *gela melaparaḳa.*
Gela-NOM he-talked-me-II-2
'Gela talked to me.'
(b) **gela melaparaḳa bevrs/bevri.*
lot-DAT/NOM
('Gela talked a lot to me.')

(14) (a) **gelam* *melaparaḳa.*
Gela-ERG
('Gela talked to me.')
(b) *gelam melaparaka bevri.*
'Gela talked to me a lot.'

In (13) the subject, *gela*, is in the nominative in Series II; in (14) it is in the ergative. In the (a) sentences, there is no direct object; in the (b) sentences *bevr-* 'a lot, much' occurs, which has the characteristics of a direct object in Georgian. To summarize, there are at least three types of speakers: (i) ones for whom the *e—ebi* forms may have their subject either in the nominative or ergative in Series II, regardless of the presence of a direct object, (ii) speakers who use the ergative with *e—ebi* forms when there is a direct object and the nominative when there is not, (iii) speakers who follow the literary norm in using only the nominative case for the subject of *e—ebi* forms in Series II.

With respect to Inversion, the *e—ebi* forms behave strictly like Class 3 verbs, as shown in (15). In (15a) Inversion has applied, in (*15b) it has not.

(15) (a) *gelas* *ulaparaḳia* *iastan.*
Gela-DAT he-talked-III-3 Ia-with
'Gela talked with Ia.'
(b) **gela* *laparaḳebula/slaparaḳebia ias.*[32]
Gela-NOM he-talked-her-III-2 Ia-DAT
('Gela talked with Ia.')

Thus, syntactically, the *e—ebi* forms show more characteristics of Class 3 than of Class 2.

To summarize, this group of verbs is ambivalent both morphologically and syntactically, showing some characteristics of Class 2 and some of Class 3. My theory predicts that they belong to Class 3. I have no explanation for their Class-2-like behavior.

3 ARSEBOBS

The verb *arsebobs* 'it exists' is ambivalent in the following way: (i) On the basis of the semantics of the verb, my theory predicts that it belongs to Class 2. Morphologically, it is a member of Class 3. (ii) Syntactically, it behaves like a verb of Class 2 or 3 ambivalently, under circumstances that are stated below. Not surprisingly, normative grammars classify it, according to its morphology, in Class 3 only.

(16) shows that *arseboba* 'exist' may trigger Inversion only if a location is stated. Triggering Inversion is a characteristic of Class 3 verbs, not of Class 2 verbs.

devebs *ar* *uarsebniat.*
devis-DAT not they-exist-III-?
('Devis do not exist.')
(b) *devebs ar uarsebniat betaniaši.*
Betania-in
'There are no devis in Betania.'

(Devis are mythological creatures; Betania is a wood near Tbilisi.) In both sentences of (16), Inversion has applied. This shows that in (16b), the verb has the characteristics of a Class 3 verb, but not in (*16a). (17) is the grammatical counterpart of (*16a); here Inversion has not applied. This shows that here the verb has the syntactic characteristics of a Class 2 verb.

(17) *devebi* *ar arsebulan.*[33]
devis-NOM they-exist-III-2
'Devis do not exist (in general).'

In a general statement of existence, beyond the control of the final subject, *arseboba* behaves like a Class 2 verb. On the other hand, in a statement of location, where the subject is in control (of its own location), *arseboba* is used as a Class 3 verb, with the syntactic characteristic of that Class.

4 SUMMARY AND CONCLUSIONS

The purpose of this appendix has been to show that the strict classifications of normative grammars and dictionaries do not always reflect the true use of the verbs in the speech of present-day dwellers of Tbilisi. In each of the examples cited above, my theory predicts that a particular verb belongs to one Class, and normative grammars classify it as belonging to another Class. The truth in each instance is somewhere in between.

Epilogue

In this epilogue, I will try to draw together related results that have been discussed in separate chapters. In addition, I will give very brief summaries of the most important conclusions reported here.

1 The grammatical relations 'subject', 'direct object' and 'indirect object'

Some linguists have expressed doubts that these notions play a role in the syntax of a language like Georgian, where the apparent subject may be marked with any one of three cases and may trigger either of two sets of agreement markers. I have shown that a large number of rules refer to these syntactic notions, regardless of the case of the nominal. In particular, the rules of *Tav*-Reflexivization, Subject Person Agreement, Causative Clause Union, Inversion, Retired Term Marking, and Number Agreement refer crucially to the grammatical relation subject. The rules of Direct Object Person Agreement, Object Camouflage, Object Raising, Causative Clause Union, Passivization, Retired Term Marking, and Unaccusative are among the rules that refer to the grammatical relation direct object. And the rules of Indirect Object Person Agreement, Object Camouflage, Causative Clause Union, the several Version rules, and Retired Term Marking refer to the grammatical relation indirect object. For Georgian, none of these rules can be stated in a simple way on the basis of case marking or linear order.

2 Simplifications in case marking

In the Introduction and early chapters of this work, it was shown that case marking appears to be very complex in Georgian. Three Patterns were identified,

	Subject	Direct Object	Indirect Object
Pattern A	ERGATIVE	NOMINATIVE	DATIVE
B	NOMINATIVE	DATIVE	DATIVE
C	DATIVE	NOMINATIVE	*tvis*

and their distribution was stated in terms of Series of tense-aspect categories and Classes of finite verb forms:

(2)

	Series I	II	III
Class 1	B	A	C
2	B	B	B
3	B	A	C
4	C	C	C

In chs. 8 and 16 it is shown that significant simplifications can be effected with two rules, Inversion and Unaccusative, whose inclusion in the grammar is independently justified. It has been shown that Inversion applies in Series III with Class 1 and 3 verbs and with Class 4 verbs in all Series. This rule changes grammatical relations such that Pattern B accounts for marking on final termhood in the inversion construction. This permits the simplification (1′–2′).

(1′)

	Initial Subject	*Initial Direct Object*	*Initial Indirect Object*
Pattern A	ERGATIVE	NOMINATIVE	DATIVE
B	NOMINATIVE	DATIVE	DATIVE

(2′)

	Series I	II	III
Class 1 & 3	B	A	B
2 & 4	B	B	B

The second simplification is effected by recognizing initial structures with intransitive direct objects (direct objects not accompanied by subjects) which advance to subjecthood. This permits (1′–2′) to be simplified in two areas. First, the notion 'Class' need not be referred to by the grammar. Second, the rules for term case marking can be stated simply as

1 If the verb is in Series I or III,

a. the final subject is marked with the nominative case.
b. the final objects are marked with the dative case.

II If the verb is in Series II,

a. an initial subject which is also a final subject is marked with the ergative case.

b. a direct object which is a final nuclear term is marked with the nominative case.

c. a final indirect object is marked with the dative case.

At the same time, these rules show that the term case marking rules in Georgian are not ergative, in the generally accepted meaning of that notion.

3 Retired Term Marking

A retired term_i is a nominal which bears the *i*-relation as its last term relation, and which is a final non-term. At least six constructions in Georgian involve retired terms: object-raised clauses, organic causatives, passives, inversion clauses, masdars, and infinitives of purpose. In ch. 11 it is shown that all of the retired relations involved in these disparate constructions can be accounted for with three simple rules:

I. A retired absolutive (=direct object or intransitive subject) is marked with the genitive case.

II. A retired ergative (=transitive subject) is marked with the postposition *mier*.

III. A retired indirect object is marked with the postposition *tvis*.

4 Rule interaction

In the investigation reported here, I have not assumed conventional extrinsic rule ordering. Rather, I have attempted to make the *minimum* specification of rule interaction that would allow all grammatical sentences while blocking all ungrammatical ones. In addition, I have not assumed any rule interaction that has been shown to exist in other languages, but have tried to state only what is supported by the data from Georgian. The statements of rule interaction can be made most simply on the basis of initial, final, and first termhood. This leads to the typology below.

Types in Georgian

I. Rules stated on initial termhood.

II. Unrestricted rules.

III. Rules stated on final termhood.

IV. Rules referring to termhood at more than one level (global rules).

Rules of the first type include the various rules of suppletion (introduced in §4.3 of the Introduction and shown in later chapters to be stated on initial termhood). Type II includes Object Raising, Version, Unaccusative, etc.; these may apply whenever their input conditions are met.

Type III includes the three rules of Person Agreement, some of the rules of term case marking (cf. above, §2), Unemphatic Pronoun Drop, and Question Formation. These rules apply to the output of rules that change grammatical relations.

Rules of the last type include *Tav*-Reflexivization, Number Agreement, and two of the rules of term case marking (IIa and IIb). The first of these refers to initial subjects that are final terms, the second to first subjects that are final terms. The third includes a rule referring to initial subjects that are final subjects and a rule referring to direct objects that are final terms.

There is one rule that does not fit neatly into this typology. Object Camouflage applies to the output of rules that change grammatical relations; these rules must not apply to its output. But the rules of Person Agreement and Unemphatic Pronoun Drop apply to the output of Object Camouflage.

Evidence to support the conclusions stated here is given above in various chapters.

5 Characteristics of grammatical relations

The investigation reported here takes into account a large body of facts and shows the systematicity and consistency in apparently disparate rules. The data assembled here do not support the notion of a 'squish' of grammatical relations (cf. Keenan (1976) and Johnson (1977) for two sides of this problem). The system analyzed here supports instead the idea of a distinction between levels of derivation (or initial and final termhood) and rules which take these into account, in something like the manner summarized in §4. Taken as a whole, the system worked out here shows that nominals in a particular syntactic construction do not arbitrarily partake of some characteristics of one grammatical relation and other random characteristics of another grammatical relation. For example, an inversion nominal does not merely have some properties of a subject and other properties of an indirect object. Rather, on the basis of facts like those summarized in the preceding section, it is absolutely predictable which subject and which indirect object characteristics a nominal will have.

Notes

Introduction

1 A problem with Chikobava's and Aronson's analysis is noted in ch. 15, n. 11.
2 Johnson (1977) discusses the difficulties of arbitrarily selecting criteria which would define the notion 'subject'.
3 Some traditional works do recognize levels of derivation to a certain extent. They distinguish, for example, between 'real subject' and 'grammatical subject' or 'morphological subject'. One example of this is Chikobava (1968: especially 136ff).
4 Class 1 corresponds to the traditional group of *gardamavali* or *akṭiuri zmnebi*. Class 2 corresponds to the group traditionally called *vnebiti, gardauvali,* and some of those called *mediopasiuri*. Class 3 contains most of the verbs traditionally called *sašualo zmnebi*. Class 4 is usually called *inversiuli zmnebi*. The problems associated with the traditional terminology are discussed in detail in chs. 12 and 16 and in Harris (to appear b).
5 Diachronically cliticization played a much more extensive role in the derivation of finite verb forms.
6 The word *unda* 'should, would, might, must' when it occurs with the optative also must intervene in this order: Q-word, NEG, *unda*, VERB. It is not clear whether *unda* is synchronically a verb (auxiliary or modal) or a particle in this use.
7 'Emphatic *-a*' is added to personal pronouns in sentence-final position, as in *šen-a*, and under certain other circumstances.
8 Both (*16b) and (*16c) can have a grammatical reading. Each requires a heavy pause to separate *çigni* from the rest of the sentence, and is equivalent to left- and right-dislocation in English, in that the isolated element represents a fore- or afterthought with respect to the sentence as a whole.
9 Relative clauses are an exception to this generalization. When the head of a relative clause is questioned, the relative clause is necessarily separated from its head, as shown in

vis icnob, vinc mušaobs biblioteḳaši?
who you-know who-REL works library-in
'Who do you know that works in a library?'
**vis, vinc mušaobs biblioteḳaši, icnob?*
**vinc mušaobs biblioteḳaši, vis icnob?*

10 It might alternatively be proposed that the suppletion described in §4.3.1 and 4.3.2 is conditioned by the animacy/number of the semantic patient, rather than that of the direct object. These positions are not distinct, however, since in chs. 4, 5, 7, and 8 it is established that it is the initial direct object that governs suppletion, and in ch. 16 it is shown that all semantic patients are initial direct objects.

11 Although prescriptive norms call for the use of *jdoma* only with singular subjects, in fact it is used with both singulars and plurals. *Sxdoma*, however, is used only with plurals, as my examples show. Cf. Shanidze (1973:501–2); Tschenkéli (1958: 286–7); Tschenkéli (1960–73).

Chapter 1

1 The dialect described here and referred to throughout this monograph is the more restrictive of two dialects I identified with respect to *Tav*-Reflexivization. Both are described in Harris (ms.).

2 These same forms occur as emphatic pronouns and as camouflaged objects (cf. ch. 3 for a complete treatment of the latter).

3 For some speakers, the form *arçmunebs* is preferred here. The meaning and grammatical relations are the same as in (1a).

4 The sentences below show that it is really the subject that is triggering *Tav*-Reflexivization, and not the nominal with which the speaker empathizes (cf. Kuno 1975; and Kuno & Kaburaki 1977).

(i) *gelas ʒma elaparaḳa mas tavis tavze.*
Gela-GEN brother-NOM he-talked-him-II-2 him-DAT self's self-on
'Gela's$_j$ brother$_i$ talked to him$_j$ about himself$_i$.'

(ii) *aḳamde aravin ar elaparaḳeboda ninos tavis tavze.*
until-now no one-NOM not he-talked-her-I-2 Nino-DAT self's self-on
'So far, no one$_i$ has talked to Nino$_j$ about himself$_i$.'

If empathy, rather than subjecthood, controlled *Tav*-Reflexivization, *tav*- should refer to *gela* in (i), since the double occurrence of this nominal in this way has established the speaker's empathy with *gela*, not with *gelas ʒmas* 'Gela's brother'. Similarly, in (ii) the speaker would not empathize with *aravin* 'no one'; yet this triggers *tav*-.

5 See Vogt (1972) for a discussion of this phenomenon in Old Georgian.

6 For many speakers, there is an additional constraint that *tavis*- cannot occur in the subject. For these speakers, both (iii) and (iv) are impossible.

(iii) **švils bans tavisi deda.*
child-DAT she-bathes-him-I-1 self's mother-NOM
('His$_i$ mother$_j$ bathes the child$_i$.')

(iv) **tavisi deda bans švils.*

Some speakers have additional constraints on this rule.

Tavis- may precede its antecedent (cf. (29–30) of ch. 8 of Harris 1976), just as *tav*- may (cf. example (3a–c)). It is more natural for the reflexive to follow its antecedent.

7 The rules of Person Agreement must introduce, not specific morphemes, but abstract elements: first person subject, second person subject, etc. Rules that specify the precise form of subject markers must be sensitive to grammatical relations, person, number, tense-aspect, Class, and morphological sub-group of the verb. A detailed proposal for agreement rules that make direct reference to abstract features of this type is given in Hale (1973).

8 The *t* of the third person plural indirect object marker is usually not triggered (cf. ch. 15); it is stated here on the basis of examples like (15a) of ch. 15.

9 The morpheme *t* (plurality marker) deletes under conditions that are specified in ch. 15.

. take a derived indirect object, as shown in ch. 6. This indirect object rrom that used with *miçera/moçera* in meaning and in the morphology it quires in the verb form.

The notion of dropped unemphatic pronouns is similar to Vogt's 'catalysts' (Vogt 1971) and to the practice common among Georgianists of listing term pronouns after verbs, e.g. *çers is mas mas* 'writes he-NOM he-DAT he-DAT'.

12 (*27b) would not be ungrammatical in those dialects where the third person indirect object marker is always zero.

13 (*38b) has a grammatical reading in English, where *and* is a clausal conjunction; the Georgian example has no grammatical reading.

14 Unemphatic dropped pronouns are distinct from *unspecified* nominals. The former are used when speaker and hearer know the identity of the referent of the nominal. The latter occur when either the speaker or hearer or both do not know the identity of the nominal. They occur in sentences like (v).

(v) *amboben, rom sakartvelo lamazia.*
they-say-it-I-1 that Georgia-NOM pretty-it-is-I-2
'They say that Georgia is pretty.'

Like its English counterpart, (v) may in context mean either that some particular people (referent identified) say this, or that in general it is said (referent not identified). In the latter case the nominal is unspecified; in the former, it is an unemphatic anaphoric pronoun.

Chapter 3

1 Sentences of this type in Series I are disambiguated by word order.

2 The (a) example, which is in Series I, is grammatical in the interpretation where *givi* is direct object. This is because, as we have seen in chs. 1 and 2, the two objects are both marked with the dative in Series I. The (b) example, on the other hand, has no grammatical reading. The (b) example is in Series II, where the direct and indirect object are case marked differently.

3 If *šedareba* 'compare' occurs in a clause in which the indirect object is not realized on the surface, the clause is interpreted as having had its initial indirect object dropped by Unemphatic Pronoun Drop. This is shown by the fact that (*i) without Object Camouflage is ungrammatical; while (ii), where Object Camouflage has applied, is grammatical.

(i) **vano (me) gadarebs.*
Vano-NOM I-DAT he-compares-you-him-I-1
('Vano is comparing me to you.')

(ii) *vano čems tavs gadarebs.*
my self-DAT
'Vano is comparing me to you.'

In (i–ii) the dropped indirect object triggers Object Camouflage obligatorily. This constitutes additional evidence for a rule of Unemphatic Pronoun Drop, since without such a rule the ungrammaticality of (*i) would be unexplained.

4 The person of the indirect object does not affect the rule in the dialect reported here. In (2–3) and (5–6), the indirect object is third person; in (iii) below, it is first person, and in (iv) second.

(iii) (a) **vanom* (*šen*) *šemadara* (*me*).
you-NOM he-compared-**me**-him-II-1 me-DAT
('Vano compared you to me.')
(b) *vanom šeni tavi šemadara* (*me*).
'Vano compared you to me.'
(iv) (a) **vanom* (*me*) *šegadara* (*šen*).
me-NOM he-compared-**you**-him-II-1 you-DAT
(b) *vanom čemi tavi šegadara* (*šen*).
'Vano compared me to you.'

(1) shows that this rule does not apply to third person direct objects with a third person indirect object. (v), which differs from (1b) only in the person of the indirect object, shows that the third person direct object is unaffected, regardless of the person of the indirect object.
(v) *vanom anzori šegadara* (*šen*).
'Vano compared Anzor to you.'

There exists another dialect in which Object Camouflage applies only if the clause contains an indirect object of the first or second person. That dialect is described in Boeder (1968: §1.6) and in Harris (1976: Appendix to ch. 3). I found that dialect only among speakers not native to Tbilisi.

5 The phrase *tavisi tavi* 'self's self' occurs, but only as a reflexive (cf. ch. 1, §1). Therefore,

vanom *tavisi tavi* *šemadara* (*me*).
Vano-ERG self's self-NOM he-compared-me-him-II-1 I-DAT

means, not 'Vano$_i$ compared him$_j$ to me', but 'Vano compared himself to me'.

6 'Personal pronouns' must here be understood to include *es*, *igi*, and *is*, which also function as demonstrative pronouns.

Chapter 4

1 I found one older speaker who did not have Object Raising at all. All of my younger informants did have the rule, though object-raised constructions do not occur frequently.

2 I have glossed the masdars with English *-ing* forms; this is not intended as a claim that the two are the same syntactically.

3 A refinement of this analysis is made in ch. 16.

4 See Introduction, §4.1 on *Aris*-Cliticization. An optional form of (11) has *aris* cliticized to *ra-*

raa ʒneli mosaʒebnad?

5 While (11) is related to (4b), (i) is related to (4a).

(i) *risi* *moʒebna* *aris* *ʒneli?*
what-GEN finding-NOM it-it-I-2 hard
'What is the finding of hard?'

The genitive in (i) cannot occur with the infinitive, as predicted by the analysis in §2:

(ii) **ris*(*i*) *mosaʒebnad aris ʒneli?*
what-GEN to-find
('What is it hard to find?')

blish that predicate nominals are marked with the nominative case in I–III, respectively.

(iii) *ekimia.*
doctor-NOM-he-is-I-2
'He is a doctor.'

(iv) *ekimi iqo.*
he-was-II-2
'He was a doctor.'

(v) *ekimi qopila.*
he-was-III-2
'He must have been a doctor.'

Chapter 5

1 The morphology of organic causatives is further described in Getsadze *et al.* (1969); Schmidt (1966); Shanidze (1973: §423); Taqaishvili (1974); Tschenkéli (1958: vol. 1, ch. 30); and Vogt (1971: §2.70–2.73).

2 (3) is an oversimplification in that it states the effect of Clause Union only on causative constructions. A more general formulation would encompass other instances of Clause Union as well. See Aissen & Perlmutter (1976), Frantz (1976), and page 241 for examples of Clause Union in constructions other than the causative.

3 The argument given here is of the same structure as that given for Japanese in Kuno (1973) and McCawley (1972).

4 The following sentence shows that a nominal that is an initial, but not final, subject can be the target of *Tav*-Reflexivization:

(i) *vanom alaparaka tavisi tavi sxvaze.*
Vano-ERG he-caused-talk-him-II-1 self's self-NOM other-on.
'Vano made himself talk about someone else.'

5 The fact that Object Camouflage applies to the output of all rules that change grammatical relations correctly predicts that this rule and Object Raising cannot apply in a derivation. (ii) bears out this prediction.

(ii) **šeni tavi ʒnelia givistan šesadareblad.*
your self-NOM hard-he-is-I-2 Givi-with to-compare
('You are difficult to compare with Givi.')

(iii) (*šen*) *ʒneli xar givistan šesadareblad.*
you-NOM hard you-SG-are-I-2
'You are difficult to compare with Givi.'

After Object Raising applies, there is no direct object; the input conditions for Object Camouflage are therefore not met, and the rule cannot apply.

6 That Causative Clause Union can apply interatively is shown by (iv), which is the causative of the causative sentence (11).

(iv) *bebia mamas açveninebs gelas*
grandmother-NOM father-DAT she-causes-cause-lie-him-him-I-1 Gela-DAT
ṭaxṭze.
couch-on
'The grandmother makes the father let Gela lie on the couch.'

But speakers dislike a double causative if it creates a retired term; this happens, of course, if the lowest clause of the would-be double causative has two or more terms. For this reason, (v b), the causative of (v a), is unacceptable.

(v) (a) *vanom daaçerina mdivans çerili.*
Vano-ERG he-caused-write-him-it-II-1 secretary-DAT letter-NOM
'Vano had the secretary write a letter.'

(b) **uprosma vanos* { *daaçerinebina* / *daaçerina* } *çerili*
boss-ERG Vano-DAT he-caused-cause-write-him-it-II-1 letter-NOM
mdivnis mier/tvis.
secretary by for
('The boss made Vano have the secretary write a letter.')

The double causative form *daaçerinebina* is said to exist 'in principle', but informants will not use it in a sentence that contains all case-marked nominals (cf. Shanidze 1973; and Vogt 1971: §2.79).

7 This example is quoted in Vogt (1971: §2.75), from Chikobava (1950).

8 Some speakers do not accept these forms as double causatives at all. For such speakers, *šemaçmevina* means 'he fed it to me'; that is, it is a single causative. Those speakers I interviewed who did accept this form as a double causative considered it ambiguously a single causative. (See also n. 6.)

9 The comparison of (vi) with (35) shows that this nominal does not trigger Person Agreement or Number Agreement.

(vi) *dedam tkven papa šemaçmevina.*
mother-ERG you(PL)-DAT gruel-NOM she-caused-feed-me-it-II-1
'The mother made me feed gruel to you(PL).'

The fact that changing the initial embedded indirect object to second person plural causes no change in the verb shows that this nominal fails to trigger both agreement rules. It can also be seen in Shanidze's and Vogt's additional examples that in other dialects this nominal fails to trigger the agreement rules.
If *tkven* 'you(PL)' is omitted from (vi), the meaning is changed:

(vii) *dedam papa šemaçmevina.*
'The mother fed me gruel.' (Cf. n. 8.)

This shows that the nominal cannot undergo Unemphatic Pronoun Drop.

10 In Old Georgian, retired indirect objects in all constructions were regularly marked with the dative, as in these idioms (Harris 1979). See ch. 11 for marking of retired indirect objects in Modern Georgian.

Chapter 6

1 There is confusion in the traditional terminology. I use the word *version* only with reference to rules that create indirect objects. The marker that they trigger in the verb I call 'version vowel' or 'version marker'. It is important to distinguish this from other uses of the so-called 'character vowel', or vowel prefix which occurs immediately before the verb root. Character vowels are used as (a) markers of version, (b) parts of the productive markers of synthetic passives, such as *icvleba* 'it changes' (cf. ch. 13), (c) parts of the markers of certain tenses including future and aorist, for Class 3 verbs, such as *imušava* 'he worked', (d) parts of the markers of causatives, such as *antebinebs* 'he causes him to light it', (e) parts of the markers of

Series III forms for verbs of Class 1 and 3, such as *dauçeria* 'apparently he has written it' (cf. ch. 8), and (f) morphologically empty markers which are attached to finite forms of some verbs, e.g. *içqebs* 'he begins it', *icinis* 'he is laughing'.

2 The same is true in the plural:

(i) *še-gv-i-ḳera.*
'He sewed it for us.'
(ii) *še-g-i-ḳera-t.*
'He sewed it for you(PL).'
(iii) *še-u-ḳera.*
'He sewed it for them.'

(iii) is not distinct from (7c); that is, plurality is not marked in the third person. This is explained in ch. 15.

3 Examples (*13) and (*14) are respectively (*34) and (*36) from Holisky (1978); transliteration and glosses have been changed to correspond to the conventions adopted here. The verb in (*13–14a) is highly irregular and not easily assigned to a Class.

4 In Harris (1976) I proposed a general constraint on Version, such that it cannot create a chomeur. While this constraint is supported by many examples, there are exceptions to it. In (iv), *gela* has been put *en chomage* by the advancement of 'me', as shown in (v). *Gela* is marked with the dative case in (iv a) and with a positional in (iv b). (As discussed in §6, indirect object chomeurs may be in the dative case in non-standard dialects.) Both sentences are marginal, but each is accepted by some speakers. The grammaticality of these examples depends on the version nominal being first or second person (cf. ch. 5, §4.2 for a similar situation).

(iv) (a) *mdivanma mimiçera çerili gelas.*
secretary-ERG he-wrote-me-it-II-1 letter-NOM Gela-DAT
'The secretary wrote a letter to Gela for me.'
(b) *mdivanma mimiçera çerili gelastan.*
Gela-at
'The secretary wrote a letter to Gela for me.'

(v)

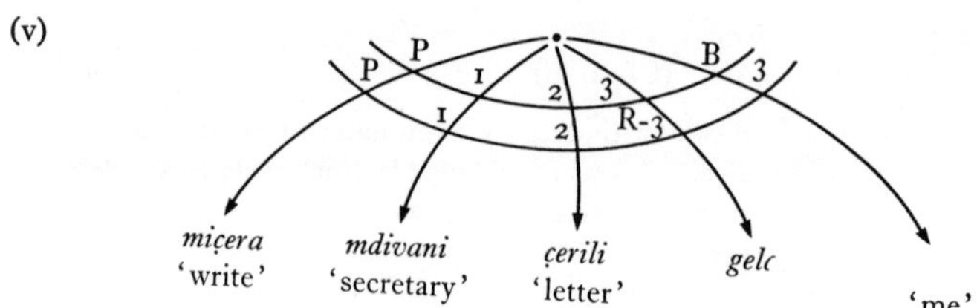

While there are exceptions like (iv), some form of this constraint must be included in the grammar to account for the non-occurrence of (15c) and many other examples.

5 The counterpart of (*17b), with the version vowel *i-* instead of *u-* is also ungrammatical:

(vi) **gela (tavis) tavs iḳeravs axal šarvals.*
('Gela is making new trousers for himself.')

6 There is no specific morpheme that corresponds to the gloss 'self'. The meaning 'self' is indicated in Georgian by the version marker *i-* without a marker of Person Agreement.

7 It can also happen that the version nominal, the subject of its clause, *and* the direct object are all coreferential. In such a case, the version nominal and direct object are reflexivized, as in (vii).

(vii) *ḳlavs* *tavis tavs.*
he-kills-him-I-I self's self-DAT
'He kills himself.'

Version may optionally apply, with Coreferential Version Object Deletion, giving

(viii) *iḳlavs* *tavs.*
he-kills-self-him-I-I self-DAT
'He commits suicide.'

The obligatoriness of Coreferential Version Object Deletion blocks (ix).

(ix) *iklavs tavs tavs.
('He commits suicide.')

Thus, the rules already proposed correctly account for these phenomena.

8 There is no form **miviçere* ('I wrote a letter to myself') corresponding to (19). While *ilaparaḳa* and *imɣera,* corresponding to (20) and (21) exist as forms, they do not mean 'he talked to himself', 'he sang to himself', but simply 'he talked' and 'he sang', respectively.

9 There is no **gaiçmendina.*

10 Among the analyses known to me, only Boeder (1968) and Nebieridze (1976) have recognized that synchronically *sataviso kçeva* is a special instance of Benefactive or Possessive Version and that the *i-* is a marker of Benefactive or Possessive Version, whether or not there is coreference between the subject and version nominal.

11 This discussion has been limited to Benefactive Version for the sake of simplicity. In fact, Coreferential Version Object Deletion also applies to indirect objects created by Possessive Version. When the latter is included, there are two additional arguments against the Extended Traditional Analysis:

A. Rule (18) is stated with respect to a 'reflexive nominal'. It could be stated instead with respect to the coreferential clausemate of the subject, but to formulate it in that way would unnecessarily repeat the conditions on full pronoun reflexivization (*Tav*-Reflexivization). Rule (23), if revised to include Possessive Version, could not make the same economy. Rule (18) refers crucially to an indirect object, but the revised version of (23) would refer to a possessor or benefactive. We have seen in ch. 1 that the conditions on possessive reflexivization (*Tavis*-Reflexivization) are different from those on full pronoun reflexivization; in particular, possessive reflexivization can be triggered by any term. Therefore, to state the revised version of (23) with respect to a 'reflexive possessor' would permit a possessor that was coreferential with the direct object to delete. This would predict that (x b) was related to (x a); but (x b) is ungrammatical in the intended meaning.

(x) (a) *avadmqopi sṭudenṭi* *gavgzavne* *tavis ekimtan.*
ill student-NOM I-sent-him-II-I self's doctor-at
'I sent the ill student$_i$ to his$_i$ doctor.'
(b) **avadmqopi sṭudenṭi gavigzavne ekimtan.*
('I sent the ill student$_i$ to his$_i$ doctor.')

To state the revised version of (23) with 'reflexive' therefore would constitute the false claim that (x b) and similar sentences express coreferentiality. Therefore (23) must be restated as (xi), which is more complex in this sense than (18) and constitutes an argument against the Extended Traditional Analysis.

(xi) *Coreferential Benefactive/Possessor Deletion*
A benefactive or possessor that is coreferential to the subject of its clause deletes.

B. Both grammars must contain a condition that Possessive Version, which is otherwise optional, is obligatory if the relation whole-part obtains with respect to the possessor-possessed (cf. Harris 1976: ch. 6, §2.2). This condition blocks the derivation of (*xii a) from an initial structure like that necessary for (xii b).

(xii) (a) **v(u)ban* *bavšvis* *xels.*
I-wash-(him)-it-I-1 child-GEN hand-DAT
('I am washing the child's hands.')
(b) *vuban* *xels bavšvs.*
I-wash-him-it-I-1 child-DAT
'I am washing the child's hands.'

((xii a) has a grammatical reading from another source, corresponding to 'I am washing *his* child's hands'.)

The Extended Traditional Analysis must include, in addition to this condition on Possessive Version, the same condition on the revised deletion rule, (xi). Such a condition is needed to block the derivation of (*xiii a), since deletion must be an optional rule, as shown above.

(xiii) (a) **v(i)ban* *čems xels.*
I-wash-(self)-it-I-1 my hand-DAT
('I am washing my hands.')
(b) *viban xels.*
'I am washing my hands.'

Thus, the Extended Traditional Analysis requires an additional constraint on deletion; this duplicates the constraint independently required for Possessive Version. The analysis proposed here, on the other hand, requires no additional constraint on deletion. (*xiii a) will be blocked by the constraint on Possessive Version and the independently necessary statement that (18) is obligatory.

12 In the Tbilisi dialect this promotion of *me* 'me' would be blocked by the constraint discussed in n. 4.

13 This can be seen in other examples, such as (xiv); here *gv-* is the first person plural marker.

(xiv) '. . . *rom migviçero* *çerili.*'
that you-write-us-it-II-1 letter-NOM
'. . . that you may write a letter for us.'

This is quoted in Shanidze (1973: §402), from Vazha Pshavela, an author who wrote in the Pshav dialect.

14 Seiter (1979), however, presents data that pose a serious challenge to both Laws.

Chapter 7

1 *Direct construction* is used in this work instead of *active*, in order to avoid the multiple ambiguity of the latter.

2 Passivization is an optional rule. If a clause undergoes the rule, the verb it contains

is a Class 2 verb. If the same clause does not undergo the rule, the verb it contains is a member of another Class.

3 The formation of the past passive participle, but not its use in the passive construction, is described in Chikobava (1950), Shanidze (1973), Tschenkéli (1958), and Vogt (1971).

4 These scholars do not agree about how a passive is derived. However, this disagreement is irrelevant to the question of whether (1–2b) are passives, since they have properties which all of the works cited consider characteristic of passives.

5 Both *čems* and *čem* (*šens* and *šen*, etc.) are used with *mier*; cf. *Tanamedrove kartuli saliṭeraṭuro enis normebi* (1970), pp. 117–8.

6 I am grateful to Hans Vogt for calling this fact to my attention and for supplying me with several examples from literature.

7 The notion 'chomeur' was first introduced by Perlmutter and Postal (cf. Perlmutter & Postal 1974). Some particular studies of their occurrence with various advancement rules are reported, for example, in Bell (1974, 1976), Chung (1976a), Perlmutter (1978), Perlmutter & Postal (1977), Postal (1977), and Sheintuch (1976). The ability of chomeurs to trigger agreement is discussed in Allen & Frantz (1978) and Lawler (1977).

8 I have no data concerning the interaction of Superessive Version and Passivization.

Chapter 8 and Appendices

1 Peikrishvili (1974), a recent work on the evidential, lists, among other uses,

a. The evidential may express an action which was not witnessed directly by the speaker.
b. The evidential may express an action which is retained as a memory in the mind of the speaker.
c. The evidential may express the simple negative of a past action (the corresponding positive being in a non-evidential past).
d. The evidential may express the result of an action rather than the action itself.
e. The evidential may express the presumption on the part of the speaker that the action took place.

2 The general analysis of Inversion which follows is due to Postal and Perlmutter. This analysis is discussed for other languages in Perlmutter (to appear b) and in Harris (to appear a).

3 Aronson (1976) gives a more detailed summary of various positions that have been taken on this issue. See also individual works, Chikobava (1950, 1968), Deeters (1930), Lafon (1963), Marr & Brière (1931), Shanidze (1961, 1963, 1973), Tschenkéli (1958), and Vogt (1971).

4 The examples in (9) are from the second evidential or 'pluperfect'. The use of the subject markers in the third evidential ('third subjunctive') is the same:

(i) (a) *ga**v**egzavno* *kalakši.*
he-sent-**me**-III-1 city-in
'May he send me into the city.'

(b) *gaegzavno* *kalakši.*
he-sent-**you**-III-1 (zero marker)
'May he send you into the city.'

(c) *gaegzavno**s*** *kalakši.*
he-sent-**him**-III-1
'May he send him into the city.'

(The third evidential is restricted in use in colloquial Standard Modern Georgian.) The markers used in the first evidential (or 'perfect') are different from those in (i) and (9):

(ii) (a) *ga*(**v**)*ugzavni***var** *kalakši.*
he-sent-**me**-III-1
'Apparently he (has) sent me into the city.'
(b) *gaugzavni***xar** *kalakši.*
he-sent-**you**-III-1
'Apparently he (has) sent you into the city.'
(c) *gaugzavni***a** *kalakši.*
he-sent-**him**-III-1
'Apparently he (has) sent him into the city.'

The suffixes in heavy type in (ii) are taken from the verb 'be': ***var*** 'I am', ***xar*** 'you are', ***-a*** the unemphatic enclitic form of *aris* 'he/she/it is'. Synchronically, these represent a secondary set of subject markers, used (a) here in the first evidential, (b) with some of the verbs discussed in §4, and (c) with a few other verbs, such as *mivdi-var* 'I am going', *vdga-var* 'I am standing', *vṭiri-var* 'I am crying', etc. In all instances this secondary set of agreement markers, like that in (8), indicates the person and number of the subject. Thus, in spite of the use of a secondary set of markers, it is clear that in (ii), as in (9) and (i), the nominative-nominal triggers Subject Person Agreement.

5 The examples in (11) are from the second evidential. The use of indirect object agreement markers in the third evidential is the same:

(iii) (a) *da***m***etesos* *simindi.*
I-sowed-it-III-1 corn-NOM
'May I sow corn.'
(b) *da***g***etesos* *simindi.*
you-sowed-it-III-1
'May you sow corn.'
(c) *daetesos* *simindi*
he-sowed-it-III-1 (zero marker)
'May he sow corn.'

The markers used in the first evidential are similar, but in the third person we find a variant of that noted in (10);

(iv) (a) *da***m***itesavs* *simindi.*
I-sowed-it-III-1
'Apparently I sowed corn.'
(b) *da***g***itesavs* *simindi.*
you-sowed-it-III-1
'Apparently you sowed corn.'
(c) *da***u***tesavs* *simindi.*
he-sowed-it-III-1
'Apparently he sowed corn.'

Notice that in the first and second persons there is a morpheme *i*, which is part of the stem formant of the first evidential; this morpheme immediately precedes the verb root and immediately follows the indirect object markers. It is quite generally the case in Georgian that the third person indirect object agreement marker (*s*/*h*/ø) combines with the formant *i*, the two morphemes together being realized as *u*. The *i* formant occurs in a variety of functions, which include its being (a) part of the marker of the first evidential, (b) part of the marker of future and aorist tense groups for one class of verbs, (c) the marker of promotion of a benefactive or possessive to indirect object (cf. ch. 6, §2.1), and (d) an empty morpheme that occurs in a few verbs. In all these functions, the formant *i* combines synchronically with a third person indirect object marker as *u*. Examples (7) and (9) of ch. 6 illustrate functions (c) and (d) respectively. Thus, in spite of the occurrence of the *u* variant in the third person, we can see that the first evidential in (iv) contains regular object markers, just as (11) and (iii) do.

6 The fact that Object Camouflage never applies in Series III with Class 1 and 3 verbs, which trigger Inversion, is accounted for by the fact that the input conditions are not met, as stated. Object Camouflage never applies in Series III with Class 2 verbs either, and these verbs do not trigger Inversion. However, there is no Class 2 verb that meets the input conditions for Object Camouflage, and therefore the rule never applies with a Class 2 verb in *any* Series. To understand why no Class 2 verb satisfies the input conditions for Object Camouflage, it is necessary to recognize that the Class 2 verbs which take a direct and indirect object are a tiny, irregular set (cf. ch. 16, Appendix B). They are all verbs of 'saying' and therefore do not take first or second person direct objects:

mama *motxrobas uqveba* *ninos.*
father-NOM story-DAT he-tells-her-it-I-2 Nino-DAT
'Father is telling a story to Nino.'
**mama me/čems tavs* *uqveba ninos.*
I my self-DAT
(*'Father is telling me to Nino.')

Without a first or second person direct object, the input conditions for Object Camouflage are not met. Thus, the proposal made above accounts for the failure of Object Camouflage to apply in Series III, with Class 2 verbs as well as with Class 1 and 3 verbs.

7 In both types, Unaccusative applies only if its input conditions are satisfied, of course. This is discussed below in §6.

8 Not all traditional descriptions of Georgian take the position summarized in (27–28). Shanidze (1963), for example, takes the view that the relations indicated in (24) are the only grammatical relations. From this position, case marking could be simplified as in (27′–28′), but the facts observed in §4.1, 5.1, and Appendix A cannot easily be accounted for.

9 This statement is refined in ch. 16.

10 Alternative forms for some speakers are *moamšives* and *moamšies*; the meaning and grammatical relations are the same as in (29b).

11 In the causative of a transitive inversion verb, the experiencer is the derived indirect object, and the stimulus is the derived direct object. This shows nothing, however, since the derived indirect-objecthood of the experiencer could arise either from its being the subject of a transitive or from its being an indirect object. Similarly, the final direct-objecthood of the stimulus could arise either from its being a direct object or from its being an intransitive subject. Since these are precisely the pairs of relations that are in question, the causative of a transitive inversion verb sheds no light on the problem.

12 There is a systematic ambiguity in examples of this type, which derives from the fact that *tvis* not only marks retired indirect objects, but also marks benefactives. Thus (30b) could also be glossed 'Apparently the king has had the palace cleaned

for you,' with the initial subject of 'clean' left unspecified. The alternative word order, *turme mepes gauçmendinebia sasaxle šentvis* is also, for many speakers, acceptable and ambiguous.

13 Example (45) below appears to provide additional support for the initial direct-objecthood of the unaccusative nominal, since it undergoes Object Raising, which is restricted to direct objects. However, as discussed in Harris (1976: 249–50), it might be argued that the infinitive in (45) is derived, not from the Class 4 verb in (42), but from a Class 1 verb with the same root. If the latter were correct, it would not be a counter example to any part of the analysis presented here. But because of this ambiguity in the form, (45) and similar examples do not provide strong support for my analysis, and are not discussed in detail from that point of view.

14 This differs slightly from Perlmutter and Postal's analyses of similar data in other languages, cf. Perlmutter (to appear b) and Perlmutter & Postal (to appear c).

15 The inability of Passivization to apply to the output of Inversion, on the other hand, is accounted for automatically by the fact that the output of Inversion (or Inversion and Unaccusative) fails to meet the input conditions on Passivization. Passivization, as stated above in §6, may only apply in clauses containing a subject and direct object. The output of Inversion (only) contains no subject. The output of Inversion and Unaccusative contains no direct object. Therefore, it is correctly predicted that Passivization cannot apply to the output of Inversion. The ungrammatical sentences that would result cannot easily be illustrated, since the forms are lacking.

The same is true of the other interactions discussed in §7.2–7.5, as the reader can confirm for himself.

16 This example is from Tschenkéli (1958: vol. II, 268, no. 3).

17 At least the following verbs require a genitive under certain circumstances: *mjera* 'I believe it', *mesmis* 'I hear, understand it', *mešinia* 'I fear it', *mrçams* 'I believe in it', *mrcxvenia* 'I am ashamed, shy of it', *mexatreba* 'I am shy of it', *mšurs* 'I envy it'.

18 It is not clear under exactly what circumstances the complement must be genitive. In (1) both animate and inanimate nominals must be in the genitive, but cf.

*mjera šeni /*šen.*
I-believe-it-I-4 you-GEN you-NOM

*mjera ?*ambavisa/ ambavi.*
news-GEN news-NOM
'I believe the news.'

Chapter 9

1 Analyses similar to this have been proposed by several scholars, including Marr (1925) and Schuchardt (1895). Chikobava (1961) considers in detail this analysis of Georgian and several others and argues eloquently in traditional terms that the ergative-nominal in Series II is both the 'real' (initial) subject and the 'morphological' (final) subject.

Chapter 10

1 The name 'masdar' is used here as it is traditionally in Georgian linguistics; masdars are also called *saçqisebi* 'beginnings'. These deverbal forms do not have all of the characteristics of the masdar in Arabic and related languages.

2 Shanidze (1973: 565) suggests that *ḳaḳani* and *saubari* are not masdars, but are *used*

as masdars; his distinction seems to be based on the derivational morphology. See also Holisky (1980a:127–9).

3 Lees (1963) characterizes these meanings as 'the fact that SUBJ VERB' and 'the way that SUBJ VERB'; both meanings also occur in English.

4 This example is from Vogt (1971:243).

5 In ch. 11, I will argue that these nominalizations have a clausal source, which Chomsky (1970) claims does not exist for 'derived nominals'. This is consistent with the suggestion made in Comrie (1976d) that it is inappropriate to make a strict bifurcation between noun-like and sentence-like nominalizations.

Schmidt (1967) considers the question of whether the masdar is a *Verbalabstraktum* or infinitive, deciding in favor of the latter. He, too, notes that masdars decline, but feels that this is not a good way of distinguishing nominals from infinitives (p. 160). In spite of examples like those in (3), he considers that masdars are morphologically relatively uniform, and in this respect like infinitives (p. 158). See Shanidze (1973:560–5) for more exhaustive lists of masdars from each of the types represented in (3).

6 The examples in (5) are from Shanidze (1973:568). I have confirmed them as Standard Modern Georgian with an informant and have added glosses.

7 In Old Georgian the infinitive had the shape of a 'masdar in the adverbial case' (cf. Chxubianishvili 1972; Matrirosovi 1955).

8 In ch. 4 I showed that the *tvis*-nominal of object-raised sentences (cf. *for*-nominal in English) is not the initial embedded subject, but is coreferential with the initial embedded subject, and that the latter gets deleted. I assume that the initial subject in (7) is also deleted by Equi. In (7) the initial subject of the embedded clause is coreferential with the initial and final subject of the matrix clause. It may be coreferential with a final subject that is not an initial subject, as these passives show:

(i) . . . *rac* *agretve* *kartulši* *mizezis* *garemoebis* *gamosaxaṭavad*
which-NOM also Georgian-in reason-GEN adverb-GEN to-depict
aris *gamoqenebuli.*
it-is-I-2 used.
'. . . which is also used to express the adverb of purpose in Georgian.'
Imnaishvili (1957:723)

(ii) *mivlinebuli* *viqavi* *udur* *enaze* *samušaod.*
sent (on a job) I-was-II-2 Udi language-on to-work
'I was sent to work on the Udi language.' Panchvidze (1937:295)

9 Some speakers find the infinitive acceptable in (iii), but most of my informants prefer (iv), with a true participle.

(iii) *bevri* *makvs* *gasaḳeteblad.*
much-NOM I-have-it-I-4 to-do
'I have a lot to do.'

(iv) *bevri makvs gasaḳetebeli.*
doing-NOM
'I have a lot to do.'

The infinitive in (v) is also generally considered grammatical.

(v) *bevria* *gasaḳeteblad.*
much-it-is-I-2 to-do
'There is a lot to do.'

[10] (vi) and (vii are grammatical variants of (*8).

(vi) *minda* *gavaketo*
I-want-it-I-4 I-do-it-II-1
'I want to do it.'

(vii) *minda misi* *gaketeba.*
it-GEN doing-NOM
'I want to do it.'

(On the occurrence of these two types, cf. Pätsch (1965).)

[11] While other orders are acceptable, these are definitely the unmarked ones.

[12] The use of this case in Modern Georgian is quite restricted. In general, it is used for the predicate nominal of a verb of 'being' when the subject of that verb is not in the clause. For example, when the subject of 'be' undergoes Subject-to-Object Raising, the predicate nominal is in the adverbial. (The verb 'be' obligatorily deletes.)

(viii) (a) *nino* *tvlis,* *rom gela* *čkviania.*
Nino-NOM she-considers-it-I-1 that Gela-NOM clever-he-is-I-2
'Nino considers that Gela is clever.'
(b) *nino tvlis gelas* *čkvianad.*
Gela-DAT clever-ADV
'Nino considers Gela clever.'

Similarly, in (ix a) the (final) subject is dropped by Unemphatic Pronoun Drop, while in (ix b) it is not present at all.

(ix) (a) *masçavlebeli aris.*
teacher-NOM he-is-I-2
'He is a teacher.'
(b) *masçavleblad qopna...*
teacher-ADV being-NOM
'Being a teacher....'

Other uses of the adverbial case are mostly translatable in English with 'as'-nominal:

(x) *mušaobs* *masçavleblad.*
he-works-I-3 teacher-ADV
'He works as a teacher.'

(xi) *kvrivad* *darča.*
widow-ADV he-remained-II-2
'He remained as a widower.'

Compare (xi) with (xii).

(xii) *kvrivi* *darča.*
widow-NOM
'He remained a widower.'

[13] The nominal which corresponds to the subject of a finite transitive verb form is, with a participle, typically marked with *mier*, as shown in (xiv) and (xv).

(xiv) a. *šipneris* *mier dadasturebul pormas...*
A. Schiefner by confirmed form-DAT
'... (paid attention) to the form confirmed by A. Schiefner...'
Panchvidze (1942:69)

(xv) *čven... vamoçmebdit* *a. šipneris mier mocemuls da čven mier*
we-NOM we-verified-it-I-1 given and us by
vartašenši šegrovebul leksiķas.
Vartasen-in collected lexicon-DAT
'We ... verified the lexicon given by A. Schiefner and (that) collected by us in Vartashen.'

Panchvidze (1937:315)

However, at least some native speakers also accept phrases like (xvi), where the nominal corresponding to the initial subject is marked with the genitive case, not with *mier*.

(xvi) *im ķacis daçerili çigni...*
that man-GEN written book-NOM
'A/The book written by that man...'

Such marking of a transitive subject is totally unacceptable with masdars:

(xvii) **im ķacis (çignis) daçera...*
book-GEN writing-NOM
('The writing (of the book) by that man...')

14 The genitive (or possessive) of each first and second person personal pronoun has several forms; two forms of the second person singular occur in (41a) and (42a) (cf. ch. 7, n. 5).

Chapter 11

1 Retired transitive subjects of participles are also usually marked with *mier* (cf. ch. 10, n. 13), but a detailed analysis of participles has not been proposed here.

There is a second postposition that is sometimes used in place of *mier*. (i) illustrates this use of the postposition *-gan* 'from', apparently marking a retired transitive subject.

(i) *es vašli micemulia bavšvisagan.*
this apple-NOM given-it-is-I-2 child-from
'This apple is given by (?from) the child.'

The use of *-gan* can be predicted from the fact that the nominal is a retired subject, together with the fact that the governing verb is *micema* 'give'. This verb permits the use of *-gan* to mark its retired subjects generally.

In this matter there is considerable variation among speakers, which I will characterize in terms of dialects. In one dialect, *-gan* is acceptable only with a very limited number of verbs, including *micema* of (i). Speakers of this dialect find (ii) unacceptable.

(ii) *gelasagan çerilis daçera...*
Gela-from letter-GEN writing
'The writing of the letter by (?from) Gela...'

It is probable that in this dialect *-gan* has only the meaning 'from' and does not mark retired subjects, even in (i). In a second dialect, *-gan* is used more widely, but it is still restricted to a particular set of verbs. Speakers of this dialect find (ii) acceptable. In a third dialect, *-gan* is sometimes preferred to *mier*; (iii) is preferred over (5).

(iii) *bavšvi dakbenilia ʒaɣlisagan.*
child-NOM bitten-it-is-I-2 dog-from
'The child is bitten by the dog.'

In this dialect *-gan* clearly functions as a marker of retired transitive subjects, as well as in the meaning 'from'. I have reported the first of these dialects in this work, as it seems to represent the majority speech.

2 While the relations between specific termhood and the markers *-tvis*, *mier*, and the bare genitive case have not previously been observed, Latsabidze (1975) suggests that genitives are transformationally related to terms. I consider that postpositions function like cases in marking grammatical relations and consider it a coincidence that *mier* and *tvis* both govern the genitive case. Latsabidze, on the other hand, discounts the importance of *mier* and *tvis* and observes that all three term relations are marked with the genitive as an alternative to the usual term cases.

Since I first proposed the correlations (14) in Harris (1976, 1977), some Georgian linguists have suggested to me that other postpositions also mark retired terms (cf. n. 1). In particular, it has been suggested in personal communication that *mešveobit*, *sašualebit*, and *šesrulebit* (said to be literary) may mark retired transitive subjects, and that the suffixes *-euli* and *-admi* may mark retired direct objects. Additional field work has shown that these mark ordinary non-terms (obliques), but do not serve the purely grammatical function of marking retired terms. The evidence concerning all of these cannot be given here, but the first is taken as an example. In the passive (iv), either *mier* or *mešveobit* may occur, suggesting that they function in the same way.

(iv) *vardi gazrdilia vanos* {*mier* / *mešveobit.*}
rose-NOM grown-it-is-I-2 Vano
'The rose is grown [?by] Vano.'

But in the intransitive (v), *vano* is not the initial subject; *mier* is unacceptable, while *mešveobit* is acceptable.

(v) *vardi gaizarda vanos* {**mier* / *mešveobit.*}
it-grew-II-2
'The rose grew because of Vano./The rose grew through the intervention of Vano.'

(The nature of constructions like (v) is discussed further in ch. 13.) I conclude that *mešveobit* means 'through the intervention of' rather than having a purely grammatical function. It is interesting that the same meaning attached to *mier* in Old Georgian, though today it is not used that way in the standard dialect (cf. Harris 1979).

3 Because I had not included sentences like (9)/(16) in my 1974–75 field work in Georgia, in Harris (1976, 1977) I reported only (16), on the basis of work with only one informant in the United States. Based on (16) and other examples of that type, I concluded that marking was as in (15). Subsequent field work in Georgia in 1977 revealed that the dialect originally reported is not widespread.

4 One fact seems to support this possibility: a very few verbs govern a particular postposition other than *tvis* or *mier* for marking a specific retirement relation. For example, *miɣçeva* 'reach' governs *-mde* 'until' for its retired object: *miɣçeva kalakamde* 'reaching the city'.

5 The relationship between grammatical relations and semantic relations is explored further in ch. 16.

6 *Mier* in Standard Modern Georgian is used only to mark retired subjects. *Tvis*, on the other hand, while it marks retired indirect objects, also marks other non-terms in the general meaning 'for'. Thus, the fact that the nominal in question in the object-raised sentences is marked with *tvis* does not indicate that it is a retired indirect object.

Chapter 12 and Appendix

1 The label 'verb' is used in this work with the systematic ambiguity that is usual in the use of that word: it may refer to the concrete inflected occurrence of a verb, or to the abstract notion 'verb'. In this chapter, I am claiming that some verbs, in the latter sense, have an obligatory initial direct object. That is, the verb *daçera* 'write' has an obligatory initial direct object, whether it is a direct form (*daçera* 'he wrote it'), a passive (*daçerilia* 'it is written'), a causative (*daaçerina* 'he made him write it'), etc., and whether it is in Series I, II, or III. Whatever the surface realization of this verb, it has an initial direct object.

There are a few instances where two verbs, in this sense, are formed on one root, and where one verb takes a preverb and the other does not. In this case, too, their initial term inventories may differ. For example, *gačorva* in (i) takes an obligatory initial direct object, while *čoraoba* in (ii) does not permit an initial direct object.

(i) (*šen*) *mčorav* (*me*) *dedačemtan.*
you-NOM you-gossip-me-I-1 I-DAT my-mother-to
'You gossip to my mother about me.'

(ii) (*šen*) *čoraob* *čemze dedačemtan.*
you-gossip-I-3 me-on
'You gossip to my mother about me.'

Gačorva and *čoraoba* belong to different morphological Classes and must be considered different verbs in the sense discussed here.

2 Verbs of the last type have corresponding organic causatives which have a direct object. But in this instance, it is not the embedded verb, but the matrix verb, CAUSE, which has an initial direct object.

3 In examples (*5) and (*8), the markers of Person Agreement do not differ from those in (4a) and (7a), respectively, because the marker of third person singular direct objects is the same as the marker of third person singular indirect objects in this phonological environment.

4 (5) has a grammatical reading, 'I had *Vano* written', where *Vano* is the direct object as the word written.

5 Nominals which are obligatory in the initial inventory of terms can be dropped by Unemphatic Pronoun Drop. Nominals which are *not* in the initial inventory of term nominals can also be dropped if they are final terms; for example, benefactives that advance to indirect object may be dropped, *dauçera* 'he wrote it for him'. I know of no counterexamples to the statement made in §2.

6 Examples (1a), (2), (10), (11), and (30a) of ch. 1, (1) of ch. 3, (9) and (22) of ch. 8, and (2) and (3) of ch. 13, as well as other examples in this work show that it is not typical for verbs in Georgian that animacy plays a role in grammatical relations.

7 I assume here that the indirect object is an initial locative and advances to indirect

object by a rule of Locative Version, similar in essential respects to Benefactive Version (cf. ch. 6). I make this assumption for the following reasons:

A. The meaning of this indirect object differs consistently from that of initial indirect objects.

B. The locative-nominal may occur either as an indirect object, in the dative case and triggering Indirect Object Agreement, or as a non-term, with the postposition *-tan* and not triggering agreement:

(i) *vanom* *dareḳa* *dedastan.*
Vano-ERG he-rang-it-II-1 mother-at
'Vano rang his mother's.'

(ii) *vanom daureḳa* *dedas.*
he-rang-her-it-II-1 mother-DAT
'Vano rang his mother.'

C. When the locative-nominal has advanced to indirect object, as in (ii), it triggers the version vowel *i-* (cf. (8) of ch. 6); when it has not advanced to indirect object, as in (i), no version marker occurs.

D. The dative-nominal in (ii), but not the locative in (i), is deletable by Unemphatic Pronoun Drop.

Since Locative Version applies optionally, there is a parallel set of sentences in which the locative has not been advanced and occurs as *dedastan* 'at mother's'. Parallel to (6), (8), and (9) are

(iii) *vanos turme daureḳia dedastan.*

(iv) *vanos mier dedastan darekva,*

and

(v) *vanom damareḳina dedastan.*

Although Locative Version is infrequent, it does apply with other verbs, such as *miberavs* 'it is blowing on me' (cf. *beravs* 'it is blowing') and *movuçre mas* 'I made it there on time' (cf. *movaçre mastan* 'I made it there on time').

8 *P̣asuxi* is one of the verbs that allows *-gan* to replace *mier* (cf. ch. 11, n. 1). *P̣asuxi* is not only a masdar, but a concrete noun; therefore, *šeni p̣asuxi* 'your answer' is also grammatical. These two uses of *p̣asuxi* may be distinguished by co-occurrence with adjectives or adverbs; *sçorad* 'correctly' may co-occur with the masdar, but only *sçori* 'correct' with the concrete noun:

šengan gaḳvetili sçorad p̣asuxi
**šeni sçorad p̣asuxi*
šeni sçori p̣asuxi.

Chapter 13 and Appendix

1 Possessive Version is not obligatory, but usual, in this environment (cf. introduction to ch. 6).

2 Within the set of verbs characterized morphologically by the circumfixes *i—ebi*, *e—ebi*, or *ø—ebi*, at least four types must be distinguished; they do not correspond to the distribution of the circumfixes:

A. *Synthetic passives* are illustrated and characterized in the body of this chapter.

B. *Potentials*, like synthetic passives, are related to direct forms, in the sense that they are formed from the same abstract verb. For example, *es xe ixerxeba* 'this tree/wood cuts well', a potential, is related to *viɣac xerxavs am xes* 'someone is cutting this wood/tree', a direct form. Potentials may be distinguished from other verb forms with the same morphology by the fact that they have no forms outside Series I.

As far as I am aware, all of the characteristics discussed in this chapter with respect to synthetic passives apply equally to potentials. I have excluded them because of lack of data.

C. Certain other verb forms which share the morphology of synthetic passives do not share some of the other characteristics discussed in §2. This group includes *içereba* 'it is written', *iɣeba* 'it is received', and *ič̣reba* 'it is cut'.

D. Forms like *vardeba* 'he falls', as stated above, share the morphology of synthetic passives, but may be distinguished from them by the fact that they do not have corresponding direct forms.

Traditionally these sets of verbs have been described together, since they share morphology. The arguments adduced in this chapter do not necessarily apply to types B–D. In ch. 16 the similarity of these four types and others of Class 2 is explored.

There are also several verb forms which are morphologically like the synthetic passive, but which are not regularly derived. These include verb forms like *igineba* 'he curses', *imaleba* 'he hides'. Some of the problems presented by these irregular verb forms are discussed in Harris (to appear b) and Harris (1976), Appendix C.

3 This definition rules out the inversion construction. This could be considered as a fourth contrasting construction, but it has already been discussed in detail in ch. 8.

4 Notice that animacy plays no role in distinguishing between the analytic and the synthetic passive; both may have animate or inanimate initial direct objects. These possibilities are illustrated in the examples of §1.

5 Some Indo-European middles correspond to the forms I refer to as 'synthetic passives', others to some of the other forms which share that morphology (cf. n. 2). Still other Indo-European middles correspond to the Georgian Benefactive or Possessive Version with Coreferential Version Object Deletion, as observed in Schmidt (1965).

While most Georgianists have called synthetic passives and the other forms described in footnote 2 'passives', Blake (1932:234) observes that they are 'in reality middle'.

6 According to Holisky, these diagnostics test for the 'presence of an agent' (1978: 150, 152). There is no doubt that the adverbs of intention and the command imperative are impossible in sentences lacking an agent, but neither are they possible in all sentences containing an agent. They may in general occur in sentences with semantic agents only if the agent is a final subject. As an exception to this, *ganzrax* 'intentionally' may marginally occur with analytic passives if the initial subject is specified and *ganzrax* is associated with it by word order, as (*i) and (ii) show; the word order of (*i) is the unmarked order.

(i) **č̣urč̣eli ganzrax gamšralia.*
crockery-NOM intentionally dried-it-is-I-2
('The crockery is intentionally dried.')

(ii) *?č̣urč̣eli gamšralia bič̣is mier ganzrax.*
boy by
'The crockery is dried by the boy intentionally.'

Holisky (1978) gives additional tests, but I have not been able to apply all of these to synthetic and analytic passives in work with informants.

7 This assumes that all semantic agents are initial subjects. It is shown in ch. 16 that this assumption is correct.

8 Lomtatidze (1952) and Machavariani (1959) argue that those synthetic passives characterized by *ø—ebi* in the present tense (illustrated by (4–6) in the present chapter) are 'dynamic intransitives', not passives as most grammarians have said. I believe that this is correct, but that the same applies, not only to those forms marked by *ø—ebi*, but also to those synthetic passives marked by *i—ebi* and *e—ebi* (cf. group E of Appendix A to ch. 16 for additional examples). From the fact that they are not true passives, Lomtatidze and Machavariani draw the conclusion that their final subjects are not initial direct objects. It is argued in this section that that conclusion is unfounded and incorrect.

9 The direct object here does not trigger Number Agreement (cf. ch. 15).

10 The verb root *ḳal* alternates with *ḳvd*, and both are derived from an original root **ḳv* (Topuria 1940:535; Kavtaradze 1954:319, footnote 2).

11 Preverbs are not agreement markers, nor are they used with all verbs. In addition to the function described here, they may indicate direction, tense, and aspect (cf. Chikobava 1950; Shanidze 1973; Tschenkéli 1958; and Vogt 1971).

12 The extent to which the synthetic passive interacts with other syntactic rules is stated briefly below.

Masdars and infinitives correspond to abstract verbs (cf. ch. 12, n. 1), not to particular finite verb forms. Thus, a given masdar or infinitive does not correspond to any specific voice form. A given masdar or infinitive may have the inventory of initial terms which characterizes the direct construction or that which characterizes the synthetic passive, but this difference is not reflected in the verb form.

Causatives offer no evidence concerning the nature of the synthetic passive. Since both an intransitive subject and a direct object are realized as the direct object of the causative (cf. ch. 5), the derived grammatical relations provide no evidence concerning initial grammatical relations in this instance.

Passivization and Unaccusative cannot apply in a single clause, since the input conditions for both cannot be met in the same clause.

Version applies freely in the synthetic passive. Pairs like (iii), where Possessive Version has applied, might be construed as the basis for an additional argument to

(iii) (a) *mixuravs* *ḳars.*
he-closes-me-it-I-1 door-DAT
'He is closing my door.'

(b) *mexureba* *ḳari.*
it-closes-me-I-2 door-NOM
'My door is closing.'

support the initial grammatical relations proposed in §3. In the direct construction, (iii a), the version object possesses the direct object; in the synthetic passive, (iii b), it possesses the final subject. However, the constraints on exactly which nominals may be interpreted as possessed by the version object are still poorly understood. No argument can be based on sentences like (iii) until this fundamental property of Possessive Version is determined.

Case marking and Inversion as evidence for the analysis proposed here are considered at length in ch. 16.

13 In the *ikna*-passive, like the *iqo*-passive, the initial indirect object is realized as a final non-term, as shown by (iv) (cf. ch. 7, §2).

(iv) *es vardi dedastvis ikna micemuli.*
this rose-NOM mother-for it-was-II-2 given
'This rose was given to Mother.'

The retired indirect object, *deda* 'mother', is marked with *tvis*.

14 The use of such phrases as tests of stativity in Georgian is established in Holisky (1978).

Chapter 14

1 This generalization is supported by many additional examples, such as (i).

(i) **es perangi šovnilia genos mier tavistvis mosḳovši.*
this shirt-NOM gotten-it-is-I-2 Geno by self-for Moscow-in
('This shirt was gotten by Geno for himself in Moscow.')

There is, however, at least one exception to the generalization. In (ii), the initial subject, which is a final non-term, triggers *Tav*-Reflexivization. I have no explanation for the grammaticality of this sentence.

(ii) *bevri sisulele iqo nalaparaḳevi vanos mier tavisi tavis šešaxeb.*
much nonsense-NOM it-was-II-2 spoken Vano by self's self about
'A great deal of nonsense was spoken by Vano about himself.'

2 Pronouns dropped by Unemphatic Pronoun Drop, on the other hand, function as final terms with respect to Causative Clause Union, Retired Term Marking (cf. ch. 12), Person Agreement (cf. ch. 1, §3), Number Agreement (cf. ch. 15), and *Tav*-Reflexivization. Nominals deleted in the course of Object Raising do not function as terms in this way (cf. ch. 4, §5). This difference is accounted for here by stating Unemphatic Pronoun Drop on final termhood (cf. Epilogue, §4).

3 It is intended that (16) be interpreted to mean that reflexivization must apply if the coreferential nominals are clausemates *at any level of derivation*; cf. (11), where coreferentiality is resolved by reflexivization whether it occurs in initial or final structure.

4 Postal himself no longer supports a crossover analysis for English (Postal 1971:v).

Chapter 15

1 I have already stated in the Introduction one constraint on Number Agreement: in some dialects all inanimates trigger singular agreement.

2 The third person plural indirect object agreement marker will not show up in the first examples considered; it is stated here on the basis of examples like (15a). The third person plural direct object agreement marker is never triggered, so 'ø' is a construct.

3 When two plural terms co-occur in a clause, the plural agreement marker of one is deleted by the rule given below as (25). For this reason, examples with two plural terms are avoided here.

4 In this example, the subject agreement marker is deleted by rule (24), given below.

5 In spite of examples like those in (6), which show that third person objects regularly fail to trigger Number Agreement, one finds rare examples of object Number Agreement in the literature. Whether such examples ever occur in the Standard Modern Georgian of Tbilisi I cannot tell. Chikobava (1941: §11) cites examples of

third person indirect object Number Agreement from eastern (non-standard) dialects.

[6] The reader may need to be reminded here that the order of elements in the analytic gloss of the verb forms reflects the *English* word order, with the initial subject first, then the verb, then the initial direct object. The gloss directly reflects the presence of a plural morpheme in this way: In (15a), *t* indicates plurality of the third person initial subject, not of the third person initial direct object. This is indicated in the analytic gloss by 'they' in preverbal position. In (15b), the fact that there is no plural marker is indicated by the use of singular pronouns in the analytic verb gloss.

[7] The notion 'first subject that is a final term' also plays a role in the statement of unmarked word order in Modern Georgian. It is this nominal that regularly occupies the first position (cf. Introduction, §4.5).

[8] (18) accounts for the selection of the Number Agreement triggers, but it does not account for the selection of the marker of Number Agreement. While the trigger is selected on the basis of final and non-final termhood, the actual marker is chosen on the basis of the final termhood of the trigger. Thus, in (12–14) final subjects trigger markers from (1), while in (15) the final indirect object triggers a marker from (3).

[9] The dialect described here is that described also by Tschenkéli (1958), Vogt (1971) and by Georgian linguists. However, most of my informants found (i) at least marginally acceptable; one preferred it to (17a).

(i) *turme* *sṭudenṭebs* *gamougzavnixar***t** (*šen*).
apparently students-DAT **they**-sent-you-III-1 you(SG)-NOM
'Apparently the students (have) sent you.'

Here a third person initial subject triggers Number Agreement, even when a second person term is in the clause. That is, the dialect represented by speakers who prefer (i) to (17a) has a simplified version of the rule (18), which lacks clause (b–ii) altogether. This dialect apparently does not differ in other respects from the one described in this chapter.

[10] Plural suffixes do not co-occur (cf. rule (25)). In general, object suffixes do follow subject suffixes, as in example (15a).

[11] This is essentially the analysis proposed in Aronson (1970) and in Chikobava (1968). Aronson defines the 'grammatical subject of transitive verbs as that member of the predication which can be marked by the verb for number in the third person' (1970:294). From the discussion it is clear that he considers the inversion construction transitive. According to his definition, the dative-nominals of (15) are grammatical subjects. But, by the same token, those of (17) are not grammatical subjects, since they cannot be marked for number. But (15) and (17) differ only in the person of the nominative-nominals and in Number Agreement.

Chapter 16 and Appendices

[1] Vogt's statement of this is among the clearest: 'Les verbes neutres [Class 3] ont été définis comme des verbes qui ne sont ni transitifs ni intransitifs' (Vogt 1971:133; also cf. 87–9). Similar analyses are made by other authors.

Class 4 is not included in many parts of my discussion of the ergative analysis. This is because I am trying to represent accurately the consensus of opinion on ergativity in Georgian; but there is no unity in the treatment of Class 4 among proponents of the ergative hypothesis (cf. Aronson 1976 comparing various analyses).

2 The term 'future/aorist' is used here and throughout this chapter to denote the set of tenses listed in (5), all of which share some formant, for each verb Class.

3 In the Conditional and Future Subjunctive, *-d-* is used generally by Class 1, *-od-* by Class 2; *-d-* is used by Class 3 verbs, except those with the thematic suffix *-i*, which use *-od-* instead.

4 While most Georgianists have labelled Class 3 'irregular', both Nozadze (1974) and Holisky (1980a) emphasize the regularity of this group. Nozadze (1974:30ff.) also traces the historical development of the morphology that sets Class 3 apart from other verbs. Holisky shows that the difference is due to the fact that the preverb in Georgian is associated with punctual aspect, and this category is inapplicable to medial verbs because they are atelic.

5 An example of this is the statement below. Emphasis is added.

> . . .there are a number of intransitive verbs that *exceptionally* require an ergative subject, though this class of intransitive verbs is *essentially arbitrary*.
> (Comrie 1976b)

6 This particular example is taken from Tschenkéli (1958: vol. 1, 293–4); it is typical of many other authors as well. See also Tschenkéli (1958:299, no. 2).

7 There are also serious problems with the details of such a theory of borrowing. First, most Class 3 verbs may not take a preverb in the future/aorist, while the corresponding Class 1 verb (causative) requires a preverb in the future/aorist. This is the case with *vibaṭone* (**gavibaṭone*) 'I reigned' and *gavibaṭone* (?**vibaṭone*) *čemi tavi* 'I made myself ruler'. Second, in the Class 1 form (causative) the *i-* results from Possessive Version and Coreferential Version Object Deletion and depends upon the identity of subject and object. In the Class 3 verb, on the other hand, there is no object at any level of derivation.

Nozadze (1974:30ff.) shows that borrowing of forms is also an untenable hypothesis diachronically.

8 Fillmore incorporates the active/inactive type in his case grammar (cf. Fillmore 1968:53–4). Klimov (1973) also discusses this type; curiously, he nevertheless analyzes Georgian as having ergative case marking, not 'active/inactive'. He states that Class 3 verbs represent a relic of an *earlier* active/inactive system (p.50) or an anticipation of a *future* accusative system (p.189). This analysis apparently arises from his theory that languages can develop from an active/inactive system to an ergative system, or from ergative to accusative, but not the reverse. See Comrie (1976b) for an enlightening discussion.

9 Although it has not previously been recognized that case marking Series II is an active/inactive rule in Sapir's sense, three Georgian linguists have observed that the use of the ergative or nominative as the subject case in Series II depends upon whether the verb is active or inactive (Jajanidze 1970; Jorbenadze 1975:219ff.; Topuria 1923:115 and 120, and 1954: no. 7).

10 The notion 'basic' will not be defined; cf. lists of examples in Appendix. 'Basic Class 1 verbs' may be taken to be Class 1 verbs that are not causative, etc.

11 The type *atetrebs* 'he makes it white' from the adjective *tetri*' white' is also a causative. The type *xerxavs* 'he is sawing it' (*xerxi* 'a/the saw') may represent an additional derivational type. In any case, its term relations are identical to those in (10).

12 Perlmutter & Postal (to appear c) propose a Final 1 Law, requiring every clause to have a final subject. If this law is correct, it obviates the necessity of making a language-particular statement that Unaccusative is obligatory.

13 Not only noun subjects, but also sentential subjects of basic Class 2 verbs are initial direct objects. This includes sentential subjects of *qopna* in sentences in which

Object Raising applies. This analysis is summarized in the network below (cf. (6) of ch. 4).

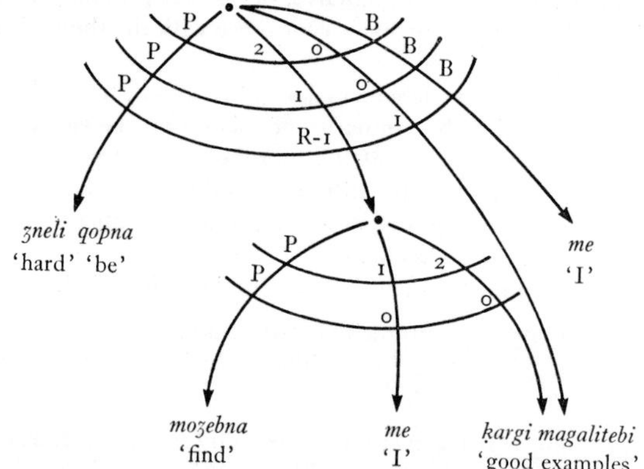

14 Inceptives may also be based on inversion predicates, as in (i).

(i)

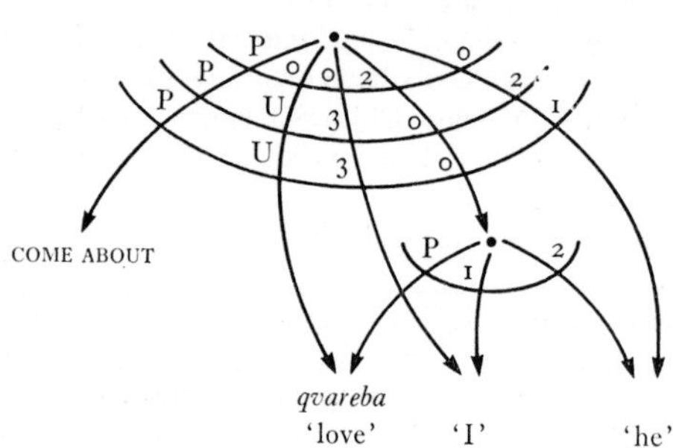

šemiqvardeba.
'I will fall in love with him.'

The analysis presented here is supported by the following facts. The initial grammatical relations represented in the dependent clauses of (18), (19), and (i), are the same as those which the unmarked form of each verb takes in an independent clause. The initial grammatical relation of the embedded clause to the abstract predicate COME ABOUT is the same as that of a non-sentential dependent to the concrete verb *axda, moxda, gaxda* 'it came about, happened, became'. The final grammatical relations are consistent with Person and Number Agreement and case marking (cf. (1)). In each of the three structures (18), (19), and (i), the initial grammatical relations are correctly related to the final grammatical relations by the rules of Clause Union and Unaccusative, with no special apparatus. (Cf. Aissen & Perlmutter 1976 and Frantz 1976 on Clause Union in constructions other than causatives.) Finally, to the best of my knowledge, this analysis violates no rule or principle of Georgian or universal grammar.

15 Basic Class 2 verbs (C) may correspond to causatives (B), which are always Class 1 verbs, e.g., *daarčina* 'he left him, he caused him to remain'. Such causatives do not provide an argument to distinguish between initial intransitive subjects and initial intransitive direct objects, since Causative Clause Union treats direct objects and intransitive subjects alike.

16 I have generalized the rules for Series I and III (rule 1) but the rules for Series II apply equally well for Series III, as the reader can verify for himself.

17 One of my informants made a revealing remark about example (22). When presented with the alternative of (22a) or (22b), he replied that he knew that (22a) was right (normative), but that it sounded strange, as though the water were dripping *on purpose*, as though the water were active (*akṭiuri*).

18 Although the use of the ergative case with verbs that irregularly govern Pattern B in the literary dialect has been much discussed in the literature on Georgian dialects, only a few linguists have observed that this phenomenon is limited to semantically active verbs that are formally in Class 2 (Jajanidze 1970:258; Topuria 1923:120, and 1954:455). Topuria, in the works cited, also shows that the use of this case is not due to the influence of Mengrelian, but that it is a process of regularizing (*unipiḳacia*).

19 With respect to complex structures, (24′) must be interpreted to mean that Inversion may apply in a clause only to the initial subject of that clause. In clause union and raising constructions, Inversion applies only to initial subjects of matrix clauses. In sentences that are finally multi-clausal, Inversion may apply in an embedded clause to the initial subject of that clause. For example, in the saying

ar ici, vardi ueḳlod aravis mouḳrepia?
NEG you-know-it-I-1 rose-NOM without-thorns no-one-DAT he-gathered-it-III-1
'Don't you know that no one has ever picked a rose without thorns?'

Inversion applies in the dependent clause only (because of the negative), demoting the initial subject of that clause (*aravis* 'no one') and marking the verb of that clause with Series III morphology.

20 Nor does the grammar need to refer to Class 4. (23a) can be restated on the basis of semantics as

(23a′) verbs having experiencers.

21 In (31) the meaning 'begin' is due to the inceptive form, which is represented morphologically by the *-d* suffix. In (32) it is due to the use of the preverb *ça*, which adds the notion 'begin' to some verbs. As shown by these examples, (31) is non-controllable, and (32) controllable; this is not easily captured in the English gloss.

22 Since these facts have not been discussed in literature on Georgian, it seems appropriate to give additional examples. The sentences given below are parallel to (31–32), in the same order.

(ii) *vano amɣerda.*
Vano-NOM he-come-about-sing-II-2
'Vano began to sing.'
čaidani amɣerda.
teakettle-NOM
'The teakettle began to sing.'
vanom imɣera.
Vano-ERG he-sang-II-3
'Vano sang.'
**čaidanma/*čaidani imɣera.*
teakettle-ERG/NOM
('The teakettle sang.')

(iii) *lek̦vi* *aṭok̦da.*
puppy-NOM he-come-about-shake-II-2
'The puppy suddenly shook/jerked (e.g. in his sleep).'
saxli *šeṭok̦da.*
house-NOM
'The house suddenly shook/jerked.'
lek̦vma *iṭok̦a.*
puppy-ERG he-shook-II-3
'The puppy shook.'
saxlma*/saxli* *iṭok̦a.*
house-ERG/NOM
('The house shook.')

The sentences in (iv) and (v) are parallel to (33), in the same order.

(iv) *vano* *amɣerebula.*
Vano-NOM he-come-about-sing-III-2
'Vano apparently began to sing.'
**vanos* *amɣerebula.*
Vano-DAT
('Vano apparently began to sing.')
vanos umɣeria.
he-sang-III-3
'Vano apparently sang.'

(v) *turme lek̦vi* *aṭok̦ebula.*
puppy-NOM he-come-about-shake-III-2
'Apparently the puppy suddenly shook.'
**turme lek̦vs* *aṭok̦ebula.*
puppy-DAT
('Apparently the puppy suddenly shook.')
turme lek̦vs uṭok̦nia.
he-shook-III-3
'Apparently the puppy shook.'

[23] Some linguists prefer to limit the notion 'ergative rule' to rules that apply in a single clause or to rules of inflection. But multi-clausal ergative rules are recognized in some important discussions of ergativity (for example, Dixon 1972).

[24] Surprisingly, it has been suggested that verb agreement in Series III of Georgian is ergative. This is based on the claim that the 'intransitive subject' and the 'direct object' trigger the same (bold type) agreement marker in sentences like (vi) and (vii).

(vi) *me* *vqopil***var**.
I-NOM I-am-III-2
'I am.'

(vii) *me* *gavgzavni***var**.
I-NOM he-sent-**me**-III-1
'He (has) sent me.'

In ch. 8 it was shown that the markers of Person Agreement here reflect the *final* grammatical relations, 'I' in both sentences being the *final subject*. Numerous arguments for this analysis have been amassed in chs. 8, 15 and in §3 of this chapter.

[25] In (35a) the initial subject (= final indirect object) triggers the plural marker *-t*,

as predicted by the rule of Number Agreement formulated in ch. 15. I am grateful to Dee Ann Holisky for bringing this example to my attention.

26 These characteristics were selected instead of some other possibilities because of (a) their high degree of mutual consistency, and (b) their high degree of correlation with syntactic characteristics (d–f). Other morphological properties include

1. the use of *-d-* or *-od-* for the formation of the conditional/imperfect.
2. the use of *-a* or *-s* as a third person singular marker in the present tense.

These properties are less regularly correlated with the syntax and semantics than are those noted in the text.

27 The verb *codna* 'know' is an absolute exception. Unlike any other verb in Modern Georgian, it uses Pattern A in some tenses of Series I; in others it undergoes Inversion.

28 Of the three morphological characteristics listed in Appendix A, only characteristic (c) (third person plural suffix in the aorist) was tested with informants. Informants consistently rejected the Class 1 suffix *-es* for all four verbs tested. In addition, they accepted only the imperfect formant *-od-*, which is used for Class 2, not Class 1, verbs.

29 **çqali iqo ševedrebuli.*
water-NOM it-was-II-2 begged
('Water was begged for.')

30 I assume here that the indirect object is an initial comitative and advances to indirect object by a rule of Comitative Version, essentially similar to Benefactive Version (cf. ch. 6). I make this assumption for the following reasons:

1. The meaning of this indirect object differs consistently from that of initial indirect objects, such as those with the verbs *cems* 'he gives it to him' or *miçera* 'he wrote it to him'.
2. The comitative-nominal may occur either as an indirect object, in the dative case and triggering Indirect Object Agreement, or as a non-term, with the postposition *-tan* and not triggering agreement:

(viii) *gela kišpobs anzortan*
Gela-NOM he-competes-I-3 Anzor-with
'Gela competes with Anzor.'

(ix) *gela ekišpeba anzors.*
he-competes-with-him-I-2 Anzor-DAT

However, the assumption that the final indirect object is an initial comitative, not an initial indirect object, is not crucial to the remarks that follow.

31 Normative grammars deprecate this use of the ergative (Tschenkéli 1958: vol. 1, 430).

32 The ungrammaticality of (*15b) is sometimes 'explained' by saying that the form does not exist in Series III. Regular Class 2 verbs with indirect objects do have Series III forms of exactly this type, e.g., *dasçqebia* 'it began for him'. If it is claimed that (*15b) is ungrammatical because the form does not exist, the non-existence of the form must still be explained. I believe that the form does not exist because the failure of Inversion to apply to the initial subject (*gela* in (*15b)) results in ungrammaticality.

33 Since normative grammars do not recognize that *arseboba* fails to trigger Inversion

when its meaning is 'exist (generally)', it seems imperative to quote examples from literary Georgian:

(x) *mis gverdit unda arsebuliqo is mçḳrivic.*
it-GEN side-INST MODAL it-existed-III-2 that screeve-NOM-too
'That screeve apparently must have existed beside this.'

(xi) . . .*romelic rogorc čans, martlac arsebula ʒvel kartulši.*
which-NOM as it-seems truly it-existed-III-2 Old Georgian.
'. . .which, as it appears, really did exist in Old Georgian.'

Kiknadze 1967:186–7

In neither example has Inversion applied. Notice that (xi) is particularly similar to (16b); but the verb here is not controllable and does not undergo Inversion.

References

Abbreviations

BSL	Bulletin de la Société de Linguistique
CLS	Papers from the (n:th) Regional Meeting of the Chicago Linguistic Society
IJAL	International Journal of American Linguistics
IKE	Iberiul-Kavkasiuri Enatmecniereba
KESS	Kartvelur Enata Sṭrukṭuris Saḳitxebi
LI	Linguistic Inquiry
LSA	Linguistic Society of America
NELS	Proceedings of the (n:th) Annual Meeting of the North-Eastern Linguistic Society
NJL(NTS)	Norwegian Journal of Linguistics
Proc. BLS	Proceedings of the (n:th) Annual Meeting of the Berkeley Linguistics Society
SLS	Studies in the Linguistic Sciences, University of Illinois

Aissen, J. (1974a) *The Syntax of Causative Constructions.* Dissertation, Harvard University.

– (1974b) 'Verb Raising'. *LI* 5:325–66.

– (1980) 'Possessor Ascension in Tzotzil'. In L. Martin (ed.) *Papers in Mayan Linguistics.* Columbia, Mo.: Lucas.

– (ms.) 'Valence and Coreference'. An earlier version was presented at the fifth annual meeting of the Berkeley Linguistics Society, 1979, under the title 'Voice and Coreference'.

Aissen, J. & Perlmutter, D. M. (1976) 'Clause Reduction in Spanish'. In *Proc. BLS* 2.

Allen, B. J. & Frantz, D. G. (1978) 'Verb Agreement in Southern Tiwa'. In *Proc. BLS* 4.

Anderson, S. R. (1976) 'On the Notion of Subject in Ergative Languages'. In C. Li (ed.) *Subject and Topic.* New York: Academic Press.

Aronson, Howard I. (1970) 'Towards a Semantic Analysis of Case and Subject in Georgian'. *Lingua* 25:291–301.

– (1976) 'Grammatical Subject in Old Georgian'. *Bedi Kartlisa* 34:220–31.

Bell, S. J. (1974) 'Two Consequences of Advancement Rules in Cebuano'. *NELS* 5:257–64.

– (1976) *Cebuano Subjects in Two Frameworks.* Dissertation, Massachusetts Institute of Technology.

Benveniste, É. (1950) 'Actif et moyen dans le verbe'. *Journal de Psychologie* 43:119–27; reprinted in *Readings in Linguistics* II, E. P. Hamp, F. W. Householder, and R. Austerlitz (eds.) (1966). Chicago: University of Chicago Press.

Berman, A. (1974) *Adjectives and Adjective Complement Constructions in English.* Report No. NSF-29 to the NSF, *Formal Linguistics*, Susumu Kuno, principal investigator.

Blake, R. P. (1932) 'Khanmeti Palimpsest Fragments of the Old Georgian Version of Jeremiah'. *Harvard Theological Review* 25:225–72.

Boeder, W. (1968) 'Über die Versionen des Georgischen Verbs'. *Folia Linguistica* 2:82–152; with unpublished *Nachtrag.*

Catford, J. C. (1976) 'Ergativity in Caucasian Languages'. *NELS* 6:37–48.

Chafe, W. L. (1970) *A Semantically Based Sketch of Onondaga.* Mémoire 25 of the *International Journal of American Linguistics.*

Chikobava, A. (1940) 'Mesame p̣iris subiekṭis uʒvelesi nišani kartvelur enebši' (The ancient marker of the third person subject in the Kartvelian languages). *Enimḳis Moambe* 5–6:13–42.

– (1941) 'Marṭivi c̣inadadebis evoluciis ʒiritadi ṭendenciebi kartulši' (Basic tendencies of the evolution of the simple sentence in Georgian). *Sakartvelos SSR Mecn. Aḳad. Moambe* 2:197–202, 561–8; reprinted as an appendix to Chikobava (1968).

– (1948) *Ergaṭiuli ḳonsṭrukciis p̣roblema iberiulḳavḳasiur enebši* I (The problem of the ergative construction in the Ibero-Caucasian languages). Tbilisi: Sakartvelos SSR Mecn. Aḳad. Gamomcemloba.

– (1950) 'Kartuli enis zogadi enatmecnieruli daxasiateba' (A general linguistic characterization of the Georgian language). *Kartuli enis ganmarṭebiti leksiḳoni* (An explanatory dictionary of the Georgian language). Tbilisi: Sakartvelos SSR Mecn. Aḳad. Gamomcemloba.

– (1961) *Ergaṭiuli ḳonsṭrukciis p̣roblema iberiulḳavḳasiur enebši* II (The problem of the ergative construction in the Ibero-Caucasian languages). Tbilisi: Sakartvelos SSR Mecn. Aḳad. Gamomcemloba.

– (1968) *Marṭivi c̣inadadebis p̣roblema kartulši* I (The problem of the simple sentence in Georgian). Second edition, Tbilisi: Gamomcemloba 'Mecniereba'.

Chomsky, N. (1970) 'Remarks on Nominalization'. In R. A. Jacobs and

P. S. Rosenbaum (eds.) *Readings in English Transformational Grammar*. Waltham: Ginn.

Chung, S. (1976a) 'An Object Creating Rule in Bahasa Indonesia'. *LI* 7:41–87.

– (1976b) 'On the Subject of Two Passives in Indonesian'. In C. Li (ed.) *Subject and Topic*. New York: Academic Press.

Chxubianishvili, D. (1972) *Inpinitivis sak̦itxisatvis ʒvel kartulši* (On the question of the infinitive in Old Georgian). Tbilisi: Gamomcemloba 'Mecniereba'.

Cole, P. & Sridhar, S. N. (1976) 'Clause Union and Relational Grammar: Evidence from Hebrew and Kannada'. *SLS* 6:216–27.

Comrie, B. (1973) 'The Ergative: Variations on a Theme'. *Lingua* 32:239–53.

– (1975) 'Causatives and Universal Grammar'. *Transactions of the Philological Society* 1974:1–32.

– (1976a) *Aspect*. Cambridge: Cambridge University Press.

– (1976b) Review of Klimov (1973). *Lingua* 39:252–60.

– (1976c) Review of Xolodovič (1969). *Language* 52:479–88.

– (1976d) 'The Syntax of Action Nominals: A Cross-Language Study'. *Lingua* 40:177–201.

– (1976e) 'The Syntax of Causative Constructions: Cross-Language Similarities and Divergences'. In M. Shibatani (ed.) *The Grammar of Causative Constructions*. New York: Academic Press.

– (1977) 'In Defense of Spontaneous Demotion: The Impersonal Passive'. In P. Cole and J. Sadock (eds.) *Grammatical Relations*. New York: Academic Press.

– (1978) 'Ergativity'. In W. P. Lehmann (ed.) *Syntactic Typology: Studies in the Phenomenology of Language*. Austin: University of Texas Press.

Davison, A. (1969) 'Reflexivization and Movement Rules in Relation to a Class of Hindi Psychological Predicates'. *CLS* 5:37–51.

Deeters, G. (1930) *Das khartvelische Verbum*. Leipzig: Kommissionsverlag von Markert und Petters.

Dixon, R. M. W. (1972) *The Dyirbal Language of North Queensland*. Cambridge: Cambridge University Press.

– (1979) 'Ergativity'. *Language* 55:59–138.

Fähnrich, H. (1965) 'Die Funktionen des Charaktervokals *i* im georgischen Verb'. *Wissenschaftliche Zeitschrift der Friedrich-Schiller-Universität Jena (Gesellschafts- und Sprachwissenschaftliche Reihe)* 14:153–7.

Fillmore, C. J. (1968) 'The Case for Case'. In E. Bach and R. T. Harms (eds.) *Universals in Linguistic Theory*. New York: Holt, Rinehart and Winston.

Frantz, D. G. (1976) 'Equi-Subject Clause Union'. *Proc. BLS* 2.

Getsadze, I. O., Nedjalkov, V. P., & Xolodovich, A. A. (1969) 'Morfologičeskij kauzativ v gruzinskom jazyke'. In A. A. Xolodovich (ed.) *Tipologija kauzativnyx konstrukcij: morfologičeskij kauzativ*. Leningrad: Izdatel'stvo 'Nauka'.

Gonda, J. (1960) 'Reflections on the Indoeuropean Medium'. *Lingua* 9:30–67, 175–93.

Hale, K. (1973) 'Person Marking in Walbiri'. In S. R. Anderson and P. Kiparsky (eds.) *A Festschrift for Morris Halle*. New York: Holt, Rinehart and Winston.

Harbert, W. (1977) 'Clause Union and German Accusative Plus Infinitive Constructions'. In P. Cole and J. M. Sadock (eds.) *Grammatical Relations*. New York: Academic Press.

Harris, A. (1973) 'On Psychological Predicates in Middle English'. LSA annual meeting.

– (1976) *Grammatical Relations in Modern Georgian*. Dissertation, Harvard University.

– (1977) 'Marking Former Terms: Georgian Evidence'. *NELS* 7:81–98.

– (1979) 'Retired Term Marking in Old Georgian'. *The Elements: A Parasession on Linguistic Units and Levels*, CLS.

– (ms.) 'Uḳukcevitobis ṭranspormaciuli analizi tanamedrove kartulši' (A transformational analysis of Reflexivization in Modern Georgian). Unpublished.

– (to appear a) 'Case Marking, Verb Agreement, and Inversion in Udi'. In D. M. Perlmutter (ed.) *Studies in Relational Grammar*.

– (to appear b) 'Vnebiṭi kartulši' (The Passive in Georgian). *Macne*.

Holisky, D. A. (1978) 'Stative Verbs in Georgian and Elsewhere'. In B. Comrie (ed.) *The Classification of Grammatical Categories* (*International Review of Slavic Linguistics* 3.1–2).

– (1980a) *A Contribution to the Semantics of Aspect: Georgian Medial Verbs*. Dissertation, University of Chicago.

– (1980b) 'On Derived Inceptives in Georgian'. In B. Comrie (ed.) *Studies in the Languages of the USSR* (*International Review of Slavic Linguistics* 5.1–2).

Imnaishvili, V. (1957) *Saxelta bruneba da brunvata punkciebi ʒvel kartulši* (The declension of nouns and the function of cases in Old Georgian). Tbilisi: Sṭalininis Saxelobis Tbilisis Saxelmc̣ipo Universiṭeṭis Gamomcemloba.

– (1977) 'Ḳvlav šereuli ḳavširebitis šesaxeb ʒvel kartulši (Once more on the mixed optative in Old Georgian).' *Tbilisis Saxelmc̣ipo Universiṭeṭis Šromebi* 187:13–24.

Jajanidze, P. (1970) 'Sinṭaksuri movlenebi gurulši' (Syntactic phenomena in Gurian). *Kutaisis Saxelmc̣ipo P̣edagogiuri Insṭiṭuṭis Šromebi* 33:249–62.

Johnson, D. E. (1974) 'On the Role of Grammatical Relations in Linguistic Theory'. *CLS* 10:269–83.

– (1977) 'On Keenan's Definition of "Subject Of"'. *LI* 8:673–91.

– (to appear) 'Ergativity in Universal Grammar'. In D. M. Perlmutter (ed.) *Studies in Relational Grammar.*

Jorbenadze, B. A. (1975) *Zmnis gvaris pormata çarmoebisa da punkciis saḳitxebi kartulši* (Questions of the formation and function of verbal voice forms in Georgian). Tbilisi: Tbilisis Universiṭeṭis Gamomcemloba.

Kavtaradze, I. (1954) *Zmnis ʒiritadi ḳaṭegoriebis isṭoriistvis ʒvel kartulši* (On the history of the basic verbal categories in Old Georgian). Tbilisi: Sakartvelos SSR Mecn. Aḳad. Gamomcemloba.

Kayne, R. S. (1975) *French Syntax: The Transformational Cycle.* Cambridge, Mass.: MIT Press.

Keenan, E. L. (1974) 'The Functional Principle: Generalizing the Notion "Subject Of" '. *CLS* 10:298–310.

– (1975) 'Some Universals of Passive in Relational Grammar'. *CLS* 11: 340–52.

– (1976) 'Towards a Universal Definition of "Subject" '. In C. Li (ed.) *Subject and Topic.* New York: Academic Press.

Keenan, E. L. & Comrie, B. (1977) 'Noun Phrase Accessibility and Universal Grammar'. *LI* 8:63–99.

Kiknadze, L. (1937) 'Zmnis otxp̣irianobisatvis kartulši' (On four-person verbs in Georgian). *Ḳomunisṭuri Aɣzrdistvis:* 8–9.

– (1967) 'Šereuli xolmeobitis mçḳrivi ʒvel kartulši' (The mixed habitual screeve in Old Georgian). *Orioni: Akaki Šanizes.* Tbilisi: Tbilisis Universitetis Gamomcemloba.

Klimov, G. A. (1973) *Očerk obščej teorii èrgativnosti.* Moscow: Izdatel'stvo 'Nauka'.

Kuno, S. (1973) *The Structure of the Japanese Language.* Cambridge, Mass.: MIT Press.

– (1975) 'Three Perspectives in the Functional Approach to Syntax'. *Papers from the CLS Parasession on Functionalism:* 276–337.

Kuno, S. & Kaburaki, E. (1977) 'Empathy and Syntax'. *LI* 8:627–72.

Kuryłowicz, J. (1946) 'Èrgativnost' i stadialnost' v jazyke'. *Esquisses linguistiques.* Warsaw, 1960. Translated from the Russian by Peter Culicover as 'Ergativeness and the Stadial Theory of Linguistic Development'. In *The Study of Man* 2:1–21.

– (1964) *The Inflectional Categories of Indo-European.* Heidelberg: Carl Winter Universitätsverlag.

Latsabidze, L. (1975) 'Natesaobiti brunvis pormata semanṭiḳuri da sinṭaksuri ḳavširi zmnastan tanamedrove kartulši' (The semantic and syntactic relation of genitive case forms to the verb in Modern Georgian). *Macne* 4:150–8.

Lafon, R. (1963) 'Notes explicatives à Chanidze' (cf. Shanidze 1963). *BSL* 58:27–40.

Lakoff, G. (1970) *Irregularity in Syntax*. New York: Holt, Rinehart and Winston.

Lakoff, R. (1968) *Abstract Syntax and Latin Complementation*. Cambridge, Mass: MIT Press.

Lawler, J. M. (1977) '*A* Agrees with *B* in Achenese: A Problem for Relational Grammar'. In P. Cole and J. M. Sadock (eds.) *Grammatical Relations*. New York: Academic Press.

Lees, R. B. (1963) *The Grammar of English Nominalization*. Indiana University Research Center in Anthropology, Folklore, and Linguistics.

Lomtatidze, K. (1952) '*Tbeba* ṭipis zmnata isṭoriisatvis kartulši' (On the history of *tbeba*-type verbs in Georgian). *IKE* 4:75–81.

Machavariani, G. (1959) ' "Unišno vnebiti" kartvelur enebši' (The 'markerless passive' in the Kartvelian languages). *KESS* 1:101–29.

Marr, N. (1925) *Grammatika drevneliteraturnogo gruzinskogo jazyka* (*Materialy po jafetičeskomu jazykoznaniju*, 12). Leningrad.

Marr, N. & Brière (1931) *La langue géorgienne*. Paris: Libraire de Paris, Firmin-Didot.

Martirosovi, A. (1955) 'Masdaruli ḳonsṭrukciis genezisisatvis ʒvel kartulši' (On the origin of the masdar construction in Old Georgian). *IKE* 7:43–59.

Matthews, G. H. (1965) *Hidatsa Syntax* (*Papers on Formal Linguistics* 3). The Hague: Mouton.

McCawley, J. D. (1970) 'Where Do Noun Phrases Come From?' In R. A. Jacobs and P. S. Rosenbaum (eds.) *Readings in English Transformational Grammar*. Waltham: Ginn.

McCawley, N. A. (1972) 'On the Treatment of Japanese Passives'. *CLS* 8:259–70.

– (1976) 'From OE/ME "Impersonal" to "Personal" Constructions: What is a "Subject-less" S?'. *Diachronic Syntax, CLS* parasession volume.

Nebieridze, G. (1976) 'Kcevis ḳaṭegoria kartulši: Ṭranspormaciuli analizi' (The category of version in Georgian: a transformational analysis). *Macne* 4:132–45.

– (to appear) 'Problema ѐrgativnoj konstrukcii v kartvel'skix jazykax'. *G. Axvledianisadmi Miʒvnili Ḳrebuli* (A Collection Offered to G. Axvlediani).

Nozadze, L. (1974) 'Medioakṭiv zmnata çarmoebis zogi saḳitxi kartulši' (Some questions on the formation of medioactive verbs in Georgian). *IKE* 19:25–51.

Panchvidze, V. (1937) 'Uduri ena da misi ḳiloebi' (The Udi language and its dialects). *Enimḳis Moambe* 2:295–316.

– (1942) 'Micemit-subiekṭiani zmnebi udur enaši' (Dative-subject verbs in the Udi language). *Enimḳis Moambe* 12:51–72.

Pätsch, G. (1952/53) 'Die georgische Aoristkonstruktion'. *Wissenschaftliche Zeitschrift der Humboldt-Universität Berlin* (*Gesellschafts- und sprachwissenschaftliche Reihe*) 1:5–13.
– (1965) 'Die konjunctionslose Verbindung zweier Verbalbegriffe im Alt- und Neugeorgischen'. *Bedi Kartlisa* 19–20:119–28.
Peikrishvili, U. (1974) 'Turmeobitebis mnišvneloba da gamoqeneba axal kartulši' (The meaning and use of the evidential in Modern Georgian). *Kartuli Enis Sṭrukṭuris Saḳitxebi* 4:53–70.
Perlmutter, D. M. (1978) 'Impersonal Passives and the Unaccusative Hypothesis'. *Proc. BLS* 4.
– (1979) 'Working 1s and Inversion in Italian, Japanese, and Quechua'. *Proc. BLS* 5.
– (ms.) Untitled paper on the rule of Object Raising in Portuguese.
– (to appear a) 'Relational Grammar'. In E. Moravcsik and J. Wirth (eds.) *Current Approaches to Syntax*. New York: Academic Press.
– (to appear b) 'Evidence for Inversion in Russian and Kannada'. In D. M. Perlmutter (ed.) *Studies in Relational Grammar*.
– (to appear c) 'Possessor Ascension and Some Relational Laws'. In D. M. Perlmutter (ed.) *Studies in Relational Grammar*.
– (to appear d) 'Multiattachment and the Unaccusative Hypothesis: The Perfect Auxiliary in Italian'. In D. M. Perlmutter (ed.) *Studies in Relational Grammar*.
Perlmutter, D. M. & Postal, P. M. (1974) Course in relational grammar given at LSA Summer Institute.
– (1977) 'Toward a Universal Characterization of Passivization'. *Proc. BLS* 3.
– (to appear a) 'The 1-Advancement Exclusiveness Law'. In D. M. Perlmutter (ed.) *Studies in Relational Grammar*.
– (to appear b) 'The Relational Succession Law'. In D. M. Perlmutter (ed.) *Studies in Relational Grammar*.
– (to appear c) 'Some Proposed Laws of Basic Clause Structure'. In D. M. Perlmutter (ed.) *Studies in Relational Grammar*.
Postal, P. M. (1970) 'On the Surface Verb "Remind"'. *LI* 1:37–120; reprinted in C. J. Fillmore and D. T. Langendoen (eds.) *Studies in Linguistic Semantics*, 1971. New York: Holt, Rinehart and Winston.
– (1971) *Crossover Phenomena*. New York: Holt, Rinehart and Winston.
– (1977) 'Antipassive in French'. *NELS* 7:275–313.
Reis, M. (1973) 'Is There a Rule of Subject-to-Object Raising in German?' *CLS* 9:519–29.
Rosenbaum, P. S. (1967) *The Grammar of English Predicate Complement Constructions*. Cambridge, Mass.: MIT Press.
Sapir, E. (1917) Review of Uhlenbeck (1916), *Het Passieve Karakter van het*

Verbum Transitivum of van het Verbum Actionis in Talen van Noord-Amerika (The Passive Character of the Transitive Verb or of the Active Verb in Languages of North America). *IJAL* 1:82–6.

Schmidt, K. H. (1957) 'Eine südkaukasische Aktionsart'. *Münchener Studien zur Sprachwissenschaft* 10:9–24.

– (1965) 'Indogermanisches Medium und Sataviso im Georgischen'. *Bedi Kartlisa* 19–20:129–35.

– (1966) 'Zur Syntax des Kausativums im Georgischen und in indogermanischen Sprachen'. *Bedi Kartlisa* 21–22:121–7.

– (1967) 'Die Stellung des Verbalnomens in den Kartvelsprachen: Historisch-vergleichend und typologisch Betrachtet'. *Bedi Kartlisa* 23–24:153–60.

– (1973) 'Transitive and Intransitive'. In G. Redard (ed.) *Indogermanische und allgemeine Sprachwissenschaft*. Wiesbaden.

Schuchardt, H. (1895) *Über den passiven Charakter des Transitivs in den kaukasischen Sprachen* (*Sitzungsberichte der Akademie der Wissenschaft, Wien, Philologisch-historische Classe*, 133, 1).

Seiter, W. J. (1979) 'Instrumental Advancement in Niuean'. *LI* 10:595–621.

Shanidze, A. (1920) *Subiekṭuri prepiksi meore pirisa da obiekṭuri prepiksi mesame pirisa kartul zmnebši* (The subject prefix of the second person and the object prefix of the third person in the Georgian verb). Tbilisi: Sṭamba 'Saxalxo Sakme'; reprinted in Shanidze (1957).

– (1922–3) 'Uʒvelesi kartuli ṭeksṭebis aɣmočenis gamo' (On the appearance of ancient Georgian texts). *Ṭpilisis Universiṭeṭis Moambe* 2; reprinted in Shanidze (1957).

– (1926) 'Kartuli enis zmnis sakcevi' (Version in the Georgian verb). *Ṭpilisis Universiṭeṭis Moambe* 6:312–38.

– (1927) 'Xanmeṭi Mravaltavi'. *Ṭpilisis Universiṭeṭis Moambe* 7:98–152.

– (1957) *Kartuli enis sṭrukṭurisa da isṭoriis saḳitxebi* (Questions of the structure and history of the Georgian language). Tbilisi: Tbilisis Sṭalinis Saxelobis Saxelmçipo Universiṭeṭis Gamomcemloba.

– (1961) 'Gramaṭiḳuli subiekṭi zogiert gardauval zmnastan kartulši' (The grammatical subject of certain intransitive verbs in Georgian). *Ʒveli Kartuli Enis Ḳatedris Šromebi* 7:207–28.

– (M. A. Chanidze) (1963) 'Le sujet grammatical de quelques verbes intransitifs en Géorgien'. Translated by René Lafon, *BSL* 58:1–27.

– (1973) *Kartuli enis gramaṭiḳis sapuʒvlebi* 1 (Fundamentals of the grammar of the Georgian language). Second edition, Tbilisi: Tbilisis Universiṭeṭis Gamomcemloba.

– (1976) *Ʒveli kartuli enis gramaṭiḳa* (A grammar of the Old Georgian language). Tbilisi: Tbilisis Universiṭeṭis Gamomcemloba.

Sheintuch, G. (1976) 'On the Syntactic Motivation for a Category "Chomeur" in Relational Grammar'. *SLS* 6:49–56.

Shibatani, M. (1976) (ed.) *The Grammar of Causative Constructions*. New York: Academic Press.

Silverstein, M. (1976) 'Hierarchy of Features and Ergativity'. In R. M. W. Dixon (ed.) *Grammatical Categories in Australian Languages*. Canberra: Australian Institute of Aboriginal Studies; New Jersey: Humanities Press.

Sommerfelt, A. (1937) 'Sur la notion du sujet en géorgien'. In *Mélanges offerts à J. van Ginneken*. Paris: Klincksieck, 183–5.

Sridhar, S. N. (1976a) 'Dative Subjects'. *CLS* 12:582–93.

– (1976b) 'Dative Subjects, Rule Government and Relational Grammar'. *SLS* 6:130–51.

Tanamedrove kartuli saliṭeraṭuro enis normebi (The norms of the literary Modern Georgian language) (1970). Tbilisi: Gamomcemloba 'Mecniereba'.

Taqaishvili, A. (1974) 'Ḳauzaṭivis ċarmoebis zogi saḳitxi kartulši' (Some questions of the formation of the causative in Georgian). *Kartvelur enata sṭrukṭuris saḳitxebi* IV: 5–34.

Topuria, V. (1923) 'Sinṭaksuri analogiis erti šemtxveva kartulši dialekṭebis mixedvit' (One instance of syntactic analogy in Georgian dialects). *Čveni Mecniereba:* 113–21.

– (1940) 'Kartvelur enata siṭqvaċarmoebidan II' (From word formation in the Kartvelian languages, II). *Enimḳis Moambe* 5–6:533–40.

– (1954) 'Gramaṭiḳul movlenata ertgvarovani procesi kartvelur enebši' (One type of process of grammatical phenomena in the Kartvelian languages). *IKE* 6:445–55.

Trubetskoj, N. S. (1939) 'Le rapport entre le déterminé, le déterminant et le défini'. *Mélanges de linguistique offerts à Charles Bally*. Geneva.

Tschenkéli, K. (1958) *Einführung in die georgische Sprache*, I–II. Zürich: Amirani.

– (1960–73) *Georgisch-Deutsches Wörterbuch*. Zürich: Amirani.

Van Valin, R. D., Jr. (1977) *Aspects of Lakhota Syntax*. Dissertation, University of California at Berkeley.

Vogt, H. (1938) 'Esquisse d'une grammaire du géorgien moderne'. *NTS* 9:5–114.

– (1950) 'Un aspect du problème actif–passif dans le verbe'. *Grammaire et psychologie*, special issue of *Journal de psychologie normale et pathologique* 43:130–8.

– (1971) *Grammaire de la langue géorgienne*. Oslo: Universitetsforlaget.

– (1972) 'Remarques sur le pronom possessif réfléchi du vieux géorgien' *NJL(NTS)* 26:91–7.

– (1974) 'L'ordre des mots en géorgien moderne'. *Bedi Kartlisa*, 32:48–56.

Xolodovich, A. A. (1969) (ed.) *Tipologija kauzativnyx konstrukcij: morfologičeskij kauzativ*. Leningrad: Izdatel'stvo 'Nauka'.

Ziv, Y. (1976) 'On the Diachronic Relevance of the Promotion to Subject Hierarchy'. *SLS* 6:195–215.
Zorrell, F. (1930) *Grammatik zur altgeorgischen Bibelübersetzung*. Rome: Pontificium Institutum Biblicum.

Index

Notes referred to here are cited by chapter; notes for all chapters begin on p. 280. Small capitals refer to sub-classes listed in Appendix A of ch. 16, beginning on p. 259. Entries in bold type indicate pages where a definition, explanation, or statement of a rule can be found.